Beginning Windows 8.1

Mike Halsey

Apress·

Beginning Windows 8.1

ISBN-13 (pbk): 978-1-4302-6358-6

ISBN-13 (electronic): 978-1-4302-6359-3

Trademarked names, logos, and images may appear in this book. Rather than use a trademark symbol with every occurrence of a trademarked name, logo, or image we use the names, logos, and images only in an editorial fashion and to the benefit of the trademark owner, with no intention of infringement of the trademark.

The use in this publication of trade names, trademarks, service marks, and similar terms, even if they are not identified as such, is not to be taken as an expression of opinion as to whether or not they are subject to proprietary rights.

While the advice and information in this book are believed to be true and accurate at the date of publication, neither the authors nor the editors nor the publisher can accept any legal responsibility for any errors or omissions that may be made. The publisher makes no warranty, express or implied, with respect to the material contained herein.

President and Publisher: Paul Manning
Lead Editor: Jonathan Hassell
Technical Reviewer: Brent Schooley and Ian Bennett
Editorial Board: Steve Anglin, Mark Beckner, Ewan Buckingham, Gary Cornell, Louise Corrigan, Morgan Ertel, Jonathan Gennick, Jonathan Hassell, Robert Hutchinson, Michelle Lowman, James Markham, Matthew Moodie, Jeff Olson, Jeffrey Pepper, Douglas Pundick, Ben Renow-Clarke, Dominic Shakeshaft, Gwenan Spearing, Matt Wade, Tom Welsh
Coordinating Editor: Katie Sullivan
Copy Editor: Kimberly Burton
Compositor: SPi Global
Indexer: SPi Global
Artist: SPi Global
Cover Designer: Anna Ishchenko

Distributed to the book trade worldwide by Springer Science+Business Media New York, 233 Spring Street, 6th Floor, New York, NY 10013. Phone 1-800-SPRINGER, fax (201) 348-4505, e-mail orders-ny@springer-sbm.com, or visit www.springeronline.com. Apress Media, LLC is a California LLC and the sole member (owner) is Springer Science + Business Media Finance Inc (SSBM Finance Inc). SSBM Finance Inc is a Delaware corporation.

For information on translations, please e-mail rights@apress.com, or visit www.apress.com.

Apress and friends of ED books may be purchased in bulk for academic, corporate, or promotional use. eBook versions and licenses are also available for most titles. For more information, reference our Special Bulk Sales–eBook Licensing web page at www.apress.com/bulk-sales.

Any source code or other supplementary materials referenced by the author in this text is available to readers at www.apress.com. For detailed information about how to locate your book's source code, go to www.apress.com/source-code/.

Four years ago I self-publiushed my first Windows book. This book is the successor to that title. I would therefore like to dedicate this book to everyone who has a dream of becoming an author... never give up.

Contents at a Glance

Contents

About the Author

Mike Halsey is a Microsoft Most Valueable Professional (MVP) awardee (2011, 2012 and 2013) and the author of many Windows books including Troubleshooting Windows 7 Inside Out, Troubleshoot and Optimize Windows 8 Inside Out and 70-687 Configuring Windows 8 Exam Ref (Microsoft Press), Windows 8: Out of the Box (O'Reilly) and Beginning Windows 8 (Apress).

Mike regularly makes help, how-to and troubleshooting videos along with writing tech and help articles on his website. He is also a teacher who lives with his rescue border collie, Jed, in an eco-home in Yorkshire (UK).

You can find mike on his website at the longclimb.com and on Facebook, Twitter and YouTube as HalseyMike.

About the Technical Reviewers

Ian N. Bennett is a Technical Evangelist with the Developer Platform Evangelism group at Microsoft, helping consumer brands design and build consumer solutions using a myriad of both client and server technologies. Ian has spent the last fifteen years in many different verticals designing, building, supporting, and leading the development of systems and applications utilizing a vast spectrum of technologies across many different platforms. You can read more about Ian's current work at http://blogs.msdn.com/ianisms.

Brent Schooley is a Technical Evangelist for Infragistics who has been working with Microsoft technologies since 2004. His interests include client and mobile application development and user experience design, with a recent emphasis on Windows 8 and Windows Phone. Other platforms he has worked with include WPF, Silverlight, Windows Forms, and iOS. He has a passion for making people's experiences with software the best that they can possibly be. Brent is the author of *Designing for Windows 8* , a Windows 8 design primer from Apress.

Acknowledgments

With thanks to Jon Hassell. Thanks for the continued support.

Introduction

When Microsoft released Windows 8 in October 2012 the reaction to such a 'bold' operating system was decidedly mixed. Windows 8.1 aims to rectify the criticisms and it is very successful in this. Ultimately though what is delivered to consumers and businesses is an operating system, so powerful, configurable and in places complex that getting the very best out of it can prove a real challenge, especially when people might have no idea that Windows 8.1 is capable of doing X or Y.

That's where this book comes in. Think of it as your introduction, your getting the best out of and your masterclass all in the one volume. Everything you will need to harness the full power of Windows 8.1 is here, from getting started to maximizing your productivity to hacking the OS.

I have tried to include everything you don't normally find in a computer book. As such there's a whole chapter on accessibility and making Windows 8.1 easier to use. This isn't just for blind or disabled, but for those with less than perfect eyesight, color-blindness, motor problems and more.

I make no assumptions here about your level of technical ability, short of to say that by the time you reach the end of this book I hope you will find yourself with a new confidence and an improved willingness to experiment and try new things that can help you get the very best out of using your PC.

I hope you enjoy the book.

CHAPTER 1

■ ■ ■

Introducing Windows 8.1

When Microsoft first began talking about "the next version of Windows" in January 2011, it used words such as "bold" and "risky" to describe both it and the venture that the company was undertaking. Microsoft was already some years behind the competition in the ever-expanding consumer tablet market and it needed desperately to catch up.

At the Windows BUILD developers' conference that September, it was actually no surprise to discover the entirely new Microsoft tablet-centric interface based on its highly praised Windows Phone user interface. What did come as a surprise, however, was the beginning of a move toward a new user interface paradigm for Windows: the relegation of the traditional desktop (the default Windows interface in previous versions of the OS) to an app.

The truth isn't anywhere near simplistic: Windows 8.1 is a far more detailed and complete OS than it was before. The new interface doesn't replace the desktop, but it does offer new ways for both power and casual users get the very best out of the operating system (OS). Moreover, many of the administrative resources are now easier to access than ever before.

In this chapter, I'll talk you through this version's most significant changes to Windows and help you decide where this operating system fits within your digital world. I'll cover the following:

- How Windows 8.1 differs from its predecessors

- Differences between the various SKUs (editions) and processor versions

- New features in Windows 8.1

- How to use, customize, and configure the new Windows 8.1 lock screen

What Is Windows 8.1?

Windows 8 was the 2012 release of the popular Microsoft Windows OS. It is based around a small kernel called MinWin, which provides all the core OS functions. MinWin is also the basis for the Windows Server OS and possibly others in the future, including Windows Phone.

Having a single kernel powering the Microsoft OSs helps maintain compatibility across devices and platforms, reduces development time, and helps increase security. It is also what Apple does; its OS X desktop operating system and the iOS operating system on the iPhone and iPad are based on the same kernel.

Windows 8.1, like Windows 7 and Vista before it, is a *modular operating system*. This means that features can be switched on or off, and some features can be removed completely without affecting the resiliency of the whole system. It is what happens with the desktop and server versions of Windows: the features and modules differ while the kernel remains the same.

This modular approach helps Windows 8.1 maintain compatibility with older "legacy" software and hardware, while still being as customizable as previous versions of the OS.

Microsoft released the free Windows 8.1 update a year later, which brought about many and significant changes to the OS. These changes included everything from the way the interface looks and how you interact with it, to how you change settings; and a couple of features were even jettisoned. Underneath, the improvements for business users were greatly expanded upon.

Windows 8.1 is available for all existing Windows 8.1 users in the Store (see page XREF for details of how to get started with the store and how to upgrade to Windows 8.1). It also comes preinstalled on all new PCs. So for the purposes of this book, I assume that you are already using Windows 8.1 on your computer.

What's the Difference Between Windows 8.1 and Windows RT?

If you are using Windows on a desktop computer or a laptop, you are almost certainly using Windows 8.1. (I use a caveat here because we never know what imaginative new computing hardware will be released during the lifetime of this book.) If you are using a tablet computer, you could be using either Windows 8.1 or Windows RT. So what's the difference between them?

The fundamental difference is the hardware they run on and the incompatibilities between the different processors used to power the device. Windows 8.1 runs on the same Intel chips of PCs of old, so it is backwardly compatible with all your existing hardware and software. Windows RT (Run Time for those of you who are interested in what it stands for) has been designed to operate on processors from ARM. These processors are much more power-efficient than Intel chips, and you will find them powering the world's smartphones, iPads, Android phones, tablets, and probably your television as well. The software that runs on ARM chips is fundamentally incompatible with Intel chips, however.

The upshot is that although Microsoft and hardware vendors have done a remarkably good job of ensuring that your existing computing hardware, especially USB devices, will work with both platforms, your desktop software, which has been written for the Intel processors, simply can't and won't work.

Within the OS, there are small and relatively minor changes here and there. Many of the differences lie underneath the skin of Windows and aren't seen unless you administer computers for a company. Where other changes exist, I will detail them at the appropriate points throughout this book.

How Windows 8.1 Differs from Windows 7 and Windows Vista

When you first start using Windows 8.1, the changes from Windows 7 are significant and very obvious. The biggest change is the use of the new user interface (UI) as the default method for interacting with software programs and apps (see Figure 1-1). The desktop has effectively been downgraded to an app, but it retains all the power and functionality of Windows 7.

Figure 1-1. *The Start screen*

Windows 8.1 is also the very first version of Windows to feature a built-in antivirus as standard. The new Windows Defender software is not like the version in Windows XP, Vista, and Windows 7, in which it was a basic malware protection tool. In Windows 8.1, it is a fully rebadged copy of the free Microsoft Security Essentials software.

The final major change is the addition of the Microsoft Ribbon interface throughout the desktop, File Explorer, and other aspects of the OS. Other than some new features (as you would expect with any new version of an OS), the underlying base for Windows 8.1 is exactly the same as its predecessor. Microsoft hasn't changed or tinkered with anything other than the Task Manager, which has had a major overhaul. What it has done is add a whole raft of new features over the top. This means that if you are familiar with using Windows 7, you won't get lost because almost everything is where you would expect to find it—certainly when you drill down into the advanced features on the desktop. Some of the new features may come as a pleasant surprise, however, because they expand the core power and flexibility of Windows in new and exciting ways.

How Windows 8.1 Differs from Windows XP

If you're moving from the "comfortable old shoe" of Windows XP to Windows 8.1, you're probably in for a very pleasant surprise. That may surprise you, given the move away from the desktop as the default UI and the fact that software and hardware compatibility is no better in Windows 8.1 than in Windows 7.

This compatibility issue, however, is one that I will come back to several times in this book. It's very common for us to have older software and possibly hardware that we're either very comfortable using or that we have to use for work or to perform another specific task. I have an aging graphics package from Microsoft that was released more than

10 years ago, so not all the features work properly now in Windows 8.1. That said, the virtualization technologies built into Windows 8.1 Pro and Windows 8.1 Enterprise, as well as the Application Compatibility Wizard, address some of the issues. Overall, the way Windows has advanced to this version makes upgrading extremely worthwhile.

The simple fact remains that all support for Windows XP is ending in April 2014. After that, there will be no further security and stability patches for the OS, so it will become a big target for malware writers and criminals. Windows XP Mode in Windows 7, while good, is based on older Virtual PC technology and it, too, will no longer be supported after April 2014 (although Windows 7 will be supported until 2020). Conversely, the Hyper-V virtualization technology built into Windows 8.1 will continue to be supported for many years.

Windows 8.1 is the most secure OS that Microsoft has ever produced, especially with its first-ever built-in antivirus protection. Security was difficult to maintain in Windows XP, but doesn't really need to be considered in Windows 8.1—as long as you are aware that criminals and malware writers will try to trick you into bypassing the OS's built-in security. I will cover this issue later in the book.

I will talk more about security and virtualization in Chapters 11 and 14, respectively.

32-bit (x86) and 64-bit (x64) Explained

Windows 8.1 is reportedly the last version of the desktop OS to come in both 32- and 64-bit variants. The reason for this is to maintain compatibility with older hardware that might still be in use in some environments.

What do the terms "32-bit" and "64-bit" mean? Well, a *bit* is a binary digit. Binary is the mathematical number base that uses only the digits 0 and 1. The number zero is represented as 0, and the number one is represented as 1; but because there is no digit 2 in binary, representing the number 2 requires an additional digit, just as the number 10 does in decimal. In binary, the number 2 is represented as 10, 3 as 11, 4 as 100, and so on.

A 32-bit number is represented by 32 digits and thus cannot be larger than 65,535. There are ways of getting around this limit using software, which involves using 2 or more 32-bit numbers together to achieve greater numbers, but this adds significant overhead and can slow down performance. With a 64-bit system, the largest number that can be processed is 18,446,744,073,709,551,616. This is significantly higher than any maximum value that can be processed by a 32-bit system. As a result, computers running 64-bit OSs can directly address vastly more memory (the limit with a 32-bit OS is 4 GB, including any graphics memory in the machine), and processing larger numbers means the computer can do more things simultaneously.

The main benefits of a 64-bit system being able to process larger numbers come not just in being able to address more memory but also in being able to perform operations in a single step. For example, if you were working with very large numbers in a 32-bit OS, let's say the number 100 billion, performing a calculation on this would require multiple memory registers to be used simultaneously. With a 64-bit OS, memory is used more effectively because fewer memory registers are required to perform calculations on numbers. All new computing hardware from the last few years can run 64-bit OSs, but the Windows 8.1 installer tells you if there is a problem. Conversely, not all older hardware has 64-bit driver support; if you have older hardware in or attached to your computer, you should check for 64-bit driver availability before changing to 64-bit.

If 64-bit compatible drivers for all the hardware in and attached to your computer exist, and you either already have or plan to upgrade to more than 4 GB of memory (including the memory on your graphics card), you should use the 64-bit version of Windows 8.1.

Windows RT is currently available only in a 32-bit version.

What's New in Windows 8.1?

As I have already mentioned, Windows 8.1 presents the biggest change to the user interface since Windows 95 was launched. Underneath this new interface, however, are hundreds of additions and changes, small and large, which I will talk about in Chapter 2.

Start Screen

First of all, what is this new UI? Why does it exist and how do you use it? The Start screen came about in Windows 8.1 because of the need for Microsoft to get into the tablet computing market. It is based on a design created for the company's Windows Phone OS and can be traced back in various forms to the Zune media player and even Windows Media Center before that.

The Start screen is based around a series of "live tiles," each of which gives you real-time information from a particular app. For example, they can display the number of e-mails you have waiting, or the sender and subject of those e-mails. They can show you calendar appointments, currency exchange rates, stock market values, or the latest photographs in your collection.

I will talk a lot more about how to use and navigate Windows 8.1 in Chapter 2; for now, suffice it to say that the system is much more powerful, useful, and flexible than it might appear at first sight.

Refresh and Reset

Windows Vista first introduced "system image" backup, in which you could create an image of your entire Windows installation—including all your settings and installed software—and restore from this backup in the event of a catastrophe. With Windows 7, this feature was included in every edition of the OS.

Windows 8.1 still contains this feature, but it also adds two more. Refresh is a system that allows you to reinstall Windows if you encounter a problem—while maintaining all your settings, data, and apps (see Figure 1-2).

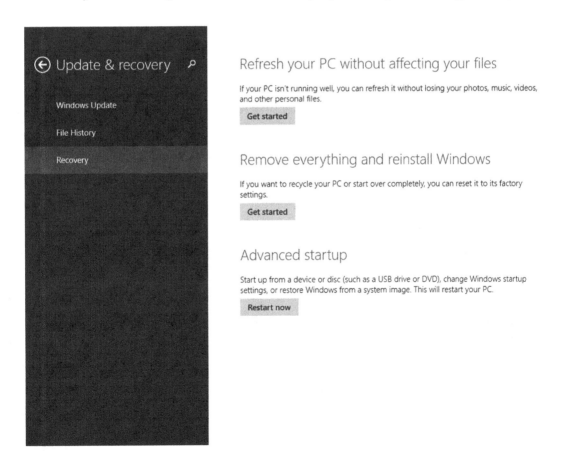

Figure 1-2. *The Refresh and Reset options in Windows 8.1*

■ **Tip** Using Refresh to fix your computer retains all your apps, but it wipes out all the desktop software you have installed on your computer. You can create a custom refresh image, however. I cover how to do this in Chapter 12, in which I also discuss how it differs from a system image backup and why this is important.

When you use the Reset feature, all your files, settings, and apps are deleted, and your computer is returned to its factory default state. This process can be useful if you want to give away or sell your computer.

Windows To Go

The Windows To Go system allows you to create a bootable USB flash drive containing your copy of Windows 8.1 with its software and settings. It is compatible with both USB 2.0 and USB 3.0 drives, and on BIOS and UEFI motherboards.

Windows To Go sounds like a takeaway for a very good reason. No longer will people have to worry about finding mobile versions of apps or using cloud services. With Windows To Go, you really can carry around your entire Windows installation, safely and securely.

Windows To Go is an Enterprise-only feature in Windows 8.1, however, so it isn't included in the standard and Pro editions of the OS or in Windows RT.

Hyper-V

Probably the most talked-about feature in Windows 8.1, after the new UI, is the inclusion of Microsoft's Hyper-V virtualization software (see Figure 1-3). First released in 2008 as part of the Windows Server 2008 OS, it is a virtualization tool that allows other OSs—including earlier versions of Windows and GNU/Linux—to be run inside the main installed *host* OS, this being Windows 8.1.

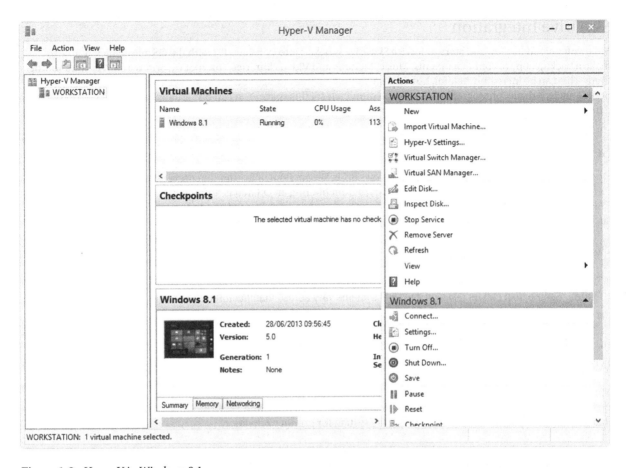

Figure 1-3. *Hyper-V in Windows 8.1*

Each virtualized OS runs effectively in a self-contained ISO disk image file. You can run multiple OSs side by side on a single Windows desktop.

Hyper-V is a Type-1 hypervisor, which means that it can communicate directly with your computer's hardware and take full advantage of it. One advantage of this type of hypervisor is that it can be programmed to take full control of a specific processor core in a multicore chip. This maximizes processing efficiency and ensures that there is no latency while each running OS waits for processing resources to become available.

By contrast, older Type-2 hypervisors used the host OS to *simulate* the hardware of a computer, not allowing access to the actual PC's hardware. This type included the now-aging Microsoft Virtual PC.

Storage Spaces

Storage Spaces is a feature that allows you to aggregate multiple hard disks into a single large storage location. For example, if you have a 750 GB HDD and a 2 TB HDD, you can pool them into a single 2.75TB drive. You can also use USB-attached disks with the feature.

Windows 8.1 manages the data distribution and can also create built-in resiliency with mirroring or striping of data across the various physical hard disks to prevent data loss.

SkyDrive Integration

Microsoft's cloud backup and storage service SkyDrive is baked into Windows 8.1 with the OS automatically able to make a backup copy of your Documents, Music, Pictures and Videos libraries; Internet Favorites; and Windows settings there. This can be incredibly helpful, but the total amount of free storage you get with SkyDrive is 7 GB. With large files on PCs such as digital photographs it is easy to completely fill this space. You can buy additional storage with SkyDrive if necessary or you can turn off this backup feature in part or in full. I will show you how to do this in Chapter 12.

Secure Boot

One of the more controversial features of Windows 8.1 is Secure Boot, a feature that prevents any Unified Extensible Firmware Interface (UEFI)–equipped motherboard from booting an OS that is not signed with a security certificate. This feature, sometimes called Trusted Boot, is most commonly found on the computers you buy from manufacturers such as Samsung, HP, Dell, and so forth, in which it will be enabled by default.

The reason behind Secure Boot is to stop unauthorized firmware, OSs, or UEFI drivers from loading at boot time. This is to prevent the spread of malware and viruses that can attack the computer at boot time.

■ **Note** Secure Boot can be disabled, but UEFI systems vary across manufacturers. To disable it, you need to refer to the documentation for the system used on your computer.

What Else Is New?

There are many other new features in Windows 8.1, including new multimonitor support; drivers for new hardware types such as USB 3.0; an improved Task Manager, Microsoft Account, and SkyDrive integration; improved boot times that make use of hibernation; and a new security system for product activation.

Configuring the Windows 8.1 Lock Screen

The new lock screen in Windows 8.1 is much more useful than those of previous Windows versions in that it can display additional information about Internet connectivity, battery status (very useful), e-mail, appointments, and more.

You can also plug third-party apps into the Logon screen as they become available. But how do you do this?

■ **Tip** On a desktop PC or laptop, you can quickly open the Logon screen without having to swipe upward with your mouse. Just press any key on your keyboard—and the Logon screen opens.

You access the Logon screen settings using the new PC Settings in the interface. This is a multistep action. If you are using touch, swipe your finger in from the far right of the screen to bring up the charms (see Figure 1-4). I talk about charms in detail in Chapter 2 and discuss touch in Windows 8.1 later in this chapter.

Figure 1-4. *The charms, located on the right side of the Start screen or desktop in Windows 8.1*

1. Press **WinKey+C** on your keyboard or move your mouse to the bottom right of the Start screen.

2. Click the **Settings** charm.

3. Click **Change PC Settings** near the bottom right of the screen.

You are automatically taken to PC Settings, in which you see a Lock Screen tile (see Figure 1-5). You can change the wallpaper for the lock screen, and add and remove apps from it.

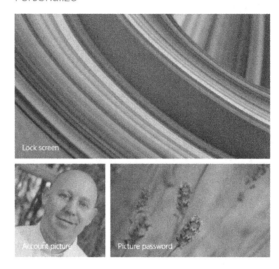

Figure 1-5. *Accessing the lock screen settings from PC Settings*

Once in the Lock Screen settings page, you see the *Lock Screen* apps section, in which you can add and remove apps from the lock screen. To add an app, click one of the available + icons; you can have a maximum of seven apps on the lock screen. To remove an app, click or tap it; and from the context menu that appears, select **Don't display a quick status here**.

■ **Note**   You cannot change the order of apps on the lock screen by dragging and dropping. You need to unpin and repin apps in the order you want them displayed.

You can choose one app to display a detailed status at the bottom of the lock screen options. By default, this is set to the calendar; but you can remove it by clicking it and selecting **Don't show detailed status on the lock screen** from the context menu that appears. You can also show an alarms app on the lock screen, which is useful if you're travelling and using a Windows RT device such as a Microsoft Surface that has great battery life and can easily last a full day on a single charge, or several days (and nights) while on standby.

Not every app is capable of displaying detailed information, and only those that are will appear in this section, in the same way that only apps capable of displaying lock screen information will show in the main Lock Screen Apps options.

Additionally, you can change the lock screen wallpaper to a static image or a slide show. By default, a static image is shown, but you can click or tap the Slide Show switch to reveal additional options (see Figure 1-6). These options include being able to choose a specific folder on your computer or on SkyDrive where the pictures you want to display are stored, or just to use your Pictures folder and its contents. Bear in mind that your device needs to be connected to the Internet to access SkyDrive pictures.

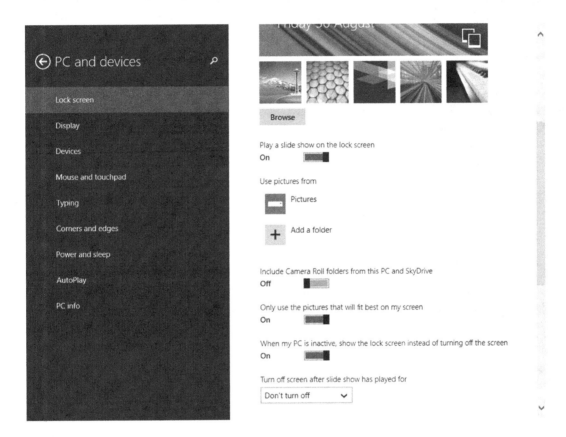

Figure 1-6. *Setting a slide show on the lock screen*

There are additional options on this page, including how to control your slide show. You can, for example, disable the screen off feature after the device sits unused for a period of a few minutes. This allows you to use your lock screen as a digital photo frame, albeit quite an expensive one.

Using a Pin or Picture Password on the Lock Screen

It is always advisable to have a strong password, but if you log in to your copy of Windows 8.1 using a Microsoft Account ID (such as your Hotmail, Outlook.com, Live, or MSN e-mail address), you don't always want to type a long string of 12 or more uppercase and lowercase letters, numbers, and symbols.

Windows 8.1 offers two alternatives, though it is up to each individual user to decide how secure they are. One is to unlock your computer with a four-digit PIN number (it is advisable to never use the same code you use for your credit card or alarm system), and the other is to use a picture password or to create a password if you do not currently have one assigned to your account (see Figure 1-7).

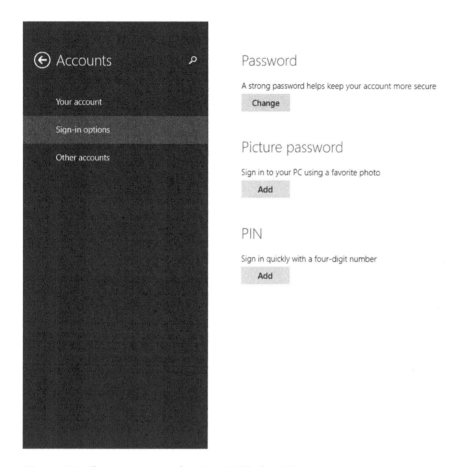

Figure 1-7. *Changing password options in Windows 8.1*

To access these options, go to PC Settings, as detailed earlier, and click or tap Accounts and then Sign-in Options. You see the options to create (or remove) a picture password and a PIN.

When creating a picture password, you are asked to select a photograph or picture from your Pictures library and to perform three actions on it. These can be taps, swipes, or a combination of both. Picture passwords are best used on touchscreens because the movement involved can be quite laborious with a mouse.

Changing Your Login Method

Creating a picture password or a PIN doesn't automatically change the way you sign in to Windows 8.1. You are still required to use your password the next time you log in. Just underneath the sign-in password box, click the new link, Sign-in Options, which displays icons allowing you to switch to a picture password, PIN, or a fingerprint (if it's configured on your computer).

Your selection is remembered and used in the future. This is where security considerations come into play; you can switch back to a full password for extra security if you are taking your computer on the road, for example.

■ **Note** A strong password is always more secure than a PIN or a picture password. If your computer contains sensitive files or is used often in public locations, you might find it best to not have a PIN or picture password configured on your device at all.

Mastering Touch in Windows 8.1

Touch has assumed a central role in Windows 8.1. Not all Windows machines currently support touch, but the technology is moving more and more in that direction. In this section, I want to briefly talk about how to use touch in Windows 8.1.

The touch interface is remarkably intuitive and operates in a way that you might expect it to work on any other tablet or touch OS. The following are the main gestures:

- **Tap** an item to open it in the new user interface.
- **Double-tap** to open an item on the desktop.
- **Swipe** either up, down, left, or right from the edges of the screen to bring up menus or options; or swipe on the screen to perform an action in an app or program.
- **Drag** an item on screen by tapping and holding it, and then dragging it to move it.
- **Tap and hold** to highlight an item on the screen.
- **Pinch inward** to zoom out of a view.
- **Pinch outward** to zoom into a view.

When you are swiping in from the edges of the screen, try to start on the actual screen bezel because doing so produces better results. For some screens, however, the bezel and screen might not be completely flat against each other. In this case, practice might be required to get the best results. See Appendix A for more information on using touch with Windows 8.1.

■ **Note** The Windows 8.1 Kinect sensor provided with the Xbox 360 and Xbox One isn't compatible with Windows 8.1, as perfect as such a union might be. However, a separate Kinect for Windows is available that can be used with your PC for an immersive experience. Alternatives also exist, such as the highly innovative LeapMotion controller, `www.leapmotion.com`.

Using the Onscreen Keyboard in Windows 8.1

Windows 8.1 is very good at detecting when you have selected something with a mouse or with a keyboard. It pops up the onscreen keyboard if it detects a finger tap on an input field such as the password box.

There are several different keyboards you can choose from in Windows 8.1. I want to describe each one for you, as follows:

- The **default keyboard** is a standard affair; you can see the QWERTY keyboard in Figure 1-8. The &123 key brings up numbers and symbols; and an Emoticon button brings up happy and sad faces for e-mail, social networking, and instant messaging. On the bottom right of the keyboard is a key that allows you to change your input method to one of the next four options.

Figure 1-8. *The onscreen keyboard in Windows 8.1*

- **Split keyboard** splits the keys to the far left and right of the screen, making it much simpler to hold a tablet in both hands and type with your thumbs.

- **Written input** allows those with a tablet stylus to input text, numbers, and symbols using Windows 8.1's excellent handwriting recognition. This is useful for writing notes while carrying a tablet.

- **Full keyboard**'s full keyboard option gives you all the keys you expect to find on a PC keyboard, including a number row across the top of the keyboard and access to function keys. You can switch on the full onscreen keyboard in PC Settings by clicking **PCs** & **Devices** then **Typing** and activating the switch for **Add the standard keyboard layout as a touch keyboard**.

- **Hide keyboard** is the final option; it allows you to hide the onscreen keyboard.

The Maximize and Close buttons are located at the top right of the keyboard window when you are viewing it on the desktop. The Maximize button expands the keyboard to fill the width of the computer's screen. It does not make the keys larger, but it does effectively put the keyboard in its own locked dock. Pressing the Maximize button again returns the keyboard to its normal mode.

■ **Tip** Tap and briefly hold a letter on the onscreen keyboard to display international variations for that letter, including accented letters.

In normal mode, the keyboard floats on the desktop and can be dragged around and placed where you want it. This is very useful if the keyboard is obscuring something that you need to see or read.

■ **Tip** The default onscreen keyboard doesn't show the full PC keyboard layout with number, row, and page control keys. You can activate a full onscreen keyboard by searching for **keyboard** at the Start screen (see Figure 1-9).

Figure 1-9. *The full onscreen keyboard*

Privacy and Security for Personal and Business Data

Throughout this book, I highlight where privacy and personal or business data security are relevant.

On the lock screen, an app showing detailed information can be displayed to anyone viewing your computer when it is locked and you are away from it. You should not leave an app showing detailed sensitive, private, or personal information on your Windows 8.1 lock screen. It is for this reason that the e-mail app displays only the current number of unread e-mails.

Summary

Windows 8.1 is very different from Windows 7, though it is built on the same code, and everything that is in Windows 7 sits underneath the new UI. In the chapters that follow, I discuss all the features in the desktop and Start screen interfaces, and show you how you can maximize the best benefits in both. I also help you learn how to use Windows 8.1 to get maximum enjoyment, maximum performance, and maximum productivity.

CHAPTER 2

■ ■ ■

Finding Your Way Around Windows 8.1

The first thing that you notice when you use Windows 8.1 for the first time is the new interface. It is very much unlike anything that we've ever seen on the desktop, and on initial inspection, it seems very focused on tablet devices.

The new Start screen dates back to early versions of Windows Media Center, but perhaps in a more pronounced way, to Microsoft's Zune HD media player, which was released in 2009.

The main purpose of the Start screen is to use the types of iconography that are commonly found in our daily lives to help us get information quickly and easily; the familiar signs and symbols that navigate us around roads, public transport systems, and in public spaces. Primarily, it involves transportation signage, which is designed specifically to give us relevant information quickly and simply.

The new user interface and the new Start screen in Windows 8.1 are aiming to do just that for OSs. The use of different shapes, sizes, colors, and iconography can help you quickly locate the information you need, and the live tiles on the Start screen can then provide better and more in-depth detail about a particular subject.

While the "traditional" desktop is still beneath this new interface and can be selected to display at startup, the Start screen is now the default way to interact with Windows and it's more usable and powerful than you might first presume.

In this chapter, I show you how to get the very best out of the Start screen and all its new features by using either touch or a keyboard and mouse.

Using the Start Screen and Apps

The main elements of the Start screen are as follows:

- Square and rectangular tiles for apps

- Square tiles for desktop software

- Live tiles for apps that show up-to-date information from within the app itself

- A pop-up menu at the bottom of the screen with main options called the *App bar*

- A pop-down menu at the top of the screen with additional options

- Thumbnails of running apps that pop in from the left of the screen

- The charms, which pop in from the right of the screen

By default, each app that runs in Windows 8.1 runs full screen, though it is possible to have two or more apps running side by side. When you run more than a single app at one time, the apps each occupies 50 percent of the screen, but you can change this by dragging the slider bar that appears between them, and larger screen resolutions can allow up to four apps to run side by side. This allows you to use a main app—perhaps the weather next to another app (see Figure 2-1).

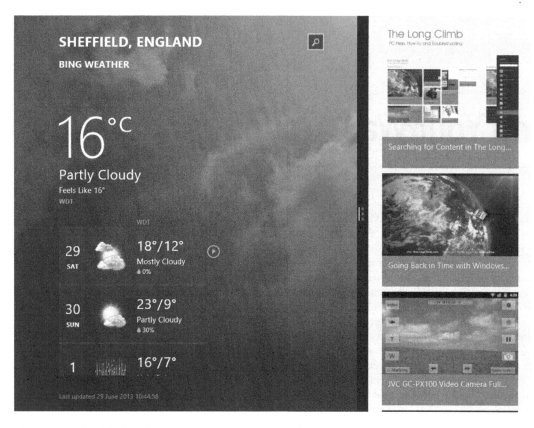

Figure 2-1. *The side-by-side app view*

To pin an app to the left or right of the screen, when the app is running, drag it away from the top center of your screen with the mouse or your finger, and it becomes a large thumbnail. Drag this thumbnail to the left or right side of the screen, and you will see a vertical bar appear to signify that the app will be docked left or right. With the keyboard, you can dock an app to the left or right of the screen with the key combination Win+ left cursor or Win + right cursor.

■ **Tip**   To switch back to a single app on your screen, drag the vertical bar all the way to the left or right to swipe other apps off the screen.

When you run a third or even a fourth app (though you need a higher than HD screen for four apps), it appears as a thumbnail between the two currently docked apps (see Figure 2-2). It can at first appear confusing, but here's how it works.

Figure 2-2. Pinning more than two apps side by side

When you drag this thumbnail left or right with your finger or mouse, you can drop it onto the left or right sides of your screen to replace the app that is running there. If you hold it *between* the running apps, you see the vertical bar expand outward to allow room to drop the new app in the middle of your screen. If the vertical bar does not expand, your screen resolution is not wide enough to support an additional app.

■ **Tip** You can quickly close an app by pressing the Windows key + down cursor or by touching the app at the top center of your screen and dragging it off the bottom center of the screen.

The Start screen is the hub of everything in Windows 8. It is where you launch not only apps and programs but also the desktop itself. In Windows 8, to reduce memory usage, the desktop doesn't load unless you call it. Some say this is reducing it to another app, but it contributes to a memory-efficient operating system (OS) nonetheless.

When you first launch Windows 8, the Start screen already has apps and programs split into different groups. You can define and name these groups as you want. I will show you how to do this later in the chapter.

■ **Tip** On some higher-resolution displays such as those over full HD, Windows 8.1 can display more tiles vertically on the screen. To activate this feature, open the Charms menu and click Settings, and then at the top right of your screen, click Tiles. If your screen can support this feature, you see the Show More Tiles option.

In a change to the way many of us are used to interacting with our computers, the tiles on the Start screen scroll left and right instead of the more customary up and down. When you install new apps or programs into Windows 8, their tiles appear on the far right of the Start screen, although they can be rearranged, as I will detail shortly.

Switching Between and Shutting Down Running Apps

There are two different ways to switch between apps and programs in Windows 8.1. If you are on the desktop, the well-known Alt+Tab key combination displays thumbnails of all your running programs *and* apps. You can switch between them, but you can't shut them down from here.

To switch between your running apps, use the Win+Tab key combination. This displays all your running apps in a bar that runs vertically on the left of your screen. Keep pressing this key combination until you get to the app you want to use. You can switch to your last-used app by swiping your finger in from the left edge of the screen.

With touch and the mouse things are slightly different. Moving your mouse to the top left or bottom left of your screen, and then moving the mouse inward to the center, displays the same vertical bar showing running apps. With touch, you access this menu by swiping inward from the left of your screen and then, in the same movement, swiping back out again.

After you open the list of running apps in one of these ways, the list remains in place. You can now either right-click an app to close it (or indeed snap it to the left or right of your screen), or you can drag it with your mouse or finger down and off the bottom center of the screen. This will close the app.

Action	Keyboard	Mouse	Touch
Switch between running desktop programs	Alt+Tab	N/A	N/A
Switch between running apps	Win+Tab	Move to top-left or bottom-left corner of screen	Swipe in from left of screen
Close the currently running app	Alt+F4 (also works for desktop programs)	Drag app (or app thumbnail) off the bottom center of the screen	Drag app (or app thumbnail) off the bottom center of the screen

Locking the Computer and Signing Out

The word "Start" appears in the top left of the screen (see Figure 2-3), but it doesn't do anything if you click or tap it.

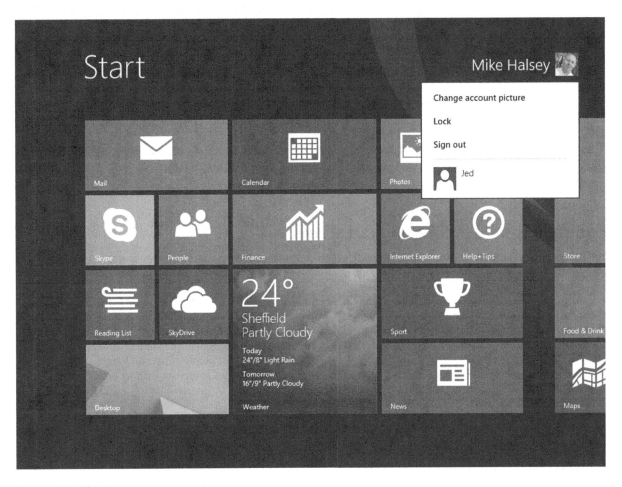

Figure 2-3. *The Start screen*

Your username and avatar appear in the top right of the screen. You can click it to perform the following actions:

- **Change the Account Picture** takes you to the Personalization options in PC Settings, in which you can upload a new profile picture; take a picture using a webcam, if you have one attached to your computer; or use an installed app, if one is compatible, to take or create a picture.

- **Lock** is the option you choose to lock the computer without turning it off. It is useful if you are leaving your computer for a short break. You can also lock the computer the more traditional way by pressing Ctrl+Alt+Del on your keyboard and selecting Lock from the options; or you can press WinKey+L to lock the computer instantly.

■ **Tip** Use WinKey+L to lock your computer quickly.

- **Sign Out** is the option to use if you are finished with your computing session and want to let somebody else use the computer with his own user account. This option does not shut down the computer.

- With **Switch users**, other people who have accounts on this PC have their names listed here. You can click a person to switch to her account. This does not log you out, so any programs and apps you have running remain open until you are logged out or the PC is switched off.

■ **Note** There is no option to restart, shut down, hibernate, or sleep the computer directly from a menu on the Start screen. To do this, you need to access the charms (more on this shortly) and select Settings.

Controlling the Windows 8.1 Start Screen

The new interface is designed with touch in mind. You can control it with a keyboard and mouse, but this can create complexity due to several ways to operate and control various aspects of the screen, and in trying to find ways to mimic touch controls with a keyboard and mouse.

You control the Start screen by swiping left and right with your finger on a touchscreen or by moving your mouse left or right on the screen to scroll sideways. When you use a mouse, you also see a scrollbar appear at the bottom of the screen. You can grab this scrollbar and use it just like a scrollbar in a desktop program.

When the scrollbar is visible, you see a small (-) button in the bottom-right corner of the screen, as shown in Figure 2-4. Clicking it shows the Start screen zoomed out so that you can quickly find and locate a specific group of programs, apps, or links. If you are using a touch interface, you can zoom out with a pinch gesture. This "scemantic zoom" is also an action that's available in many apps and also in Internet Explorer and Microsoft Office on the desktop.

Figure 2-4. *The Zoom control next to the Start screen scrollbar*

■ **Tip** Hold down the Ctrl key and use your mouse's scroll wheel to zoom in and out of the Start screen to see all your app groups.

When you are looking at the zoomed-out Start screen, you can see buttons for individual apps, programs, and links. This helps you locate things that you may have difficulty finding should you have a lot of tiles or groups on your Start screen.

You cannot run any app or program directly from the zoomed-out view; however, clicking or tapping anywhere on that view zooms back into that place on the Start screen (see Figure 2-5).

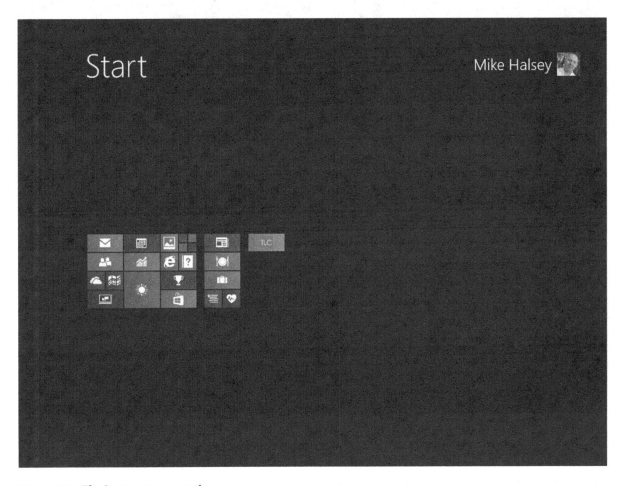

Figure 2-5. *The Start screen zoomed out*

■ **Tip**   In this zoomed-out view, you can also rearrange entire groups in the same way that you would move tiles on the Start screen: simply by dragging and dropping.

Context menus, known as the *App bar*, appear on the Start screen from the top and bottom of the screen, depending on the app or feature you are using. You can swipe downward from the top of the screen or upward from the bottom to bring up a context menu. If you are using a mouse, right-click in any unused space to bring up the context menus, as shown in Figure 2-6. When opening this menu from the keyboard, the combination WinKey+Z opens the context menus for you.

■ **Tip**   Use WinKey+Z to open the App bar.

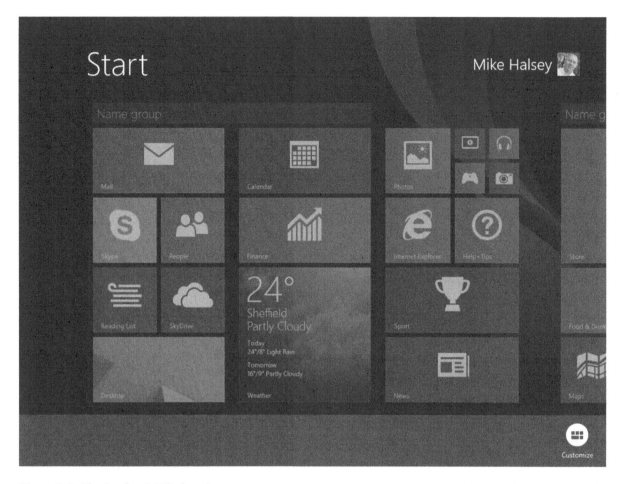

Figure 2-6. *The App bar in Windows 8*

Controlling Apps and Live Tiles

You open (launch) an app or program (I'm going to make the distinction between *apps* that are downloaded from the Windows Store and *programs* that run on the traditional Windows desktop) from the Start screen with a single click or tap. This launches an app full screen or switches to the desktop to run a program. You want to be able to organize and perform additional actions on apps and programs, which includes running them as an administrator, resizing the live tiles, and so on. More importantly, you will want to arrange these tiles into groups that make it easy to find your most-used apps and programs, and hide the ones you don't use as often.

■ **Tip**   You can get back to the Start screen at any time by pressing the Windows key on your keyboard.

Performing Functions on Apps and Live Tiles

The equivalent of a right-click in a tile in Windows 8.1 is *still* a right-click; but if you are using touch, you need to touch a tile and hold it for a second to perform the same task.

■ **Tip**   You can deselect a tile or select multiple tiles by touching and holding or right-clicking. There is no need to hold the Ctrl or Shift keys when selecting or deselecting multiple tiles.

The actions you can perform on a tile vary depending on what you have selected:

- **Unpin from Start** allows you to remove a tile from the Start screen. It is still available in the All Apps view (more on this shortly) and it can be launched from there. It is useful for programs and apps that you use only occasionally.

- **Pin to/Unpin from Taskbar** is useful if you want quick access to desktop programs from the Windows desktop taskbar. This option adds or removes a button on the desktop taskbar for a particular program. Apps cannot be pinned to the desktop taskbar.

- **Uninstall** is the option you use to uninstall *both* an app and a program from your computer. You can still manage and uninstall programs from Programs and Features, as with Windows 7, but this new quick method makes it easier to remove software from your PC.

- **Resize** allows you to resize compatible app tiles between up to four sizes (depending on which sizes the app supports). For example, you may have a live tile for e-mail that gives you previews of the weather as a small square in which you only see limited information about the current weather, but as a large square you can see more information and details of the next day as well (see Figure 2-7). You may decide that you want to make some tiles smaller so that your organized groups on the Start screen take up less space or look more organized.

Figure 2-7. *The four live tile sizes*

- **Turn Live Tile Off** deactivates the live component of a compatible tile. You may want a larger rectangular tile for e-mail to make it easier to find and open, but not have the tile display the subjects and senders of your most recent e-mails.

- **Open New Window** allows you to open multiple instances of a program. Let's say, for example, you have Internet Explorer open from the Start screen and you want to open a web site, but not in a new tab because you want to view two web pages side by side. This option on compatible apps and programs allows you to open a new instance of the app or program.

- **Open File Location** works only on installed desktop programs and Windows desktop components. It opens a File Explorer window and navigates directly to the folder on your hard disk in which the program or link you have selected is located. (I discuss File Explorer in Chapter 5.)

- **Run as Administrator** allows you to run the program or feature with full admin privileges.

- **Clear Selection** cancels the current selection apps and/or programs.

■ **Note**   Tiles for desktop programs can only be resized between small and medium squares.

Arranging Live Tiles into Groups

As I have already mentioned, you can arrange your tiles on the Start screen into customizable groups and rearrange them within those groups. This is something that can be used to bring your most commonly used programs to the beginning (left) of the Start screen and to group together related tiles such as Internet links or development software.

You do this by invoking the Start screen customization mode by tapping and holding or right-clicking a tile. In this mode, the tiles fade slightly and move farther apart to make them easier to work with but also as a visual identifier that you're in this special mode.

■ **Tip**   You can also invoke the Start screen customization mode by clicking Customize from the App bar (see Figure 2-8).

Figure 2-8. *You can click Customize on the app bar to invoke the Start screen customization mode*

You can rearrange tiles within a group or move one to a different group by dragging and dropping it using touch or the mouse. You can work with as many tiles as you want while in Customization mode.

■ **Tip** When you are finished arranging and performing other actions on Tiles, *double* tap or click in any blank space to lock your changes and finish. You can also lock your changes by pressing the Windows key on your keyboard.

When you move a tile between groups, a highlighted vertical bar appears between groups as you move from one to another. If you drop a tile onto this highlighted bar, a new group is created.

By default, the Windows 8 Start screen does not give names to groups, but it is possible to do this and you will see the words *Name group* appear above each group of tiles. You might want to name your groups, work, games, Internet, and so on (see Figure 2-9).

Figure 2-9. *You can name groups on the Windows 8.1 Start screen*

Hiding and Adding Apps and Tiles

When you customize and arrange your Start screen, you will want to hide tiles, which can be done by selecting one or several, and from the App bar selecting Unpin from Start. Having a lot of apps and programs pinned to the Start screen can create a very messy environment. You certainly want to remove unwanted and unused tiles from the Start screen.

But what if you want to restore some of these afterward? What if you want to restore all the Start screen programs that you weren't previously using, but now want easier access to?

You can do this by opening the All Apps view. This is invoked either by swiping upward on the Start screen with your finger or by clicking the down arrow that appears near the bottom left of the screen when using a mouse (see Figure 2-10). This displays a screen showing all the apps and programs that are installed on Windows 8, including those tiles that are hidden from the Start screen or the desktop taskbar.

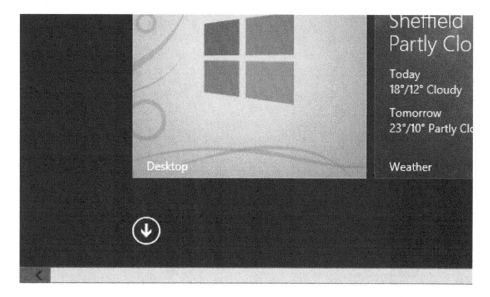

Figure 2-10. *Opening the All Apps view with your mouse*

On the left of this screen, which also scrolls left and right, you are first shown all the apps that are installed (see Figure 2-11). Further to the right, you find Windows features and all the software you have installed in Windows 8.1 sorted into groups as they would appear in the Start menu.

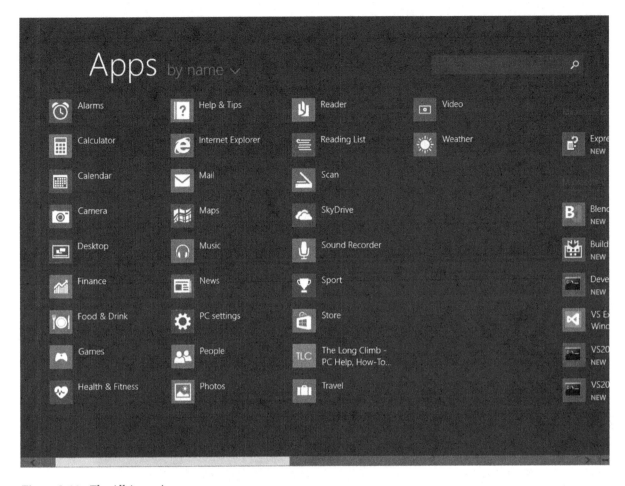

Figure 2-11. *The All Apps view*

You cannot edit this screen as you do in the Start menu, which allows you to drag and drop programs and Windows features between folders.

There are different ways to arrange the All Apps view and these are accessed by clicking the *by name.* link at the top of the screen.

The options here allow you to arrange the all apps view in four different ways:

- **By name** is the default way, with all your apps listed alphabetically, followed by all your desktop programs listed alphabetically and arranged by program folder (publisher).

- **By date installed** allows you to arrange your apps according to when they were installed, with the most recently installed apps (and programs) featured first in the list.

- **By most used** lists your apps and programs according to how often they are used on your PC.

- **By category** arranges your apps according to their Windows Store category (education, games, etc.) but it can also be used to display your desktop programs *before* your installed apps. (I will show you how to make this change in Chapter 9.)

■ **Tip** You can pin an app or program back to the Start screen by selecting it and clicking Pin to Start in the App bar.

You can also zoom out from the All Apps view. This additional zoomed-out view (see Figure 2-12) shows apps arranged alphabetically. Software packages and Windows features are arranged by folder.

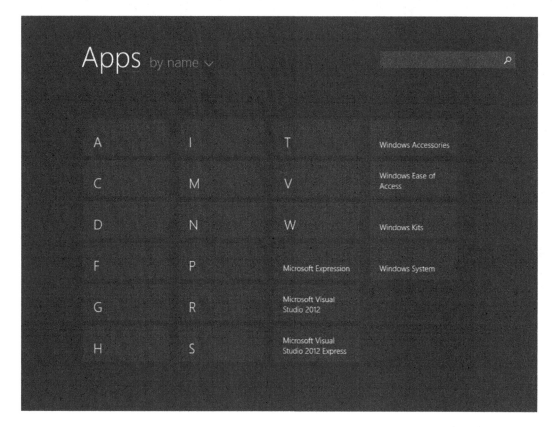

Figure 2-12. *You can zoom out of the All Apps view to see programs and apps arranged into groups*

With this view, you can quickly navigate to Microsoft Office, Windows Accessories, Windows System, or other folders and groups that appear in the All Apps view by simply clicking or tapping.

Using the Charms

The charms provide the central controls for interacting with apps and interacting with and configuring Windows. They include the Start button, also known as the Windows flag; search; and several features that are new to Windows 8.

You open the charms (see Figure 2-13) in several ways: by swiping your finger in from the *bezel* (the area around your touchscreen) on the right of your screen, by moving your mouse to the top left or bottom right of the screen, or by pressing Win+C on the keyboard. The charms open in both the Start screen and the desktop.

Figure 2-13. *The charms*

There are five charms:

- **Search** allows you to search apps, settings, and files and the Internet, all from a central location.

- **Share** is a new feature in Windows 8.1 that allows you to share text, images, and other items between apps, including sharing a photo with a social networking app to publish it there. You can use the Share charm to send somebody a screenshot from your PC or to save app or web content as a Reading list bookmark to view later. I will show you how to use Reading lists later in this chapter on page 35.

- **Start** is now where the main Start button appears. In Windows 8.1, it has been redesigned with a new look. Pressing it, just as with pressing the Windows key on your keyboard, cycles between the Start screen and the most recently running app or program.

- **Devices** is a quick way to access devices such as USB peripherals and secondary displays. This is also where you go to print content from apps (more on this in Chapter 6).

- **Settings** is the new home for the touch-friendly Control Panel, now renamed PC Settings. It is also where you will find controls for connecting to networks and the Internet, and restarting and switching off your PC.

The charms are not configurable; you cannot manually add apps or hardware to the Share and Devices charms. You also cannot customize the Settings options or add extra charms. When Windows 8.1 detects apps and hardware that are compatible with the Share and Devices features, they are added automatically.

Tip There is a second Start button hidden in the bottom left of the Start screen that you can click with your mouse.

Share is a new feature that allows apps to share items, similar to the way that we copy and paste things between programs. This share functionality works with apps *only*, not with programs on the desktop.

Using the Desktop in Windows 8.1

Using the desktop in Windows 8.1 is the same as with any previous version of the OS. You can pin programs to the taskbar by right-clicking them on the Start screen or All Apps view, and selecting Pin to Taskbar from the App bar. Pinning programs to the taskbar offers a very quick and efficient way to open programs on the desktop without having to interact with or even see the Start screen.

There have been changes with the desktop since the first version of Windows 8, all of which I will detail in this chapter. These changes include the ability to start (boot) your PC directly to the desktop. You can also tweak the OS in other ways, too, including using the category view on the All Apps screen I mentioned on page 16 to display your desktop software *before* your modern apps. I will show you how to implement this change in Chapter 9.

All the usual desktop clicks, such as right-clicking with the mouse to bring up a context menu, still work. On a touchscreen, you can tap and hold to simulate a right click. This is the same way that touch has worked in Windows going back to Windows XP, and it's also consistent with other touch-based OSs including Windows Phone and Android, which makes it intuitive and easy to use.

Start Button

Gone in Windows 8 and back in Windows 8.1, clicking the Start button doesn't open a traditional Start menu, though in fairness you simply don't need one any more with the ability to pin both programs and files to the taskbar (see the following section for instructions on how to do this) and also being able to program the Start button to display the All Apps view instead of the Start screen (this is detailed in Chapter 9). Clicking or tapping the Start button returns you to the Start screen, though it is possible to modify the behavior of this button so that it instead takes you to a customized All Apps view that prioritizes your desktop programs. I will show you how to make this change in Chapter 6.

Right-clicking the Start button also opens the Windows 8.1 Administration menu (see below) which provides additional options.

Windows Administration Menu

Although the Start menu has been removed from the desktop in Windows 8, it isn't gone completely. On both the desktop and the Start screen, right-clicking with your mouse in the very bottom left of the Start screen or by right-clicking the Start button on the desktop (also accessible by pressing Win+X) brings up a menu of options typically found in the Start menu, such as the Run and Command prompt. This menu offers a great many administration options plus quick access to Restart, Shut down, and Sleep controls (see Figure 2-14).

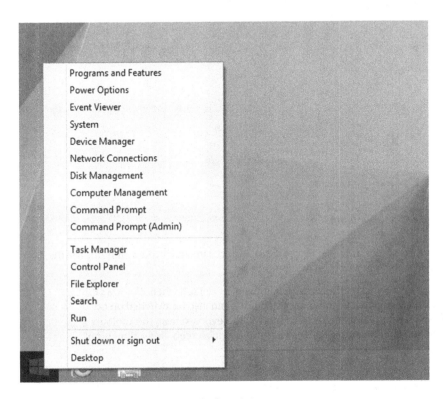

Figure 2-14. *The Win+X menu in Windows 8.1*

One important thing to note in this screenshot is that the *Command Prompt* and *Command Prompt (Admin)* links have been replaced by Windows PowerShell. This is because you can switch these links in the WinX menu between the two different scripting environments. I will show you how to make this change in Chapter 9.

Using the Desktop Taskbar

The Windows 8.1 taskbar is the same as in Windows 7. You can pin programs that can be launched with a single click, or that on a click up-and-drag-upward motion (also on a right-click) opens a Jump List with additional options (see Figure 2-15). I will talk more about Jump Lists shortly. To pin a program to the taskbar, right-click (touch and hold) its icon on the Start screen or All Apps view, and from the App bar click the *Pin to Taskbar* option. Icons on the taskbar (including non-pinned but running programs) can be dragged left and right to change their ordering. This can be very useful for grouping similar or commonly used programs together.

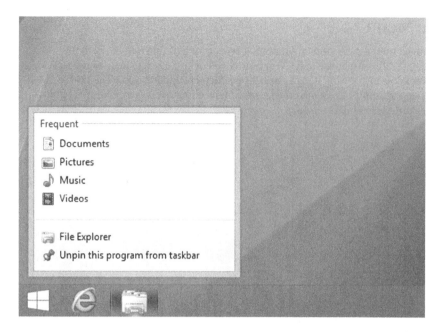

Figure 2-15. *The Windows 8.1 desktop and taskbar Jump Lists*

On the right side of the taskbar sits the system tray (see Figure 2-16), the area in which you commonly see the time and date. The following list describes the other icons in the system tray:

- The **Keyboard icon** brings up the onscreen keyboard. It appears by default when Windows 8.1 detects a touchscreen interface attached to your computer, but it can also be switched on by right-clicking in a blank space on the taskbar and clicking Touch Keyboard from the Toolbars option that appears. Note that if your computer does not have a touchscreen, this option is not visible.

- The **system tray** is represented by a small white up arrow. This is the bucket container for all the system tray icons that are hidden. I will show you how to customize the system tray in Chapter 9.

- The **Action Center** is the central location for Windows messages, including those about antivirus, backup, problems, and errors. When there is a notification for you, the icon will change to display a small alert symbol superimposed on it. The irony that the icon for the Action Center is a white flag has never been lost on me!

- The **Battery icon** shows only when you are running Windows 8.1 on a computer containing a battery. This icon gives you a visual representation of the battery's charge level and overlays a Plug icon if your computer is currently connected to mains electricity.

- The **Network icon** changes depending on whether you are connected to your network and the Internet by a physical Ethernet cable, Wi-Fi, or a mobile Internet connection such as 3G or LTE via a SIM card in your computer or via a dongle. This icon changes to an airplane if you have airplane mode switched on.

- The **Volume icon** offers a quick way to turn the computer's volume up or down, mute it and also to control your sound devices. If you click this icon, a volume control appears. I talk more about the additional functionality of this icon in Chapter 9.

- The **Date and Time** format can be changed. I talk about how to customize and configure the Date and Time settings in Chapter 9. If you click the time and date in the system tray, a dialog box shows the current month's calendar, the currently displayed clock(s), and any messages relating to Daylight Saving Time. I talk more about using this window shortly.

- The **Show Desktop button** was a visible button on the Windows 7 taskbar, but it is hidden in Windows 8. Clicking over this button temporarily hides all open windows on the desktop. Clicking the far right of the taskbar, however, minimizes all the windows currently open on your desktop, showing just the desktop and any gadgets you may have on it. Clicking the button again restores all previously minimized windows (refer to Figure 2-14). It is also possible to switch back on the "Peek" functionality that was introduced in Windows 7 (I will show you how to do this in Chapter 9).

Figure 2-16. The system tray icons on the desktop taskbar

Using the Date and Time Dialog Box

The Date and Time dialog box, which is viewable by clicking the date and time on the taskbar, is very powerful, and one of its best features is the calendar. (I explain how to configure the settings in Chapter 9.) At the top of the calendar are left and right arrows that navigate to either side of the current month (see Figure 2-17).

Figure 2-17. The date and time accessible from the taskbar

Clicking the month changes the display to show all the months in the current year. Clicking it again displays all the years in the current decade, and clicking it a third time displays all the decades in the current century. This makes it an excellent tool for quickly locating dates. You can also add up to two additional clocks to this view that will display graphically when you click the time and date on the taskbar, see Figure 2-18, or that will display as a pop-up when you hover your mouse over it. (Again, I will show you how to configure this in Chapter 9.)

Figure 2-18. *Using the calendar and additional clocks*

Viewing Taskbar Thumbnails

When you hover your mouse over a button on the taskbar, a pop-up showing a live thumbnail image of the running program appears (see Figure 2-19). If that program is minimized, mousing over the thumbnail image temporarily brings that application to the foreground without having to restore it to the desktop. This is an excellent way to get a quick peek at what is going on in a program. Because the thumbnails are completely live, you can see any progress bars or motion in the thumbnail that is occurring in the window at that time. This is useful for keeping an eye on programs that you only want running in the background while they complete tasks.

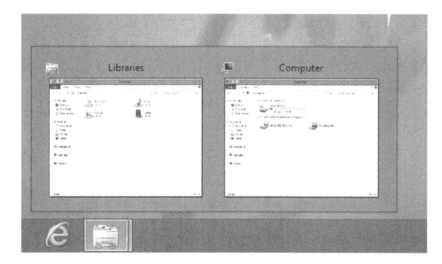

Figure 2-19. *Using live thumbnail previews on the taskbar*

■ **Tip**　When you move your mouse over a thumbnail, a close button appears in its top-right corner. You can click it to quickly close the program.

Using Taskbar Jump Lists

I find Jump Lists to be one of the most useful features of Windows (see Figure 2-20). I use them all the time. They are pop-up menus that appear above program buttons on the taskbar. You display a Jump List by right-clicking a taskbar button, or by clicking it and dragging upward with your mouse or finger. Jump Lists can make all manner of actions with desktop programs simple, including include quick access to your commonly or recently used files, for opening multiple instances of a program and closing windows that may be hidden deep in the background of a busy working desktop environment.

Figure 2-20. *A Windows 8.1 taskbar Jump List*

■ **Tip**   You can open multiple instances of an already open program with a single click by clicking the Taskbar icon with the center button on your mouse if you have one (sometimes pressing down on the mouse scroll wheel performs the same action).

Jump Lists can contain any of the following elements:

- **Recently opened files** in a program for quick access

- **Pinned files** that will always display in the Jump Lists for quick file access

- **Tasks** that can be performed with a program

- The **Program Launch**, which can be very useful if you want to start multiple instances of a program

- The **Unpin button** for unpinning the program from the taskbar

- The **Close Window button** for closing the program

▪ **Tip**   You don't need to open a file to pin it to the Jump List for the associated program; just drag the file's icon onto the Program's icon on the taskbar to pin the file there.

Jump Lists are programmable, not only by software packages but also by web sites. You can drag the icon for a web site from the address bar in the desktop version of Internet Explorer and pin it to the taskbar by dropping it there. Many web sites, such as Facebook and Outlook.com, are programmed to provide quick links to specific parts of the site or specific features.

Managing Windows on the Desktop

When you have a lot of windows open on your desktop, things can get very muddled. You can use the taskbar thumbnails to give you previews or quick views of windows. But what if you want to clean away all but the current working window or work on two windows together?

Both of these tasks are easy in the Windows 8 Shake and Snap features. Shake allows you to grab and shake a window. This has the effect of automatically minimizing every window except the one you're shaking. If you want to return the desktop to the way it was, just shake the window again, and all the minimized windows are restored.

Sometimes you will want to work on two documents side by side, perhaps to move data from one to another, or to compare two web pages or documents. You can do this by dragging windows to the far left or right of the desktop. When you do this, an outline appears, indicating that the window will fill exactly half the screen. You can use this feature to snap windows to both sides of the desktop screen, which can be useful for comparing documents, working on two windows simultaneously, or moving or copying from one location to another. I will show you how to get the best out of this functionality in Chapter 8.

Common Ways to Work with Windows Apps

Windows 8.1 comes with a large amount of preinstalled apps, with hundreds of thousands more available to download via the Windows Store. There are commonalities in the way you interact with apps, and I want to detail these here.

▪ **Tip**   You can quickly open the App bar at any time and in any app by pressing Win+Z in your keyboard.

These commonalities all focus on the charms, and some charms perform specific actions within apps.

- **Search:** The Search charm adds search results from the currently running app to its main results panel (files, settings, Internet results). You can read more about search in Chapter 5.

- **Share:** The Share charm allows you to share content and links from the running app directly with other apps you have installed on your PC. They can include mail, messaging, and social networking apps; as well as being able to save content to your Windows 8.1 Reading list. (More on this later in this chapter.)

- **Devices:** The location in which you print from the running app if you have a printer installed. It is also from the Devices charm that you can play audio and video playlists that can be embedded directly into web pages and apps.

- **Settings:** Displays in the top right of your screen options and settings for the running app. If you want to change a setting, such as adding an e-mail or social networking account, or changing the way the app displays information, you can always find these options by clicking or tapping the Settings charm.

Preinstalled Windows 8.1 Apps

There are a great many apps provided with Windows 8. Many are the standard apps that you now expect to find bundled with an OS or are there to showcase the capabilities of the system. I will discuss the apps with features that can genuinely aid productivity. I won't detail all the included apps with Windows 8.1, partly because they may vary depending on where you bought your PC, but I discuss the most commonly used apps.

■ **Note** One of the biggest advantages of the default apps in Windows 8.1 is that they are more regularly updated than we previously experienced with desktop programs.

Alarm

The Alarm app is most useful on PCs that are always plugged in to mains electricity or that have long battery lives, such as Windows RT tablets (including the Microsoft Surface RT tablet). This app does exactly what you might expect, allowing you to set multiple alarm clocks on your PC (see Figure 2-21). Additionally the app includes timer and stopwatch functionality.

Figure 2-21. *The Alarm app in Windows 8.1*

Calculator

The Calculator app exists in Windows 8.1 as an additional option to the desktop Calculator program (see page 38). It is a simple and touch-friendly calculator with scientific and unit conversion functions (see Figure 2-22).

Figure 2-22. *The Calculator app in Windows 8.1*

Calendar

When you log in to Windows 8.1 using a Microsoft account linked to a Hotmail, MSN, Live, or Outlook.com account, Windows Calendar automatically syncs your appointments and shows any upcoming appointments on the lock screen. This is especially useful if you use a Windows Phone and manage your calendar there or if you log in using an ID linked to an Exchange server.

By default, the Calendar app shows several different calendars, perhaps birthdays and national holidays (see Figure 2-23). You can switch these individual calendars on and off by opening the Settings charm and clicking Options in the top right of your screen. You can also change the colors of displayed calendars here, perhaps to highlight differences between them.

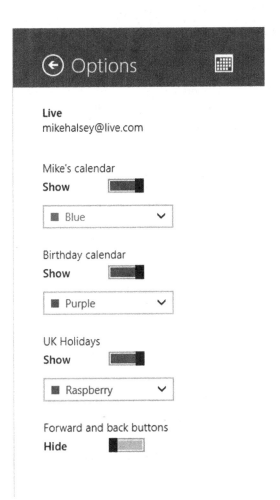

Figure 2-23. *Turning individual calendars on and off*

It is also in these options that you can turn forward and back buttons for the calendar on and off. These buttons can make the app much easier to use with a mouse.

To add a calendar account to the app, open the Settings charm and then click Accounts in the top right of your screen.

Camera

The Camera app lets you take pictures and record video from your tablet, laptop webcam, or the webcam built into or attached to your desktop PC. This app is probably more useful on mobile devices, but eliminates the need for third-party software to do the same job.

In the options for the Camera app you can control important features such as whether the app is allowed to use location information and attach it to photos and videos (note that your PC no longer needs installed GPS for this to work, as the information can also be extracted from your IP address). Additionally here are controls for controlling the aspect ratio and mega-pixel density of pictures and video and also a very useful video stabilization feature.

The features that appear, such as flash, depend entirely on the hardware support in your PC. If your PC does not support a specific feature or doesn't even have an installed camera, you do not see controls for that feature.

Maps

Maps is one of the most useful and powerful apps in Windows 8. It does everything you expect a standard mapping app to do, such as support both road and aerial views, but it also contains a quick and effective route planner with the ability to use an Internet connection to show traffic congestion and its built-in GPS (or location information obtained from your IP address) to pinpoint your location.

Music

Music as an app has been greatly improved since the first release of Windows 8. It now focuses on the music library on your PC while also enabling you to stream and purchase music from the Xbox Music store. You can also build custom "radio stations" based on your personal preferences for music.

Outlook

When you sign in to Windows 8.1 using a Microsoft account linked to an e-mail account or an Exchange server, your e-mail is automatically synced to Windows 8. There is no need to configure the account separately. The Mail app is basic e-mail software, however, with features that allow you to arrange mail by folder. It is a good package for very light usage and as a way to separate your home and work e-mail (work e-mail may be best read with Windows Live Mail or Outlook).

You can add e-mail accounts from the app by opening the Settings charm and you will see an Accounts link appear in the top right of the screen.

The options for the Mail app are slightly different from other apps as some options can be set on a per-account basis. To access these additional controls, see Figure 2-24. These include controlling when the Mail app checks for new e-mail, how much e-mail is downloaded, whether pop-up (toast) notifications are displayed on your screen when new e-mail arrives, and what (if any) your e-mail signature can be.

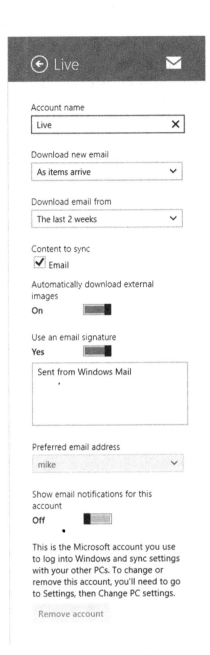

Figure 2-24. *Settings per-account options in the mail app*

■ **Note** If the e-mail account you use in Mail has a calendar and contacts, those features appear in the Calendar and People apps.

People

On the face of it, the People app doesn't look very useful—maybe a bit like a stripped-down social network aggregator. It is actually more powerful than you might imagine. But before you can use it to its full effect, you need a Microsoft account to which you can connect third-party services.

To connect other services to your Microsoft Account, go on the web to `account.live.com`. After logging in, click the *Permissions* link followed by the *Add accounts* link (see Figure 2-25). There are links on this page to connect you to additional services, including social networking and messaging providers.

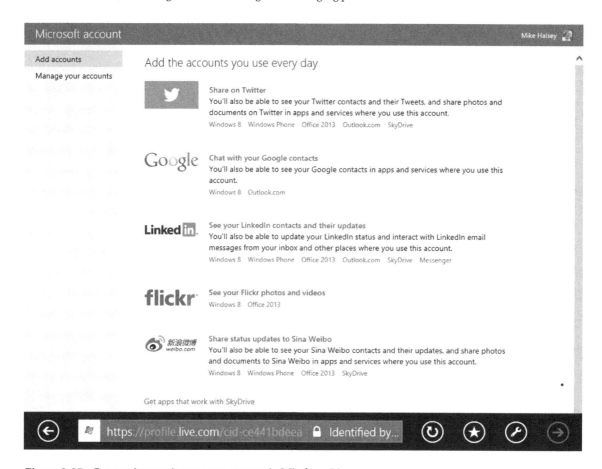

Figure 2-25. *Connecting services to your account in Windows Live*

You can also use the *Manage Other Accounts* and *Manage Apps and Services* links to modify permissions for and also remove services and apps to which your Microsoft account is already connected.

There are dozens of services that can be integrated into Windows Live, including Facebook, LinkedIn, YouTube, Flickr, and more. Linked services appear in your People app, making it much more useful and interesting.

■ **Tip**   After you have connected services to your Microsoft account, you can also activate them within the People hub on a Windows Phone to see updates from your contacts on those networks while on the move.

Photos

The Photos app is a good way to organize and view the photos on your PC. This app also includes some of the more common editing controls such as cropping, brightness, and contrast.

Reading List

As you move between various pages and web sites online, and also within information from apps such as recipes and news, you might find yourself coming across an article that you simply don't have the time (or perhaps the inclination) to read there and then. A new app in Windows 8.1 called the Reading List integrates with the Share charm to enable you to save this content for viewing later.

You can save a page of content in compatible apps (and many older apps are compatible by default with no need for updating) by opening the Share charm and from the sharing options that appear, clicking or tapping *Reading List (bookmark for later)*. The item to be bookmarked is highlighted on the right of your screen, and you can confirm this action by clicking the circular Add Bookmark icon near the top right of your screen (see Figure 2-26).

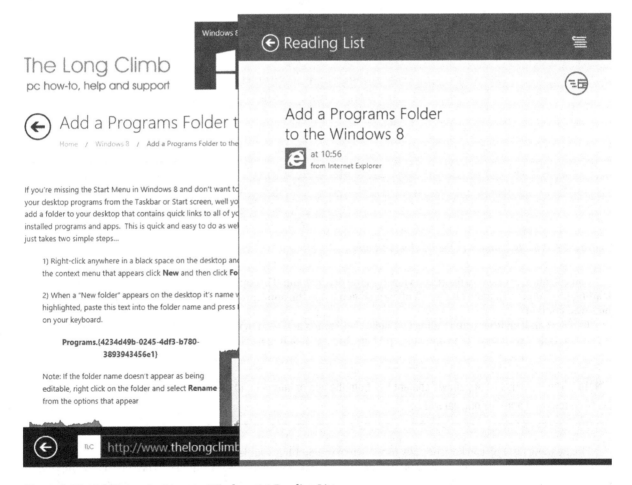

Figure 2-26. Adding content to your Windows 8.1 Reading List

When you want to read content that you have bookmarked, open the Reading List app from the Start screen or the All Apps view and you will see all the content you have bookmarked listed there, along with appropriate imagery or subtitles (see Figure 2-27).

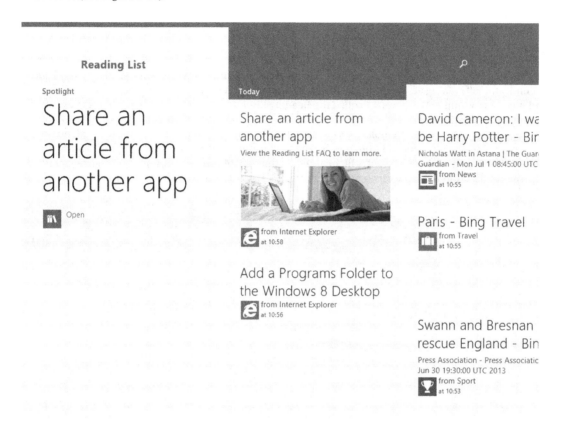

Figure 2-27. *Viewing content in the Reading List app*

You can click any item to open and view it in the original app. This opens a split screen view where your Reading List moves to a pane on the left of your screen while the appropriate app fills the rest of your screen with the saved content.

To delete an item from your reading list, right-click (touch and hold) it to either display a trash icon next to the item in the split-screen view, or to open the app bar when the Reading List is running full screen.

■ **Note**   The Reading List app draws content live from the app or Internet and does not display anything if the content has been removed from the original source.

The Reading List app can be especially useful when researching a subject or subjects, such as for a school, college, or university student, or even when you're undertaking a task at home that interests you such as tracing your family history or reading about the background to a current new story. I personally can see many occasions when the Reading List app will be invaluable in my own life, so it's definitely worth trying.

Video

Video is a basic video-playing app that connects to other services such as Xbox video through a Microsoft account.

Preinstalled Desktop Programs

As you might expect to find with Windows, the bundled desktop programs are much more powerful than their app equivalents. Not much has changed in recent years, but improvements have been made, and some of the apps are indeed very powerful and flexible.

Calculator

If you are used to the basic Windows calculator from XP, you're in for a surprise and a treat. The calculator in Windows 8.1 is extremely flexible. In addition to the default standard mode, there are scientific, programmer, and statistics modes available in the View menu (see Figure 2-28).

Figure 2-28. *The calculator in Windows 8*

You can also use the Windows calculator for unit conversions and date calculations, and there are additional worksheets integrated to help you figure out common calculations, including fuel economy.

Character Map

The Character Map allows you to view all available text characters from the installed fonts on your computer. You can copy these characters, many of which are not available via a keyboard combination, and paste them into your documents.

■ **Tip** You can get quick access to common international characters with the onscreen keyboard by pressing and holding the associated root letter. International variants then appear around it and can be individually selected.

Math Input

If you have a stylus for your computer or tablet, Math Input is useful for turning scribbled equations and formulas into text that can be inserted into your documents. It is extremely good at recognizing handwriting, as you can see in Figure 2-29 (it's not easy writing on my laptop's screen, honest).

Figure 2-29. *The Math Input window*

Notepad

Notepad is still here. The old favorite hasn't changed at all. Why would you want it to? This basic text editor and note taker has always been a popular inclusion in Windows, especially with programmers.

Paint

If you have used Paint in Windows 7, you are familiar with the Ribbon interface. For basic graphics work, such as cropping images and light touchup work, it's fine, too. I have used it extensively in creating the images for this book.

Snipping Tool

Although Windows 8's new feature for automatically saving screen grabs using the Win+PrntScrn key combination is welcome (Win+VolDown on a Microsoft Surface tablet), sometimes you just want to capture a specific window or a part of the screen. This is where the Snipping Tool is useful. It can grab any part of your screen, in any shape, and save it as a file (see Figure 2-30).

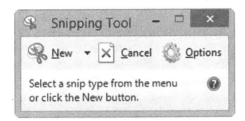

Figure 2-30. *The Snipping Tool*

Sound Recorder

As a basic sound recording tool, the Windows Sound Recorder has always worked well. It records everything passing through the current sound device on your computer and is very good at what it does and has also been carried over from previous versions of Windows. I will show you how set and configure your current audio recording device in Chapter 9.

Sticky Notes

Sticky Notes were formerly gadgets on the Windows Vista sidebar, but in Windows 7, they made their way into the Start menu as a full program. Sticky Notes exist in Windows 8.1 as a useful way to put notes on your desktop without getting glue all over the screen (please don't try that at home!).

Windows Fax and Scan

Despite the fact that every scanner and multifunction printer in the world comes with its own custom scanning software, the scanning software in Windows is extremely accomplished in its own right—with excellent configuration and management options as standard (see Figure 2-31). The app has full faxing capabilities too, including fax history, header pages, and more if you have a compatible modem installed in your PC and are connected to a phone line. See Chapter 6 for details of how to install and manage scanners and cameras in Windows 8.

Figure 2-31. *Windows Fax and Scan*

Windows Journal

The Windows Journal is a note-taking app designed primarily for touchscreens. It is the "little brother" of the incredibly powerful and flexible Microsoft OneNote, a free app for which, OneNote MX, can be found in the Windows Store. The little brother hasn't had a makeover in Windows 8, but for tablets and touchscreen laptops, it still exists as a free alternative to OneNote (see Figure 2-32).

Figure 2-32. *Windows Journal*

Windows Media Center/Windows Media Player

I'll talk in-depth about Windows Media Center and Windows Media Player in Chapter 7, but they exist to allow you to view pictures and video, to listen to music, and to watch and record live TV.

WordPad

Unless you have bought a Windows RT tablet, which comes with full versions of Word, Excel, OneNote, PowerPoint, and Outlook preinstalled, your PC is unlikely to come with an Office package, with Office Starter from Windows 7 having long since been retired in favor of Microsoft's Office web apps (http://office.live.com). WordPad is bundled with Windows 8.1 though, and it is an effective basic word processor that comes with every version of Windows 8.1, including retail copies. It also supports the latest Microsoft Word file formats (see Figure 2-33).

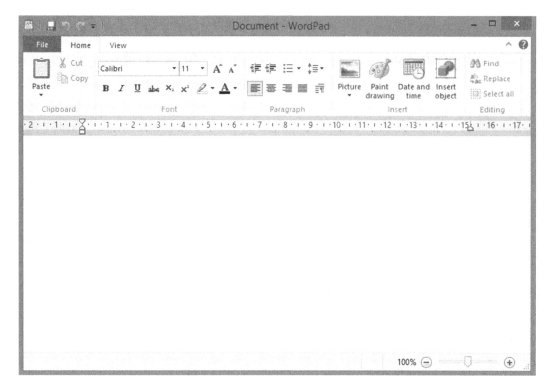

Figure 2-33. *WordPad in Windows 8*

XPS Viewer

XPS has long been Microsoft's alternative to Adobe's PDF file format, and although it's not as popular, it's not going anywhere. Whereas Windows Reader is set as the default app for opening XPS views, the desktop XPS Viewer exists to open XPS files when you don't want to use the app.

Installing and Uninstalling Apps and Programs

When you install an app onto Windows 8, you can't get them from web sites as you can with desktop programs. Instead, you install them from the Windows Store. This makes it very simple to find, install, and update your apps. If updates are available, they will be automatically installed, although you can turn automatic updating off if you want. To do this, in the Store open the Settings charm; then click *App Updates* near the top right of your screen. On the settings page that appears, you can control whether apps are automatically updated (see Figure 2-34).

Figure 2-34. *Updating apps in the Windows Store*

■ **Note** If you manage your computers through Windows Server, you can deploy, manage, and remove apps and desktop programs and apps in Windows 8.1 using AppLocker. AppLocker is not available on Windows RT devices.

You can install Windows desktop software the same as always: by inserting a CD or DVD with the software installer or by running it from a USB flash drive or other external storage through File Explorer. You can't install desktop software on Windows RT because of fundamental differences in the processors used to power Windows 8.1 PCs and Windows RT devices. Attempting to install a desktop program in Windows RT produces an error (see Figure 2-35).

Figure 2-35. *You can't install desktop programs in Windows RT*

■ **Tip** Always choose advanced options when installing software because many software packages also want to install third-party toolbars and utilities that you don't need and may not want.

To uninstall software in Windows 8, you can access Programs and Features from the Control Panel. Here you find all the desktop software installed on your computer. You can click the column headers (Name, Publisher, Installed On, etc.) to sort and arrange the software to make it easier to organize (see Figure 2-36). You may want to arrange it by date, for example, to see the most recently installed software first; you can do this by clicking the column headers (Name, Publisher, Installed on, etc.,) to sort your programs in ascending (one click) or descending (two clicks) order.

Figure 2-36. *The Programs and Features page in Windows 8*

To uninstall apps (and desktop software) from the Start screen, right-click (touch and hold) an app and select Uninstall from the App bar (see Figure 2-37).

Figure 2-37. *Uninstall software from the Start screen*

■ **Tip** When uninstalling apps, you can select multiple apps from the Start screen or All Apps view before pressing Uninstall. Doing so uninstalls all the apps at the same time.

If you uninstall an app this way, it is uninstalled immediately. If you uninstall a desktop program this way, you are redirected to the Programs and Features page—from where you will need to select and uninstall it.
Windows 8.1.

■ **Note** Uninstalling an app might additionally ask you if you only want to uninstall the app from this PC (see Figure 2-38). This occurs if you are logged in to the PC with a Microsoft account and have that app installed on more than one PC. Checking this box uninstalls the app *only* from the PC you are using, but leaving it unchecked also uninstalls the app from *every* PC on which you use the same Microsoft account.

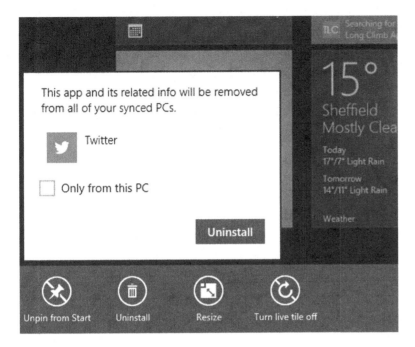

Figure 2-38. *When uninstalling an app, you may be asked if you want to remove it from your other PCs*

Summary

The Start screen is a completely new way of working with Windows. It offers its own challenges and its own learning curve. Some people will love and enjoy it, other people will prefer to use the desktop. In Windows 8, it is much easier to stay on the desktop than you might think, and with the exception of the Start menu, all the functionality from previous versions of Windows remains.

In the next chapter, you will look at how to get Windows 8.1 connected to your home and work networks, devices, peripherals, and the wider world via wired, wireless, and mobile broadband connections.

■ ■ ■

CHAPTER 3

Getting Connected

Windows 8.1 is the best-connected version of the Windows operating system (OS) yet. It includes support for new wireless standards such as 4G mobile broadband. With this added flexibility, however, come some pitfalls. Getting online and connecting to networks is now far more than turning on a connection and entering a password.

In this chapter, I want to take a holistic look at safely and securely connecting to networks and the Internet. You don't want to worry about securely checking your e-mail. Worse still, you don't want to worry about your business or personal data being open and available to hackers and drive-by Wi-Fi thieves.

I will give you the knowledge you need to use network and Internet connections safely and securely, whether you are at home, at work, or on the move. This is especially important as we keep more of our personal and business lives in digital files and in online cloud services. With all our precious photographs, music, documents, and business projects now stored digitally, we need to be certain that we're protected on any device because everything is now interconnected in ways we've not previously experienced.

Getting Online with Windows 8.1

One of the very first things you do with a computer is connect it to the Internet. So much of what we do these days is online, with e-mail and social networking now part of the fabric of society. Long gone are the days when we might use an MSN or IRC chat client for a couple of hours on a weekend. Now it's constant access to chat via PCs and smartphones; social updates across multiple platforms; and access to e-mail, even work e-mail, 24 hours a day.

There really is no getting away from the Internet wherever we go. If you are a web enthusiast, a gamer, an IT pro, at work, or running a business; or even just on your daily commute looking for something to occupy yourself with, odds are that you'll be on a computer and that you'll be online. Tablets recently out from major manufacturers offer features not seen in other tablet OSs, including multiuser setups. Use of Windows 8.1 will be more widespread than in the previous Windows editions that were used only on desktop PCs and laptops. We really do need to make sure that all our data is safe and secure.

Understanding Public and Home and Work Networks

When you connect to a network for the first time, Windows 8.1 asks you this question: "Do you want to find PCs, devices, and content on this network, and automatically connect to devices like printers and TVs?" (See Figure 3-1.) This question is asked because there are differences between home, public, and work networks that determine how the security on your PC should be set up. I want to spend a little time explaining the difference between these three types of networks.

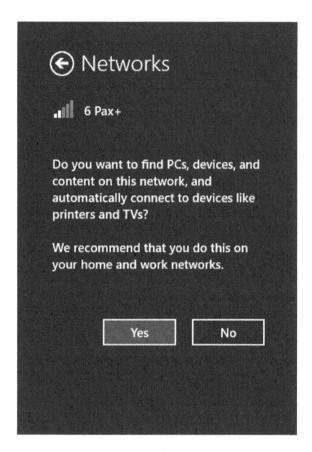

Figure 3-1. *Setting network sharing and security on first connect*

Home Networks

Home networks are the types where you simply trust everything. You are, after all, in complete control of the network and all the hardware attached to it, including other computers, smartphones, tablets, game consoles, and maybe even storage attached to your home Wi-Fi router. What could possibly go wrong with all this?

Well, for starters, many people are confused by or simply don't understand home network security. Why should they? As consumers, we're used to home electronics being like a television, a microwave, or a Blu-ray player. It's not true that all consumer electronics are simple to use. Take the new Internet-connected televisions, for example. Some of these TVs can take three-quarters of an hour to set up the first time you use them. They have myriads of menus controlling different tuners, movie and TV downloads, plug-in services, and 3D and surround sound. A friend of mine bought a new TV in 2011 that he couldn't tune into at all. He simply couldn't get a signal on it, so he called me to look at it. I figured out that both the digital and the old analog tuners had completely different onscreen menus, and they were accessed by pressing different buttons on the remote control. The reason he couldn't get a signal was because he'd been using the wrong tuner in a place where the old analog signal had been switched off.

With home computer equipment, it can be even more complicated. The most common piece of hardware at fault is the router that connects your home to the Internet. While Internet service providers (ISPs) are much better than they used to be at programming individual Wi-Fi passcodes into devices, they still usually leave the administration password as the default.

When coupled with the fact that the name of your Wi-Fi network commonly includes the make and model of the router, it's simple for a neighbor or a drive-by hacker to casually access the router and gain access to your network and the devices on it.

While this type of drive-by hack is rare, it is commonly blamed in file-sharing cases in which unsuspecting people are accused by the authorities and big movie studios of downloading the latest Johnny Depp movie.

The first thing to do with your own home network is make sure that you have unique passwords on both your Wi-Fi access and your router's administration interface. How you do this depends on the make and model you have, but your ISP can talk you through it, and the router should come with a manual or help files.

You don't always connect only to home networks in your own house; you may also connect to home networks at friends' and family members' houses. You have no control over their network or hardware, nor do you have any idea whether they have adequate antimalware protection on their network-connected computers and devices.

When you connect to their Wi-Fi, however, you know whether they have a strong password or even no password at all (be very careful when connecting to networks in which you don't know whether any of the computers are infected with malware).

Home networks are really for use only in your own safe and secure environment, your little bubble in which you absolutely know the state of your security, and where you can implicitly trust the person who put it all together.

Work Networks

Workplace networks are inherently more trustworthy than home networks because they are managed by qualified personnel (mostly). In a work network, the other computers attached to the network can't see the documents, pictures, music, or video you have shared in a HomeGroup (more on this in Chapter 4), but well-written malware can still infect network-connected computers.

Work networks are really only useful only in managed server environments in which a company is running its own Windows Server and you have access to shared storage. If you are connecting to a work network that's run from a Windows Server system, for example, telling Windows that you want to be able to connect with other computers is essential to ensuring that all the relevant network systems in Windows 8.1 have permission to talk to the server and receive data back from it.

If you are in a workplace, however, in which you are using the network only for Internet access, and your computer is stand-alone or not connected to a server (for example, when you're visiting a client), I don't recommend turning on the sharing settings unless you really have to. The reason for this is that in your own company, you have to take it on trust that the IT department has set security appropriately on the network. You may even manage that network yourself. If it's somewhere else, though, and especially if it's a small business, you don't have any reliable knowledge about how security is set on the network and the router.

Public Networks

For everywhere else, and for your peace of mind, there are public networks. It is what you should *always* use if you are in a public place such as a coffee shop, library, or even connected via a mobile dongle or SIM card.

When you tell Windows you do *not* want to connect to other PCs and devices, the OS throws up its full defenses against other computers and network nasties, not allowing file sharing or other sharing unless you explicitly permit it, and thus preventing people on other computers from getting access to your own PC and its files.

If you are ever uncertain about the network you are connected to or perhaps only need to get on the Internet, I recommend you tell Windows 8.1 not to find other PCs. This is the best way to avoid problems and security concerns.

Connecting to Networks in Windows 8.1

Connecting to networks in Windows 8.1 is slightly different from previous versions of the OS. If you are on the desktop, you can still click the network connection icon in the system tray area of the taskbar; but from the Start screen, you first need to open the charms and then click Settings. (You can open the charms with a touch swipe in from the right of your screen; by moving your mouse to the bottom right of the screen; or by pressing Win+I on your keyboard, which is a shortcut that opens the Settings charm.)

In Settings, your network connection button is in the group of six small buttons that pop out from the right of the screen. It is the first of the six, in the top left of the group.

When you click it, you are shown various options (see Figure 3-2). I want to talk about each of these in turn.

Figure 3-2. *The network connection window in Windows 8.1*

Airplane mode was first introduced on mobile phones because radio signals given off by the phones can cause interference with airplane computer systems during takeoff and landing; they can also interfere with other equipment, such as sensitive medical equipment in hospitals. You also find airplane mode settings on GPS-enabled equipment such as some digital cameras. The airplane mode feature is present in Windows 8.1 because people now commonly use laptops and tablets with mobile broadband while traveling. Switching on airplane mode in Windows 8.1 deactivates all communication signals, effectively cutting off all radio communication from being sent and received by the computer. You are reminded by signage onboard the aircraft or by the cabin crew with a polite tap on the shoulder when you need to activate airplane mode on your computer.

Mobile broadband networks are those you access through a SIM card in your laptop or tablet; through a USB mobile broadband dongle; or by sharing the data connection from your mobile phone, which is now the most common. There are data usage concerns with mobile broadband in Windows because of networks commonly capping data usage. I will talk more about this shortly.

Wi-Fi networks are standard home, workplace, or public networks. They have limited range and do not work when you move away from the router or base station.

When you choose a network to connect to, you are asked for the network password if there is one. (Remember to be extremely wary about networks that don't because anybody with nefarious motives can connect and get access to any shared PCs.) There is a box that allows you to see the full characters of the normally hidden password. This is useful to make sure you are typing a complex password correctly. But don't select this option if someone might be looking over your shoulder!

You are also asked if you want to always connect automatically to this network; this box is checked (selected) by default, but unless you want to connect to this network regularly, you should uncheck it. Just because you are fairly sure that a given network is safe, don't assume that it will always stay secure into the future. All it takes is for a single setting to be changed.

Managing Mobile Broadband

As I mentioned earlier, one of the problems with network connections in Windows is that they can be set (deliberately or accidentally) to connect automatically whenever you are in range. I will show you how to manage your network connections shortly, but with 3G or 4G/LTE mobile broadband, this can be a problem, especially if your laptop or tablet has a built-in SIM card.

Mobile data packages regularly cap usage and impose heavy charges for additional data use, so it's bad if your computer connects to such a network when you don't specifically want it to. This can result in hefty data usage bills if you go over your allotted limit (or you may also find you can't get a connection when you need to because you used up your allotment).

While you can set your mobile broadband connection to *not* connect automatically, the only way to be completely safe and secure is to switch it off when you don't need it. Why do I recommend this? Simply because while we're all used to uncapped Wi-Fi usage at home and at work, mobile broadband is still very expensive. Personally, I am not prepared to risk running up huge bills on my laptop and Windows tablet (both of which have a SIM card slot), so I always have mobile broadband switched off in Windows when I'm not using it.

You can independently switch mobile broadband and Wi-Fi on or off (they'll be on by default) in the network connections panel (refer to Figure 3-2). Here you have switches to the right of the Mobile broadband and Wi-Fi headers that control these two network types independently of one another.

Connecting to Hidden Wi-Fi Networks

Wi-Fi networks that are hidden (usually to improve their security) don't appear in the general network connections panel; you have to enter their settings manually. These are settings that you need to have provided to you by the people responsible for maintaining that network.

To connect to a hidden Wi-Fi network, follow these instructions:

1. From the desktop, right-click (or touch and hold) the network icon on the far right of the taskbar. From the pop-up that appears, click *Open the Network and Sharing Center.* You can also search for the Network and Sharing Center from the Search charm.

2. In the Network and Sharing Center, click the *Set up a New Connection or Network* link roughly in the middle of the page.

3. Click *Manually Connect to a Wireless Network* in the dialog that appears and click *Next* (see Figure 3-3).

Figure 3-3. *Connecting to a hidden wireless network*

4. On the next page, you are required to enter information that has to be provided by the Wi-Fi network manager. This information includes the name of the network, its security key, and its security encryption type.

You may find it helpful to also check the *Start this Connection Automatically* box, which autoconnects your PC to the hidden Wi-Fi network whenever you are in range of it. This is a different default behavior than if you connect to a network using the network connections panel from the Settings charm.

Connecting to a Mobile Broadband Network

When you connect your PC to a mobile broadband network, which you do in much the same way as when connecting to a Wi-Fi network, you are presented with an additional option: *Roam Automatically* (see Figure 3-4). You may want to leave it unchecked because checking it allows your PC to stay connected to the Internet even if you roam outside of your own mobile network, perhaps even on to one in a different country.

Figure 3-4. *Connecting to mobile broadband*

This can be a particular problem for people who live or work close to a country's border where mobile signals from both countries can be detected, and where your phone or computer can become confused about the country in which it is located. Roaming charges, especially for data, can be considerable, and the ability to automatically prevent data roaming on your PC is a very helpful addition.

■ **Note**　If you tell a mobile network to roam (or not), you can't change this setting later without deleting the network and connecting again from the beginning. This process must be done from the Windows command prompt, so you may find it simpler to enable roaming if you want it occasionally, but disable the mobile broadband connections in the networks panel when you are close to a country's border and do not want it to be used accidentally.

Connecting to a Company Workplace

If you use your Windows 8.1 laptop or tablet at work or have been provided with a Windows 8.1 PC by your employer, you probably need to connect to the company network (often called a *domain*). Sometimes, however, you want to use your own computer, so for this purpose Microsoft introduced a new feature called *Workplace*. This feature allows the IT department to grant certain network access permissions to computers and staff members who are not directly connected to the company domain.

1. To connect to a workplace, open the Settings charm (Win+I from the keyboard).

2. Click *Change PC Settings* in the bottom right of your screen.

3. When in PC Settings, click *Network* on the left of the screen.

4. Click *Workplace* on the left of the screen (see Figure 3-5).

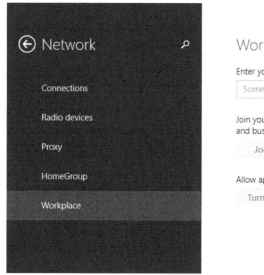

Figure 3-5. *Connecting to a company domain*

When you're in the Workplace settings, enter the ID provided by your company in the *Enter your ID* box, and the *Join* button becomes available to click. You may optionally be asked for a password at this point.

Below this, you see a box labeled *Allow apps and services from IT admin*. This is a feature that allows system administrators to remotely install apps and programs that are essential for your role in the workplace. This feature saves you having to install them manually and helps the IT department ensure that the correct versions are installed and updated in the proper manner. You may be asked by your IT department to click the *Turn on* button to activate this feature.

Connecting to a Company Domain

If your company doesn't support the Workplace feature on your PC or if the PC is *only* used in the same workplace, you may need to manually join a company domain. Doing so gives your computer access to the company network and shared files and drives, and it also grants the IT department management control for your PC.

To connect to a company domain, follow these instructions:

1. Open *System* either by selecting it in the Control Panel or by searching for it with the Search charm.

2. In the *System* panel, click the *Change Settings* link in the Computer name, domain and workgroup settings section (see Figure 3-6).

Figure 3-6. *Click the Change Settings link on the right side of the panel*

3. In the dialog that appears, click the *Change* button.

4. In the next dialog, shown in Figure 3-7, change the Computer name if instructed to do so by your IT department.

Figure 3-7. *Changing the domain settings*

5. Check the radio button for *Member of Domain* and in the box below, enter the name of the domain (e.g., `thelongclimb.com`), as instructed by your IT department.

6. The computer now attempts to connect to the domain, and you are asked to enter the username and password provided for your domain account.

7. When prompted, restart your PC.

The next time, and at all future times unless and until you change these settings again to once more make the computer part of a workgroup instead, you are presented with a login screen when starting your computer that requires your domain username and password credentials.

Connecting to Virtual Private Networks

By default, Windows 8.1 shows you only networks that are not hidden; it's designed to make things as easy as possible for you. To connect to a workplace virtual private network, (VPN) perform the following steps. Note that if you are connecting to a VPN that has been set up for your company, you need settings that can be provided by your network administrator.

1. Open the Settings charm (Win+I from your keyboard).

2. Click *Change PC Settings* in the bottom right of your screen.

3. When in PC Settings, click *Network*.

■ **Note**   You can also connect to VPNs from the Network and Sharing Center. Right-click the network icon in the taskbar system tray and click *Open the Network and Sharing Center.* After this is open, click *Set up a Connection or Network* in the center of the panel.

4. In the *Connections* section of the network settings, click *Add a VPN Connection*. It should be visible right away.

5. You need the VPN details from your workplace to enter at the next screen (see Figure 3-8).

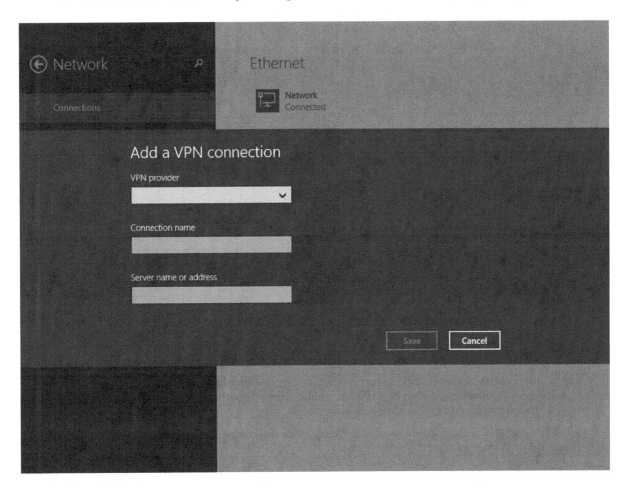

Figure 3-8. *Network and Sharing Center in Windows 8.1*

6. To connect to the company VPN, click *Save.*

The wizards to connect to hidden Wi-Fi networks and VPNs are very straightforward and easy to use, but you need specific information for them, such as the hidden network's SSID name and security passphrase type, or the IP address of the VPN.

Managing and Deleting Wireless Network Profiles

Sometimes, perhaps because the settings for a Wi-Fi network have become corrupt or because the passphrase for the network has changed and you find yourself locked out, you might want to change or even delete and start again with one or more of your connections.

Alas, there's no easy way to do this in Windows 8.1 because the Forget this Network feature was removed from Windows 8.1. It is still possible and relatively simple to manage and delete these network profiles, however:

1. Open the *Command Prompt* from the WinX menu (Press Win+X on your keyboard, right-click in the bottom left of your screen or search for Command Prompt from the Search charm).

2. In the Command window, type **netsh wlan show profiles** and press Enter. A list of your stored WiFi networks appears (see Figure 3-9).

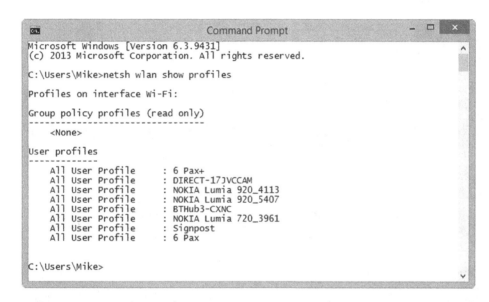

Figure 3-9. *Wireless networks appear in the Command window*

3. Choose the wireless network you want to delete and type **netsh wlan delete profile name="ProfileName,"** where *ProfileName* matches the name of the network you want to delete as it appears in the list; then press Enter.

The wireless network profile is now deleted, and the next time you connect to that network, it will be as if you never connected to it before on that PC.

■ **Tip** You can manage saved mobile broadband profiles in the same way by substituting **wlan** in these commands for **mbn**.

It is also possible to recover the password for a wireless network if you forget it and need it to connect another PC. To do this, follow these instructions:

1. Make sure that your PC is already connected to the wireless network.

2. Open the *Network and Sharing Center* by right-clicking the network icon in the system tray (on the right of the taskbar) or by searching for it using the Search charm.

3. In the Network and Sharing Center, click the name of the wireless network in the *Connections* section (see Figure 3-10).

Figure 3-10. *You see the name of the currently connected network*

4. In the dialog that appears, click the *Wireless Properties* button. If you do not see this button, you are connected to an Ethernet or 3G/LTE network for which these properties do not apply.

5. In the next dialog, click the *Security* tab.

6. Now check the *Show characters* box (see Figure 3-11); the passphrase for the wireless network is revealed.

Figure 3-11. *You can display the passphrase for the current network*

Managing Network Connections

You also use the Network and Sharing Center for managing your main network connection hardware, whether Ethernet, Bluetooth, Wi-Fi, mobile broadband, or other connection types. You can access the Network and Sharing Center by either searching for it or navigating to the desktop and right-clicking the Network button, in which there is an option to open it.

To see the network hardware you have installed on your computer, click Change Adapter Settings in the left pane. The window that opens contains all the network connections that you have on your PC (see Figure 3-12).

Figure 3-12. *Managing network connections in Windows 8.1*

You can right-click these connections to perform various actions, but the following actions are also available on the toolbar at the top of the window:

- **Disable** the connection so that you keep it in your network settings, but the network cannot be accessed.

- **Connect** or **Disconnect** from the network.

- Check the **Status** of the network, which is useful if you are having connection difficulties.

- **Diagnose** a problem or a fault with the connection. This runs an automated troubleshooter that resets the connection to its default state.

- Check the **Properties** of the connection. This is where you can change specific settings with the network adaptor. Use your computer to share this connection with other computers by turning your PC into a mobile hotspot, or turn on/off specific features that may be causing problems, such as IPv6.

- There is no direct option to delete a connection or change its autoconnect or stored password settings. To delete a connection, highlight it and press the **Delete (Del) key** on your keyboard.

■ **Note** Windows 8.1 only allows you to select the status of a connected network or Internet connection. Sometimes it is simpler to delete the connection and have Windows rebuild it on a restart.

Network Management Best Practice

If you manage a network at home or at work, you should take a holistic view of security and network management, including consideration for who will be using the network.

It is worth the money, especially in a small business environment, to buy a router that allows you to set up multiple main and guest SSIDs. The advantage of doing this is that you don't have to worry about visitors to your work environment having accidental access to your computers, the files stored on them, or any shared storage you have in the workplace.

Many high-end routers offer this functionality, and in the workplace I couldn't recommend it more. It can also be useful in the home, especially if you have shared network storage, such as an NAS drive or a USB hard disk attached to your router, on which you keep backups and private files.

You should always make sure that the router has two passwords on it: one for the administration interface and another for the Wi-Fi. These passwords should *always* be different. If you have a router that supports multiple SSIDs, each one should have its own unique password. This is the best way to guarantee—as much as is humanly possible, anyway—that you have excellent security on your network.

■ **Tip** To create a secure password, make sure it is at least 12 characters long and includes a mixture of uppercase and lowercase letters, numbers, and symbols. You can also use some numbers and symbols to represent letters, such as 5 instead of S, 1 instead of i or L, and & instead of A.

Securing Wi-Fi Networks

When you set up your Wi-Fi network, it can be difficult to decide which type of security to use on the password; after all, there are so many. Do you choose WEP, WPA-Personal, WPA2-Personal, WPA-Enterprise, or WPA2-Enterprise encryption? Because they are all combinations of letters and numbers, what does each one mean? There is a temptation to choose a basic encryption type such as WEP because it allows for the use of short passwords that are easy to remember. This makes it very insecure, however. The higher the level of encryption you add, the longer and more complex the default password requirement is.

Suffice it to say that WEP, WPA, and WPA2 can all be compromised, especially in the business space, by an experienced and determined drive-by hacker (a person sitting outside the building in a car or on a bench who hacks into a network from a laptop). So unless your router offers additional security options that can be used in conjunction with the key—such as AES encryption or a RADIUS authentication server—you are never completely protected.

Each type of secure encryption and authentication you add to a Wi-Fi network makes the password longer with requirements that are more stringent. On the upside, it has to be entered on each computer only once; but on the downside, it still has to be entered.

I bring this up because it's a legitimate security concern, especially for business. On the other hand, you need to think about the likelihood of a drive-by hacker trying to crack your security.

What do you have on your network? How sensitive are your files and documents? Are you really a hacking target? Most enthusiasts and IT pros reading this have the same types of files on their networks as any consumer, but also have business files. Only if you store particularly sensitive data on your network—you work in the biochemical industry or for a government agency, for example—are you likely to be the target of drive-by hackers. And if the last few years have shown us anything, it is that data theft from governments is much more likely to come from within than from outside.

This isn't to say hacking will never happen to you, but I want to present a balanced argument. For home users, I recommend WPA2 encryption. The minimum password length might be a bit long to remember, but it is always recommended by security professionals to have long passwords. You should keep the password written in a safe location—a desk drawer in your home or workplace, for example, is good because it is unlikely that someone will physically break into the building to access your Wi-Fi network. If they did, they could just plug a physical network cable into your router and bypass the passphrase anyway. WEP and WPA simply don't offer enough security, so I recommend you avoid them.

Managing Mobile Broadband Data Usage

If you use your computer on a mobile broadband connection (3G/4G), you probably want to make sure that you don't go over your usage limits.

Windows 8.1 can help you both monitor your usage and limit the amount of data used by displaying the amount of data you use in the network connections panel. When you connect to a mobile broadband network, Windows tells you the amount of data you have used so far. If you are on a monthly contract in which you have a fixed amount of data, you can reset the data counter every month by clicking Reset.

You need to switch this feature on for individual networks however (and can also switch it on for Wi-Fi networks) by following these steps:

1.   Open PC Settings.

2.   Click the *Network* settings.

3.   Click the name of the network for which you want to display the data usage.

4.   In the *Data Usage* section, turn on the switch called *Show my estimated data use in the Networks list* and, optionally, you can force Windows 8.1 to treat this network as a metered connection (see Figure 3-13). Setting a connection as a metered connection prevents Windows and your apps from sending and receiving too much data to avoid excessive charges.

Find devices and content

Find PCs, devices and content on this network and automatically connect to devices like printers and TVs. Turn this off for public networks to help keep your stuff safe.

On

Data usage

Show my estimated data use in the Networks list

Off

Set as a metered connection

Off

Figure 3-13. *Windows 8.1 helps you monitor your mobile broadband usage*

■ **Tip**   For mobile broadband networks, you also see an option here to protect your data connection with a PIN. You can use it to prevent unauthorized use of the network that can run up expensive bills, or even to prevent its accidental use when you are out and about.

The live tiles on the Windows 8.1 Start screen consume data every time they automatically update. You can limit the amount of data they consume, however, by doing the following:

1. From the Start screen, open the Settings charm (Win+I from the keyboard).

2. At the top right of the screen, click **Tiles**. Note that this option doesn't appear if you open the Settings charm from the desktop.

The Tiles window (see Figure 3-14) allows you to specify the maximum amount of data that live tiles are allowed to use each month. Once this limit is reached, the live tiles no longer update over your mobile broadband connection.

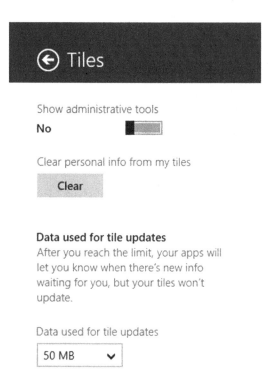

Figure 3-14. *Control the amount of mobile data that live tiles use*

Using Internet Explorer 11

Windows 8.1 comes with two different versions of the Internet Explorer web browser. One of these is an app run from the Start screen, and the other is the more traditional desktop program. Although these two browsers might appear completely separate, they do share favorites and stored information, such as web site usernames and passwords.

As you might imagine, however, the versions operate in different ways. The Internet Explorer 11 (IE11) app is a slimmed-down version containing just the controls most people need for everyday web browsing. The desktop version, on the other hand, is a full-featured browser with support for plug-ins, toolbars, and the more advanced features that many computer users like to have. In this section, I will talk you through the differences and show you how to get the best from each browser.

Using the Internet Explorer 11 App

Life is usually complicated enough, but Windows 8.1 includes two versions of the Internet Explorer web browser. There are two fundamental differences between them.

IE11 in Windows 8.1 does not support *any* plug-ins, so web content written in languages such as Java simply do not display or work, although many web sites with Flash content still work because the Flash player software is built into Windows 8.1.

That said, it isn't all bad news. For starters, the lack of plug-ins and a focus on the new HTML5 web standard makes the browser much more secure. This isn't just a decision Microsoft made; it was Apple that first blocked browser plug-ins on the iPad and iPhone. The reasoning behind the move, which was deeply unpopular at the time, was that it made the browser more secure and prevented third-party plug-ins from slowing down the browser. Plus, with HTML5 web sites beginning to appear, there was a shrinking need for plug-ins.

■ **Tip**　You can save pictures from web sites in the IE11 app by right-clicking (touching and holding) them and selecting *Save to Pictures Folder* from the options that appear.

If you want to use plug-ins and toolbars in Internet Explorer in Windows 8.1, the desktop version of the browser and some third-party web browsers continue to support them.

As with all apps, Internet Explorer runs fullscreen. A swipe upward from the bottom of the screen or down from the top brings up the App bar (see Figure 3-15).

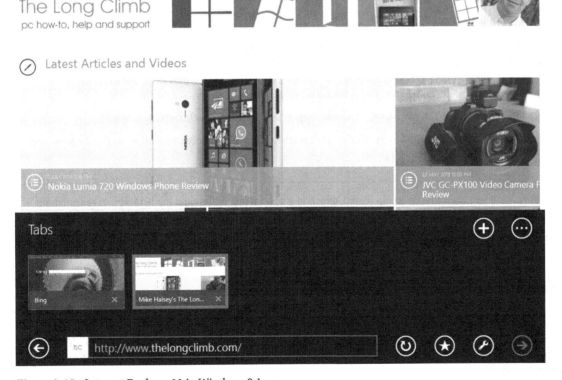

Figure 3-15. *Internet Explorer 11 in Windows 8.1*

The controls in this version of Internet Explorer are limited. It is not as full-featured as its desktop counterpart is. On the App bar, you find the following features:

- The **Back button** takes you back to the previous web page.

- The **address bar** allows you to tap and enter a web address or a search term. The **Refresh button** reloads the current page.

- The **Add to Favorites** button can be used to pin web sites to your Start screen.

- The **Settings button**. The only available settings for IE11 are the following:

    - **Find on Page**, where you can search for text on the currently displayed web page.

    - **View on Desktop** opens the current page in the desktop version of IE11.

    - **View Downloads** lets you see files that you have downloaded to your PC.

- The **Forward button** takes you forward one page if you have already moved back.

■ **Tip** When typing at the address bar in the IE11 app, tapping the *Favorites* button on the App bar displays all your Internet favorites, as shared with the desktop version of Internet Explorer. They are displayed as you have saved them, which include folders you can drill down in to. This is a very quick way to open previously saved web sites.

Above the controls, you see the following:

- **Thumbnail images of the open browser tabs**; you can click one to display it fullscreen.

- **Plus (+) button** to open a fresh tab.

- A button with three dots with two more options:

    - **New in Private Tab** opens a tab in private browsing mode. In this mode, no history is stored of the web pages you visit, and no cookies or downloadable files from the web site are stored on the computer (this is useful when shopping for gifts).

    - **Reopen Closed Tab** allows you to easily reopen a tab if you have closed it accidentally.

All the usual touch-and-swipe gestures in Windows 8.1 work in Internet Explorer, including on the desktop, and have pinch gestures to zoom in and out of a page.

■ **Tip** IE11 may ask if you want to turn on flip ahead, which is a special mode that gets the IE11 app to guesstimate what the next page of a web site will be. When you swipe from the right of the screen inward, it moves to that page. You can also swipe at any time in from the left of your screen to move backward one page.

Using Favorites in Internet Explorer

You can display your favorite links in IE11 by clicking or tapping in the address bar. The screen changes to show your favorites, including all your frequently used ones and those that are pinned to the Start screen.

You can select a favorite to load by tapping or clicking it. If you want to open a favorite in a new tab or delete it, you can right-click it with your mouse (you can select only one at a time this way) or tap and hold to bring up the context menu with touch.

Unless you choose to turn off the Windows 8.1 syncing feature in the Sync Your Settings page of PC Settings, all your Internet Explorer favorites are automatically synced between computers that you log on to using a Microsoft account. It can also sync your tabs so you can have continuity in your browsing when you move from one Windows 8.1 PC to another. This is a tremendous timesaver because you can go to any Windows 8.1 computer, log in with your Microsoft account, and all your favorites in both versions of Internet Explorer—standard Windows 8.1 and desktop—are there.

Using Internet Explorer 11 on the Desktop

Unlike its slimmed-down cousin, Internet Explorer on the desktop is the fully featured version with all the trimmings. It is the same cosmetically as Internet Explorer 9, and if you are familiar with that browser in Windows 7, you will feel at home right away.

It is a very powerful browser (see Figure 3-16) and highly configurable, too, so I want to spend some time in this chapter showing you how to get the very best from it.

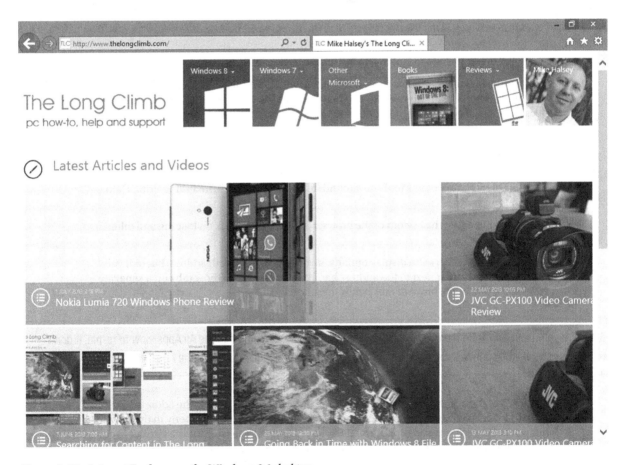

Figure 3-16. *Internet Explorer on the Windows 8.1 desktop*

One of the most useful features of the browser is in its toolbars and extras, which can be switched on by right-clicking anywhere in the blank space at the top of the window (see Figure 3-17).

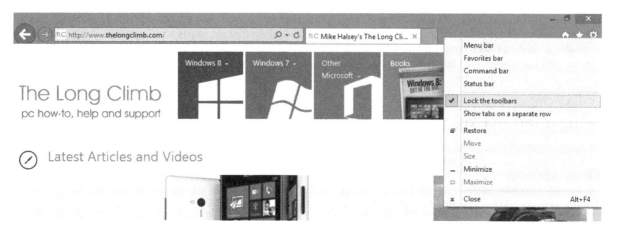

Figure 3-17. *Right-click the top of the IE11 desktop browser to display additional options*

IE11 toolbars and extras include the following features:

- The **menu bar** is the traditional drop-down menu with the typical Internet Explorer options displayed. There is really no need for this now because the options are all easy to get at and because almost nothing else in Windows 8.1 has drop-down menus. This is only a legacy feature.

- The **Favorites bar** is a quick way to launch commonly used links to web sites. It is a far quicker way to launch web sites than the Favorites menu.

- The **Command bar** contains tools now found in the Settings menu, including Print, Home, RSS, and Safety.

- The **Status bar** sits at the bottom of the browser and gives feedback on loading and other aspects of the page.

- The **address bar** offers extra display options. If you want a full-width address bar or if you want to place a toolbar next to the address bar, you can choose to **Show tabs on a separate row**, which moves the browser tabs below the address bar.

■ **Tip** If you unpin IE11 from the taskbar and then worry that you can't find it in the All Apps view to re-pin, it don't worry. You can select the Internet Explorer app, and a *Pin to Taskbar* option appears in the App bar.

- To the left of the address bar are the **Back** and **Forward buttons**. Inside the address bar are buttons for Search, Compatibility (for a web site that doesn't display properly in the browser, but worked in earlier versions of Internet Explorer), and Refresh (reloads the current page). To the far right of the tabs are buttons for Home, Favorites, and Settings.

■ **Tip** You can pin a web site to the Windows taskbar by dragging its button (found to the left of the address bar) onto the taskbar. Some web sites contain their own custom Jump Lists, enabling you to quickly access different pages or features within the web site.

Managing Browser Tabs in IE11 on the Desktop

Web browser tabs in Internet Explorer 11 work in the same way as they have in previous versions of the browser and in other web browsers. Each tab, when you mouse over it, displays a Close button (represented by an ×) on its right. You can also drag and drop browser tabs to rearrange them in any order you want.

▪ **Tip** You can drag a tab out of Internet Explorer to open it in its own Window and also drag tabs from other IE11 windows to amalgamate them into a single window with multiple tabs.

Internet Explorer 11 Safety Features

Some features in the Settings menu may be familiar, but there are some that deserve special attention. The Safety options are chief among these because Internet safety is very important to us all (see Figure 3-18).

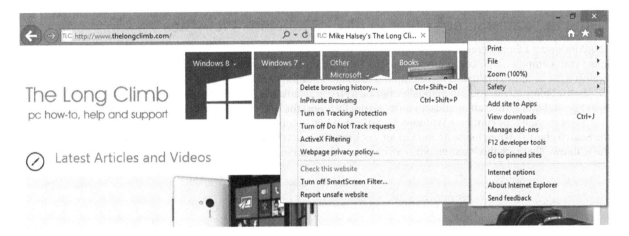

Figure 3-18. *The Safety options in Internet Explorer*

IE11 includes the following safety features:

- **Delete browsing history** deletes all records of the web sites that you have visited in Internet Explorer. You may not want anyone else seeing the web sites you have visited because they appear automatically in the address bar when a user clicks in it or searches in it.

- **InPrivate Browsing** is a special mode within Internet Explorer that doesn't keep any record of the web sites you visit and that doesn't allow those web sites to leave cookies or other tracking files on your computer. This mode is useful for gift shopping.

- **Tracking protection.** Sometimes you visit web sites in which cookies are placed on your computer by third-party web sites, often through advertisements. Tracking protection is disabled in IE11 by default, but you can turn it back on here if you want.

- **Turn off Do Not Track requests**. IE11 requests, politely of course, that web sites do not track it or your online activity. If you want to turn off this functionality, you can do so here.

- **ActiveX Filtering** is a feature that blocks small programs, sometimes used to play video, from running in your web browser. ActiveX controls can be programmed to run malicious code on your computer when activated.

- **Webpage privacy policy** displays the privacy policy, if available, of the web site that is currently displayed.

- **Check this website**, which is available for some (but not all) web sites, enables you to check the web site against the Microsoft master list of known safe and unsafe sites to see whether there is a potential security risk. Fortunately, my own web site, shown in Figures 3-15 to 3-18, is known to be safe ☺.

- **Turn off SmartScreen Filter**. Microsoft SmartScreen, which I will talk about shortly, helps prevent malicious code from web sites from running on your PC. If you want to turn this feature off, perhaps because it interferes with a company intranet, you can do so here.

- **Report unsafe website** is where you can report a web site to Microsoft and the relevant authorities that you know contains malware or that is being used for criminal purposes.

Using the SmartScreen Filter to Block Malicious Web Sites

The Windows 8.1 SmartScreen Filter runs in IE11 to help prevent malicious code from running on web sites that can infect your computer. Unless you turn it off in the Safety options, it automatically checks every web page you visit against a list of known malicious sites compiled in collaboration with other browser makers and security companies.

In the Safety menu, you can manually check a web site against the SmartScreen database. If you suspect a web site to be malicious, you can use this menu to manually report the web site as potentially unsafe to Microsoft.

You can manually configure Windows SmartScreen in the Action Center (or by searching for SmartScreen from the Search charm). When in the Action Center, click the *Change Windows SmartScreen Settings* link in the top left of the window. There are three settings you can choose with SmartScreen, as shown in Figure 3-19.

Figure 3-19. *Changing Windows SmartScreen settings*

1. The default setting is to **Get administrator approval before running an unrecognized app from the Internet**. Microsoft recommends this, and so do I. It offers the best level of protection while still giving you the choice of running a suspect app if you want to.

2. **Warn before running an unrecognized app, but don't require administrator approval** allows Standard users on your PC to run suspect apps. This could pose a security risk to your PC and files, especially if the person running the app is inexperienced in such things, such as a child.

3. **Don't do anything (turn off Windows SmartScreen)** isn't a setting I recommend at all. It should be set only if you use your PC for work, and SmartScreen is blocking essential features of your company intranet.

Managing Add-ons, Toolbars and Search Providers in IE11

Toolbars and add-ons are incredibly useful in Internet Explorer, including the Flash Player and Java (though the Flash player is now built into IE11). Occasionally, however, they can get in the way, slow down your browser, or even be malicious and hijack your search submissions.

You can manage and remove toolbars from Internet Explorer 11 in the Settings menu by selecting Manage Add-ons. In the window that appears (see Figure 3-20), you can highlight an add-on or a toolbar; Enable and Disable buttons appear in the bottom-right corner of the window.

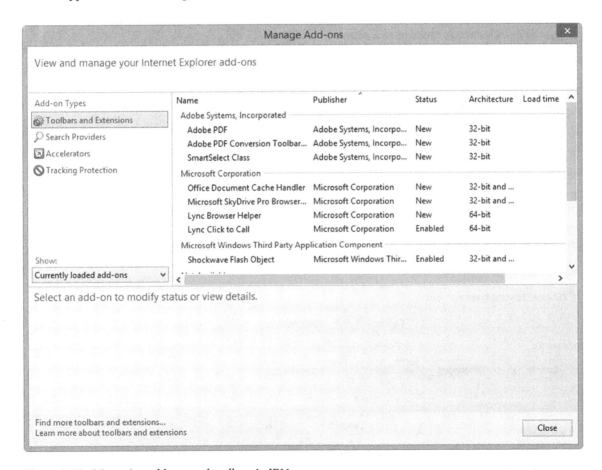

Figure 3-20. Managing add-ons and toolbars in IE11

■ **Note** Disabling an IE add-on or toolbar is not the same as uninstalling it from your computer. You can uninstall add-ons and toolbars in Programs and Features in the Control Panel.

I mentioned at the beginning of this section that abusive toolbars can hijack your search providers. Having this happen can be as annoying as having a problem toolbar, and disabling the toolbar won't fix the problem, either. In the left column of the Manage Add-ons window, you can click *Search Providers* and it is here where you can remove problem search providers and even add in new ones, such as Google or Yahoo!.

Internet Explorer 11 Options and Configuration

The extensive Internet options in IE11 (see Figure 3-21) also need a mention. I want to talk you through some of these settings. You access Internet Options from the Settings button to the far right of the browser tabs.

Figure 3-21. The General tab in Internet Options

■ **Note**   Windows 8.1 automatically syncs your browser tabs across different Windows 8.1 computers in the IE11 app. It can't be controlled here, but it can be switched on and off in PC Settings. I will show you how to do this in Chapter 9.

The first tab to appear in Internet Options is the General tab (see Figure 3-21). Under this tab, you can set a single or multiple (write each one on a different line) home pages for your web browser. You can also set IE to automatically reload all the pages from your last browsing session when you start it. Note that this is something the IE11 app does automatically.

The Tabs options are interesting. When you open a tab from another browser tab, IE color-codes them automatically. It also opens all new tabs next to the existing one. These are features that some people find irritating. It is here where they can be switched off.

You can also turn off tabbed browsing completely if you want, forcing each new web site to open in its own window.

■ **Tip**   You can completely delete your web browsing history in the Settings panel by clicking the *Delete* button. Optionally, you can force Windows to delete your browsing history every time you close your browser by checking the *Delete browsing history on exit* check box.

Managing Safety and Privacy in Internet Explorer 11

Two things that concern people greatly these days, especially parents whose children use the Internet, are safety and privacy. Internet Explorer 11 comes with built-in options to help with this. Click the Settings button near the top right of the window and select Internet Options from the menu.

The Safety options, also selected from the Settings button in IE11, block potentially unsafe web sites or allow web sites that IE11 blocks by default. These settings can be further customized, but unless you have real reasons for changing this control, you will probably find that it proves more of a hindrance than a help because all manner of useful and perfectly legitimate web sites are blocked if you turn the settings up.

The Security tab (see Figure 3-22) allows you to set general rules for your Internet security, such as whether to allow or block certain types of cookies, which are small tracking files placed by web sites on your computer to permit actions such as remembering login passwords.

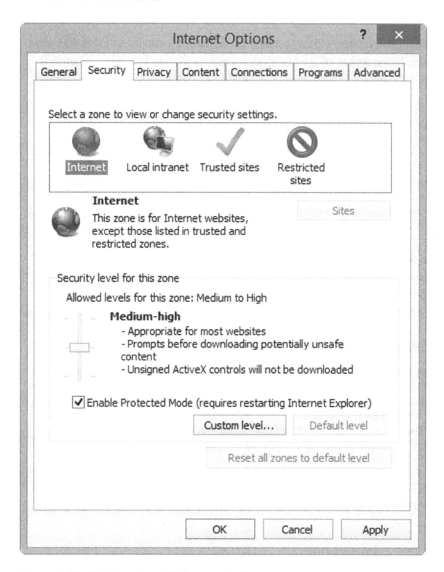

Figure 3-22. *The Security tab in Internet Options*

Of more interest are the Privacy options (see Figure 3-23), which allow you to block tracking and other cookies from web sites, depending on your own criteria. The feature also allows you to import whitelists and blacklists from third parties (perhaps parental or privacy groups).

Figure 3-23. *The Privacy tab in Internet Options*

In the Location Services section of this tab, you can block web sites from being sent to your physical location. This is useful not just because computers now come fitted with GPS systems but also because your location can often be determined from your PC's IP address.

It is also on this tab that you can turn Internet Explorer's built-in pop-up blocker on and off. It is turned on by default, but if it interferes with your company intranet, for example, you can deactivate it.

The Content tab (see Figure 3-24) is commonly of interest to parents. Windows 8.1's Family Safety can be accessed from here. It is also where you can manage the AutoComplete settings whereby IE11 remembers passwords, usernames, and more from your browsing history. Individual components in AutoComplete can be switched on and off here.

Figure 3-24. *The Content tab in Internet Options*

Recovering Lost Web Site Usernames and Passwords

While I'm on the subject of stored usernames and passwords, this is a good time to tell you that Windows 8.1 can show you your usernames and passwords for web sites if you forget them. You can do this by searching for **credentials** and running the *Manage web credentials* settings.

The Web Credentials panel lists all the web sites you have stored usernames and passwords for (see Figure 3-25). You expand the details for a web site by clicking the down arrow to the right of its name. Then details such as your username and whether the credentials are permitted to roam (i.e., if they are be synched between Windows 8.1 PCs) are displayed.

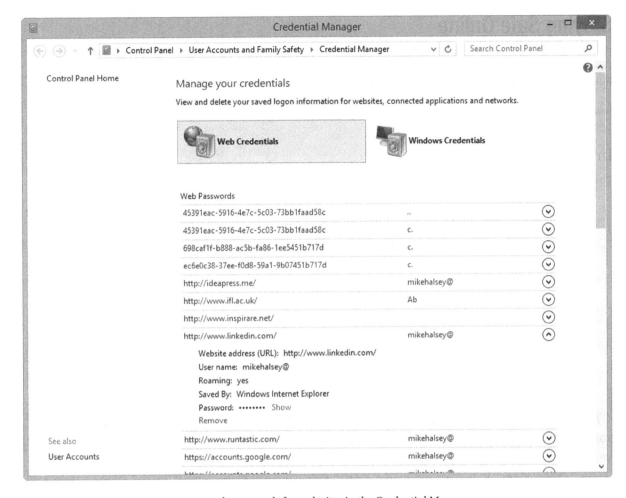

Figure 3-25. *Recovering usernames and passwords for web sites in the Credential Manager*

By default, the password is blanked out, but you can click the *Show* link next to a password to display it. If you have a password on your Windows 8.1 user account, you are asked to enter it here as authorization.

If you want to remove the credentials for a certain web site, you can click the *Remove* link; they are deleted from stored memory in the Credential Manager.

What is InPrivate Mode?

I want to insert a quick note about InPrivate mode here because it is relevant to your privacy online. This mode, which can be easily activated in both the desktop and app versions of IE11, as I have detailed earlier, is a special mode that prevents the web browser and web sites you visit from collecting any information about you.

This mode is useful for a wide range of activities, including shopping for secret birthday presents and for communication inside a country where Internet activity can be monitored. (Some regimes have mechanisms in place that track you anyway, and additional software such as a mobile browser or Tor, www.torproject.org, may be required for complete anonymity.) Generally speaking, and especially for present shopping, InPrivate Mode is a great way to hide what you've been doing from the people who use your PC and user account.

Staying Safe Online

Staying safe online is a challenge these days. Criminals are everywhere, ready to infect our computers with malware or steal our credit card information or identities. So when we increasingly spend our time on online social networks and Internet shopping sites, how can we know that we are safe and secure?

I want to discuss online threats; how you can spot them; and how you can protect yourself, your friends, and your family against them.

Internet Threats Explained

There are several major types of Internet threats.

- **Malware** is malicious software that infects a computer to steal information, steal or encrypt files, or simply corrupt a machine and delete things. It can come from various sources, including *macros* (small programs than run inside files, usually word processor or spreadsheet files); *keyloggers* that record everything you type, including credit card information and bank logins; and browser plug-ins that pretend to be something that you need, such as a codec required to view a video online.

- **Phishing** e-mails try to trick you into revealing sensitive information, such as passwords, by pretending to be from a reputable bank or business institution.

- **Compromised web sites** may look perfectly legitimate, but they ask for sensitive information that can be used to hijack your account or that are programmed to download and run infected files to your computer.

▓ **Tip**   No legitimate web site will *ever* e-mail you asking you to confirm your security details. If you notice the web site that you regularly use has changed and is asking for additional login information, e-mail abuse@companyname.com (where *companyname.com* is the web address of the company) to report it.

Identifying Safe and Unsafe Web Sites in IE11

Internet Explorer is great at telling you whether a web site is safe. It displays a padlock in the address bar that indicates the site is a known, secure web site. Also, the address bar is green when the URL is a safe web site, and it is red when it is known to be used by criminals (see Figure 3-26).

Figure 3-26. *IE11 desktop version highlights a safe web site*

Unfortunately, these features are best highlighted in the desktop version of IE11 because the address bar is hidden from normal view in the IE11 app. If you are doing financial transactions or shopping on a laptop or desktop PC, I recommend you use the desktop version of IE because it gives you more and better feedback about web sites.

The web site safety reporting in Internet Explorer, or any web browser for that matter, is not infallible and is only as good as its last update.

Making the Desktop Version of IE11 Your Default Browser

When you install Windows 8.1, the default browser (the one all web links open in) is the IE11 app. If you want to change this to the desktop version of IE11, it's easy to do:

1. Open Settings in the desktop version of IE11 by clicking the *Settings* icon in the top right of the window.

2. In the options panel that appears, click the *Programs* tab.

3. In the *Choose how you open links* section at the top of the panel, change the drop-down option from *Let Internet Explorer Decide* to *Always in Internet Explorer on the desktop* (see Figure 3-27) and then click OK to confirm the change.

Figure 3-27. Changing the default browser in Windows 8.1

Summary

Windows 8.1 offers new ways to connect to the Internet and these new ways also bring challenges (the worry that comes from being accidentally connected to your 3G or LTE network and using expensive data, for example).

There are also challenges with staying safe on the Internet. Internet Explorer does an excellent job of keeping you safe, but the weak link is always the user. Malware writers and criminals will prey on you, trying to trick you into entering sensitive information on the pretense that it's perfectly safe to do so.

On my web site (`www.TheLongClimb.com`), I write and make tutorial videos about regularly maintaining your security and privacy online. You can always find more information there.

■ ■ ■

CHAPTER 4

Sharing with Family and Friends

Windows 7 introduced the concept of HomeGroup, enabling us to share our files, music, photos, and video easily within small networks. Windows 8.1 is taking sharing to the next level with built-in sharing for apps of all descriptions.

With Windows 8.1, apps that send or receive information, such as pictures, don't need to be programmed to import and export files to and from other programs. Windows 8.1 now handles it all. This opens new opportunities for sharing, but some of the traditional methods of sharing files, folders, and network hardware still exist. In this chapter, I'll show you how to share a wide variety of hardware, file types, and data libraries in Windows 8.1.

Working with User Accounts

One of the traditional strengths of Windows has been its support of multiple users. On the face of things, this may seem relatively minor, but when you work from home, do schoolwork, or just want some privacy, the usefulness of this feature steps up to another level. At the time of writing, handling multiple user accounts on a tablet device is still something few non–Windows 8.1 devices are capable of doing, straightforward as you might think it would be. This is a major feature of Windows 8.1, and you'll be pleased to hear that the operating system handles user accounts admirably.

Windows 8.1 practically begs users to log on with a Microsoft account—the same ID you use to log on to a Live, Hotmail, Outlook.com, or MSN e-mail account. When you do this, much of the system is automatically set up for you, including the Windows Store and the e-mail and calendar apps. This presents issues for multiple user systems, however, because you might not want other people in your household or workplace reading your e-mail.

There is also the matter of file security. We generally trust the people we live with, but accidents do happen. If somebody doesn't know the importance of a particular file or Internet favorite, it can be deleted all too easily.

The ability to set up Windows 8.1 so that each user has his or her own account is a benefit. It is also a task that's simpler than ever to perform.

Setting Up Users

In Windows 8.1, Microsoft has removed the need to navigate through the full Control Panel to add users. This task was often seen as complicated and off-putting. Now you simply add users through the PC Settings panel, with the whole process clearly detailed.

To create a local user account, follow these instructions:

1. Open the charms and select Settings.

2. At the bottom right of the screen, click More PC Settings.

3. In PC Settings, click *Accounts*.

4. In the *Accounts* section, click *Other Accounts* (see Figure 4-1).

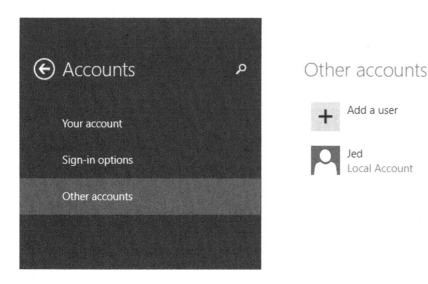

Figure 4-1. *Creating a new user account in PC Settings*

■ **Tip**   If you are creating an account for another person using a Microsoft account ID, she doesn't need to be present. Just enter her e-mail address and you're done. The PC won't ask for the password until the first time *she* logs in to the PC.

---

5.   Next, click **Add a user**, which opens the screen shown in Figure 4-2.

How will this person sign in?

What email address would this person like to use to sign in to Windows? (If you know the email address they use to sign in to Microsoft services, enter it here.)

Email address

Sign up for a new email address

This person can sign in to easily get their online email, photos, files, and settings (like browser history and favorites) on all of their devices. They can manage their synced settings at any time.

Add a child's account

Privacy statement

Sign in without a Microsoft account (not recommended)

Next   Cancel

Figure 4-2. *Adding a new user*

■ **Note**   So what difference does it make to you whether you create a local account or a Microsoft account? A local account has advantages if you use only one PC in which everything is stored locally, so there's nothing in the cloud if you're concerned about privacy. However, you can't use the Windows Store to purchase apps and your Internet favorites, and other settings won't be synched to other Windows 8.1 PCs.

---

6. To create a local account, click **Don't want this user to sign in with a Microsoft account?** to open the screen shown in Figure 4-3.

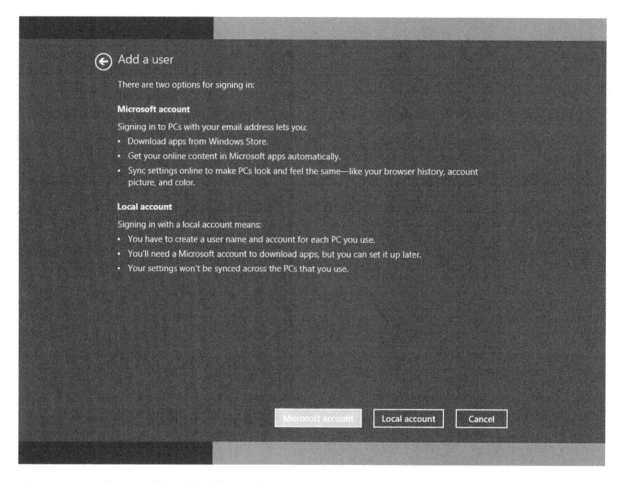

Figure 4-3. *Windows 8.1 tells you the difference between a Microsoft account and a Local account*

7. Click the Local account button. You are asked for a username and (optionally) a password for the new user (see Figure 4-4).

Figure 4-4. *It is not necessary for local accounts to have a password, which is especially helpful for young children*

8. Enter the name of the user and, optionally, a password and password hint (in case you forget the password). When you are finished, you are asked if you want to turn on Family Safety to get reports of what a child does online (see Figure 4-5).

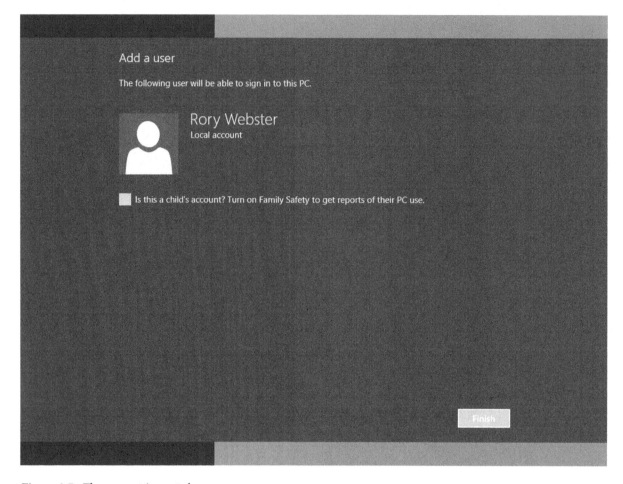

Figure 4-5. *The account is created*

■ **Note**   The "Using Family Safety" section, which appears later in this chapter, covers this topic. When you check this option, that user will be notified when they log in to the PC that the activity is being monitored. This is a privacy feature to prevent people from using this tool to spy on other PC users.

---

9.   The local account is created. Click Finish to complete the process.

Creating a Password Reset Drive

If you have a local account on your PC, you can create a Password Reset drive to help you if you ever forget the password to the computer. To create it, you need a blank USB flash drive (any size will do, so it's a good use for an old one) already plugged into the PC. Search for **Password Reset** from the Search charm and run *Create a Password Reset Disk* from the options that appear.

This displays a wizard that will quickly walk you through creating a password reset system on the USB flash drive.

If you forget your password at logon, insert your password reset flash drive into a USB port and then click the *Reset Password* link below the password input box (see Figure 4-6).

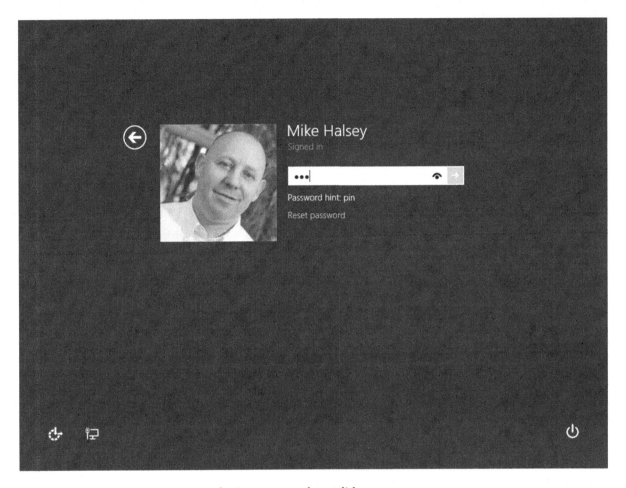

Figure 4-6. *You can reset your password using a password reset disk*

The password reset wizard will appear and ask which port or drive you have inserted your password reset disk into. It will use this to reset your password, enabling you to log in to the computer again.

Resetting Your Microsoft Account Password

If you log in to your PC using a Microsoft account, you don't have the option to create a password reset disk. Instead, you will be pointed at the Microsoft account password reset web page at http://account.live.com/password/reset (see Figure 4-7). You need to do this on a PC or account you can log in to, or perhaps on a smartphone.

Microsoft account

Reset your password

To reset your password, enter your Microsoft account and the characters in the picture below.

Microsoft account

Example: someone@example.com

Enter the characters that you see
New | Audio

Next   Cancel

Figure 4-7. *Resetting a Microsoft account password*

Here you are prompted to enter the e-mail address associated with your Microsoft account and to confirm the security captcha code that displays. You are then asked if you want Microsoft to e-mail you a temporary password (if you have set up a backup e-mail address in your Microsoft account) or send you a text message by phone (assuming that you have a current mobile phone number registered to your Microsoft account).

If these are not suitable for you, you are asked to enter an alternative e-mail address that somebody from Microsoft can contact you about. They typically contact you within 24 hours, which is a good incentive to set up an alternate e-mail address or a mobile phone on your account! I will show you how to manage your Microsoft account online later in this chapter.

■ **Tip**   If you have another administrator account on the PC you can log in to, your password can be reset in the User Management panel; see the following for details of how to do this.

Managing User Accounts

There are two types of users in Windows 8.1: *administrators*, who have authority to make any changes to the operating system and computer's files that they want to; and *standard users*, who can make only changes that affect their own user account. Typically, a PC has one administrator, the account that was set up when Windows 8.1 was first installed or activated, and all accounts created after this will be standard users. For general use, this is the most secure way to run the operating system (OS), but you might find that a second user needs to install software and needs the administrator password to do so. Under this circumstance, you may want to consider having more than one administrator account on the PC.

The first user account created when you start using Windows 8.1 will always be an administrator, but any accounts you create for the computer after that will be standard users unless you specify otherwise. As we just saw in the preceding section, you create a new user account in the Users panel of PC Settings.

There are two ways to manage user accounts: one in which you can simply change the account type in PC Settings, and another with more controls in the full Control Panel. To do this, you first need to be logged in to the PC as an administrator; then in PC Settings, click *Accounts* and then *Other accounts*. When you click *Other accounts* on the PC, an *Edit* button appears (see Figure 4-8). Clicking this button enables you to change the account type between administrator, standard user, and child.

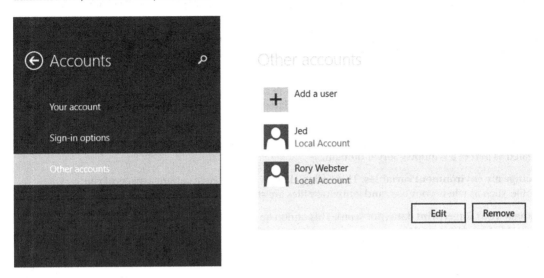

Figure 4-8. *You can change the account type in PC Settings*

■ **Tip**   You can also remove user accounts in the Other accounts section of PC Settings.

When you need more control over user accounts, you need to open the full Windows 8.1 Control Panel, which you can do by searching for **control** at the Start screen. Managing user accounts is done from the User accounts section of the Control Panel. When you load this panel, you are first shown your own user account (see Figure 4-9). Here you can perform various actions, as follows.

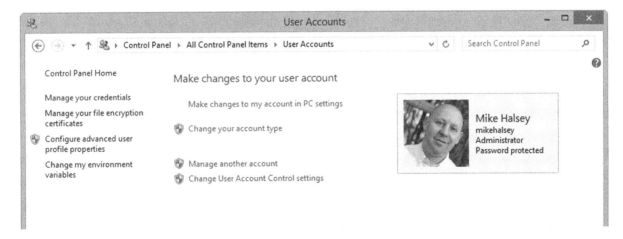

Figure 4-9. *Managing user accounts in Windows 8.1*

- **Change your account type**: You can change from standard user to administrator (or vice versa). This might be useful to upgrade a user to an administrator.

- **Manage your credentials**: You can view, edit, and delete the stored password for Windows, Windows software, and web sites that are associated with your account. This can be useful if something has become corrupt, and Windows or Internet Explorer gets confused when you change your password.

- **Create a Password Reset Disk** (not seen): This option appears only for local user accounts and allows you to create a USB flash drive that can be used to reset your password if you forget it.

- **Manage your file encryption certificates**: This option allows you to back up and restore any Encrypting File System (EFS) encryption keys associated with this account. For more on this, see Chapter 12.

- **Change advanced user profile properties**: This option is used if your user account has been created as part of a Windows Server domain.

- **Change my environment variables**: This option allows you to change certain aspects of your profile, such as where your user and temporary files are stored by default.

- **Manage your fingerprint data** (not seen): This option appears if your computer has a biometric fingerprint reader.

■ **Tip**　If you have friends or family members using your computer occasionally, but you don't want to configure specific user accounts for them or have them use your account, you can turn on the Guest account by clicking Manage Another Account in the User Accounts panel. The Guest account gives you a quick and secure way to allow other people to use your computer and is a basic standard user account.

If you click Manage Another Account, you are shown a list of the other user accounts on your computer. Clicking an account allows you to change the settings for that user (see Figure 4-10).

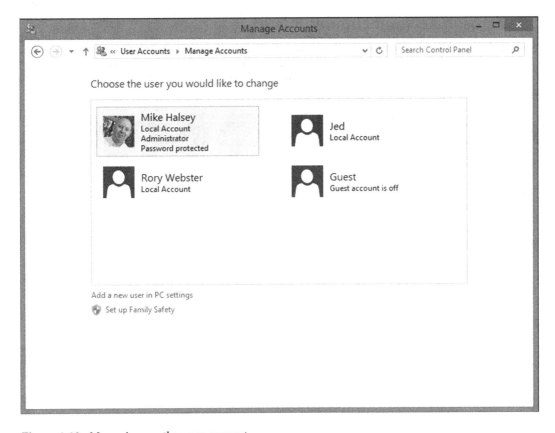

Figure 4-10. *Managing another user account*

The options found for managing other users include the following:

- **Change the account name**.

- **Create a password** for the account if it doesn't have one. If it does, you will see options to change or remove the password.

- **Set up Family Safety** allows you to place the Family Safety feature on the account.

- **Change the account type** from standard user to administrator (or vice versa). All secondary users are standard users by default.

- **Delete the account** gives an alert that the user has files on the computer and gives the opportunity to save these files to a desktop folder before the account is deleted.

▪ **Tip**   If you log on to someone else's computer with your Microsoft account, but you don't use that computer very often, be aware that Windows 8.1 might have downloaded your Internet Favorites or other personal files to the computer. Obviously, you don't want them to remain on someone else's computer, so you can remove them by performing a few steps. When logged on as another user, open User Account in the Control Panel; otherwise, open Manage Another Account. Click the name of the account you want to delete. Next, click Delete the Account and, when prompted, click Delete Files. This process removes the files, but you should make certain by checking the C:\Users folder. If a folder still exists for that user account, delete it manually.

Managing a Microsoft Account Online

The management tools for your Microsoft account can be found online at http://account.live.com. Here you can control all aspects of your account: display name, date of birth, billing and credit card information for the Windows Store; and your alternate e-mail address and mobile phone number if you forget your password or for some other reason, such as being hacked, you become locked out of your account.

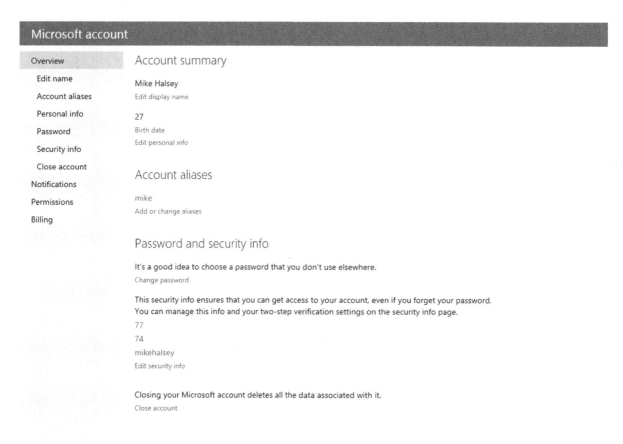

Figure 4-11. *You manage your Microsoft account at* http://account.live.com

There are a great number of options to be found on this web site, and even if you have had your Microsoft account for some time, it can be well worth looking through the options here to ensure everything is as it should be and that all the correct account permissions have been set.

Using Family Safety

With children using the Internet at ever-younger ages, it's more important than ever before to shield them from inappropriate games, web sites, and images. Windows 8.1 comes with an excellent suite of tools that enables you to do this and more, including determining when children can use their PCs, and it all comes with a reporting tool with which parents can monitor children's Internet usage.

When you create a new user account in Windows 8.1, you are asked if the user you are adding is a child (see Figure 4-12). Checking this option activates Family Safety activity reports, which is accessed through the Family Safety page. You can specify that an account is for a child by checking the **Is this a child's account?** box after you input the name and other details about the new user.

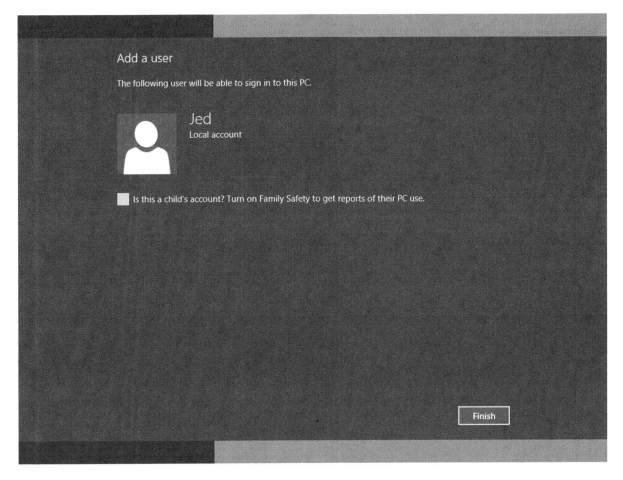

Figure 4-12. You can specify if a new user is a child

Family Safety is very powerful and flexible in Windows 8.1 and includes web filtering for the first time. The activity report is a very helpful addition to these controls because they show you the types of activities your child is participating in online and which web sites they visit.

You access the activity report from the main Family Safety page. To open it, search for **family safety** from the Search charm. When you have opened the Family Safety controls, on the right side of the window, you can View activity reports of your child's time on the computer (see Figure 4-13). Your child cannot see these reports; they are visible only to administrators on the computer, but the child is informed when logging in to the PC that the account's activity is being monitored. This is a privacy and safety feature to prevent unwanted snooping.

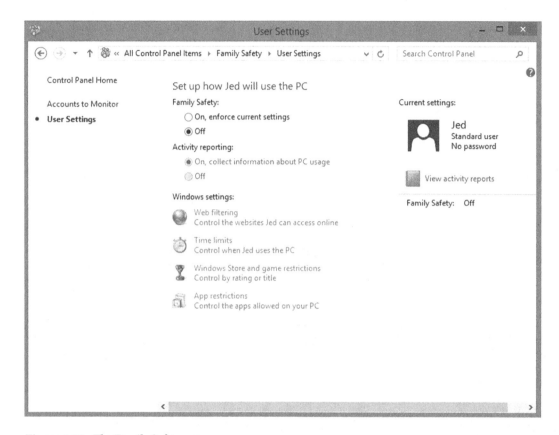

Figure 4-13. *The Family Safety page*

Although the content filtering in Internet Explorer is useful, it is much easier to use the Windows 8.1 Family Safety (see Figure 4-14). You find it by searching for the word **family** from the Search charm. There is more about searching in Chapter 5.

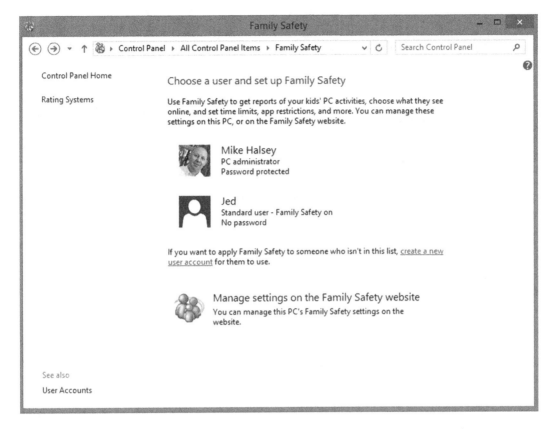

Figure 4-14. *Windows 8.1 asks you for which user you want to have Family Safety controls*

At the main Family Safety screen, select the user you want to set controls for. You can set Family Safety only for standard users because administrators have permission to perform whatever actions they want, including deactivating Family Safety controls.

■ **Note**   You need to have a password on your main user account to use Family Safety in Windows 8.1.

After you select which user you want to set Family Safety for, you are taken to the main Family Safety page (see Figure 4-15).

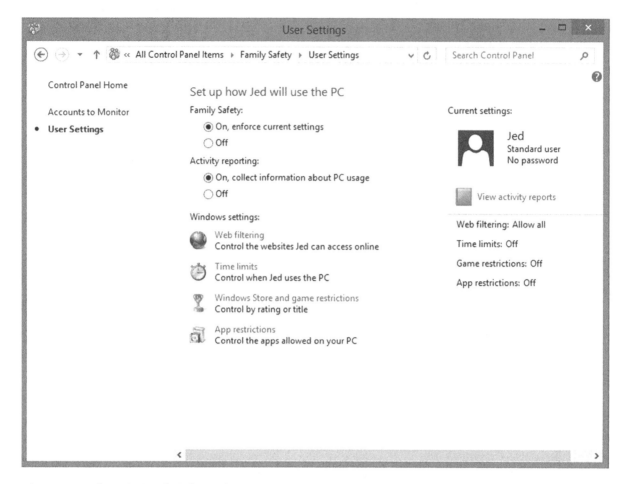

Figure 4-15. *The main Family Safety options*

On the Family Safety page, you have several options:

- Turn the controls on or off for a particular user.

- Set **Web Filter** parameters to decide which web sites are suitable for your children.

- Set **Time Limits** on when children are allowed to use the computer.

- Choose what types of **Windows Store and Game Restrictions** are suitable for your children.

- Choose which **App Restrictions** will be required for your children.

I want to spend a little time discussing each of these settings in detail. Web filtering in Family Safety (see Figure 4-16) is much simpler than it is in the Internet Explorer 10 (IE10) Content Advisor page. In Family Safety, you can choose from five web category types:

- Allow list only (in which you can manually specify which web sites to allow)

- Designed for children

- General interest

- Online communication

- Warn an adult

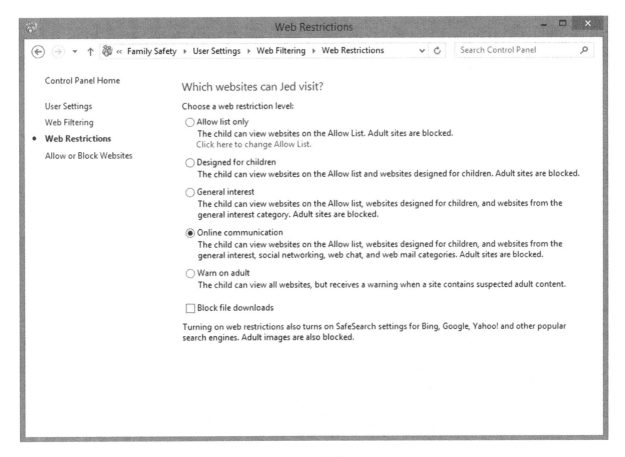

Figure 4-16. *Choose the web sites that are suitable for your child*

Each category has a clear description of what it is, so you can feel certain that your children are seeing only appropriate web sites. You can also block Internet downloads, which helps protect your computer from malware.

Additionally, if you click the *Allow or Block Websites* link in the left panel, you can choose specific web sites to permit or completely block (see Figure 4-17). You might want to allow your child to view web sites in the Online Communication category, but you want to block Facebook and Twitter until she is slightly older. This is a very useful feature because the white and black lists of web sites maintained by Microsoft are not completely perfect for every parent and child; they could block a school web site, for example. A parent might also want to block access to a web site even if Family Safety has deemed it suitable for the child.

Figure 4-17. *You can allow and block specific web sites in Family Safety*

The Time Restrictions page is extremely useful (see Figure 4-18). Here you can set the times your child is allowed to use the computer. There are two options: you can set how many hours the PC can be used each day, and you set the number of hours for each day of the week independently, perhaps to allow more time on weekends. You can also set a curfew and, by filling in blocks of time, you can specify the earliest and latest times each day the PC can be used, which is useful for enforcing bedtimes. This again can be set independently for each day.

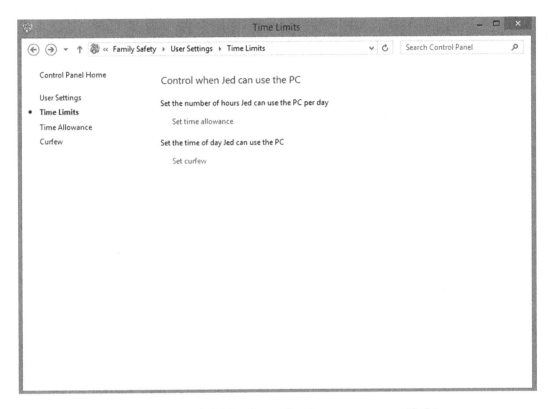

Figure 4-18. *Family Safety can block children from using the computer at specified times*

Not all apps and games come with ratings, and there is no guarantee that inappropriate games won't slip through. Parents may find, however, that the age ratings system on games is a great indicator for which games are suitable for their children (see Figure 4-19).

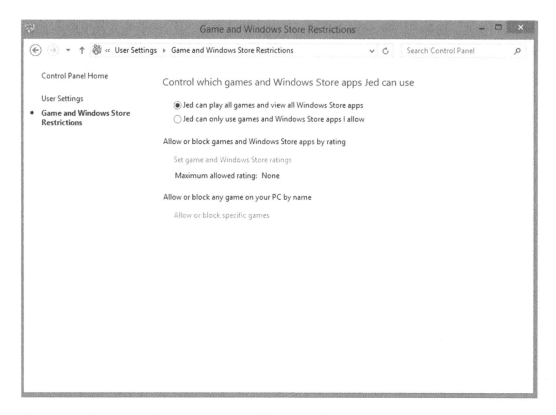

Figure 4-19. *Parents can choose the games suitable for their children*

Select a maximum game rating, and all ratings below that are automatically included in your selection. These ratings map to the standard ratings system for games in your own country, which makes them easy to understand. This means that you can block games rated as more mature from running on your computer.

The last section of options, App Restrictions, relates to the desktop software on the PC, some of which, when installed, is automatically set up for use by all the users on the PC (see Figure 4-20). On this page, you can choose the software that your child is allowed to use.

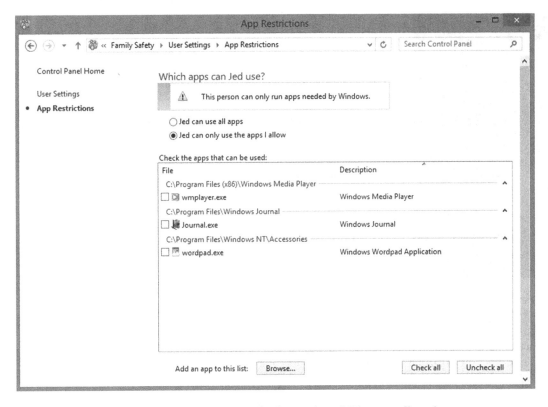

Figure 4-20. Parents can select the programs and software their children are allowed to use

The App Restrictions feature is at its most useful when you use a computer for both home and work, and want to stop children from accessing your work programs.

Sharing Files and Folders with HomeGroup

HomeGroup was introduced in Windows 7 as a means of sharing documents, pictures, music, video, and printers across small, protected home networks. Think of a HomeGroup as a quick way to share files between your home computers. This is because Windows knows which environment you're sharing things in, and as a result, automatically sets all the correct permissions and parameters on the files, folders, and networking settings for you, minimizing your configuration.

HomeGroup still exists in Windows 8.1. It's easy and straightforward to set up and configure. HomeGroup is in PC Settings (see Figure 4-21), which is available by opening the charms on the right side of the screen and selecting Settings. Once in PC Settings, click *Network* and then click *HomeGroup*.

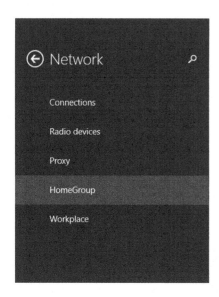

Figure 4-21. *The HomeGroup page in PC Settings*

If a HomeGroup has already been set up on another computer, you are asked to enter the password. You may have a Windows 7 computer on which you have previously set up and configured a HomeGroup, for example.

If a HomeGroup does not exist, or if Windows 8.1 can't detect one on the network, you are asked if you want to set one up.

■ **Note**   HomeGroup works only over Wi-Fi for networks on which you have said you want to find other PCs and devices. It is automatically disabled and blocked on work and public networks to help maintain your file and PC security.

Once you are connected to a HomeGroup, the HomeGroup page in PC Settings gives you controls for sharing files and devices, including documents, pictures, music, videos, printers, and devices such as USB attached storage and external hard disks (see Figure 4-22).

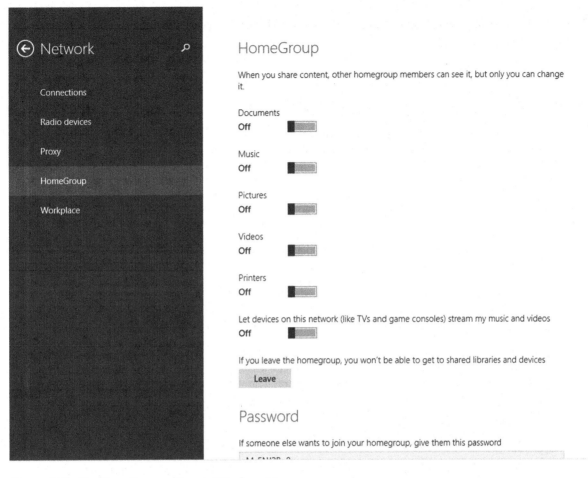

Figure 4-22. *The HomeGroup settings in Windows 8.1*

Next, however, is a very interesting option. Do you want to allow your TVs and other devices, such as game consoles, to share the media on your home network? HomeGroup allows you to use your computers as Universal Plug and Play (UPnP) devices.

UPnP devices can share media, commonly pictures, music, and video over a network. They are used by media streamers to play music from your PC on your Hi-Fi or video from your laptop on your television. You can use this, for example, to share your media with your Xbox 360 or Playstation 3 to view on a big screen or to listen to an Internet radio station in the garden.

There are security concerns to take into account, however. With a HomeGroup, you have a secure password, which is also shown in the HomeGroup page in PC Settings, but when you share media via this setting, all that is required is access to your network. You need not worry about having a very secure password on your Wi-Fi router because media connectors and modern routers have a pairing button on them, usually called WPS, which connects secure devices without the need to enter complex passwords using awkward interfaces.

If you do not have a password on your Internet router, you should create one right away. Unsecured routers provide outsiders with access to your home Internet connection and the shared files on your computers and devices.

Media shared on a HomeGroup cannot be deleted from your computer, and they don't include your documents. It is always wise to know who has access to what before you share it, however.

■ **Tip** You can still manage a HomeGroup from the full Control Panel, but the management options in PC Settings are so much better that I wouldn't bother.

Sharing Files and Folders on a Network

There are several ways to share files and folders across a network in Windows 8.1. First, I want to discuss why you might want to share files and folders, and in what environments you should do it.

In the home environment, by far the simplest way to share files and folders is in a HomeGroup, as I have detailed already. HomeGroup gives you easy ways to share devices such as printers, which means you save money from not having to buy expensive new Wi-Fi printers.

You may have set up a HomeGroup and decided to share your pictures, music, and video, but not your documents. You may decide to keep your documents private, but want to share a folder or two's worth of documents with another person in the family.

HomeGroup can sometimes have connection difficulties, however, and you may want to share only a particular folder with another person or persons. Let's say, for example, that you are collaborating with another individual in a home office or at work, and you want to be able to share the resources and workflow documents.

In a Windows Server environment, you have all this managed by System Center Configuration Manager, SharePoint, or a similar or alternative service such as Microsoft Office 365; but many small businesses can't afford their own server system and don't have an Office 365 cloud-services subscription. This is where the built-in sharing in Windows 8.1 is very useful.

Again, in an office environment, you may want to set up a computer as a file store. I've done this myself, placing project documents and resources—in my case, teaching resources, lesson plans, schemes of work, and contractual paperwork—on a single machine (with a backup kept on another). I provided network access to the main PC with a desktop shortcut to the shared files to make it easy for everyone to access them.

Sharing with Individuals

Let's say several people use the same computer in your home, and you want to be able to share files such as household documents, bills, legal documents, and perhaps homework assignments. File Explorer and Microsoft have made this type of sharing simpler than ever.

In File Explorer, navigate to and highlight the folder you want to share. Then, in the Ribbon, click the Share tab; you see a section called Share With. Here, you highlight to share file(s) and/or folder(s) and click the name of the person(s) with whom you want to share. Windows 8.1 automatically and silently sets the sharing permissions.

If you want to choose a specific user, perhaps because he doesn't appear on the list, or if you want to choose the privileges for users, select Specific People to display a full list of the users on your computer (see Figure 4-23).

Figure 4-23. *Sharing with individuals in Windows 8.1*

This dialog comes in handy when you want to choose specific privileges for a user, such a Read Only, so that files can be accessed but not modified—and, crucially, not deleted!

■ **Caution**   Be careful giving others access to files and folders that you do not want changed or deleted.

For most sharing scenarios within a home with one PC, this is all you need; but many homes now have multiple computers to share across. In a business environment, it is rare for several people to use the same PC, except in instances of small businesses in which people need only occasional access to a computer.

Sharing with Groups of People

If you have a multicomputer setup and don't want the risk that comes with sharing absolutely everything in your Documents folder, you will want finer control over sharing. Windows 8.1 offers finer control in an easy-to-manage way.

This is managed by right-clicking a folder and selecting its properties. A Sharing tab contains all the controls (see Figure 4-24). There are only three, the first of which takes you to the settings dialog similar to the one I talked about in the last section.

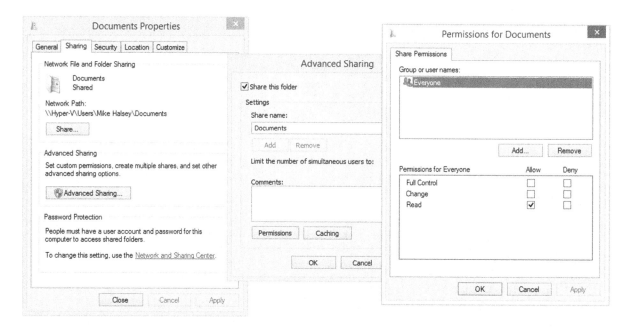

Figure 4-24. *Setting advanced file and folder sharing in Windows 8.1*

Click the Advanced Sharing button to get access to the settings for sharing a folder across a network. There is a simple check box to turn sharing on and off, making it simple to rescind sharing at a later stage, perhaps when a project has completed and you want to archive the folder. You can also give the shared folder a custom name. By default, sharing gives others permission to read files within the folder, but nothing else. This means that although others can access the files in a folder and read them, if they modify a file, they can't save it back to that folder. They also can't create or copy new files into the folder.

To change these settings, click the Permissions button. You are offered a variety of permissions options for separate user lists:

- **Full Control** enables you to create new files, and copy files to and delete files from a folder. This is something you should be aware of when setting full control on any shared folder.

- **Change** allows people to make changes to files that already exist in the document; for example, opening, working on, and saving the updated copy of the file in the folder.

- **Read Only** grants permission to only open and read the contents of a folder.

■ **Note**   If you want to share folders from a computer running Windows 7 or Windows Vista with a Windows 8.1 computer, the sharing setup works the same way as described here.

Sharing with Non-Windows Computers

Setting the advanced sharing properties for folders is also useful if you want to share with non-Windows computers, such as Apple computers or PCs running GNU/Linux, for example if one person in your household has an Apple iMac computer. These network shares are accessible, although additional configuration may be required on the other computer to deal with minor incompatibilities that can arise from time to time.

■ **Caution**   Be cautious about sharing files with a computer running Windows XP unless you are certain that the security on that computer is properly maintained. Any files hosted on an XP machine are far more vulnerable to malware than those in Windows Vista, Windows 7, and Windows 8.

Sharing Files with Windows 8.1 and RT Tablets, Ultrabooks, and Laptops

ou should never consider any mobile computer as being completely secure because they are so prone to opportunist theft or sudden loss. Although some laptops (and perhaps even a few tablets such as Microsoft Surface and Surface RT and ultrabooks) come with Trusted Platform Module (TPM) security chips onboard to support full-disk encryption via BitLocker, most do not. These chips store encryption and keys for your hard disks in their firmware, and as such are very secure. I talk more about TPM chips and encrypting your files and computer in Chapter 12.

If you are carrying volumes of data around, it probably includes personal and sensitive information; and the simple fact remains that tablets, ultrabooks, and laptops are highly desirable items for thieves.

The next consideration is what you will actually be able to *do* with those files on these portable devices. Do you want Word, Excel, and PowerPoint documents? Do you want your entire photo or music library when you'll likely only ever access a small portion of it when you're on the move? One advantage is that Windows 8.1 is capable of synching mobile devices with your SkyDrive account, and keeping a local copy of files once you've accessed them once. I will show you how to use this effectively in Chapter 8.

I believe it is folly to assume that any portable device is completely secure, even when it is encrypted properly with a TPM chip and a technology such as BitLocker. There are just too many variables associated with carrying around your entire libraries of documents, photos, and more to justify carrying it around when in unfamiliar places.

The final consideration is whether the computer is properly password protected. You may have a local account on your tablet (or other device) that doesn't require a password, which means that anyone picking up your device has complete access to all your files.

Alternatively, you may have a Microsoft account that you use to log on to your device. This could be a long, super-secure password containing a mixture of uppercase and lowercase letters, numbers, and symbols at least 10 characters long. But there's a temptation to create a PIN or picture password for Windows 8.1 access because you won't want to have to enter such a long password every time you start your device.

A PIN code instantly reduces a secure multicharacter password to a simple, four-digit numeric code, which isn't anywhere near as secure; and although a picture password might be more secure if presented with a photo of three or more people, the temptation would be to poke the first three people on the nose or draw circles around their faces. Is this what you would do? Is this what you might consider for a picture password? Although web enthusiasts and IT pros are generally more security aware than consumers are, a great many people think that a "plonk, plonk, plonk" approach to picture passwords in a pattern that's a bit fun would also be secure. Believe me, it isn't any more secure than having a password that's the name of your dog.

Windows 8.1 and SkyDrive File Backup

Microsoft's cloud backup and sync service, SkyDrive, comes built into Windows 8.1, and the implementation can really help you gain access to your files and documents when you're using devices with small amounts of storage, such as tablets and ultrabooks.

It works by downloading pointers and thumbnail images for all the files you have stored in SkyDrive already and storing them on your PC's hard disk. These files consume almost no space, so even if you have 100 GB of files stored in SkyDrive, you can store the pointers on your PC.

These files appear in the SkyDrive link in File Explorer and are accessible when you click SkyDrive storage from the SkyDrive app, see Figure 4-25.

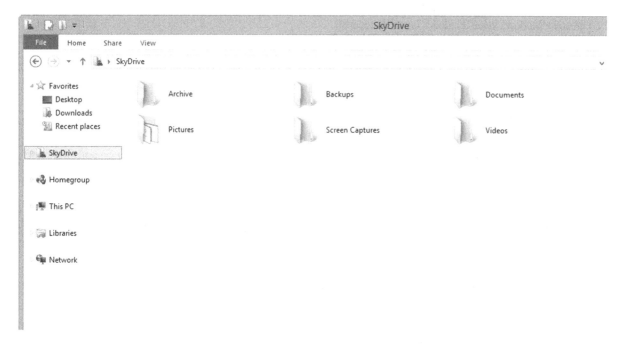

Figure 4-25. *You can access SkyDrive apps in File Explorer or from within apps*

■ **Tip**   Some apps that allow you to access the files on your PC also provide access to SkyDrive.

When you open a file in SkyDrive, it is quickly and silently downloaded from the cloud and stored on your PC as long as you have an active Internet connection. The file is then kept on your PC so that any changes you make are synced back to the cloud. This is a great way to avoid filling your valuable storage on low-storage PCs with files you won't open on it.

You can turn on SkyDrive file save (and sync) in PC Settings by opening *SkyDrive* and then *Files*. Here you can turn on the switch for *Save documents to SkyDrive by default*. This activates the full sync feature with SkyDrive, and from this point on any file you create on or save to your PC will be auto-synced to the cloud as well, creating a secure file backup.

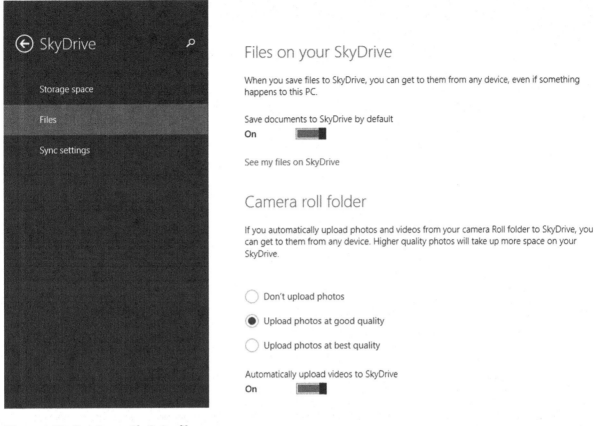

Figure 4-26. *Turning on SkyDrive file save*

For the more technical of you, Windows 8.1 SkyDrive sync works by switching the default file save location on your PC from the C:\Users\[Username]\ folders to the C:\Users\[Username]\SkyDrive folders, which is where it downloads its pointer files. There is no facility to move this file location from within PC Settings or the Control Panel, so it won't let you store the files you want to back up to the cloud anywhere else, such as on a different partition or hard disk. However, there is a workaround, and I will show you how to hack SkyDrive to allow for the moving of this folder in Chapter 13.

If you take photographs using your Windows 8.1 PC, there is also an option in the *SkyDrive ➤ Files* section of PC Settings that allows you to switch on or off automatic uploading of those photos to SkyDrive. This works independently of the full file sync and includes three different options for the quality you want for uploading the photos.

Downloading SkyDrive Files to Your PC

You can force SkyDrive in Windows 8.1 to download and sync files directly to your PC, useful if you have a good sized hard disk or if there are files you want to carry with you and have access to even when you won't have an active Internet connection. You can do this in File Explorer by opening the SkyDrive folder in the left pane of the window and then right-clicking the file(s) or folder(s) you want to keep offline. You can also change this setting back so that files and folders are kept only online (in the cloud); see Figure 4-27.

Figure 4-27. *You can tell Windows 8.1 to download files or whole folders from SkyDrive*

Using Microsoft SkyDrive to Share Files

Sometimes you might want to share a file that you have stored in SkyDrive with other people. You can do this at the *SkyDrive.com* web site. Right-click the file(s) or folder(s) you want to share with other people and click the *Sharing* link at the top of the screen. A dialog then appears, asking who you want to share the files with and what permissions you will give them (see Figure 4-28).

Figure 4-28. *Sharing files from SkyDrive*

■ **Caution**   You can also right-click a file in File Explorer and select *Share with* followed by *SkyDrive* to open a SkyDrive browser window.

Be careful what permissions you grant people when sharing your files. You might, for example, not want to give them permission to delete the file(s) because accidents can very easily happen.

Sharing Content Within Apps

One of the best new features in Windows 8.1 is the capability to share content directly from one app to another. This is done without the apps having to know how it is done and without the developers having to add any code into the app other than support for the sharing service because the sharing mechanisms are part of Windows 8.1.

How this will actually be used over time remains to be seen as industrious app developers will no doubt constantly find new and innovative ways to use the feature. At its most basic, however, it is a way to share photos vie e-mail or with photo-sharing services such as Flickr, Facebook, and PhotoBucket.

You can also highlight text, perhaps on a web page, and share it between apps; you can share any type of content, really. This is where it will be fascinating to see how app developers use this feature. There's not really been anything quite like it in an operating system before, so anticipating how it will be used over time is impossible to guess right now.

You can share in Windows 8.1 by highlighting the item or items you want to share, opening the charms, and clicking Share or just opening the Share charm to share a whole page or article. All compatible apps for that type of content appear (see Figure 4-29). Click the app you want to share the content with, and the content is transferred to the other app for sharing without kicking you out of the app you are currently using.

Figure 4-29. *Sharing via Windows 8.1*

Of course, this sharing feature comes with risks. The easier it is to share content with apps, web sites, and the like, the easier it becomes to accidentally put content where you didn't intend for it to go, or for it to go on web sites where your privacy settings mean that it is generally accessible to the whole world. I always recommend, strongly in fact, that you make sure your privacy settings on web sites are set to automatically block all content from those you have not *deliberately* invited to view it.

Sharing Optical Drives

One of the biggest challenges facing users of Windows tablets and ultrabooks is the lack of an optical drive. Sure, you can install software (and even Windows 8.1) from a USB flash drive or the Internet, and Windows 8.1 will allow you to mount ISO files; but there will be occasions when you'll need an optical drive.

One solution is to buy a USB optical drive, but this isn't always a practical solution. Indeed, I bought one the other year for my Windows tablet and then promptly left it at a Microsoft research event in Cambridge, where it isn't doing me much good.

A better solution is to share the optical drive on another computer. To do this in both Windows 8.1 and Windows 7 (because the instructions are the same), do the following:

1. On the host computer (the one with the optical drive), open File Explorer (Windows Explorer in Windows 7) and click Computer in the left pane.

2. Right-click the optical drive you want to share. From the options, click Share With ➤ Advanced Sharing (see Figure 4-30).

Figure 4-30. *Select an optical drive to share*

3. In the dialog, click the Advanced Sharing button (see Figure 4-31).

Figure 4-31. *Select the Advanced Sharing settings*

4. Check the Share This Folder box and then give the share an appropriate name, such as **DVD Share** (see Figure 4-32).

Figure 4-32. *Share the drive and give it a name*

    5.   Click OK. You are shown the full network name of the share, in this case
\\HYPER-VDVD-Share (see Figure 4-33). You also see a small share icon in the bottom left
of the drive's icon in File Explorer to indicate it has been shared.

Figure 4-33. *The full share name of the drive*

■ **Note**　For the drive to be visible on other computers, you need to have File and Printer Sharing turned on in the Advanced Sharing Settings of the Network and Sharing Center. Users of other computers may also need the username and password of the host computer to gain access to the shared drive.

This optical drive is now accessible to people on other computers when they are attached to the same network and the computer containing the optical drive is switched on; this includes those using ultrabooks and tablets.

Streaming Music and Video to Devices and Computers

At the beginning of the chapter, I showed you how to set up a HomeGroup to share your documents, music, pictures, and videos with other Windows 8.1 and Windows 7 computers. Among the HomeGroup settings was one to "Allow devices such as TVs and games consoles to play my shared content."

Activating this feature turns your computer, when it is switched on anyway, into a Universal Plug and Play (UPnP) server. Many devices support this feature, including Internet radios, MP3-playing hi-fi systems, external network-attached storage (NAS) and USB hard disks, game consoles, and even devices you wouldn't normally expect to work happily with Windows, such as smart TVs.

Not only can Windows 8.1 (and previous versions of Windows) share content in this way, it can also stream content from other UPnP devices that are connected to your home network. UPnP devices are found in the Network section of File Explorer (see Figure 4-34).

Figure 4-34. *Displaying network media devices in Windows 8.1*

■ **Note** Microsoft does not include DVD and Blu-Ray playback support as standard in Windows 8.1. Instead, it has made it a chargeable extra. You can use Add Features to Windows in the Control Panel to purchase and upgrade to Windows 8.1 Pro with Media Center. Doing this adds these features, but only within Windows Media Center, not through the Video app or Windows Media Player.

Here you can check whether Windows 8.1 is sharing your content properly and also, I think somewhat crucially, to check that nothing is being shared by accident.

Windows 8.1 shares only media files such as pictures, music, and video; you can be sure that your documents will not be shared with media devices. This comes in particularly handy if you have downloaded movies or TV shows onto your computer and you want to watch them on your TV, perhaps through your Xbox 360.

Changing the Advanced Sharing Settings in Windows 8.1

Sometimes you may have trouble with network sharing in Windows, which could be caused by something switched off in the Advanced Sharing Settings page. Alternatively, you may want to deliberately switch something off if you no longer want a certain type of sharing to take place from a specific computer.

You can access the Advanced Sharing Settings page from the Network and Sharing Center, itself accessible from either the Ribbon in the Network view of File Explorer, or by right-clicking the Network icon on the desktop taskbar.

Once in the Network and Sharing Center, there is a link to Change Advanced Sharing Settings in the left pane.

There are a great many options in the Advanced Sharing Settings page (see Figure 4-35), and some are very important and significant.

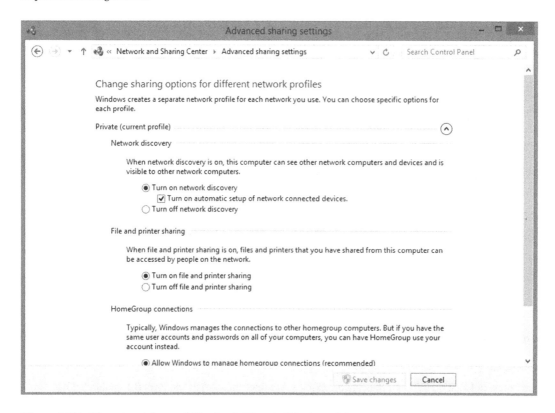

Figure 4-35. *Changing Advanced Sharing Settings in Windows 8.1*

The network settings are separated into three groups: Private, Guest or Public, and All Networks. The sharing settings for Public networks are understandably different from those for Private networks. The following describes the main settings:

- **Network Discovery** is the setting to go to when your computer can't be found on a network or you can't see any other computers and devices. There is a switch here to automatically turn on setup for network connected devices. You may not want this on, however, if you are commonly in environments in which networked devices such as storage might be prone to malware infection and distribution.

- **File and Printer Sharing** is the main switch for sharing all your files, documents, pictures, music, and videos on networks. Printer sharing affects only printers physically attached to the computer.

- **HomeGroup Connections** is a useful setting if you want to choose between Windows automatically managing user access from computers in HomeGroup and finer control with specific user accounts and passwords required.

- **Public Folder Sharing** isn't what you might first believe. It's not about sharing your files and folders with the public. Instead, it is about the public folders that Windows has always set up in user accounts to aid the sharing of files. These folders are not commonly used, however.

- **Media Streaming** controls the options for live broadcasting of pictures, audio, and video over a network to UPnP devices. Uncheck this if you do not want your music, videos, and pictures to show up on your network as shared media.

- **File Sharing Connections** is the setting for controlling the amount of encryption used on the network when sharing files. This should not ever be changed from the default unless you are requested to do so by a company IT administrator because making changes can potentially compromise your PC's security.

- **Password Protected File Sharing** is something that you shouldn't normally change; however, if you do not have a password on the computer from which you use to share files, you will find that you can't access those files from another computer unless you turn this setting off.

Connecting to Network Shared Storage

These days, most networked shared storage automatically appears in the Network section of File Explorer. This is the case whether you're on a home or a work network, and can include NAS boxes, file servers (though you may need to log in to access these), and USB hard disks plugged into compatible routers.

In Windows 7, you can view a full network map through the Network and Sharing Center to locate devices. You can no longer do this in Windows 8.1, but the operating system is much better at connecting to network resources than its predecessors.

Unfortunately, with the removal of the network map, the option to automatically log in to the network storage administration interface is also gone. In Windows 8.1, if you want to change a configuration option, you have to know the IP address of the device, which you can get through your router or through the Devices and Printers page.

■ **Note** The default IP address of a router is normally 192.168.0.1 or 192.168.1.1. You can type this into your web browser address bar to gain access.

Why You Might Not See Network Storage on Your Computer

Sometimes network resources fail to appear. This is usually a problem caused by your router. A typical home router provided by your ISP can be unreliable at simultaneously managing multiple devices on the network.

In my own home, for example, I regularly have a desktop PC, a laptop (perhaps even a second laptop), an Xbox 360, a Windows phone, and an NAS drive on at the same time—so six devices plus the router. I regularly find that Windows starts with a message that it has detected an IP address conflict. This is where the router has incorrectly assigned the IP addresses of the computers and devices on the network, and one device thinks it has a different IP address from the one the router has assigned it.

In practice, however, Windows is very good at sorting out these types of problems on its own. It is very rare that you are completely unable to see a networked device.

You can manually set the IP addresses for computers and devices on your router, but the facility to manually set IP addresses in Windows has been removed from previous versions. If a device still fails to appear, then restarting that device (and the router) normally rectifies the problem.

Another thing that can prevent your computer from seeing network storage is a firewall that has settings that are too aggressive. I have found that some security suites have this problem with the default configuration. The solution depends on your security suite and the way its configuration options work. It is always worth checking if you experience problems. You can best check by temporarily switching the firewall off. After you are successfully connected to your network storage, you can turn the firewall back on again without interrupting the connection in the future.

Viewing the Status of Network Drives

When you use the Network page in File Explorer, it's simple to view and access other hard disks and attached storage on your network. The ability to see the amount of remaining storage is more difficult. There's no point in performing a backup to a network drive; for example, if you don't know that you first need to clear some space.

You can do this by connecting your computer to a folder on the drive; any folder will do, but it's usually a good idea to create a root folder on the disk into which you put everything else. This way, when you open the shared drive, you can to see and work with all its contents.

To do this, follow these instructions:

1. Open File Explorer and click Network in the left pane.

2. Double-click the network drive you want to attach to your computer.

3. Right-click a folder within that drive. From the options, click **Map network drive** (see Figure 4-36).

Figure 4-36. *Connecting a network drive*

4. In the dialog, choose any free drive. If you want Windows to automatically connect to this drive every time you start your computer, make sure that Reconnect at Logon is checked. If the mapped drive is on another computer, you may need to log in to it with different credentials; they will be the username and password for the host PC (see Figure 4-37).

Figure 4-37. *Map Network Drive options*

5. Click Finish when you are done.

The network drive now appears in File Explorer in the Network Location section of the Computer window. It displays the total size of the drive along with the amount of available free space (see Figure 4-38). As you can see from this screen shot, it's good that I checked.

Figure 4-38. *Viewing a mapped drive in File Explorer*

■ **Tip** Sometimes your network drives don't show up in File Explorer, perhaps because they're on a subnetwork such as a powerline system in your home or office. You can manually connect to them in the Address bar by typing \\ followed by the name of the network drive; for example, \\N3 to connect to the drive called N3.

Summary

There are more ways to share documents, media, and network resources in Windows 8.1 than ever before offered in a Windows operating system. The new sharing integration with apps is something that I am personally excited to see developers use to push sharing in new directions.

Of course, there are security considerations. You should always make sure that you have up-to-date antivirus protection.

The Devices and Printers page is far more powerful than it first appears to be. The networking settings for sharing are also very powerful. When it comes to sharing media files and printer access, Windows 8.1 is a great operating system to use, especially with its helpful wizards—something Microsoft has always been good at—walking you through each step.

Despite the removal of a couple of Windows 7 features that I personally found very useful, it is still very possible to robustly work with network resources.

CHAPTER 5

■ ■ ■

Organizing and Searching Your Computer

Our computing devices—be they desktop PCs, laptops, tablets, smartphones, or new ultrabooks—are all about content. We either make it or consume it, but we all have ever-growing quantities of it. You may store it on a network share, in the cloud, on an external hard disk, or on the computer's hard disk or solid-state drive (SSD)—but there will probably be a lot of it wherever it is stored.

Of this content, you'll likely have an ever-ballooning collection of digital photographs, a big music Library, and possibly a growing video collection. These files take a lot of space to store and can make finding exactly what you're looking for problematic, especially with photos.

At the other end of the file-size scale are all your Microsoft Word, Excel, PDF, and other file types, which you have for personal, household, work, and school purposes. Although they may not take up large amounts of space, these files can be equally difficult to find and organize.

Traditionally, the way to organize files and documents was to use a folder structure. I remember using software such as XTree on the first IBM PCs to perform this task (see Figure 5-1).

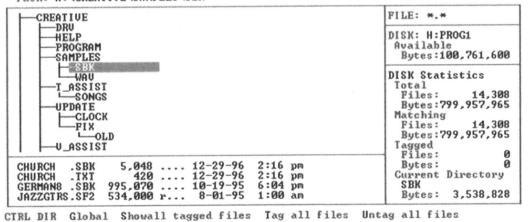

Figure 5-1. *XTree on the original IBM PC*

Folders aren't always a suitable way to organize our files and documents because some have crossovers between categories; and as the volume of files, music, pictures, and videos we collect expands, even the most organized folder structure can become unwieldy and difficult to navigate.

For many years now, Windows has tried to help us organize our files through user folders, My Documents, and so forth. They still exist, but there are much more powerful ways to help you organize. In this chapter, I'll show you how to optimize file organization and access.

Using File Explorer

Before moving into newer features, the place to start a discussion about organizing your files is File Explorer, sometimes referred to in Windows 8.1 as *This PC*. In Windows 8, it has been significantly overhauled with the inclusion of the Ribbon interface, which was first introduced in Microsoft Office 2007.

■ **Note**   The Ribbon interface is minimized by default in Windows 8.1, appearing only when you click a tab header. You can show or hide the Ribbon at all times in File Explorer by clicking the small arrow on the right of the Ribbon headers (see Figure 5-2).

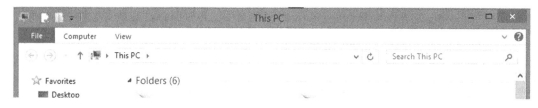

Figure 5-2. *File Explorer in Windows 8.1*

File Explorer in Windows 8.1 is split into several different sections, and some can be used with great effect to aid productivity or save time when searching for and working with files. At the very top left of the File Explorer, there is a File Explorer button that can be clicked to perform various actions on the program, including minimizing it and closing it.

■ **Tip**   Clicking a program button in the top left of its window first displays a menu of window controls; with a second click, the program closes.

Quick Access Toolbar

The Quick Access Toolbar remains next to the program button at the top of the window (see Figure 5-3). This area allows you to single-click access to commonly used commands. It is customizable too, with the Down arrow to its right bringing up a list of additional buttons that you can add to the toolbar, including Undo, Delete, and Rename.

Figure 5-3. *The Quick Access Toolbar in File Explorer*

You can add and remove items from the Quick Access Toolbar by selecting and deselecting them in the toolbar options menu.

The Address Bar

Just below the Ribbon, which I will talk about in depth shortly, is the address bar, sometimes known as the breadcrumb bar. On the left of it are buttons to move backward and forward in the current view. These buttons remember where you have been and allow you to return to locations, even if they are out of the current folder tree (see Figure 5-4).

Figure 5-4. *The address bar in File Explorer*

Next to these buttons is an up arrow that takes you one level up in the current folder hierarchy. To the right of the address bar is a search box that allows you to search for any type of file or text within a file. By default, the search prioritizes the contents of the current folder. For example, if you are looking at pictures, those pictures are prioritized in your search results over other types of documents.

The address bar is so called because it offers you ways back in the current folder tree that provide easy access to other parts of that tree (see Figure 5-5). Each of the two folder names has a small black arrow separating them.

Figure 5-5. *Using the address bar in File Explorer*

■ **Tip** The address bar displays a list of recent places on your PC and your network that you have visited when you start using it. You can clear this history from the *File* tab on the Ribbon by clicking *Delete History* and then clicking *Address bar History*. Similiarly, deleting the *Recent Places List* clears the recent places history for the *Recent Places* link in the *Favorites* bar in the Navigation Pane (see Figure 5-5).

If you click one of the arrows between folders, you are given quick links to jump to any other folder in that part of the tree. This can make it extremely quick and easy to navigate to different parts of your hard disk(s) and find what it is you are looking for.

■ **Tip** To find out the exact current folder location or to manually type a folder address into the address bar, click the button located on the far left of the address bar. The exact current folder address will appear, highlighted, so you can immediately start typing a new folder address; you can also press Ctrl+C to easily copy it while its highlighted.

The Navigation Pane

To the left of the window is the Navigation pane, which is split into different categories. In the first, Favorites, you can drag and drop folders (not files) that you want quick one-click access to, perhaps because you use them often.

■ **Tip** You can pin Favorite Links, folders, and files to the Start screen by right-clicking them and selecting Pin to Start.

Beneath the Favorite Links in the Navigation Pane are quick, expandable groups for the following:

- **SkyDrive** displays if you log in to your Windows 8.1 PC using a Microsoft account. It displays all the files and folders you have stored on SkyDrive and gives you quick access to them. If you are syncing your PC's files with SkyDrive, this duplicates the user folders in *This PC*.

- **HomeGroup**, which I discuss in detail in Chapter 4, provides access to documents, pictures, music, and video that is shared on your home network using the HomeGroup feature.

- **This PC**, formerly known as Computer in File Explorer, displays all the hard disks and attached storage on your computer in addition to your user folders for your Desktop, Documents, Downloads, Music, Pictures, and Videos.

- **Network** displays all available attached network locations, networked computers, and network storage.

Customizing the Navigation Pane

You can customize the Navigation Pane by clicking the *Navigation Pane* button on the *View* tab in the Ribbon, see Figure 5-6. The options available include

Figure 5-6. *You can customize the Navigation Pane in File Explorer*

- Turning the **Navigation Pane** off altogether

- Displaying a folder list underneath the clicked item in the Navigation Pane that automatically **Expand**[s] **to** [the currently] **open folder**

- **Show**[ing] **all** [the] **folders** on your PC in a traditional tree view (yes, this is where you can find it!)

- **Show** [the] **Libraries** that are hidden by default in Windows 8.1 but still exist. Libraries, which I will show you how to use later in this chapte,r can be extremely useful.

- **Show** [the] **Favorite** links section at the top of the Navigation Pane

Status Bar and Folder Options

Running along the bottom of File Explorer is the Status bar. It gives basic information about the current folder of the currently selected items, such as the number of files. Unlike with Windows 7, this Status bar doesn't contain details about files; they have been moved to a Details pane, which I will talk about shortly.

You can turn the Status bar off in the Folder Options for File Explorer. It can be accessed by clicking the *Options* button under the *View* tab on the Ribbon and then clicking *Change folder and search options*. In the options that appear, you find the Folder Options under the *View* tab (see Figure 5-7).

Figure 5-7. *The Folder Options for File Explorer*

In this list, you find a check box for *Show status bar*. Other controls are also very useful and include being able to uncheck the option to *Show Drive letters* for your hard disks; showing compressed NTFS drives in color; or unhiding protected operating system files, which can prove useful if you need to troubleshoot and repair a problem with Windows.

Another useful feature in the Folder Options is the *Apply to Folders* button that you can use to make all the folders on your PC (for general and mixed document types) look the same as the current folder. I will show you how to customize the views in File Explorer later in this chapter.

Tip At the far right of the Status bar are buttons to quickly access two of the most common views in File Explorer: the Details view and the Thumbnail view. Clicking these buttons immediately changes the File Explorer view of the current folder.

Main Explorer View

In the main File Explorer pane, you see all your files and folders, which can be arranged in a great many ways. You can also select files in the main view in several ways, including the following:

- **Right-click:** You can right-click a file or folder with your mouse to bring up a context menu of the actions you can perform on it.

- **Tap and hold:** You can tap and hold a folder or file to bring up the actions context menu.

- **Hover the mouse:** You can hover your mouse over a file or folder to bring up a check box to select the item. You can use this method to select multiple items if you want.

■ **Tip**   To select multiple files and/or folders with your mouse and keyboard, you can use one of these options. To select everything between two items, click the first item, hold down the Shift key, and then click the item at the end of the list. To select multiple, randomly placed items, hold the Ctrl key while clicking the items you want to select.

Hiding Picture File Names

One very useful feature that has not made it into the Ribbon is the ability to hide the file names of pictures in File Explorer. If you are looking at holiday photos or similar, why do you need to look at reams of DSCxxx file names anyway?

You can hide the file names for pictures by right-clicking in any blank space; then in the View menu, select **Hide file names** (see Figure 5-8).

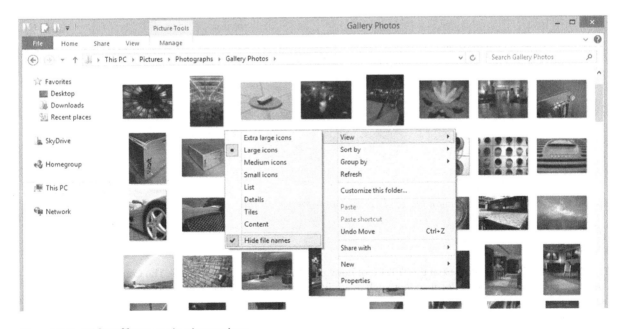

Figure 5-8. *Hiding file names in picture views*

File Explorer Ribbon

I have left the Ribbon until last because I want to spend a little more time on it and talk about each tab.

By default, the Ribbon in File Explorer is hidden, and you display it by clicking one of the tabs at the top of the window: File, Home, Share, and View. Other tabs can appear, however, such as Computer, Library, or Picture. These extra tabs contain functions specific to those file types. When the Ribbon is open, a *pin* icon appears on the right of the window. You can click this to lock the Ribbon so that it is always displayed.

I won't discuss every Ribbon function in depth here, but I do want to concentrate on the Ribbon functions that I think are most useful, most interesting, or most likely to give you a valuable productivity boost.

You may find that the Ribbon is hidden in File Explorer and you can see only the tab names. If you click one of these, the Ribbon appears temporarily, but you can show and hide the Ribbon by clicking the small up/down arrow (this changes depending on whether the Ribbon is currently displayed or hidden) that appears next to the Help button on the far right of the tab name on the right of the window.

File Tab

The main file tab, which is blue—a different color from the other tabs—is where you find options such as Open or Open in a New Window. As well as having options for deleting your File Explorer history a list of your frequently accessed folders appear here. You can click the pin icon to the right of them to pin any to this *Frequent Places* list (see Figure 5-9).

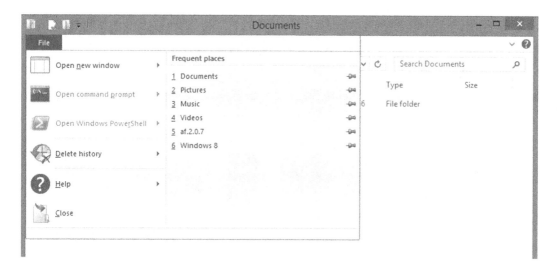

Figure 5-9. You can perform general File Explorer options from the File tab

Computer Tab

The Computer tab is accessible from the This PC or network main drive (see Figure 5-10). The Computer tab provides context-sensitive options to perform actions such as adding a network location to File Explorer. You also get easy access to the Windows 8.1 Control Panel and the Programs and Features panel, in which you can uninstall desktop programs.

Figure 5-10. *Computer tab*

Home Tab

The Home tab (see Figure 5-11) is where you find all the common options associated with files and folders in Windows. These options include Cut, Copy, Paste, Move, and Delete. You can also create new folders and files in the New section of the Ribbon. Of particular interest are the History button and the Selection buttons.

Figure 5-11. *The Home tab in File Explorer*

■ **Tip**   You can perform cut, copy, and paste actions in Windows using the Ctrl+X (Cut), Ctrl+C (Copy), and Ctrl+V (Paste) hot keys.

Windows 8.1 includes a better file versioning system than what was included in Windows 7. I discuss how to use the feature in depth in Chapter 12, but if you have a single file selected, the History button brings up the versioning for that file, including any previous versions of the file that Windows 8.1 has backed up.

Also, the Open section has a Properties button that you can click to quickly bring up the Properties dialog for any file, folder, or a selection of files and/or folders. In the Properties dialog for files, you can change or update information about a file, including artist and track information for music, as well as tags and ratings.

In the Selection section, very handy buttons for Select all, Select None, and Invert Selection have been included. It can be very helpful when you want to work with some files, perhaps to change their properties, and then need to perform another action on all the other files in the same folder.

Note that if you select a location such as a DVD or non-hard-disk location, the options on the Home tab change to better reflect the actions you can perform with that device.

Share Tab

The Share tab (see Figure 5-12) contains the tools and utilities you need to share and back up your files and folders. These options include syncing and backing up to Microsoft's SkyDrive service, sending files via e-mail, creating a zipped archive file, burning files to disc (CD/DVD/Blu-ray), and printing or faxing files.

Figure 5-12. *The Share tab in File Explorer*

If you are sharing files on your computer or across a network, or would like to, you can set who you want to share files with by using this tab.

View Tab and Customizing File Explorer

In the View tab (see Figure 5-13), you can customize File Explorer to look and work the way you like.

Figure 5-13. *The View tab in File Explorer*

There are different panes that can be switched on and off in File Explorer. The Navigation Pane has a button to switch it off or to customize it. There is no way to turn on the traditional folder view, not that you were necessarily used to it in earlier versions of Windows anyway, but turning on Show All Folders in the Navigation Pane displays the same result in the This PC section.

The Preview and Details panes are slightly different, though they can be confused with one another. Both these panes appear on the right side of the Explorer window and cannot be displayed simultaneously. If you turn on the Preview pane, a live image of the file appears, which you can review (this will work for the most common file types, but won't work for custom or less common files). This includes being able to scroll through an entire Word, Excel, or Acrobat document.

■ **Tip**　Grouping, which is a great way to clearly organize your files and folders in File Explorer, can be activated for a folder by clicking the [■] button in the *Current* View section. It seperates the content of a folder by a category that you specify, such as the size or file type. When you group items in File Explorer, each group is separated by a horizontal line. You can click this line to select all the items in the group or right-click the line to display an option to hide the group (or all the groups). This makes folders that contain many files easier to navigate.

The Details pane in File Explorer gives you detailed information about a file that you select. The information presented in the Details pane is editable, meaning that you don't have to bring up the separate Properties dialog to edit information such as Author, Track Number, or Rating.

In the Layout section of the Ribbon are some very useful tools for customizing the current view:

- The **Small**, **Medium**, **Large**, and **Extra Large buttons** change the default thumbnail size in the current view.

- **List** displays all items in view as a simple list, such as was the case in the very early versions of Windows.

- **Details** is a very common view. It can also be accessed from a button on the Status bar at the bottom right of the window. This view displays extra information about files and folders that many people find useful, such as the file size and the date/time the file was created and last modified.

- **Tiles** and **Content** present files and folders in much friendlier ways than the default view, in my opinion. Tiles is an upgraded thumbnail view. Content presents more details about files in a way similar to the Details view.

In the Current View section are tools to help you sort and group content in different ways. You may want, for example, to sort items by Date Modified or Created By. Grouping files and folders is an excellent way to keep yourself organized so that you know exactly what you have and where. Grouping files and folders by Type, for example, groups all the folders together, all the Word documents together, all the PNG images together, and so on.

■ **Tip**   At the bottom of the Sort By and Group By drop-down menus is a Choose Columns option. If you select it, many more sort and group options appear, including album artist or rating for music or EXIF data for digital photographs.

In the Show/Hide group are two functions previously hidden to many Windows users: the ability to show and hide file extensions. These are hidden by default for all known file types. The second option is to show and hide hidden files. This option is extremely useful if you need to drill down into the Windows system folder or your User folder to find specific information or a specific hidden file.

■ **Tip**   In the Ribbon, you can set all folders to display in the same way as the current folder by clicking Options ➤ Folder and Search Options ➤ View ➤ Apply to Folders.

Copying and Moving Files in File Explorer

The feedback you get when copying and moving files in Windows 8.1 has significantly improved. There is more feedback and more control when duplicate copies of files are found. The copied file dialog is shown in Figure 5-14.

Figure 5-14. *The improved copy/move file dialog in Windows 8.1*

One of the most significant improvements to copy and move file operations is that all operations now appear in the same window. This means that if you have several copy or move operations running simultaneously, you now only have one window on your screen that contains them all.

The other significant improvement is the addition of a Pause button to the dialog. You can now pause, copy, and move operations if you need to do something else or put your computer to sleep at the end of the day. When you return to Windows, you can continue with the operation by unpausing it.

When you click More Details on a copy or move file dialog, you are shown a graph of the copy or move operation. This graph gives you live feedback on the current speed of the copy, the number of megabits per second being copied, and a filled graph showing how the speed of the copy has changed. This is useful for diagnosing problems with copy or move operations when something else is happening in the background.

The Replace dialogs have also been upgraded in Windows 8.1 (see Figure 5-15), as you will notice when you copy or move files into a folder or onto a drive where another copy already exists.

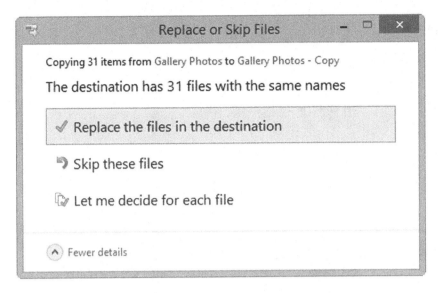

Figure 5-15. *The improved Replace or Skip Files dialog*

The Replace or Skip Files dialog is now much simpler with choices to replace or skip all the files, or to choose which ones you want to keep in the destination folder.

If you want to choose which files you want to keep or overwrite, this dialog has improved as well. You still have a check box to select everything to keep or replace, but each individual file is more easily identifiable.

▪ **Tip** To keep all the source *and* destination files in a copy or move operation, check the Files From and Files Already In check boxes at the top of both the left and the right columns (see Figure 5-16).

Figure 5-16. *You can easily select files to overwrite in Windows 8.1*

Pictures have a thumbnail image, but other file types just display the associated program's icon. This new dialog makes it much easier to decide which files to keep and which to replace than with Windows 7, in which you were given only text information such as the date and time stamps.

Managing Files and Folders from Apps

Managing files and folders in Windows 8.1 apps is a much simpler affair, and you can get easy access to files across your network or stored in SkyDrive (see Figure 5-17). However, the new interface can make it difficult to manage large volumes of files or to perform complex actions because the commands available in the App bar are not as extensive as in the desktop File Explorer.

Figure 5-17. You can easily find files in different locations from within apps

To select any file in an app on which you want to perform an action, tap and hold it. You can also right-click it with a mouse. You can select multiple files, but the options available for working with those files in the App bar may change depending on the app in which you are currently working.

Using Libraries in Windows 8.1

The common view of Windows 7 users is that Libraries are the same as the shell user folders—those folders with "My" in front of their names. Libraries actually are aggregated storage for many locations. They are customizable for specific types of content. They're actually very powerful with the way that content can be displayed.

By default, Libraries aren't displayed in Windows 8.1, although you can turn them on by clicking the *Navigation Pane* button on the *View* tab in the Ribbon and selecting them there. They then appear in the Navigation Pane as in Windows 7 and 8; additionally opening File Explorer now takes you directly to your Libraries (see Figure 5-18). However, if you still want to see *This PC* as the default File Explorer view, I will show you how to do this in Chapter 13.

Figure 5-18. *Accessing Libraries in File Explorer*

By default, there are Libraries of documents, music, pictures, and videos; although if you install other software (such as the Microsoft Zune player), others (such as Podcasts) may be added.

You can create your own Libraries to view and arrange content in specific ways; for instance, you might want one for your work or school documents, and so on.

Creating a Library

You can add new folders to an existing Library (I show you how to do this shortly), but you can also create your own custom Libraries. I have one for Photos, in which where all my pictures are arranged by their tags. You might want a separate Library for your school, work, or household documents. You can have a Library for anything, and it's a great way to organize files.

■ **Tip**　You can add SD cards and other removable media to Libraries in Windows 8.1. This is useful if your ultrabook or tablet comes with a memory card shot for additional storage. To add these file locations, right-click them; from the context menu that appears, click *Include in Library*. From the list that appears, click the Library in which you want to include the folder.

To create a new Library, perform the following steps:

1.　Open File Explorer on the desktop.

2.　Click Libraries in the left pane.

3.　Right-click (or tap and hold with your finger) any blank space in the main Explorer window (see Figure 5-19).

Figure 5-19. *Creating a new Library*

4. From the context menu, select New and then Library. You are presented with a new empty Library to which you need to give a name.

5. Once the Library is created, double-click it to open it.

6. Click the Include a Folder button and choose a folder to display in the Library (see Figure 5-20). You can add additional folders later (I will show you how to do this shortly).

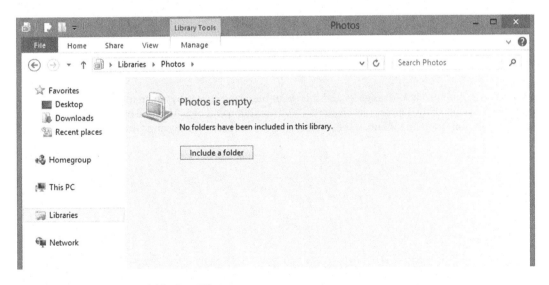

Figure 5-20. *Including a folder in a Library*

Changing the Way a Library Displays Files

You now see your folder listed in the Library, but it just looks like an ordinary explorer Window. It is now that the full flexibility of Libraries can be used because they can display content in ways that the normal Explorer folder view cannot.

1. To change the view, right-click (or tap and hold with your finger) in any blank space in the main window (see Figure 5-21).

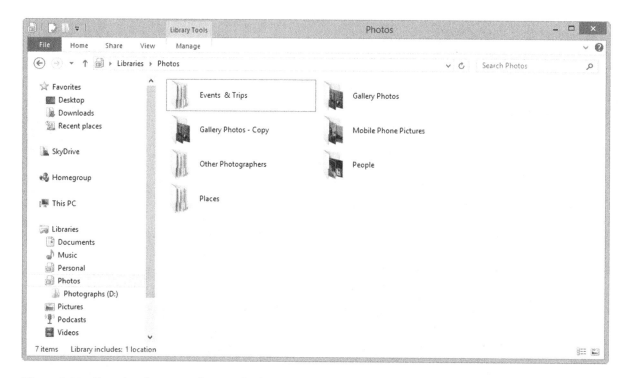

Figure 5-21. *Changing the way a Library is displayed*

2. From the context menu, click Arrange By and then your preferred choice by which to arrange the contents of the Library (see Figure 5-22). This action can be performed only by a right-click, not from the Ribbon. It is different from the Ribbon's Sort By and Group By views.

Figure 5-22. *Choosing how to arrange files in a Library*

You see that the Library is now arranged as you want it. In Figure 5-23, I have arranged a Photo Library by tag. Regardless of what folder the photographs are stored in, I can view all pictures of Brighton Pier (for example) just by opening the tagged group. A nice benefit.

Figure 5-23. *Viewing photos by tag in Libraries*

These Brighton Pier photos may reside in a dozen or more different folders on my hard disk, but because they all have the same tag, they are all displayed together in the Library when I arrange the files by tag.

■ **Note** Within Libraries, you can arrange files by type, which display the files as stacked groups for Word documents, PDFs, and so on. Sadly, you cannot specify just a single file type to be shown in a Library, only complete folders.

Managing Libraries

When you are viewing a Library, a *Manage* tab appears on the Ribbon (see Figure 5-24). This Library Tools tab contains tools for managing the library, including which folders are included within it, what type of content the Library is optimized for (to aid in displaying that content correctly), and whether the Library is displayed in the Navigation Pane. Here you can also change the icon for the Library to one of the standard Windows icons or to a custom .ico file of your choosing.

Figure 5-24. *You can manage a Library from the Ribbon in File Explorer*

The folders included by default in the standard Windows 8.1 Libraries are the default folders found in C:\User\[Username]. In addition to the default folders, you can include other folders and remove folders in a Library. To add or remove folders from a Library, click *Manage Library* on the *Manage tab* in the Ribbon.

■ **Tip**   Although Libraries don't allow you to add external hard disks and network locations, it can still be done through an easy cheat. See "Adding Network Locations to Libraries," later in this chapter.

Clicking the Manage Library button on the Ribbon brings up the Photos Library Locations dialog with its simple Add and Remove buttons for Library locations. You must have at least one location for a Library, but you can specify as many as you want (see Figure 5-25).

Figure 5-25. *Adding and removing folders to Libraries*

■ **Tip**   You can also add local folders on your PC and SD card storage to Libraries by right-clicking them and selecting *Include in Library* from the menu that appears.

Changing the Default Save Location

A question mark can be raised about where the default save locations for Documents, Music, Pictures, and Video will be when you add new folders to a Library. After all, when you save a file, where does it go? Into your Users folder on the C:\ drive? Into the Library somewhere? Into a specific folder in the Library?

In Chapter 12, I talk about how and why you should move your files away from Windows and onto a separate hard disk or partition to safeguard them, but one way to do it is to change the default save location for a Library. You can do this from the Library Tools tab on the Ribbon in File Explorer when a Library is being viewed.

On the left of the Ribbon, there is a Set Save Location button, which offers a drop-down menu of the folders contained within that Library. To change the default save location, simply click the relevant folder that you want all new files saved to (see Figure 5-26).

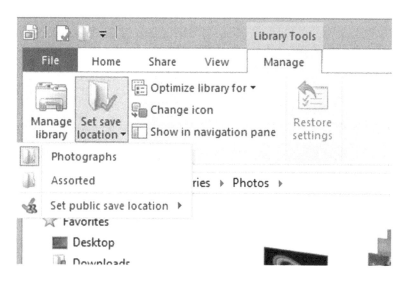

Figure 5-26. *Setting the default save location for Libraries*

Adding Network Locations to Libraries

It's fairly well known and established that you can't add network locations to Libraries in Windows 8.1, as was the case with Windows 7 … or can you? In fact, it's always been possible to add network locations to your Music, Pictures, and Videos Libraries. You do it in two ways in Windows 8.1.

The first way is to create a symbolic link between the Library and the folder on your network that contains the files you want to include:

1. Create a folder in your C:\Users\[Username] folder named after the folder you want to include.

2. Add this new folder to your Library.

3. Delete the folder from C:\Users\[Username], but *do not* delete it from the Library.

4. Open the *Command Prompt* window from the Win+X menu.

5. Type **MKLINK /D C:\Users*Username**FolderName* *NetworkLocation***, substituting the correct paths to the folders.

This process adds the network location to the Library, but does not add it to the index, which means that the Library may be slow to refresh when you open it. (I will talk more about the Windows index later in this chapter.) A friendlier way to add a folder to a Library can be done using Windows Media Center. Note that in Windows 8.1, Windows Media Center is no longer a standard feature in the operating system, but is available as a chargeable add-on for Windows 8.1 Pro and brings with it DVD and Blu-ray playback. You can purchase an upgrade by clicking Add Features to Windows in the Control Panel.

Open Windows Media Center to add network locations containing Pictures, Music, and Video (but not Documents). From the main menu, click Settings ➤ Media Libraries.

You are presented with a wizard that allows you to add or remove folders to/from the Libraries. When asked where the files are located, select On Another Computer (see Figure 5-27). This displays network drives and allows you to add these locations to the Libraries.

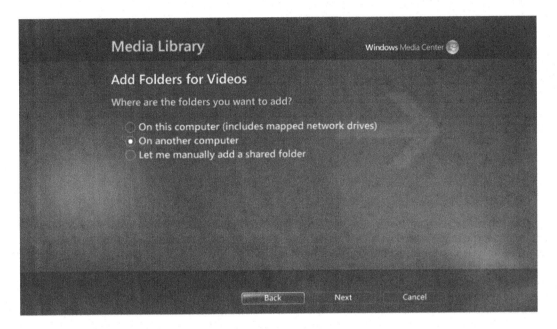

Figure 5-27. *Using Media Center to add network locations to Libraries*

All available network locations, including other computers on your network (that are switched on), appear in a collapsible list (see Figure 5-28). You can check and uncheck media folders to add to the Library. This is a fantastically simple workaround to what is otherwise a missing functionality in Windows Libraries.

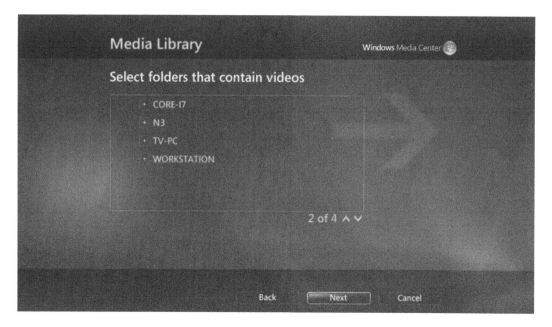

Figure 5-28. *Viewing network drives to add to Libraries in Media Center*

Using Tags and Ratings to Organize Files

Tags and Ratings are two of the best ways to organize and categorize files. Tags are labels that help you find relevant documents. For example, you might have documents tagged as "work," "school," "household," or "auto." Thus, tags might help you locate documents related to your car quickly and easily.

If you have a lot of photos, you might label them "vacation," "children," or "Germany" to help you find them quickly for display to friends and family (this is, after all, why you took them in the first place).

You might already be familiar with tags called *metadata* with your music files, where the artist, album name, track number, track name, and more are all tags. They are labels used to help you identify the contents of a file.

You don't need to be limited to a single tag per file, either. You can stack multiple tags together so your recent vacation photos in Orlando might be tagged "vacation," "Orlando," "Disney," "Janell," and "Lidia."

Ratings are slightly different but easier to understand. Ratings in Windows 8.1 use one to five stars that indicate how significant the file is. In your music, you probably already use 4- and 5-star ratings to identify your favorite tracks; you may have been doing this for years. If you use the Like tag for music tracks in the Zune Desktop software, for example, it automatically adds a 5-star rating to each file you like.

You can view the tags and ratings for any file or files in File Explorer by clicking the Details pane button on the Ribbon under the View tab (see Figure 5-29). This opens a pane on the right side of the windows, showing all manner of information, which changes from file type to file type. Tags and Rating are always at the top of the list.

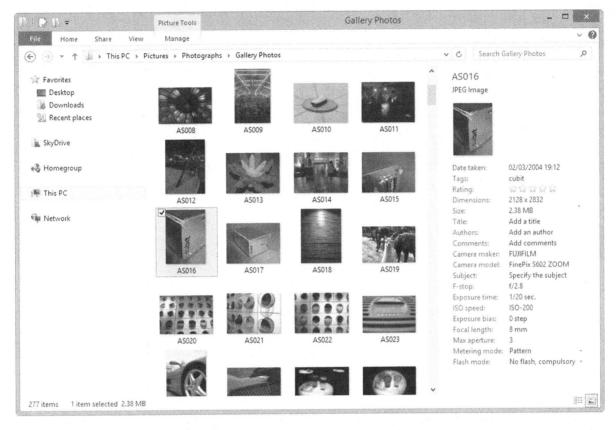

Figure 5-29. *The Details pane in File Explorer*

To add a tag or multiple tags to a file or a selection of files (remember you can press Ctrl+click to select multiple individual files, and click followed by Shift+click to mark a selected group), click next to Tags in the Details pane and type as many as you like, each one separated by a semicolon (;). When you have finished adding tags, click the Save button to finish.

You can add a rating or change a rating by clicking the appropriate number of stars. Click Save when you are done.

■ **Tip** You can remove all the metadata in a file by opening the file's properties (right-click and select Properties from the menu that appears) and under the *Details* tab click the *Remove Properties and Personal Information* link at the bottom of the properties panel.

Simplify Adding Tags and Ratings with Windows Photo Gallery

It can be a laborious process adding tags and ratings to files, but the important thing to remember is that *you need to do this only once.* There are tools that can make the process much easier for you as well. Windows Photo Gallery, part of the Windows Essentials suite, can be downloaded for free from download.live.com. In the View tab on the Ribbon, you have the option to view files by tag (see Figure 5-30).

Figure 5-30. *Tagging photos in Windows Live Photo Gallery*

The View tab features a button to open the Tag and Caption Pane (the button is on the far right of the Ribbon). This pane offers a great way to simplify the addition of tags to photos and pictures because it lists all your photos by tag category, and shows all the photos that are *not tagged*. You can select these photos for tagging, making it much easier to know which pictures are already tagged.

When you import new photos to Windows 8.1 from your digital camera or memory card, the default import utility, the Photos app, doesn't permit adding tags. You can add tags automatically when you import photos to your PC however by doing this from within Photo Gallery. This is a good time to do it because all the photos are probably related, and having Windows automate the process of adding tags makes things much simpler.

You can also remove and amend tags and ratings later in Windows Live Photo Gallery using simple controls. The options for this appear in the right pane when a photo or photos are selected.

You can import photos from your camera or digital memory card by clicking the Import button under the Home tab on the Ribbon.

You will first be asked to identify the media you are importing your photos from and you can then click Add Tags and type your tags (see Figure 5-31). This automatically adds the tags you enter to all your imported photos. You may want to use general tags such as "vacation," "family," or "Germany." I talk more about importing photos and videos in Chapter 7.

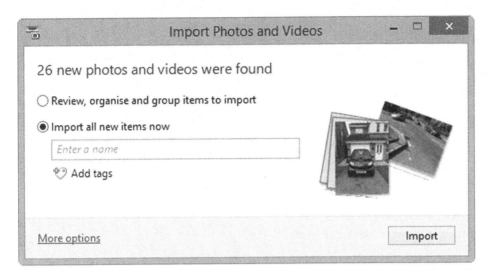

Figure 5-31. *Tagging photos on import from a camera*

■ **Tip**   Most music players help automate adding tags to your music by finding the correct album from an extensive online database.

Managing Folder Options

Folder Options offers a huge amount of control over File Explorer and the way files and folders are viewed.

The first tab in this window, General, gives you the option to open files and folders with a single-click instead of a double click. This is especially useful for people using a Windows 8.1 tablet (see Figure 5-32).

Figure 5-32. *Changing the general folder view options*

The option to show all folders in File Explorer's Navigation Pane may be the most popular. If you aren't a fan of the new Favorite Links pane, either you can switch it off completely in favor of the legacy folder view (see Figure 5-33) or you can combine the two. You can also set File Explorer to automatically expand the folder view of the currently viewed folder.

Figure 5-33. *Showing the folder view in File Explorer*

The View tab gives you extra control over the way files and folders are viewed and organized (see Figure 5-34). At the top of this window are buttons to **Apply [the current folder view] to [all] Folders** or to **Reset [all] Folders** to their default view. This enables you to decide the way you want your folders to look. If you want your folders tiled with items grouped by file type, for example, you can apply this quickly and easily to all the folder views on your computer.

Figure 5-34. *Changing advanced folder view options*

Brief descriptions of some of the more noteworthy options follow:

- **Display the full path in the title bar** forces the address bar to display the full drive and folder location at all times.

- **Hidden files and folders** allows you to show or hide all hidden folders on your computer.

- **Hide empty drives in the Computer folder** is checked by default. It hides empty USB flash drives or memory card drives that you might want to copy files onto.

- **Hide extensions for known file types** is checked by default, but some users want to know the file extensions for all their files.

- **Hide protected operating system files** can be unchecked to display hidden system files that you may need to work with.

- **Show drive letters** shows the legacy drive assignments (C:, D:, and so on) on File Explorer views. Uncheck to remove the ability to see the drive letters.

- **Show encrypted or compressed NTFS files in color** highlights files in blue when an encryption service such as EFS is turned on. Many people like to uncheck this option.

The last tab, Search, contains options for searching files and folders. For example, by default, Windows 8.1 doesn't search the content of compressed ZIP, CAB, or RAR files. You might want to turn on this option if you work with compressed files often (see Figure 5-35).

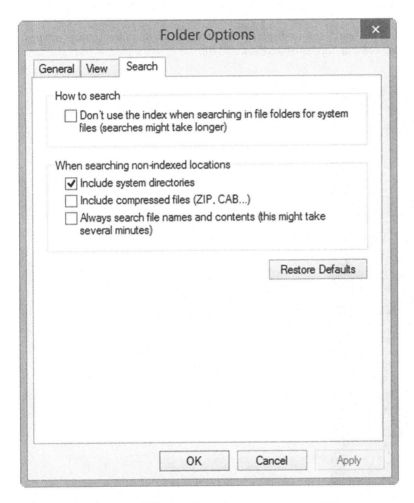

Figure 5-35. *Changing folder search options*

Using Search in Windows 8.1

It seems that with each new version of Windows, the methods by which we search for programs, settings, and files changes again. Windows 8.1 is no exception. In its simplest terms, basic search has been greatly improved since Windows 7. In Windows 7, you open the Start menu and simply type a search result; whereas in Windows 8, you just start typing at the Start screen.

Windows 7 always contextualizes your searches, so a search in the Start menu always prioritizes programs and settings. Windows 8.1 searches by default for files, settings, and apps; and also searches online at the same time. Searching directly in File Explorer, however, still prioritizes the type of content displayed in that window.

Searching from the Start Screen

You can now search in Windows 8.1 directly from the Start screen by simply typing. Whatever it is you are doing, as long as you are looking at the Start screen (even if you have right-clicked on a tile), you can begin typing, and the search results instantly appear. You can also search directly from the Start screen or the Windows desktop by pressing the Win+S key combination.

When you begin a search in Windows 8.1, the search results display relevant results, be they files, settings or apps, with Internet search results (provided by Bing.com) underneath (see Figure 5-36).

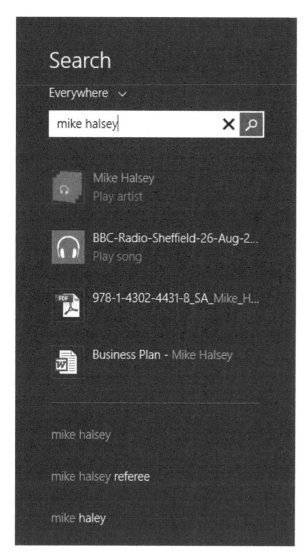

Figure 5-36. Searching from the Start screen in Windows 8.1

If you press the Enter key or the Search button to the right of the search box, then a full screen results page appears, containing many more contextualized results (see Figure 5-37). These results are displayed in columns, and underneath is a *See all* link that, when clicked, expands that section if more results are available.

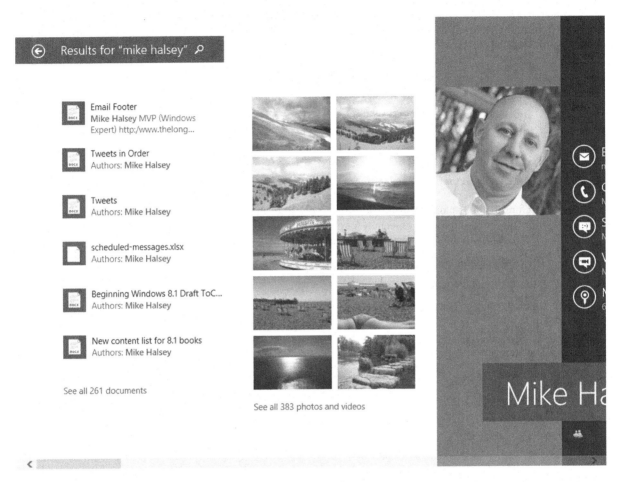

Figure 5-37. *You can get very detailed and contextualized search results*

■ **Note** Sometimes when you search, the first item in the Search pane results list is highlighted because Windows 8.1 believes this to be exactly what you're looking for. Pressing Enter here opens that selected item, *not* the full search panel. If you see a highlighted item, click the search button to the right of the search box to open the full results panel instead.

Search is intelligent, so it does not search for the words literally as you type them. A search for **Control**, for example, brings up relevant Windows features, including the Device Manager, Remote Assistance, and Accessibility options.

This means that you do not have to know the exact name of the feature in Windows you are looking for. When you are searching for apps and desktop programs (for which the results appear in the Apps results), the results depend more on how the developer has described and programmed it, but generally the search facility in Windows 8.1 is excellent.

Searching in File Explorer

File Explorer contains its own context-sensitive search box. In some ways, using it is a more efficient way to search for files and documents in Windows 8.1 than using the Start screen.

The search box prioritizes the content. It might be prioritized by documents, pictures, music, video, a specific disk drive (internal or external), a network location, or something else (see Figure 5-38). In this way, it is flexible and more dynamic than the Start screen search.

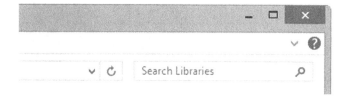

Figure 5-38. *File Explorer has its own search box*

When searching in File Explorer, a Search tab appears on the Ribbon. It contains tools and buttons to make search even more powerful and useful, especially for people who are less familiar with search syntax.

The Search tab on the Ribbon (see Figure 5-39) allows you to filter your search by

- The current folder and all subfolders

- Libraries, e-mail, notes, or the Internet

- When the file was last modified (opened)

- The type of file

- The file size

- File names

- Specific folders

- File tags

Figure 5-39. *The Search tab on the Ribbon*

These options cover just about any search you will undertake in Windows 8.1. The Search tab on the Ribbon appears automatically the moment you type anything in the search box in File Explorer.

■ **Note** The Search tab on the File Explorer Ribbon allows you quick access to recent searches you have made, so that you can repeat them.

When you search from an Explorer window, you can also use Advanced Query Syntax (AQS) to narrow your searches (see Figure 5-40). I detail the full AQS in Appendix C, but some of the most useful search syntax options include Kind, Datemodified, Type, and Name. as shown in Tables 5-1 through 5-4.

Figure 5-40. *Using AQS to search in an Explorer window*

Table 5-1. *Kind (to Search the Properties of a Document Type)*

Option	Example
Kind:=email	Jake Webster kind:=email
Kind:=task	Meeting kind:=task
Kind:=note	project kind:=note
Kind:=document	Apress kind:=document
Kind:=music	Metallica kind:=music
Kind:=song	Equinoxe kind:=song
Kind:=folder	Book kind:=folder
Kind:=program	paint kind:=program

Table 5-2. *Datemodified (to Search by the Date a File Was Modified)*

Option	Example
Datemodified:MM/DD/YYYY	Report datemodified:10/22/2012
Datemodified:MM/DD/YY	Report datemodified:7/4/12
Datemodified:MM/DD/YY..MM/DD/YY	Report datemodified:7/4/12..10/22/12
Datemodified:yesterday	Orders datemodified:yesterday
Datemodified:lastweek	Orders datemodified:lastweek
Datemodified:pastmonth	Orders datemodified:pastmonth

Table 5-3. *Type (to Search by File Type)*

Option	Example
Type:	Type:image
	Type:image jpeg
	Type:.doc
	Type:.pdf

Table 5-4. *Name (to Search by File Name or by a Property Name of a File)*

Option	Example
Name:	Name:vacation
	Name:wedding
	Name:budget

Typing **type:** initially displays a drop-down list of all the file types on your computer (for example, DOC or PDF), as shown in Table 5-3. If, for example, you continue by typing **type:image**, you can filter your search by various image types or search for all image types. You also can use other file types, such as type:document, type:audio, type:video, type:presentation, and so forth.

As you begin to type a search filter in File Explorer, a drop-down list (with all the supported filter options) is displayed. Clicking the appropriate one for your search helps you find what you are looking for more quickly. If you are searching for dates, a calendar assists you.

Expanding Libraries with Saved Searches in Windows 8.1

One of the criticisms of Libraries is that you can add only folders to them; you cannot specify that a Library should contain only one or two file types, say Word and Excel files. Nor can you specify that Libraries should contain only documents created by "Rory" or tagged as "college".

This is where the true power of search in Windows 8.1 comes into play. It's such a cool feature that it will probably save you countless hours of lost productivity all on its own!

After you complete a search, you can save it by clicking the *Save* Search option on the Search tab on the File Explorer Ribbon. Saving a search adds a quick link, named whatever you want, to the Favorite Links pane in File Explorer (see Figure 5-41).

Figure 5-41. *Saving searches in Windows 8.1*

The upshot of this is that you can create those custom-aggregated folders whenever you want, and each one is automatically and dynamically updated whenever you open it.

Let's say, for example, that you search for **type:.pdf** in the search box when looking at your Documents Library. This brings up a list of all your PDF document files in your Documents Library and all subfolders. Saving this search creates something that looks and behaves like a Library consisting entirely of PDF files, which you can use whenever you need. Each time you open this saved search, the search is re-run (it literally takes a fraction of a second if the locations being searched are part of the Windows index), and the contents are updated automatically.

You can further sort, organize, and group the contents of this search however you want, perhaps by the date they were created or the tags associated with them.

I simply cannot overstate how powerful and useful this feature is, especially when used with properly tagged files. As a way of organizing home or work documents, it is a true time-saver!

Harnessing the Full Power of Saved Searches

Let me give you an example of how powerful I believe saved searches really are. In Figure 5-42, I searched for ***.ppt? authors:mike halsey**, which displays all PowerPoint files created by Mike (and optionally) Halsey.

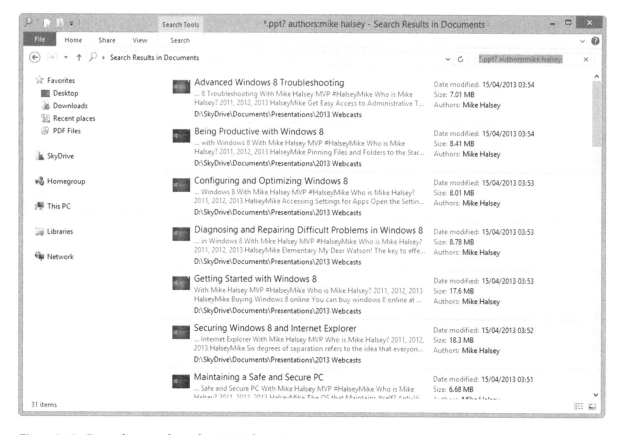

Figure 5-42. *Expanding saved searches in Windows 8.1*

Saving these search results creates dynamically updated folders in which you can quickly and easily find the information you need. Having a saved search for all documents relating to a project name, for example, enables you to keep track of all the documents related to the project at a single and always up-to-date location.

Saving and Sharing Your Saved Searches

Once you have created a saved search, you can create a copy of it to back it up or perhaps to share with a friend or colleague. You can do this by right-clicking the saved search in the Favorites pane in File Explorer and selecting Open Folder Location from the context menu.

You now see the saved search(es) listed and you can create copies in the same way you would with any other file on your computer. They can be backed up or shared with other computers. Note, however, that if drive assignments are different on the other computers, the search may not function correctly because searches work with drive letters and folders that all have absolute references on your computer.

Tagging Files in Microsoft Office

I've talked about adding tags to documents as you create them to help find them later on, but how do you do this? Obviously, the method by which you can add tags to documents as you save them varies considerably from one software package to another, and it can be expected that many software packages won't support this feature at all.

Microsoft Office has supported tags for some time, however, and if you use Office 2007 or later, it is a simple matter to add tags to documents as you save them.

When you first save a document in Microsoft Office (or select Save As), you have the option to Add a Tag (see Figure 5-43).

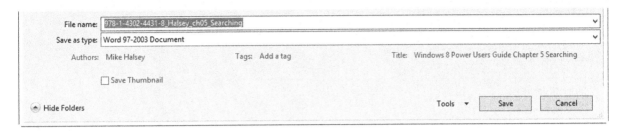

Figure 5-43. *Adding tags to documents in Microsoft Office*

You can add other details here, including authors and title, although the software will probably automatically add some information.

All Microsoft Office programs and many programs from other software vendors support adding tags to your files when you save them. In Microsoft Office, the Save dialogs for Word, Excel, PowerPoint, and so forth, allow you to add tags in the same way. You can also add information such as subjects and project managers to make files easier to find.

With other software, you need to check whether tags can be added when the file is saved. If not, you can always add tags afterward in the Details pane in File Explorer.

Managing the Search and File Index in Windows 8.1

The reason why search works very quickly in Windows 8.1, at least for internal storage on the computer, is that details about the files are all stored in an index database. By default, this database stores information on anything in your user folders and default Libraries. You can move, add, or remove folders (or even entire hard disks) to or from the index.

You can find the Indexing Options in the Search tab on the Ribbon in File Explorer, but you need to perform a search for the tab to appear. A simpler approach is to type **Index** at the Start screen and run Indexing Options from the Settings search results.

In the main Indexing Options are all the indexed drive and folder locations and their current indexing status (see Figure 5-44).

Figure 5-44. *Managing the search index in Windows 8.1*

You may find that not many files are indexed, perhaps because you have a relatively new Windows 8.1 installation and a great many files, it can take some time initially for Windows to build its index. In that case, the results you expect won't appear in the search results. You might see that some critical or important folders don't appear in the index.

Adding Folders to the Index

You can add (or remove) folders to the index by clicking the Modify button on the Indexing Options screen. It displays a folder list of all the drives on your computer. The current folder locations are checked (see Figure 5-45).

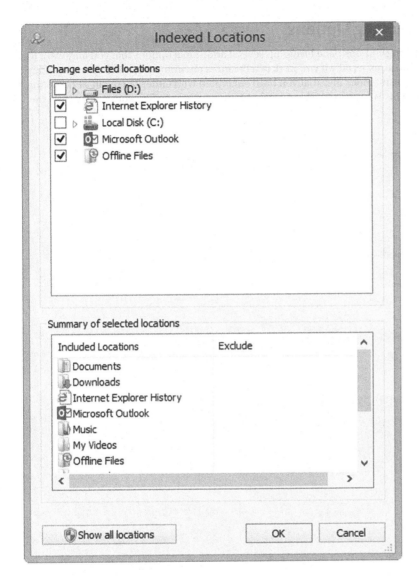

Figure 5-45. *Adding folder locations to Indexing Options*

To add or remove folders or entire drives to the index, simply check or uncheck their boxes. You can expand and collapse folders by clicking the chevrons next to folder names. When you press the OK button, the index is refreshed to include or exclude the folders you have updated.

■ **Note** It can take some time for Windows 8.1 to index the contents of your hard drive, and the process slows when you are using the computer. If you need the index built quickly, leaving the computer switched on overnight can speed up the process significantly.

Changing the Advanced Indexing Options

Clicking the Advanced button in the Indexing Options pane brings up several additional options that you may want to consider (see Figure 5-46). Chief among these, especially if you work in a business environment, is the option to index encrypted files. By default, Windows 8.1 doesn't index files that you have encrypted with either Microsoft's Encrypting File System (EFS) or third-party software. This is because the key searchable contents of the files contained within the index aren't encrypted.

Figure 5-46. *Modifying the advanced index options*

For most scenarios, it is perfectly acceptable to tick this box. If you work in a governmental, financial, medical, or research and development organization, you should seek advice, although the choice will probably be made for you, and Indexing Options will not be available.

■ **Note**   The Windows 8.1 automatic indexing of encrypted files does include hard disks in the computer encrypted with BitLocker if you are a user who has access to those drives because this is a full disk encryption system. It is assumed that if you are successfully logged in to a Bitlocker-encrypted PC, you will have permission to access its files.

The next option in the File Settings section enables you to turn off Windows 8.1's automatic correction feature to accommodate the different (albeit correct) spellings of words and the oddly spelled word.

In the Index location section is an option to change the default location of the index. I'd like to discuss why you might want to do this and what the benefits are. The most obvious reason to do this is to increase the speed of your hard disk or to improve the resilience of an SSD. If you have a large number of files to index, this is the only circumstance when it's possibly worthwhile to move the index.

If you have an SSD in your computer (the number of maximum write operations is finite over the life of the disk), you may want to move the index. On modern SSDs, it shouldn't make a difference because the overall lifespan of the disk should be more than adequate. But you may have an older SSD or perform duties that involve huge amounts of file work and modification every day.

To change the location, type the *new* location of the index into the empty box with its full drive assignment (e.g., D:\Index\) and click the Select New button.

■ **Note**   When you move the index, it is rebuilt from scratch when you restart your computer. Also, you cannot reuse an existing index when you reimage your computer; it rebuilds when you restart your computer.

Searching Network Locations in Windows 8.1

When you add extra folders and drives to the Windows 8.1 index, the system does not allow you to add network or other locations to the index. If you are a manager in a small office in which files are shared on a network attached storage (NAS) drive, for example, and you want to create a saved search to monitor the progress of a project, you cannot add this location to the index. While they also won't be indexed, you can also add network locations to Libraries by creating a symbolic link between the two locations. I described how to do this in the *Adding Network Locations to Libraries* section on page XREF earlier in this chapter.

However, you can open a network location in File Explorer from Network in the Navigation Pane. When you are at the correct location, you can then perform a search and save that search.

Searches of network locations can take longer than searches of files on your own computer because the search system has to read each file every time instead of referring to its information in the index.

If you are logged in to a domain on a Windows Server system, the index usually allows you to add mapped server locations to the index.

Using Search Syntax in Internet Explorer

In the science fiction book *The Hitchhiker's Guide to the Galaxy* (Pan Books, 1985), author Douglas Adams wrote, "Space is big. You just won't believe how vastly, hugely, mind-bogglingly big it is. I mean, you may think it's a long way down the road to the shops, but that's just peanuts to space." As a quote, this is an excellent analogy for the Internet.

The problem is how to find what you are looking for online when there are usually millions and sometimes billions of search results. After all, the major search engines, Bing, Google, and so forth, do a reasonable job of filtering the results for you. How do you know, though, that you're getting the *correct* results for what you type? Surely you're just getting the most popular generalized results.

This is where you can use search syntax options that are commonly supported by all online search engines:

- **"Enclose a few words in double quotes"** to search for those words as a complete sentence. By default, typing the words without quotes returns search results that include one or more of all the words; it does not treat them as a combined whole.

- Use a plus (+) symbol at the front of a word (e.g., **+halsey**) to guarantee that this word *must* appear in the search results. You can also use a plus symbol in front of a string of words (see preceding bullet).

- Use a minus (–) symbol to exclude a particular word or string from the results. You may want to exclude the word **-buy** or **-shopping** if you are looking for technical details of a product and want to exclude shopping and price comparison sites from the results.

- Search only a specific web site for a term by typing **site:*sitename*.com**. You may want to search for **"windows 8.1" site:thelongclimb.com**, for example.

- Use ***** and **?** wildcard operators. The asterisk represents a selection of letters, and the question mark represents only a single letter; for example, you want to search for **"Mike H*"** or **Hals?y** if you are unsure of a spelling.

- Include Boolean operators **OR**, **AND**, and **NOT** in your search to narrow down the results. **Adobe software 2011 OR 2012**, for example.

There are other search operators that are specific to individual search engines. The ones I listed here I find to be the most useful and the easiest to remember. I personally only ever use double quotes and the plus and minus signs, for example, and I get search results that I am happy with.

Appendix D features a full list of the AQS options that you can use for Windows 8.1 searches.

■ **Note**   You can use these operators directly from the Start screen when searching for things online.

Summary

Search in Windows 8.1 is incredibly powerful, but the full features can be hard to remember. I believe that by far the best feature for searching is the saved search, which allows you to search by subject, workflow, author, contributors, file type, location, and more. It also allows you to search for multiple parameters simultaneously. This truly powerful feature can help you get the best out of file management and organization in Windows 8.1.

Elsewhere, however, the ability to search from the Start screen by simply typing is very welcome. We can expect both Microsoft and third-party providers to plug some extremely useful functionality into this feature in the coming years. It's not quite as powerful and flexible as search in File Explorer, however.

Libraries are also significantly more powerful than you might first believe, with saved search and Windows Media Center able to extend their functionality considerably. I have long argued that Libraries should be more flexible by default, but the ability to create flexibility through simple workarounds greatly increases their usefulness.

CHAPTER 6

Printing and Managing Printers

In these days of external hard drives, flash drives, TV tuners, graphics tablets, HD webcams, cordless headphones, and more, it is always a printer that is commonly the first and most important peripheral that we purchase for our computers.

These days, wireless printers are becoming so common that you no longer need to have the machine physically connected to your computer. It can easily be shared between multiple computers and hidden out of sight where it isn't noticeable when you're relaxing.

Network printers in the workplace have already been common for years now, and you'll be pleased to hear that setting up and managing printers in Windows 8.1 is as straightforward as ever.

Installing Printers in Windows 8.1

Windows 8.1 performs a very neat trick that no other version of Windows has ever done before with printers (and other network devices). If these devices exist, and Windows 8.1 sees them on the network, it automatically installs them for you.

This means that the first time you try to print a document, you'll probably find that your network printer is already listed. Windows 8.1 searches Windows Update for a driver and installs these devices quietly in the background. So ordinarily, you simply plug in your printer, and Windows 8.1 takes care of the installation.

It is unlikely, however, that Windows 8.1 can install printers with drivers not included in Windows 8.1 or not available on Windows Update. If this is the case, you have to uninstall and reinstall the printer. There are two main ways to install printers and other devices in Windows 8.1, the simplest of which is using PC Settings. Open the PC Settings panel and navigate to *PCs and Devices* and then *Devices*. A list of all the devices that are currently installed is displayed, but at the top of the screen is an *Add a Device* button. Clicking or tapping this button starts the Windows 8.1 auto-detect for new hardware (see Figure 6-1).

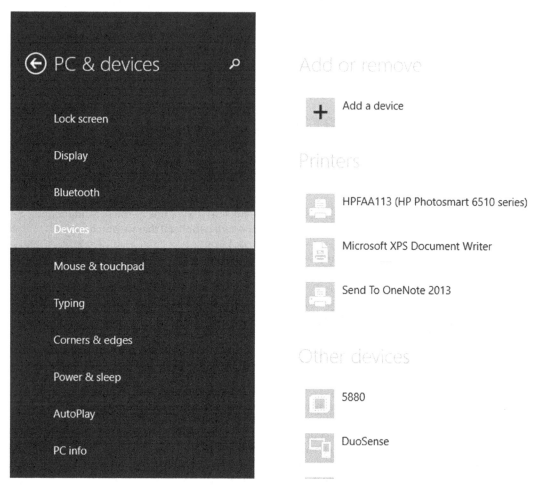

Figure 6-1. *You can install new printers in PC Settings*

If you want more control over your printer installation, or if a printer isn't being detected in PC Settings, you can open the *Devices and Printers* panel (see Figure 6-2). Type **devices** at the Start screen and you see Devices and Printers listed in the search results.

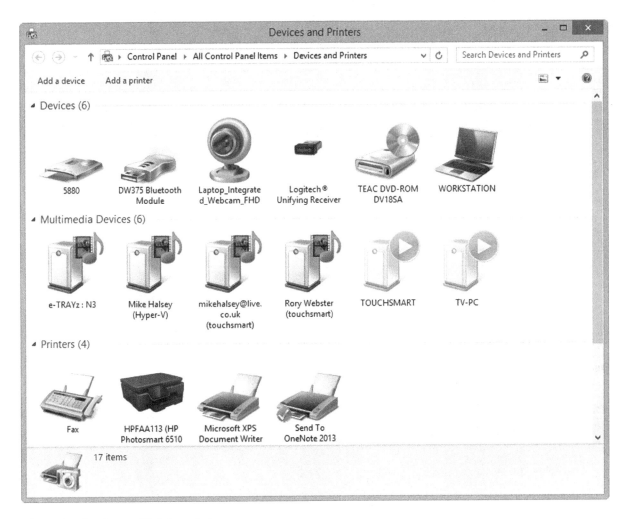

Figure 6-2. *Devices and Printers window*

■ **Tip** To uninstall a printer or another device in the Devices and Printers panel (perhaps because the driver is not properly installed), right-click the device and then select Remove Device from the options.

There are two main ways to add printers to Windows 8.1 using Devices and Printers. On the toolbar at the top of the window, you can select the link to **Add a device** or you can choose the **Add a printer**, both of which will work.

Initially, as you see in Figures 6-3 and 6-4, these options operate in exactly the same way, though they look slightly different. Both options search for network printers and other devices and then display them for you. Where they differ most is in the driver installation for the hardware.

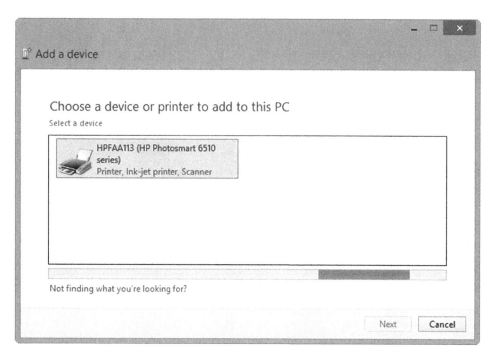

Figure 6-3. *Adding Devices and Printers to Windows 8.1 in the Add a Device dialog*

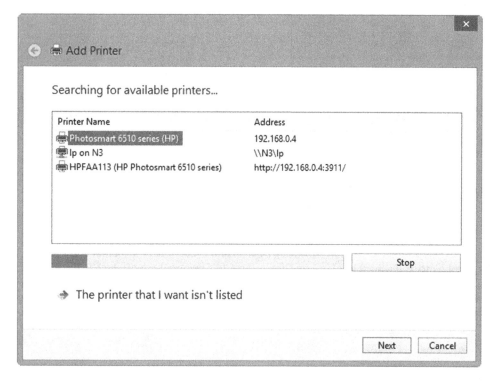

Figure 6-4. *Adding a printer to Windows 8.1 using Add Printer*

In the Add a Device dialog (see Figure 6-3), Windows 8.1 simply installs what it thinks is the best available driver for that piece of hardware. If Windows 8.1 has previously found your printer on its own and installed it with an incorrect driver, it reinstalls *the same* incorrect driver.

If the printer isn't found automatically, which is common in business environments, the *Not finding what you're looking for?* link simply opens a Help window with a note telling you how the problem may be fixed.

It is the Add Printer dialog (see Figure 6-4) that you will find helpful for all but the hardest to install printers.

If the printer is not automatically found, you can click *The printer that I want isn't listed* to bring up additional installation options for the device (see Figure 6-5).

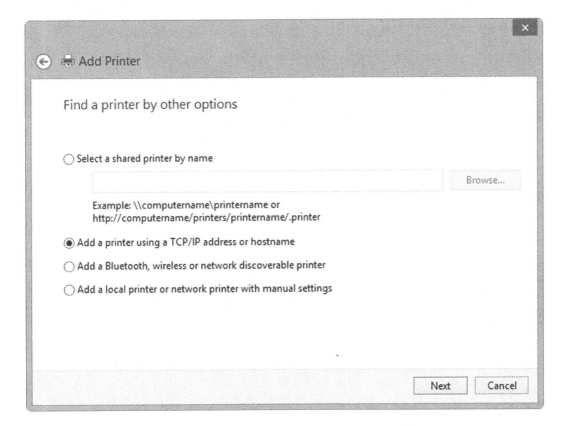

Figure 6-5. *Manually adding a printer*

In the Add Printer window, you have the following options:

- You can add a printer by its name on the network (if you know it; it is usually provided by your IT department).

- You can add it by its IP address (more on finding this in a minute).

- You can add a Bluetooth printer, if you have one.

- You can choose to manually configure the printer depending on which port it is located.

■ **Tip**   If you need to discover the IP address of a wireless printer, it is commonly available within the settings for the printer on its own display. You should refer to your printer owners' manual for the exact way to retrieve the IP address because it changes from one printer to another.

All things being equal, you probably don't know the IP address or the network name of a printer. One quick way around this is to check how the printer is configured on another computer. You can do this in Devices and Printers (in Windows 7 and Windows 8.1). Right-click the printer and select Printer Properties. Under the Ports tab, you should see the address of the printer (see Figure 6-6).

Figure 6-6. *Checking the address of a printer*

■ **Tip** Let's say you want to add an older parallel device to Windows 8.1. Choosing the *Add a local printer or network printer with manual settings* allows you to select the LPT port that the printer is plugged into.

On a home or small business network, finding a printer's IP is relatively straightforward, though the actual method varies, depending on the make of your router. The following steps provide a general approach that you should be able to tweak for your own setup:

1. Open Internet Explorer.

2. Access your router login by typing **192.168.0.1** (sometimes 192.168.1.1 or 192.168.2.1) and pressing Enter.

3. Log in to your router with your username and password (if these are still *admin* and *password*, you should change them!).

4. Find the LAN settings.

5. Look for the Ethernet settings.

6. Look for the name of your network printer; its IP address is listed as shown in Figure 6-7.

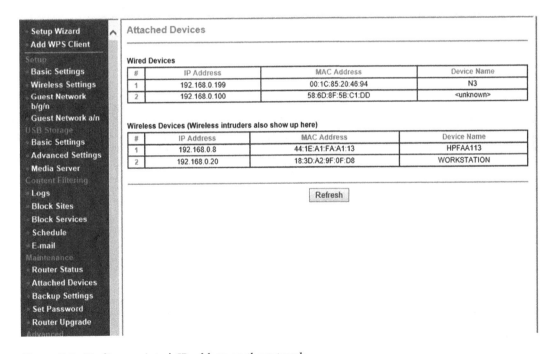

Figure 6-7. Finding a printer's IP address on the network

■ **Note** If you have to reset your router, perhaps because your Internet connection has gone down, the IP address of your printer might have changed. This requires that you uninstall and reinstall the printer on all your computers because Windows locks the driver to a specific IP address. To get around this problem, you can set the printer to a static IP address in your router setup. Consult your manual or your ISP for details on how to do this.

Setting Default Printers for Different Places

If you use the same computer in different places, perhaps both at home and at work or in different office locations, you don't want to spend time setting and resetting the default printer whenever you want to print a document.

Windows 8.1 allows you to set the default printer, depending on the network that you are connected to at the time. In Devices and Printers, select a printer and then click the Manage Default Printers on the toolbar at the top of the window.

In the dialog (see Figure 6-8), you can set a different default printer for each network you connect to. The networks and installed printers are all listed by name and are available from drop-down menus with the defaults showing in the main pane of the dialog.

Figure 6-8. *Setting different default printers for different networks*

Using this feature, you can set Windows to automatically change the default printer on your computer the moment you connect to a different network. So if you have been on this network before and have already installed the printer driver(s), you can be sure that whatever you print is sent to the correct printer.

Managing Printers in Windows 8.1

Long gone are the days when printers did only a single thing: accept an input and print it onto paper. Now printers come with a huge number of options for controlling every aspect of that output and the hardware. This, coupled with new ecoprinting features intended to save both ink and paper, can make printers very difficult to manage.

Printers and their driver software differ by make and model, but most of the functionality across devices is the same. Thus, you may find that some of the following screen shots don't match up exactly with what you see on your own computer. Windows 8 does a good job of standardizing the settings for printers, however.

You can manage your printer in Devices and Printers by right-clicking the printer and selecting Printer Properties from the options.

In the main printer properties dialog under the General tab (see Figure 6-9), you find the name of the printer (which you can change by simply typing a new name). You can also input comments about the machine's physical location as well as other notes (perhaps about how to insert paper for double-sided printing if there is no duplex unit installed).

Figure 6-9. Working with general printer properties

The Preferences button opens the printing preferences, which I discuss in the "Managing Printing in Windows 8.1" section later in this chapter. You can also print a test page here to check that the printer is working.

■ **Note** The configuration and options in the printer dialogs vary according to the make and model of the printer.

On the Sharing tab, you can choose whether you want to share the printer over your network (the computer that is sharing the printer needs to be left on for the printer to be accessible) and you can give it a name (see Figure 6-10).

Figure 6-10. Working with Sharing printer properties

■ **Tip** Earlier, I discussed finding a printer by its name. A printer with a simple name is easier for people to find and remember. Easy names may include a floor number, room number, and/or printer type.

Shared printers may be accessed by computers running other versions of Windows, such as Windows 7, Windows Vista, or Windows XP. If this is likely, click the Additional Drivers button to choose drivers that automatically load from your computer as needed.

You probably don't want to change anything in the Ports tab (see Figure 6-11), but if you have had to reset your router, the IP address of the printer may have automatically changed. Thus, after resetting a router, you may find that you can no longer print to a particular printer—and you have to reinstall it, though you will often find out that Windows 8.1 can often automatically rectify the problem on its own.

Figure 6-11. *Working with printer ports*

The Ports tab is also useful if you are using older parallel or serial printers, which are very complicated to install and configure correctly, but are still in use in some business environments.

There are many useful options available in the Advanced tab (see Figure 6-12), including the following:

- **The ability to specify that a printer is only accessible between certain hours**: This option is useful if you are trying to cut down on waste.

- **The ability to choose how the printer prioritizes print jobs that are sent to it**: You might want to set this option on a shared printer to spool a job only after the previous one has finished (if the printer doesn't have much internal memory). Generally, you should not need to do this because Windows 8.1 is excellent at managing print jobs.

Figure 6-12. Working with advanced printer properties

■ **Tip**   Setting printers to be available only between certain hours of the day is not just a great way to cut down on printing waste but also a useful way to avoid causing inconvenience to others. My own printer is located in my home office, which is next to my guest bedroom. When in use, this printer can be heard through the wall and can inadvertently wake somebody up. Setting available *from* and *to* times can prevent accidental annoyance for other people.

The Color Management options (see Figure 6-13) allow you to set a color profile that matches your monitor. This is especially useful if you have a carefully calibrated screen for color accuracy. (I will talk more about color management shortly.)

Figure 6-13. *Working with printer color management*

The options on the Security tab allow you to specify who can control what on the printer (see Figure 6-14). Here you may want to make changes, including giving users computer permissions to manage print jobs (such as deleting stuck jobs).

Figure 6-14. *Working with printer security*

To change permissions, select the appropriate users in the top pane. You can then change their options by checking the boxes in the bottom half of the tab. These basic controls are all you need to grant and deny users access to a printer. If you require more control over access to printers, such as printer availability time and which users can print and how often, click the Advanced button.

It is now common for printer manufacturers to add a custom tab that provides extra information, such as ink and toner status, and links to purchase official consumables and accessories online.

Managing Color Profiles for Printers and Displays

Sometimes you absolutely *must* have color accuracy, perhaps if you are a photographer or graphic artist. To help with this, you can load specific color profiles into Windows 8.1 for both printers and displays. Open the Color Management window by searching the word **color** at the Start screen and running Change Advanced Color Management from the Settings results.

In Color Management (see Figure 6-15), you can load specific color profiles for both printers and displays if they have the correct manufacturer profile file. The file formats are Color Device Model Profile (*.cdmp), Color Appearance Model Profile (*.camp), Gamut Mapping Model Profile (*.gmmp), and ICC (*.icm).

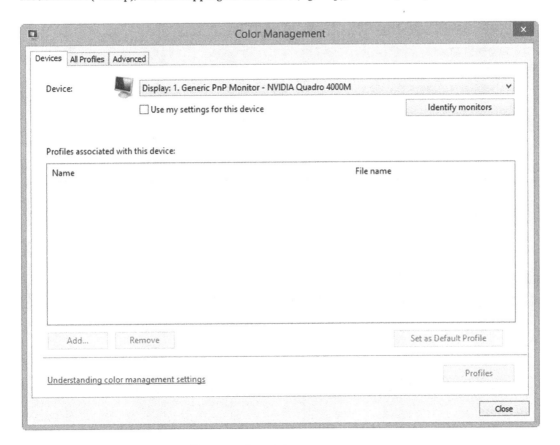

Figure 6-15. *Managing color profiles in Windows 8.1*

Choose the device in which you want to view the current color profile from the drop-down menu at the top of the window. To add a color profile to the currently selected device, check the **Use my settings for this device** box. You can then select an installed color profile.

You can add a profile from the All Profiles tab, in which you find the currently installed color profiles. Click the Add button at the bottom of the window to load a new color profile.

There are controls and options on the Advanced tab that enable you to further specify the way your color profiles are used for different types of images and art. You can also run a tool that helps calibrate the brightness, color, and contrast settings for your monitor so that what you see on screen are faithful representations of true color.

Managing Shared Printers in Windows 8.1

In the previous section, I talked a little bit about managing the security of a shared printer, which you can do directly from the Devices and Printers window. When a printer is selected, you can open Print Server Properties from the toolbar.

You can also manage security properties for the printer in the Print Server Properties dialog (see Figure 6-16), which offers additional security options, such as whether users can edit the print queue or change the print settings.

Figure 6-16. *Managing print server properties*

Managing Printing in Windows 8.1

Although there are many options for managing your printer(s), there are usually even more for managing printing. These features differ from one printer to another, but the general printing preferences are the same.

■ **Tip** To print from an app in Windows 8.1, click the *Devices* charm and then the *Print* button. Your available printers are listed, and you can click/tap the one you want to print to. Note that not all apps support printing.

When you want to print from within an app in Windows 8.1 open the *Devices* charm and click the Print option. Your available printers are listed in the top right of your screen. Once you click the printer you want to print to, a page preview appears, along with basic controls for determining how the page is to be formatted (see Figure 6-17).

Figure 6-17. *You can control your printing from within apps*

You can tap the *Use these settings in all applications* switch after setting your print settings to the way you want them to make those settings the default for all in-app printing in the future. Additionally, you can also click the *More settings* link to open more-advanced settings for your printer (see Figure 6-18). Note that these settings vary, depending on your printer's model and features.

Figure 6-18. Advanced print settings are available within apps

When you are printing from the desktop, you can't do so from the *Devices* charm because it is not supported. You print from within your desktop program, either from a File menu or a dedicated Print button. To access the print options for your printer, however, perhaps to set the global printing preferences, you can most easily access the printing preferences by right-clicking a printer in the Devices and Printers window and selecting Printing Preferences from the options.

On the first tab in this dialog, which may vary in name (see Figure 6-19), are the most common options, including the default page size, page orientation, and whether the printer uses single- or double-sided printing by default (you need an internal duplexing unit to take advantage of this).

Figure 6-19. *Working with basic printing preferences*

■ **Tip**   Once you know whether your printer's duplex unit flips the paper on the long or short edge of the paper, I recommend writing this information on a label and sticking it to the printer so that it is easy for others to use double-sided printing on their own computers.

The options on the Paper tab allow you to choose the default paper size, collation of multipage print jobs (a very useful option in an office), and the printer's default source tray.

■ **Tip** If you want to change the default printing options for the printer, perhaps to set it to print only in black draft mode to save ink or toner, you can do it in the Advanced settings. Every time someone prints from that printer (and on that computer) afterward, these are the default print options (unless changed manually for just one job).

If you want finer control over the printer's settings, click the *Advanced* button (see Figure 6-20), which displays a list of all the controls.

Figure 6-20. *Working with paper preferences*

■ **Tip** If you are printing photographs, you want to make sure that eco and draft features are switched off so that you get the best quality prints.

Working with Wireless Printers in Windows 8.1

I mentioned earlier in the chapter that resetting your router may also reset the IP address on your network wireless printer.

If this happens, the best option is to uninstall and reinstall the printer. Although you can set the printer to have a static IP address, not all routers support this functionality. Check the router's manual or consult your ISP's support department.

Sometimes it is difficult to figure out how to connect a wireless printer to your network. If you have a wired printer, it's easy enough to just plug the printer into the router or switch panel with an RJ45 Ethernet cable.

To connect a wireless printer to your network, you need to find the WPS buttons on both the router and the printer. These buttons allow you to pair the two devices wirelessly without a password.

1. Press the WPS button on your router.

2. As soon as you can (within 30 seconds), press the WPS button on the printer.

These two devices should now pair. Occasionally, however, a router refuses to see a printer, even when the WPS buttons have been pressed. In this event, you should contact your ISP's support department or consult the router manual to find the best way to pair the router with a wireless device.

■ **Tip** You can also pair computers, printers, and other devices by pressing the WPS button on your router if the computer—normally tablets or laptops—or device also has a WPS or similarly labeled button. Check the documentation that came with the device to see if this function is supported.

Obtaining the IP Address of a Network Printer

The Devices and Printers page panel (see Figure 6-21) is a very useful way to manage network resources that your computer can see. You can best access it by searching for **devices** on the Start screen and running it from the search results, which you will find in Settings. All printers and other network devices that Windows 8.1 can see are displayed here. You can use the information provided to find the IP address of a device.

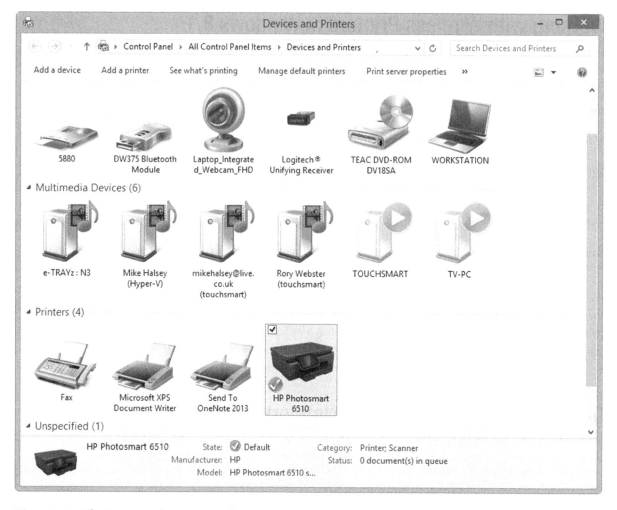

Figure 6-21. *The Devices and Printers panel*

Perform the following two steps to find the IP address of a device in the Devices and Printers page:

1. Right-click the printer you want to find the IP address for.

2. Click the Hardware tab in the window that appears.

The IP address is commonly listed in the location information at the bottom of the window. If you don't see the IP address listed here, check the onscreen display on the printer. The IP address is usually available through its settings menus, although the exact method of retrieving the IP address from the printer varies, depending on the manufacturer and model.

■ **Note**   Windows may display the IPv6 address for a device. If this happens, you can get the numeric IP address from your router.

Top Printing Tips

There are some great ways to get a little more out of your printer's ink and toner. They begin with purchasing the right printer. When purchasing a printer, follow these tips:

- If you can afford it, buy a printer with in-built duplexing (double-sided printing). This saves paper.

- Check the cost of full-price consumables (ink cartridges and toner) and compare it against prices for similar printers by other manufacturers.

- Do some research online about the printer's TCO (total cost of ownership). This information may be provided in a magazine review or in a product group test.

- Find out if you can use cheaper compatible ink and toner cartridges. Some printers have "chipped" cartridges that require you to use official manufacturer ink.

To get more life out of your ink cartridges and toner, there are a few things you can do to prolong their life.

- If you are not going to use your printer for a while, keep the ink cartridges in a cool, dry place (you can even wrap them in plastic film and put them in the refrigerator). This prevents the ink from drying up. This *does not* apply to toner, which does not dry out.

- When your toner cartridge is low, you can shake the cartridge to loosen up more toner, which results in a longer lifespan. If you do this, you *must* read the following cautionary note!

- Think about if you *really* need to print something. Most of the people I know don't actually use most of the printed material they create.

▪ **Caution**   When shaking a toner cartridge, you should always make sure your arms are fully covered, that you are wearing disposable gloves, and that you do not breathe in any waste toner. Some laser printer toners are carcinogenic. You should always wash your hands thoroughly after handling cartridges, especially refillable ones.

Summary

Working with and managing printers is always something people ask me about because these peripherals are generally used more than other devices. The one piece of eco advice I give on using printers is to first ask yourself the question, "Do I really need to print this document?" By far the best way to save paper, ink, and money is to not print a document or picture.

The controls for installing and managing printers in Windows 8.1 are excellent, although some of the most useful ones are hidden. These controls include the ability to autoset the default printer at different locations and networks; and the color management tools, which are essential to creative professionals and very useful to anybody printing high-quality photographs at home.

■ ■ ■

CHAPTER 7

Having Fun with Games, Photos, Music, and Video

Despite the business origins of the PC, Windows has always been a gaming platform. Despite predictions on the death of PC gaming in favor of consoles, Windows 8.1 brings some new features to the mix that put gaming front and center of the PC for the first time.

There is new integration between Windows 8.1 and other Microsoft platforms such as the Xbox that will be built upon and expanded in coming years, such as the ability to start a game on one device and then continue it on another.

With gaming on a PC comes some responsibility, especially if you are a parent. Controlling the games your children play is becoming increasingly difficult because the Internet provides access to games, entertainment, and content that may not be suitable for children.

When it comes to nongaming fun, Windows 8.1 is as good as any version before it—with excellent photo, music, and video playback and editing facilities, and Media Center for watching and recording live TV.

Finally, there is what will probably become the perennial Windows 8.1 gaming platform: tablets. With their sensors and accelerometers, these devices are perfect gaming platforms.

In this chapter, I'll talk you through how to have fun with your PC: integrating your PC with your Xbox 360; enjoying the latest gaming technologies, including 3D; and viewing your photos and videos.

Managing Games in Windows 8.1

If you've used the Games Center in Windows Vista or Windows 7 to manage, launch, and update your games, you'll find that it's gone in Windows 8.1. It has been replaced by the new apps.

The reasons for this change include a shift toward apps on the part of Microsoft, but also the rise of game management and delivery platforms—such as Steam—that are central locations for purchasing, updating, and managing your games, your account, and other things. These platforms provide central locations for purchasing, updating, and managing games, player settings, and achievements.

Microsoft has also expanded its own Xbox Live service to cover the Windows Phone platform, Windows 8.1, and Windows RT.

■ **Note** If you install a Windows game that is not managed by Steam, Xbox Live, or another management service, you need to update the game manually. Updates are posted on the web site of the game's publisher.

One of the biggest issues for gamers is updates, which is primarily why platforms such as Steam and Origin have taken off in such a big way. Through these platforms, users no longer have to manually find, download, and install sometimes complicated updates.

The Games App

Windows 8.1 comes with a Games app (see Figure 7-1), in which you can buy games for your PC and also manage and maintain gamer scores and other attributes associated with your Xbox Live account.

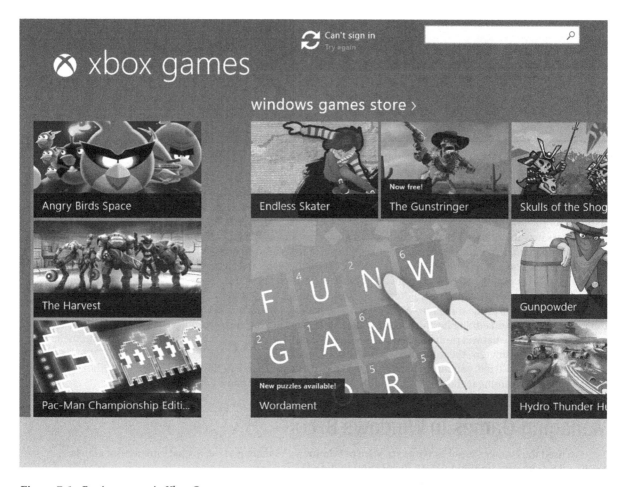

Figure 7-1. *Buying games in Xbox Games*

In Chapter 2, I said that Windows Store alerts you when updates are available for your downloaded apps and games. The Games app also alerts you when updates are available for your games.

Although Microsoft wants the Games app to be a hub for Xbox games that run in Windows 8.1, these are not the only games that can be bought there. All Xbox Live–branded PC games are available and there are thousands of non-Xbox-branded games available.

Xbox SmartGlass

Although the Xbox Games app is a central location to buy and manage games and to manage your account, the Xbox SmartGlass app is a tool for remotely controlling your Xbox console and for providing companion experiences for select Xbox games.

With this downloadable app, which you can find in the Windows Store, you can control many aspects of your console from your PC. This includes the ability to remotely control your games without having to use the dedicated Xbox controller (see Figure 7-2).

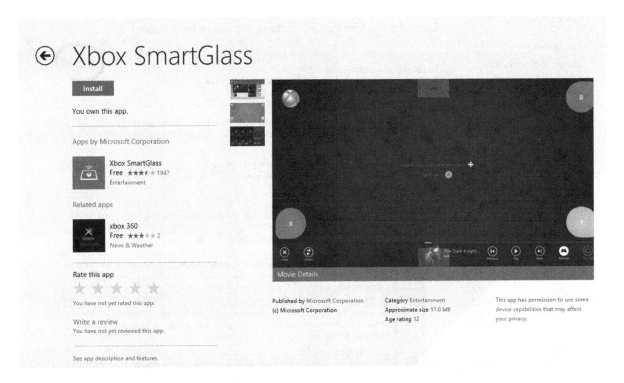

Figure 7-2. Using your Windows 8.1 PC as a remote Xbox console controller

You need to be logged in to the Xbox SmartGlass app to use it, Windows 8.1, and your Xbox console on the same Live ID. You must also have SmartGlass enabled on your Xbox console. So if you are playing a game that is logged in to the Live ID of another user, for example, the Xbox SmartGlass app won't connect to the console.

Managing Game Ratings for Children

One of the biggest concerns for parents is the suitability of the games their children play in Windows. With the Windows Vista introduction of the Games Center, you could set age ratings for games so that children could play only games that were appropriate.

In practice, however, this worked only with games that had bought into the Games for Windows branding, which few did. With the removal of the Games Center, this facility is gone, but not completely. Windows 8.1 Family Safety provides all the facilities you need to block unsuitable games (see Figure 7-3).

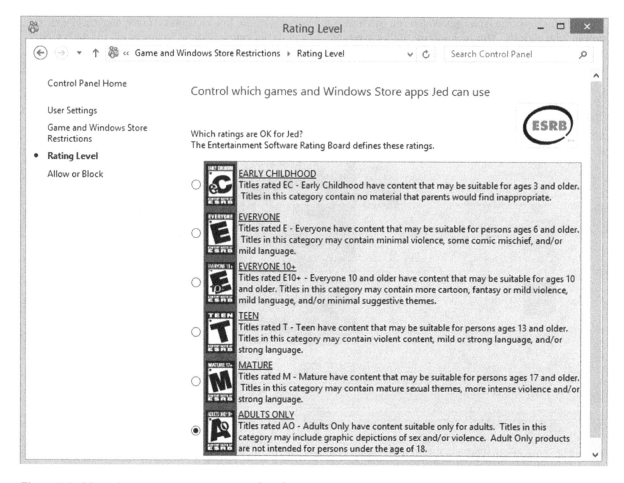

Figure 7-3. *Managing game age ratings in Family Safety*

I showed you how to set up Family Safety in Chapter 3. It is a fully featured way to manage your children's game playing. I recommend it. With these controls, you can choose which games your children are allowed to play, the types of web sites they can visit, *and* the times they can use the computer.

To use this facility, each user must have an account on the computer. If you use local accounts rather than signing in with a Microsoft account, you need to create specific accounts for your children. This is most likely if you have very young children who do not need access to services such as e-mail.

■ **Note**   The desktop games from Windows 7 have gone in Windows 8.1, indeed this new operating system (OS) doesn't come with any games at all, but Microsoft has substitutes for many of the common ones, Minesweeper, Solitaire, and so on, which are available in the Windows Store and from the Games app.

Configuring Windows 8.1 for the Latest Games

Casual gamers will have little trouble playing the latest games from the Windows Store or Games app on Windows 8.1 and RT computers and tablets. Indeed, for some years now, games have been far more popular on tablets than on desktop computers because of the new and fun ways in which we can interact with them and because the lower hardware specification of tablets means that game companies have had to create simpler games overall.

But what if you're an enthusiast? How can you configure your computer to run the latest first-person shooters?

I won't recommend specific graphics cards and other hardware because they change so often that anything I write is quickly be out of date. There are some things you can look for when purchasing a new computer or computer parts, however, which I discuss in the next section. There are also things that you can do with Windows 8.1.

So how can you configure Windows 8.1 to run the best and newest games? One of the first considerations is your antivirus software. Windows Defender, which is installed by default in Windows 8.1, is an excellent choice for games, primarily because it is lightweight but also because it doesn't do any major scanning when you use the PC for other things.

Some third-party antivirus solutions also detect when games are running—usually by detecting something running fullscreen—and hibernates their scanning engines.

As a power user, I find Windows Defender perfectly adequate, so I don't use third-party antivirus software. If you are a gamer, however, this is something you should think about if you are considering purchasing a third-party package.

The amount of software you have running in the background can also make a difference. For example, you might have Microsoft's SkyDrive software running in the background, keeping a cloud backup of your files; or perhaps you have an alternative such as Google Drive, Dropbox, Mozy, and so on. They can slow down your Internet connection. If you are gaming, you might want to switch them off if there's a lot of network traffic going on in the background.

■ **Tip** The upload speed on your Internet connection is as important for gaming as your download speed. If you have an older ADSL connection with a healthy download speed of 5 Mbps but only a 0.6 Mbps upload speed, for example, it can result in being kicked from servers. One player's slow connection adversely impacts the other players' experience (see Figure 7-4). The reason for this is that when you are gaming online, you are sending almost as much data as you are receiving.

Figure 7-4. *You can test your Internet connection speed using services like* http://www.speedtest.net

Do the following to close an app with the keyboard and mouse:

1. From the Start screen, move your mouse to the top left of the screen.

2. When the thumbnail for the most recent running app appears, move the mouse downward to reveal all the running app thumbnails.

3. Right-click the app you want to close. Select Close from the options that appear.

Do the following to close an app with touch:

1. Swipe inward and then immediately outward from the left edge of the screen to display the running apps list.

2. Touch the thumbnail of the app you want to close and drag it out of the list.

3. Drag the thumbnail image of the app off the bottom center of the screen to close it.

Do the following to close a desktop task:

1. From the desktop, click the Show Hidden Icons arrow in the far right of the taskbar. This is the small up arrow next to the system tray. If you don't see this arrow, there are no minimized programs running in the system tray.

2. Right-click the program you want to terminate (hovering over an icon tells you what the program is).

3. Select Exit or Close from the options that appear.

You may also have software and driver updaters running in the background that are slowing down your computer. You may be able to shut these down from the desktop in the same way, but perhaps you don't need them running to begin with.

Some of these updates can be very useful and are very important indeed, including the updaters from Adobe, which are used to fix security flaws that are very commonly exploited by malware. There may be other programs that you don't need, however, including quick launchers for your scanner, printer, or Blu-ray software. Auto-running software also includes utilities that came preinstalled on your computer, such as a quick launcher for media files.

To shut down these programs so that they don't autostart with Windows, do the following:

1. Press Win+X on your keyboard.

2. From the options that appear, select Task Manager (it can also be launched by right-clicking the taskbar).

3. Click the Startup tab in the Task Manager (see Figure 7-5).

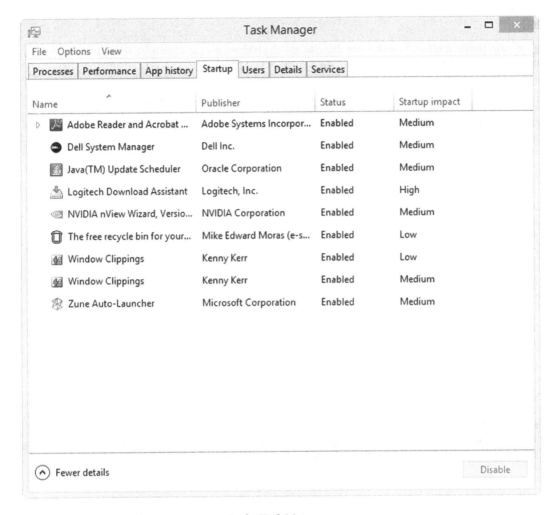

Figure 7-5. Managing Startup programs in the Task Manager

4. Click the program you don't want to run at startup.

5. Press the Disable button.

You should repeat steps 4 and 5 for all other software you want to disable at startup.

■ **Note**   Once you configure your Startup programs, you should not need to switch off programs when you are gaming.

Choosing and Upgrading Your Gaming Hardware

Building a good gaming PC is a challenge, not least because the hardware can be extremely expensive for the best kit. But it is possible to choose or build a PC specifically for gaming on a budget. I want to talk you through what to look for and what to purchase. This applies not just to traditional "tower" desktop PCs but it's also very relevant when you're choosing a desktop all-in-one or a laptop PC to purchase.

Motherboard

When choosing a motherboard, it is best to select one that can run the highest overall speeds (in GHz), even if it makes the board capable of running much faster than the hardware you plug into it. This is to ensure that the motherboard is upgradable in the long-term. It will save you money and give you greater flexibility when it comes to upgrading.

Try to choose a board that offers the new SATA 600 ports so that you can attach the new generation of high-speed solid-state drives (SSD)—more on these shortly. Also, try to choose a board offering support for either Crossfire (AMD) or SLI (nVidia). I will talk more about this shortly.

Processor

The processor is probably the least important consideration when it comes to choosing or building a gaming PC because most of the gaming processing is done by your graphics card. The important considerations here are the clock speed (again in GHz) and, most importantly, having a processor with the same socket type as your motherboard.

A computer can run only as fast as its slowest component, so if you have chosen memory that runs faster than your processor, its overall speed throttles to match that of the processor. The same applies to the motherboard. If it has a slow clock speed, nothing can run faster than it can. Bear in mind, especially if you are buying a gaming laptop, that a more powerful processor negatively affects your overall battery life, sometimes dramatically.

Memory

With your computer's memory, it's long been established that if you don't have enough memory installed on your computer for Windows and your installed programs, the computer does not run as quickly as it otherwise could. This is certainly true of a low-end laptop or desktop PC upgraded from 1 or 2 GB of RAM to 4 GB.

Above the 4 GB level, the speed benefits decrease significantly. You can still get noticeable speed increases on some machines by installing 6 GB or even 8 GB of RAM, but there is no need to install more than this unless you are also using your computer for very memory-intensive applications such as mega-multipixel digital photo editing, video creation, or computer-aided design. When purchasing RAM, you need a type that's compatible with your motherboard.

■ **Note** If you are using the 32-bit version of Windows 8.1 on your PC, your computer can "see" only a maximum of 4 GB RAM, including any memory on your graphics card. If you have 2 x 2 GB memory cards and 1 Gb graphics card memory, Windows 8.1 ignore one of the 2 GB memory cards completely because it only sees complete cards.

Hard Disk

If you can afford it, put your money into a fast SSD, preferably (if your motherboard supports the standard) one running on the new SATA 600 sockets. However, purchasing SSDs is more complicated than traditional hard drives because manufacturers' memory chip speeds vary wildly. It is wise to seek up-to-date reviews of SSDs online before you buy. You can normally find them on computer magazine web sites.

Having an SSD as your main hard disk can significantly improve the speed of Windows 8.1 and your games. You need to make sure, however, that the main hard disk is of a suitable size. This is where the cost can rise sharply. In Appendix D, I will show you how to best determine the size of the hard disk you need.

Graphics Card

Some motherboards come with onboard graphics that can handle HD video and nondemanding gaming. You might find that you want a separate graphics card, however, perhaps for online gaming or video editing. Earlier in this chapter, I spoke about SLI and Crossfire. These are technologies—by nVidia and AMD, respectively—that allow you to connect two or three graphics cards so that they can be used in parallel. This doesn't *actually* double or triple the graphics processing power—each extra card adds about an extra 50 percent of the overall computing power of the first card. You need to choose your motherboard carefully, however, because you are locked into using cards from a specific company if you use the multicard feature.

Some laptops come with switchable graphics, effectively giving you two graphics cards: a low-end one suitable for general work and watching movies that are part of the motherboard chipset, and a second one for gaming that either auto-switches when needed or that can be manually turned on. This is a great way to extend the battery life of a laptop; if you are buying a new gaming laptop, it's worth looking for.

If you want to use only a single graphics card on your computer, whether the motherboard supports SLI or Crossfire doesn't matter—you can use an nVidia or AMD card as you desire.

Some people have strong preferences regarding AMD and nVidia graphics cards. There is tremendous brand loyalty to one or the other. The overall quality and speed of the cards, especially in the price/performance mid-range, does vary quite substantially—with different companies pulling ahead periodically with new, faster, and more powerful hardware, only to lose ground to a competitor's innovation.

Before you choose a graphics card, or even a motherboard in this respect, it can be well worth checking out the online test reviews of graphics cards by PC magazines and other gaming web sites.

Working with Gaming Peripherals

Sometimes you have USB gaming hardware attached to your PC, which could include a joystick or paddle controller. To access the controls for managing them in Windows, search for **game** at the Start screen and select **Set up USB game controllers** from the Settings results to run the Game Controllers dialog (see Figure 7-6).

Figure 7-6. *Managing game controllers in Windows 8.1*

In this dialog, you can manage and change the properties of gaming controllers, such as inverting the horizontal and vertical axis of a joystick (see Figure 7-7).

Figure 7-7. *Managing gaming hardware such as joysticks*

3D Gaming on Windows 8.1

Three-dimensional gaming is relatively new to PCs. Windows 8.1 requires third-party drivers for it to work, although some graphics cards are increasingly coming with their own 3D drivers and controls.

To take advantage of 3D gaming on your computer, you need a screen capable of displaying double the number of normal frame rates, upping the standard frequency from 60 Hz to 120 Hz. You also need a graphics card that supports 3D.

To use 3D gaming on your computer, you will commonly launch your existing games through a 3D game management program or app into which you probably have to download individual profiles for your games.

There are downsides to 3D gaming on PCs, however. First and most importantly, stable 3D profiles may not be released until well after the launch of the game. Also, 3D has a darkening effect on the image, especially in first-person shooters, which can make distances more difficult to see. Finally, the 3D effect can cause headaches when used for more than 30 minutes.

That said, I've used a 3D-equipped gaming laptop and have played several 3D games on it. The effect can be extremely immersive and this can add, if you'll excuse the pun, a whole new depth to your existing games titles.

Viewing and Editing Photos in Windows 8.1

The new Photos app is your default software for viewing photographs. The old Windows Photo Viewer is gone forever. This doesn't mean that there aren't many other options for viewing and editing your digital photographs, and there are many apps of this type in the Windows Store, including those by big-name companies.

Adobe, for example, first showed how powerful touch photo-editing apps can be on Android tablets. For everyone who doesn't want to use an app or who wants finer control over their photos, there are other options, including the excellent Windows Live Photo Gallery from Microsoft.

The Photo App

The Windows 8.1 Photos app is a relatively basic way to view your photos and pictures. By default, it has a view that shows thumbnail images of the pictures and photos on your PC. It separates the different folders on your computer in which you store your pictures and also includes some basic photo editing features (see Figure 7-8).

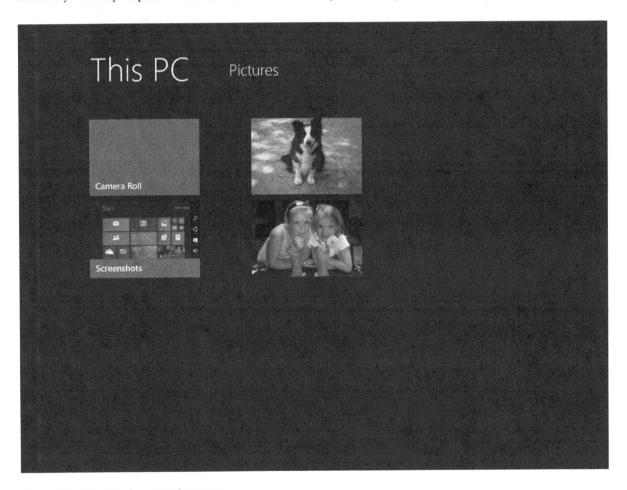

Figure 7-8. *The Windows 8.1 Photos app*

You can share photos and pictures by clicking the Share charm. Windows 8.1 tells you which installed apps you can share the picture with (see Figure 7-9).

Figure 7-9. *Managing photos in Windows 8.1*

The editing facility in the Photos app has been greatly expanded since the first release of this app, and includes a full range of the most basic and commonly found controls. They will no doubt be expanded upon in future releases of the app, but, as I mentioned earlier, there are plenty of third-party photo editing apps available for Windows 8.1. You can find them in the Photo category of the Windows Store.

When you are viewing a single photo in the Photos app, there are options you can display in the App bar (see Figure 7-10). These options include making a photo your Windows 8.1 lock screen image or setting it as the default picture for the Photos app live tile, which cycles through all your pictures by default. From here, you can also display a photo slide show.

Figure 7-10. *The App bar contains options for working with photos and pictures*

Windows Photo Gallery

Microsoft's free Windows Photo Gallery software is part of the company's Windows Essentials suite, which you can download from download.live.com. It is based around the company's Ribbon interface, so it is instantly familiar to users of Microsoft Office 2007 and above (see Figure 7-11).

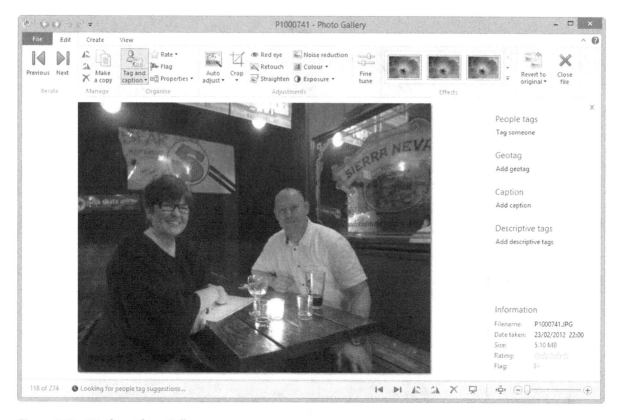

Figure 7-11. *Windows Photo Gallery*

The package allows you to perform many actions on your photos and pictures, such as the following:

- Managing your photo library with drag-and-drop actions between folders

- Uploading photos and videos to cloud services, including Flickr and YouTube

- Basic editing (including automatic editing) of photographs

In Chapter 5, I discussed adding tags and ratings to your photo library to make individual images easier to find. I'll talk about this in more detail shortly when I show you how to import photos and video from a digital camera, but Windows Photo Gallery offers excellent, easy-to-use methods for adding tags and ratings to photos.

Windows Photo Gallery also includes excellent face recognition software that can help tag friends and family, making it much easier to find photographs of specific people.

Other Third-Party Photo Editing Packages

There are many other photo management and editing apps, programs, and cloud services available. You may already have your favorite. I want to highlight three that I think are especially noteworthy.

Adobe Photoshop Express

Photoshop Express is available as an app in the Windows Store, and it's proven extremely popular since its launch. Offering more control than the Windows 8.1 photos app, and with some additional controls available through in-app purchases, this is a great tool for basic photograph editing on a tablet or other touchscreen PC.

Adobe Photoshop Elements

Adobe's Photoshop software has long been the king of desktop photo editing, but the full package is extremely expensive and very complex. It's really only for creative professionals. At the lower end of the price range, however, is Photoshop Elements, which you can download from http://www.adobe.com. It is an excellent desktop program that provides a significant amount of power and flexibility while still being very easy to use.

Pixlr

If you want something closer to the full version of Photoshop—but without its high price—I have never found a cloud service better than http://ww.pixlr.com. It is an extremely powerful, flexible, and (best of all) free cloud-based photo-editing service that offers many of the features you find in the full desktop version of Adobe Photoshop (see Figure 7-12).

Figure 7-12. Pixlr.com

Importing Digital Photographs and Videos from a Camera

When you insert a memory card from your digital camera or camcorder into your computer, you are asked if you want to import photos and video from the device.

There are several advantages of allowing Windows 8.1 to import photos and video rather than manually copying the files using Windows Explorer. The first advantage is that the import wizard allows you to add tags to the files. The second advantage is that Windows 8.1 is fantastic at determining the correct "up" position for photos and automatically rotates them for you.

To import photos or video, follow these instructions:

1. Insert your memory card, card reader, or camera into your Windows PC.

2. The photo import wizard appears (see Figure 7-13). Click Import to import all the photos to your computer. You can select or deselect images by clicking with your mouse or dragging down with your finger.

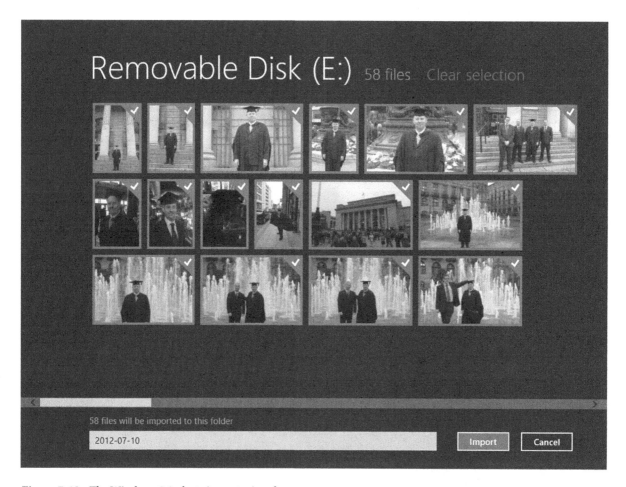

Figure 7-13. *The Windows 8.1 photo import wizard*

You can also specify a folder for the photos to be imported to. By default, this folder is named after the current date.

Sometimes you want more control over importing images. Let's say, for example, that you have been on vacation and visited several different places or countries. You might not want all your photos stored in the same folder.

You can use Windows Photo Gallery to import photos from your digital camera or camcorder. To do this in Windows Photo Gallery, click the *Import* button on the far left of the *Home* tab.

With the Import Photos and Videos Wizard (see Figure 7-14), you can simply choose to import all the items on the memory card or to first review, organize, and group items to import. I'll show you how to do this in a moment, but if you want to import all items now, you can click **Add tags** to include descriptive tags with the images.

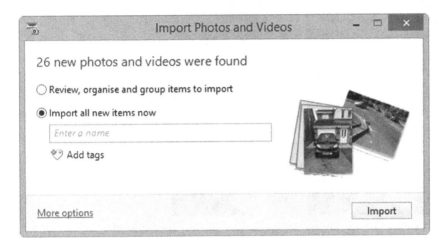

Figure 7-14. *The Windows 8.1 Import Photos and Videos Wizard*

These descriptive tags, which you separate with a semicolon (;), help you find and organize photos on your computer and enable you to search for files. For example, you can search for "Dusseldorf" or "Gilbert" to bring up all the related files and images in the Files search results after tags have been set (see Figure 7-15). For more information on using tags to organize files and photos, see Chapter 5.

Photos and videos of "gilbert"

Figure 7-15. *Searching for images is easier when they are tagged*

The Import Photos and Videos Wizard in Windows Photo Gallery also includes an option to **Review, organize and group items to import**. It brings up a page in which you can see photos and videos on the disk and select which ones you want to import (see Figure 7-16).

Figure 7-16. *You can choose the photos to import*

A slider near the bottom right of this window is particularly useful when it has been a while since you downloaded photos and videos from your camera. Let's say, for example, that you have been on vacation for 2 weeks, during which time you visited several European cities (Amsterdam, Dusseldorf, and Cologne).

Using this slider, you can separate the photos by the date they were taken. You can then tag photos as "Amsterdam; Netherlands", "Dusseldorf; Germany", and so on.

Clicking More Options on either of the import pages offers storage locations for the imported items, the ability to batch-rename imported items, and automatic rotation of photographs. If you want, Windows 8.1 can delete items from the device or memory card after they have been imported (see Figure 7-17).

Figure 7-17. *There are additional import options available*

Manually Adding a Scanner to Windows 8.1

When you add a scanner to your PC, either one that's built in to your printer or one that is separate, Windows 8.1 does a great job of automatically detecting and installing it. There might be some situations in which this doesn't happen, however, and you need to install the scanner manually. You can do this by searching for **scanner** with the Search Charm and clicking *View Scanners and Cameras* from the results.

This panel (see Figure 7-18) allows you to manually install a scanner using the driver software that was provided by the scanner's manufacturer.

Figure 7-18. *You can install scanners manually using the Show Scanners and Cameras panel*

Once a scanner is installed, you can click the *Scan Profiles* button to manage the resolution at which it scans images and the file type used to save your scanned images.

Playing and Enjoying Music and Video in Windows 8.1

Windows 8.1 also ships with Music and Video apps and Windows Media Player (note that Windows Media Player isn't available in the ARM version of the operating system). Unlike Windows Media Player, in which you play and manage your music and video libraries all in the same place, the Music and Video apps in Windows 8.1 are separate from one another, but both operate in the same way.

When you load the app, you are taken directly to the music and video you have stored on your PC (see Figure 7-19), though it may take a few minutes on first loading to index all your files.

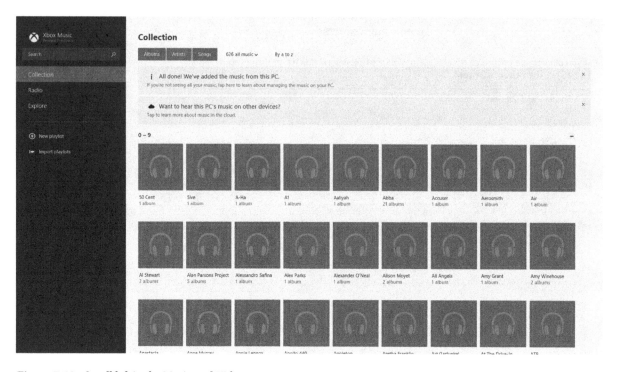

Figure 7-19. *Scroll left in the Music and Video apps to see your own content*

In the top left of the app are links to play music from Xbox Music Radio or to *Explore* new music and video that you can buy online from the Xbox Music service.

The music and video players in Windows 8.1 are rather good, having clearly evolved from Windows Media Center. They feature large onscreen controls that are simple to use with both touch and mouse; and, as with all apps, they can be docked to the left or right of the screen.

Creating and Managing Playlists in the Music and Video Apps

You can create music and video playlists in Music and Videos apps by selecting the artists, tracks, videos, or genres you want by clicking the New Playlist button on the left of the screen (see Figure 7-20). If you already have playlists created, they appear here as well, so you can add items to any of them with a single click.

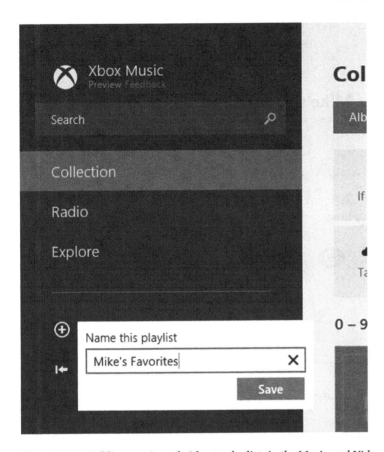

Figure 7-20. *Adding music and video to playlists in the Music and Video apps*

You manage playlists in the main My Music or My Videos view, in which a link to your playlists is on the left of the screen. Clicking it displays your current playlists. Click to open one and you can select tracks to remove from the playlist (see Figure 7-21).

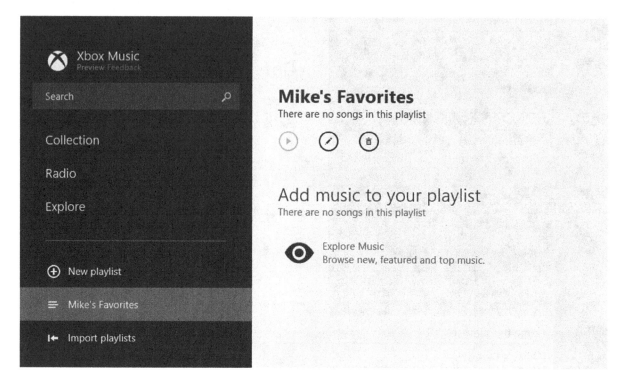

Figure 7-21. *Managing playlists in the Music and Video apps*

Audio and Video Codecs in Windows 8.1

Windows 8.1 comes with excellent audio and video support. Out of the box, it supports more music and video file types than any other version of Windows before it. There are three notable exceptions, however: the popular MKV video format (an open-source video codec) and support for both DVD video and Blu-ray video discs.

The MKV codec can be added using a codec pack such as the popular shark007.net, which is the only one I recommend. Adding the Blu-ray and DVD codecs requires an upgrade to Windows 8.1 Pro and purchasing Windows Media Center.

There are free third-party programs that can provide you with DVD and perhaps even Blu-ray playback codecs. Probably the best and most widely used is the VLC player, which you can download from http://www.videolan.org.

Windows Media Center

Windows Media Center doesn't come with Windows 8.1 as standard unless it is included by the manufacturer of your computer. It can be added to Windows 8.1 Pro, however, through purchasing the Media Center add-on that you can get by clicking *Add Features to Windows* in the Control Panel. If you don't have Windows 8.1 Pro, you can upgrade the standard Windows 8.1 to this version here as well. After you purchase Windows Media Center, an icon for it appears on the Start screen.

Visually and functionally, Windows Media Center has not changed from the Windows 7 version except that it now supports Blu-ray disc playback. The interface, which is a precursor to the one now used for the Start screen (yup, that's where it all began!), operates on a four-directional crosshairs system (up, down, left, and right) and supports viewing pictures, music, video, and live television if your computer has a compatible TV tuner (see Figure 7-22).

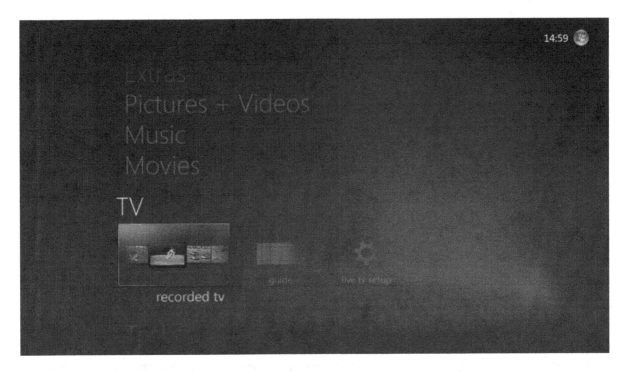

Figure 7-22. Windows Media Center

■ **Note** The DVD and Blu-ray codecs provided with Windows Media Center allow playback only within the Media Center software, not through any other app or program. You can add additional DVD and Blu-ray codecs to support playback through video players obtained from third parties. Your computer may have been provided with software that plays DVD videos and Blu-ray discs.

You can also purchase a separate remote control and sensor (if your computer did not come with one) specifically for use with Media Center in what is commonly known as the 10-foot interface. It is great for viewing across a room and has made the all-in-one PC with TV tuner popular in student dorm rooms worldwide.

Organizing Your Media Libraries in Media Center

Your Windows Media Center Media Libraries automatically include all the pictures, music, and video that are in your File Explorer libraries. Crucially, Windows Media Center allows you to do something that's impossible with File Explorer: add network locations and external hard drives to these libraries.

Any network and external file locations that you add to the Media Libraries in Windows Media Center are automatically added to the main libraries in Windows 8.1. This is a great workaround for a missing feature in the operating system.

Manage the Media Libraries in Media Center by clicking Settings on the main menu. It is listed at the bottom of the main Settings screen (see Figures 7-23 and 7-24).

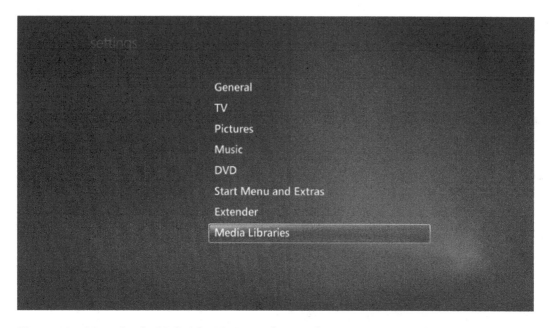

Figure 7-23. *Managing the Media Libraries in Windows Media Center*

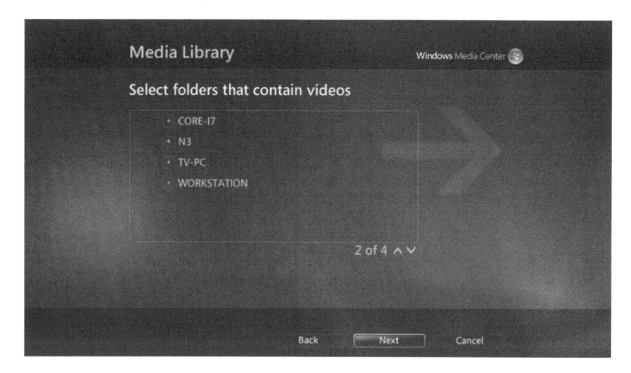

Figure 7-24. *Adding media to libraries in Windows Media Center*

Setting Up, Watching, and Recording Live TV

If you have a compatible television tuner card built into your computer or attached via USB, you can set up Live TV from the main menu. After it confirms the country and region that you live in, Windows Media Center scans for TV channels automatically (see Figure 7-25).

Figure 7-25. *Setting up Live TV in Media Center*

■ **Tip**   Windows RT supports almost all the USB hardware that's compatible with Windows 8.1, which includes many USB Television Tuners.

Windows Media Center supports a wide variety of television tuners, including cablecard, digital terrestrial, and digital satellite.

The automatically updating electronic program guide (EPG) is where you set programs to record. To record a television program, click the Record button on your remote control or right-click the program name. Press the Record button twice to record the entire series.

As with the very best digital TV recorders, Media Center is clever in that if you miss a program that was set to record (perhaps because you switched the computer off instead of putting it to sleep), it looks for a repeat of the program; if one exists, it records it.

In the TV section of the main menu, you can also search for television programs by name, genre, or other filters, such as actor or director.

■ **Tip**   MillieSoft provides a Windows Media Center plug-in called TunerFree MCE, which gives you access to on-demand Internet television services around the world (provided that those services are available in your country), including the BBC iPlayer and the complete Hulu catalog. It also provides live streams from organizations, including NASA and TWiT (This Week in Tech) podcasts (see Figure 7-26). You can download TunerFree MCE from http://www.milliesoft.co.uk.

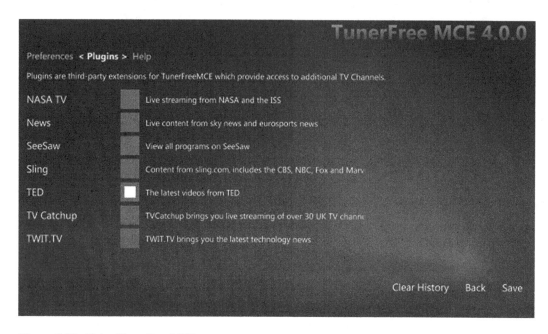

Figure 7-26. *Using TunerFree MCE*

Managing Windows Media Center

The main Settings screen in Media Center, shown in Figure 7-27, allows you to control all aspects of the software:

- You can determine the way Windows Media Center starts up and appears onscreen; for example, whether it runs fullscreen, whether the Media Center window is always on top of other windows, and whether it runs automatically when you turn the computer on.

- You can add a pin code so that children can't view programs with an inappropriate rating.

- You can edit the EPG to remove unwanted channels or that have a poor reception.

- You can control how and when subtitles appear in programs.

- You can control the default language and subtitle options for DVD and Blu-ray discs.

- You can set up an Xbox 360 console in another part of the house to work as a Media Center extender, including the broadcast of live television to that extender if you have a compatible TV tuner in your computer.

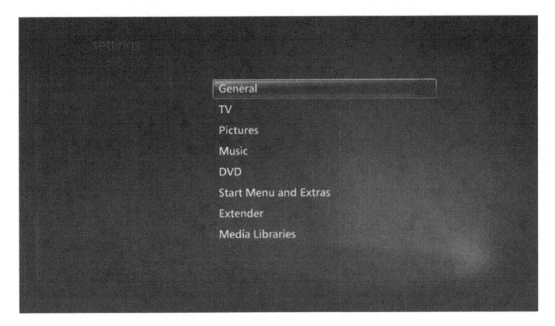

Figure 7-27. *You control Windows Media Center through its Settings*

■ **Tip** By default, subtitles appear onscreen when you mute the sound while watching live television in Windows Media Center.

Using Xbox 360 to Access TV, Music, Video, and Pictures from Windows 8.1

You can use your Xbox 360 console to stream music, video, and pictures from your PC if it has Windows 8.1 Pro with Media Center. You can do this through the Add Features to Windows 8.1 link in the Control Panel. Note that the Xbox One console cannot be used as a media Center Extender.

To do this from the Xbox 360 dashboard, select Media Center in the apps section to launch the connection wizard. The PC hosting the video and other content has to be switched on and logged on to.

As a part of the setup process, you are given a Setup Key. Enter your Setup Key by clicking Add Extender from the main Windows Media Center menu. Once you have done this, you can add the Xbox 360 console to Media Center on your PC by clicking *Add Extender* in the *Tasks* section of the main menu. The process is simple and wizard-driven (see Figure 7-28).

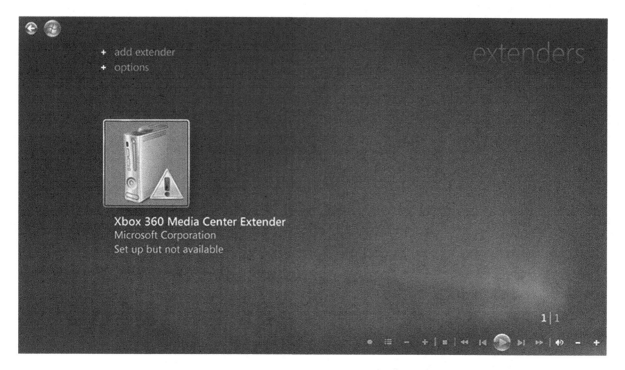

Figure 7-28. *Connecting an Xbox 360 to Windows Media Center*

Once you have successfully paired your Xbox 360 console and PC, you can launch Windows Media Center on the Xbox 360 console to stream music, video, and pictures whenever the PC is switched on.

Converting Recorded TV to DVR-MS Format

When you record a television program using Windows Media Center, the video file is captured in a Windows TV (.wtv) format. Not every video editor opens WTV files, although the free Windows Live Movie Maker does. So if you want to edit the program, you can convert it in Windows 8.1 to the widely supported DVR-MS video format used with Windows Media Center in Windows XP.

To convert recorded TV WTV files to DVR-MS format files, Windows Media Center *must* be the default playback program for your recorded television. You may find that this isn't the case even with Windows Media Center installed, so you can change this by right-clicking a WTV file and clicking Choose Default Program from the options that appear (see Figure 7-29).

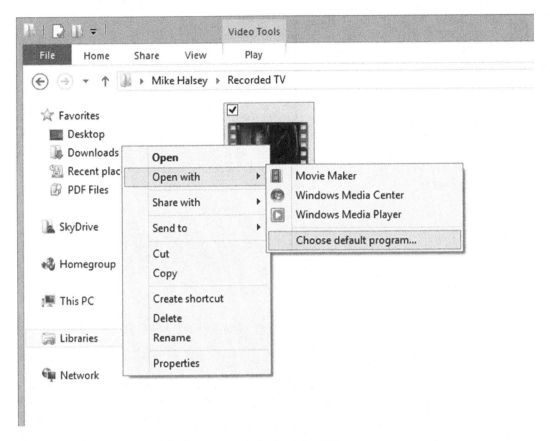

Figure 7-29. *Changing the default program to play back live TV*

When Windows 8.1 prompts you to choose the default playback program for this file, click Windows Media Center (see Figure 7-30).

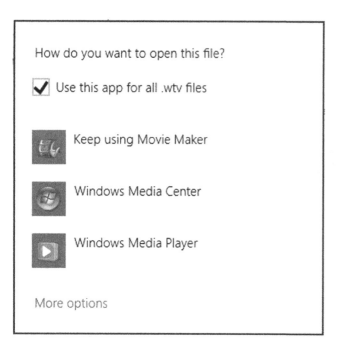

How do you want to open this file?

☑ Use this app for all .wtv files

Keep using Movie Maker

Windows Media Center

Windows Media Player

More options

Figure 7-30. *Select Windows Media Center from the options*

The file starts playing automatically, but you can close it. When you want to convert your recorded television programs to the DVR-MS format, you can right-click them and select Convert to .dvr-ms Format in the options that appear (see Figure 7-31).

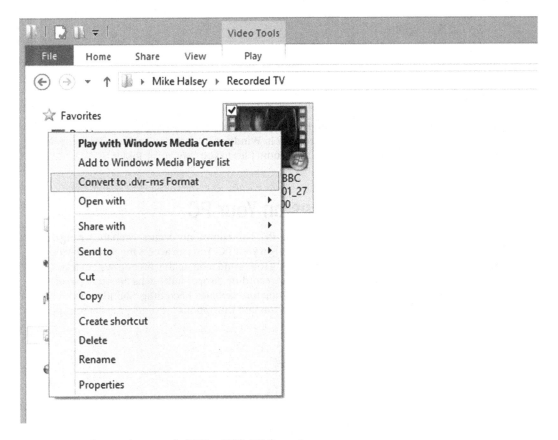

Figure 7-31. *Converting recorded TV to DVR-MS format*

This procedure doesn't delete the original WTV file—you are still left with it—but it does create an additional video file that can be edited. My favorite free editing programs for recorded TV are DVREdit and DVR-2-WMV, which need to be used together for the best results. Although the official download sites for these software packages are long gone, you can still easily find them available for download through a quick search online.

The good news is that if you don't want to use or can't find these tools, you can also edit your WTV and DVR-MS files in Windows Live Movie Maker, which is available for free download as part of the Live Essentials Suite at download.live.com.

Recording Audio Directly to Your PC

Sometimes you want to be able to record audio on to your PC. The good news is that Windows has had, for many years now, its own tool to enable you to do this. Called the Sound Recorder, this tool has been refined over the years and is now a very capable audio recorder (see Figure 7-32).

Figure 7-32. *The Sound Recorder in Windows 8.1*

This little desktop utility records automatically using the default recording device in your PC, and I will show you how to change the default audio devices soon. The Sound Recorder in Windows 8.1 also now includes an equivalent app for the first time. Both the app and the desktop program save audio files to your My Music folder.

Changing the Default Audio Devices on Your PC

Sometimes you find that you have no sound or microphone on your PC. This commonly occurs when the wrong device is incorrectly assigned as the default because you might have several on your PC. You can access the Sound devices panel by searching for **Sound** from the Search charm or right-clicking the sound icon on the desktop system tray and selecting *Playback Devices* from the options that appear (though the recording devices link opens the same panel).

In the Sound panel (see Figure 7-33), you have tabs across the top for Playback, Recording, Sounds, and Communications. It is under the Playback and Recording tabs that you find the options for setting the default speakers and microphone.

Figure 7-33. *Sound devices panel*

To set the default, click the item you want to make the default and then click the *Set Default* button. Sometimes, however, you might want different audio devices for music and for communications, such as Skype. You can set different systems, such as speakers and a headset, to be just the default audio device for communications by clicking the chevron to the right of the *Set Default* button. From the options that appear, click *Default Communication Device*.

Burn CDs and DVDs Directly from the Desktop

Although USB Flash drives are inexpensive and readily available, people still want to want to burn CDs and DVDs directly from their PC. In Windows 8.1, you can do this from the desktop but only with data CDs and DVDs. The difference with these is that they are intended to be read by other PCs and don't play in a standard CD or DVD player.

To burn content to a disc, follow these instructions:

1. Put a blank disc in your computer's optical drive.

2. Select it in File Explorer (you don't need to select every file at once).

3. Right click the file(s); from the menu that appears, click *Send to* and then click the name of the optical drive.

4. A panel appears, asking whether you want to create a disc like a USB Flash drive (which you can add more files to after it's burned) or a standard CD/DVD that can't be added to later (see Figure 7-34). Make your choice and click *Next*.

Figure 7-34. *You can create fixed and multisession discs in Windows*

5. The files are copied to a temporary store, and a new File Explorer window opens, into which you can add additional files. Remember, however, that a CD has a maximum capacity of 650 MB, and a DVD has a maximum capacity of either 4.7 or 9.5 GB, depending on whether it is single- or double-layered.

6. When you're ready to burn your disc, click the *Finish Burning* button under the Drive Tools tab on the ribbon (see Figure 7-35).

Figure 7-35. *Drive Tools tab on the File Explorer ribbon*

Burn Audio CDs in Windows Media Player

If you want to burn audio CDs, you can do this in Windows Media Player. In the top right of the Windows Media Player window are three tabs: Play (for creating custom playlists), Burn (for burning audio CDs), and Sync (for copying music to a compatible MP3 player), as shown in Figure 7-36.

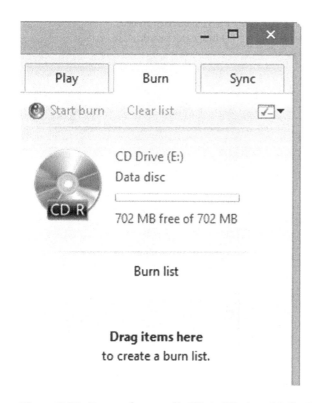

Figure 7-36. *You can burn audio CDs in Windows Media Player*

You can burn music that is already in your music library to an audio CD by dragging it from the main music details panel in the middle of the Windows Media Player window onto the Burn tab. You see how much time is left on the CD, enabling you to properly manage the amount of music that will fit on the disc.

When you have added all your music to the Burn panel and are ready to burn the CD, click the *Start burn* button near the top right of the window.

Summary

Windows 8.1 is a very consumer-oriented OS and has some great apps for photos, music, video, and more. The finer control is still available in tools such as the Import Photos and Videos Wizard.

If you're an enthusiastic gamer, you might find Windows 8.1—with Xbox Live and Xbox console remote control built in for the first time—to be just the platform for you. With support for gaming technologies such as 3D gaining ground, it will be interesting to see the innovative uses for this operating system.

The new Music and Video apps are excellent and can be easily docked to the side of the screen while you work. Although you now have to pay extra for Windows Media Center and DVD/Blu-ray playback, it is a fantastic addition that allows you to customize the Windows 8.1 libraries in ways that are otherwise impossible.

CHAPTER 8

■ ■ ■

Maximizing Your Productivity

Windows was born into the business space. It was the original IBM PC, equipped with software such as Lotus 123 or WordPerfect, that was the powerhouse of the "modern" office in the 1980s. The introduction of the Windows user interface and the Microsoft Office suite solidified the PC's position as the productivity tool of choice. It was the flexibility of PCs that eventually brought them into homes, and now we take it for granted that we'll have access to our own PC at work. Many people expect to be provided a laptop—and a smartphone as well—and others have begun using their personal PCs, tablets, and smartphones at work.

Despite all this, the computer is probably the biggest barrier to productivity in the workplace. Enormous barriers occur during a power outage or when the Internet connection goes down. There are ways to keep working in these circumstances, however, some of which are cleverer than buying laptops.

Some 90 percent of all e-mail is spam. There are alternatives to the spam mountain, though, and some people argue that the days of e-mail are numbered and that instant messaging is the way forward.

As computers become more ubiquitous and we all get older, the ever-higher pixel densities on our screens can make text and other information difficult to read. Couple this problem with the barriers encountered by the disabled and people with fine motor control problems. Windows 8.1 includes some excellent tools to include everybody in a computing life. There is also excellent support to be found elsewhere.

These topics are just a few of the ones that I'll cover in this chapter, the aim of which is to help you maximize your productivity with the operating system.

Managing and Arranging Running Apps

One of the features (some might say "limitations") of the new interface is that apps are designed to run full-screen, with only the *in focus* app displaying on your screen at any given time. On a small tablet screen, this isn't a problem, but you still might want to have a second window open showing e-mail or messaging.

You can open up to four apps side by side in Windows 8.1, though this number will vary from two to four, depending on the resolution of your screen. Some people can find the multiapp approach in Windows 8.1 confusing at first, but I will explain in this section how easy it is to use.

Think of your running apps in Windows 8.1 as a stack of playing cards from which the Start screen is excluded. The card on the top is the one you are currently looking at. The card directly under this one, the most recently used card, is the one you can bring alongside if you want.

There are several ways of displaying two applications side by side: by touch and with the keyboard. The easiest method is to drag the app downward from the top center of your screen by using either a mouse or touch. It becomes a large thumbnail as you approach the center of the screen and can then be dropped on the left or right of the screen to dock it.

Another method is with the current app displaying on your screen: drag inward from the bezel on the left side of your screen, and the previously running app slides in from the side of the screen as a card.

Windows 8.1 then signifies that it is ready to dock that card to the first quarter of the screen. Separating the apps is a vertical bar with three dots on it. You can drag this bar left and right of the screen to change the primary focus from the main app to the side app. For example, if you have an app locked to the left quarter of the screen and you then drag the bar separating the two apps to the right side of the screen, the app that was on the left side now occupies the left three-quarters of the screen. The app that previously filled most of the screen now resides in the right quarter.

▪ **Note**   You can also select a running app by swiping inward from the left of the screen and then outward again to display the running apps list. You can then drag app thumbnails out from this list and dock them on your screen.

In Figure 8-1, the desktop counts as an app insofar as viewing two apps side by side is concerned. This means you can view the desktop in most of your screen while also seeing an app pinned to the left or right side.

Figure 8-1. *Two apps side by side in Windows 8.1*

There is one way to snap any running app to the left or right side of the screen, regardless of where it sits in your stack of running apps. If you move your mouse to the top left of your screen (note that this cannot be done by touch), thumbnails of all running apps appear. You can right-click any running app and select an option to snap it to the left or right side of your screen.

To add a third or even a fourth app if your screen resolution supports it, you can add the additional app in the same way as you added the second. It appears on your screen as a large thumbnail (see Figure 8-2). When you drag this thumbnail to the left or right sides of your screen, the thumbnail indicates that if dropped it replaces the app running on that side. If you move the thumbnail over the vertical bar separating the running apps, however, a gap opens, into which you can drop the additional app. If this gap doesn't appear, your screen resolution isn't wide enough to support an extra app, and you can drag the thumbnail off the bottom of the screen to close and discard it.

Figure 8-2. *You can have three or four apps on screen at any one time*

When you have two or more apps onscreen, you can drag the vertical bar separating them left or right to change the size or the apps. This can be useful for having one app in a thin bar along one side of the screen while the other fills the rest of the space or for having two apps the same size. Not all apps are compatible with varying sizes, however, and might not display the way you want.

Switching Between Running Apps

You can switch between any of your running apps by using the Win+Tab keyboard shortcut. In Windows Vista and Windows 7, it displayed the Flip 3D view, in which you could switch between running desktop apps in a three-dimensional stack. Flip 3D is not a part of Windows 8.1.

■ **Note**   It is important to note that Win+Tab, which is used to switch between apps, doesn't allow you to select a running desktop program. To do this, you should use the Alt+Tab keyboard shortcut.

You can also use a mouse to switch between running apps from the Start screen. To do this, move your mouse cursor to the bottom left or top left of the screen; you see the Start button at the bottom of the screen and thumbnails at the top of the screen.

You can mouse up or down in this view to select the app to switch to and then click it.

■ **Tip**   You can shut down an app in this view by right-clicking it and selecting Close. You can also snap any app to the left or right side of the screen in this right-click menu.

To switch between running apps with touch, you can drag apps in from the left of the screen. Start your swipe gesture on the left screen bezel, and the apps appear one at a time in reverse order from when they were last used. Swiping an app inward makes it run full-screen. You can then continue swiping, one app at a time, until you reach the app that you want. This is one of the features in Windows 8. Alternatively, swipe inward from the left of the screen and then out again to display the running apps list. You can then tap the thumbnail image of the app you want to switch to.

You can snap the current window to the left and right of the screen using the keyboard combinations Win+right and left cursor keys. The reason to refer to these key combinations in this way is to remind you that there is no need to hold down the Shift key.

The next app you launch from the Start screen then automatically fills the remaining space, leaving your snapped app where you put it.

Arranging Two Apps Side by Side

Working with side-by-side apps is straightforward; you can have up to four onscreen at once. This view is called *split-screen* and it enables you to have one app in a side bar docked to either the far left or far right of the screen, while another app takes up the remaining space on your screen (see Figure 8-3).

Figure 8-3. *Side-by-side apps*

■ **Tip** You can snap an app to one side of the screen using a mouse. Click the top of the app and drag it from the top of the screen toward the left or right of the screen, where the dock bar appears.

There are several ways to get apps to display side by side. It depends on whether you're using a touchscreen or a keyboard and mouse. To run side-by-side apps using touch, perform the following steps:

1. Open the app you want to pin to a side pane.

2. Grab the top center of the app and drag it to the left or right side of the screen. A vertical bar appears, indicating that the app will be docked.

3. Return to the Start screen.

4. Open the app you want to pin in the rest of your screen. This app opens to fill the remaining space.

You can drag the vertical bar separating apps from the left to the right of the screen to change the focus between the two running apps.

To arrange split-screen apps using a keyboard and mouse, perform the following steps:

1.   Run the app you want to pin in a sidebar.

2.   Press Win+right cursor key on your keyboard to pin this app to the right of your screen.

3.   Return to the Start screen and run the second app.

4.   Move your mouse to the top left of your screen to display app thumbnails.

5.   Click the app you want to run in the main part of the screen.

Another way to snap apps to the left or the right of the screen is from the thumbnails of running apps.

1.   Move your mouse to the top left of the screen to display the thumbnails of running apps.

2.   Right-click the app you want to snap to the left or right of the screen.

3.   From the context menu, click Snap Left or Snap Right.

Working with Multiple Programs on the Desktop

Some people argue that running two apps side by side can be limiting, but this is what I tend to do on the desktop, with everything else minimized. So how can you maximize your desktop window productivity?

Hiding and Restoring All Windows on the Desktop (a.k.a. Boss Mode)

If your desktop is getting *really* cluttered and you're struggling to concentrate, there is a quick and easy way to minimize all the windows open on your desktop. On the far right of the taskbar, click the blank space to the right of the clock (see Figure 8-4). There is a hidden button here that automatically minimizes all the Windows on your desktop.

Figure 8-4. *The hide-all-windows button is on the far right of the taskbar*

▦ **Tip**   The best way to find the Minimize All Programs button is to press Win+M on your keyboard, however you can also click in the far right of your taskbar.

Clicking this button again restores all the windows to their previous positions onscreen. This feature is sometimes referred to as *boss mode* because if you're having a moment of downtime at work and the boss walks past, he doesn't have to see that you're playing a game on Facebook or shopping on Amazon.

▦ **Note**   Some laptops come with a feature that allows you to run your fingers downward on the trackpad (usually four fingers) to automatically minimize all windows.

Minimizing and Restoring Windows Using Shake

Another way to minimize and restore all the windows on your screen is to shake your mouse. Doing this minimizes everything; another shake restores everything. It is useful for many people, but for those who have fine motor control problems, this feature can prove annoying. You can switch it off in the accessibility options (see Chapter 10).

Snapping Two Windows Side by Side

One of the most useful features in Windows, which I use all the time, is Snap. It allows you to view two windows on the desktop side by side, with each occupying exactly 50 percent of the screen. You can use it by dragging windows to the very left or very right of your screen, or by pressing the Windows key + the left or right cursor keys. As you drag a window to the left or right of your screen, a ghost outline of the program appears onscreen to show you that when you release the window, it will snap to one half of the screen.

This feature is useful for many scenarios, including moving or copying files from one location to another, comparing two documents side by side, or working with two Internet Explorer windows side by side (see Figure 8-5).

Figure 8-5. *Snap in Windows 8.1*

Peeking at and Closing Windows from Thumbnails

Another extremely useful way to arrange Windows on the desktop is through the use of taskbar thumbnails. When you move your mouse over the taskbar button of an open program, thumbnail images of that program appear. There are several actions you can perform here:

- Hovering your mouse over a thumbnail for about 1 second displays that window in the main screen, even if the program is minimized. It shows only that program and temporarily hides all others that are open.

- You can select this window to bring to the foreground by clicking the thumbnail.

- You can close a window by clicking the Close button in the top right of the thumbnail (see Figure 8-6).

Figure 8-6. *You can view thumbnails of running desktop programs from the taskbar*

Pinning Programs to the Desktop Taskbar

You can pin a program to the desktop taskbar in Windows 8.1 by right-clicking its tile in either the Start screen or the All Apps view, and selecting Pin to Taskbar from the App bar (see Figure 8-7).

Figure 8-7. *You can pin programs to the taskbar from the Start screen*

■ **Tip**   You can select multiple programs on the Start screen or All Apps view and pin them to the taskbar together, which is a good way to save time if you have many programs you want to pin.

Once you have your programs pinned to the taskbar, you can rearrange them by dragging and dropping them so that they are in the order that best suits you. My advice is to use the taskbar to pin all the programs that you use on a regular basis because it makes it much easier to launch them.

You can still access lesser-used utilities when you need them because they are always available on the All Apps view, but the aim is to keep the taskbar relatively uncluttered by showing only the program tiles that you *genuinely* use on a regular basis.

■ **Tip**   It is possible in Windows 8.1 to not just start your computer directly to the desktop but also to show the All Apps view when you press the Start button and display your desktop programs first in that view. I show you how to make these changes in Chapter 9.

Maximizing Productivity with Jump Lists

Jump Lists, first introduced in Windows 7, are a great way to organize the files you work with on a regular basis or for a current project. You can open a Jump List from the taskbar in one of two ways:

- Tap and push up with your mouse or finger.
- Right-click with your mouse.

Jump Lists show the files or places that have been opened most recently in a program. By default, it's the ten most recently opened documents.

You can pin documents, as many as you like, to Jump Lists by clicking the Pin button that appears next to the document name when you mouse over it. Pinning a document to a Jump List ensures that it always appears at the top of the list (see Figure 8-8). This makes access to commonly used files extremely quick and simple.

Figure 8-8. *Pin and unpin recently accessed files to Jump Lists*

Jump Lists commonly also provide quick access to certain features within programs, including quick links to specific features and controls, in which links to the main sections of Microsoft Outlook can be found in the program's Jump List (see Figure 8-9).

Figure 8-9. *You can get quick access to a program's features from Jump Lists*

Using Microsoft SkyDrive with Windows 8.1

Microsoft's SkyDrive cloud storage service is built into Windows 8.1 in a significant way, and in Chapter 1 showed you how to use the built-in SkyDrive file backup and sync feature. Windows 8.1 easily provides access to the files you have stored in SkyDrive when in any compatible app that works with files (see Figure 8-10). It allows you to view and open any files you have stored in Microsoft's cloud backup service. It can be very helpful on tablets and ultrabooks, where local storage space is at a premium, or if you want to access the same file on multiple computers.

Figure 8-10. *Viewing your SkyDrive folders and files in Windows 8.1*

Additionally, any files you have stored in SkyDrive is immediately available if you log in to Windows 8.1 using the same Microsoft account regardless of whether you want to sync files locally to the PC. This can be extremely useful for low-storage devices such as tablets and ultrabooks, in which you want occasional access to files without the storage problems (and associated security concerns) of keeping a local copy all the time.

■ **Tip**   You can change the location of the SkyDrive folder in Windows 8.1 by *right-clicking* the SkyDrive link in the left panel of File Explorer. From the menu that appears, select its *Properties*. Then in the window that appears, click the *Location* tab and then click the *Move* button. You can now select a different folder location for your SkyDrive sync folder.

To access files from SkyDrive from the desktop on your Windows 8.1 PC, click the *SkyDrive* link in File Explorer; you see all your files and folders right away (see Figure 8-11).

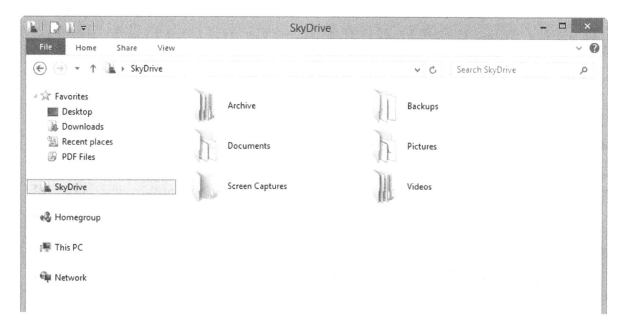

Figure 8-11. *You can access all the files you have stored in SkyDrive, even if they're not synced to your own PC*

When you open a file on the PC that is stored in SkyDrive it will be downloaded and a local copy kept and synced. This allows you to work on and make changes to the document or file locally on the PC and know that when you save it, the changes are automatically synchronized back to the cloud.

Sometimes, however, you will want to force Windows 8.1 to keep, or not to keep, a local copy of SkyDrive files, or even entire folders. You can do this through a simple right-click, where you will find a *Make available offline* or *online* command (see Figure 8-12).

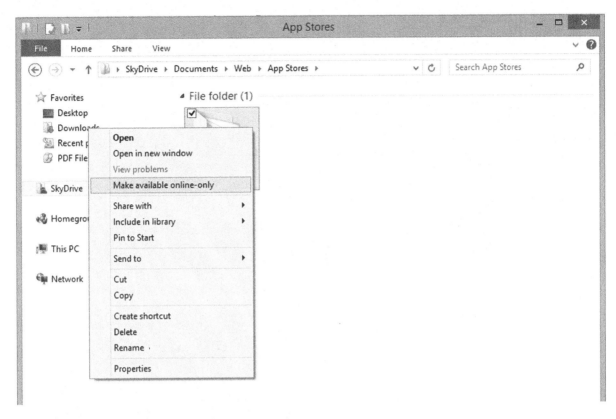

Figure 8-12. You can force your PC to keep individual files and whole folders online or offline

By default, a SkyDrive account gives you 7 GB of free storage, which is plenty for a lot of people. You can expand this amount, however, at the SkyDrive web site by purchasing additional space for reasonable rates.

SkyDrive is a good service to use with Windows 8.1, primarily because the amount of free storage you get is quite generous, but also because it is easily accessible by other Microsoft products, such as Windows Phone.

Using the Windows 8.1 Spell Checker

Windows 8.1 comes with a built-in spell checker so that this facility is available to you most of the time (the spell checker doesn't work in every program), even when filling in web forms in Internet Explorer. When Windows 8.1 detects a work that is incorrectly spelled, it underlines it for you to highlight it. You can then click the word to either correct it from a list of options, ignore it, or add it to the dictionary (see Figure 8-13).

Figure 8-13. *The Windows 8.1 spell checker works both in desktop programs and apps*

You can turn the spell checker on and off in Windows 8.1 through the PC Settings panel. Navigate to *PC & Devices* and then click the *Typing* link in the left panel. Two options for controlling the spell checker then appear at the top of your screen. The first enables or disables the autocorrect, which is where Windows 8.1 automatically correct a word for you if it believes you've misspelled a very common word; the second option turns the spell checking on and off completely (see Figure 8-14).

Figure 8-14. *Managing the spell checker in Windows 8.1*

Sometimes, however, you might find that you added a word or words to the custom dictionary in Windows 8.1 that you didn't mean to, perhaps because they are also misspelled. This isn't a problem, though. In a File Explorer window, click in the address bar, type *%AppData%\Microsoft\Spelling*, and press Enter. This process opens the file location for the custom dictionary (see Figure 8-15).

Figure 8-15. *The custom dictionary can be edited in Windows 8.1*

The file you want to edit is one of the *default* text document files (usually the one with the largest file size, and if you can see its file extension, it is called *default.dic*). This file opens in Notepad as a plain text list of the words that have been added to the dictionary and in the order they were added. You can simply edit or delete items from this list to change the custom dictionary.

▪ **Tip** If you work in an environment with many custom dictionary words, such as engineering or the legal profession, they can be added by system administrators by injecting a dictionary file into a custom Windows installation image.

Taking Screen Shots in Windows 8.1

Sometimes you need to get a captured image of what you can see on your PC screen, and this is where the Windows 8.1 useful screen shot features come in handy. You might be surprised to hear this, but there are actually four different ways to capture screen shots in Windows 8.1, and the ones you use vary, depending on what device you are using.

- Opening the **Share charm** from the desktop displays a list of programs with which you can share a screen shot. You can't share anything else from desktop programs, so whichever program you select here, a screen shot is shared with instead. From within apps, a drop-down list appears on the top right of your screen when you open the Share charm. This drop-down includes an option to take a screen shot, which can then be shared with whatever app you click next (see Figure 8-16).

Figure 8-16. *You can share screen shots from the Share charm*

- You can use the **Windows key + Prnt Scrn** key combination to take a screen shot that will be saved to a *Screenshots* folder in your Pictures library.

- On tablet devices you can commonly press the *Windows button* on the bezel of the device while holding down the *Volume down* key. It saves a screen shot to your Pictures ➤ Screenshots folder.

- You can use the **Snipping tool** to capture screen shots of specific windows or partial screens, (see the following section).

Using the Snipping Tool

You can run the snipping tool by searching for it at the Start screen or running it from the All Apps view. There are four different ways you can snip: a free form, in which you draw around an object, a rectangular snip, a window snip to capture a whole window, and a full-screen snip (see Figure 8-17).

Figure 8-17. *The snipping tool is a flexible screen capture utility*

After creating a snip, an editing window appears, in which you can annotate, highlight, or erase parts of the snip. It is also in this editing window that you save the image, and there are a wide variety of file formats that can be used.

■ **Tip**   Your productivity can be boosted further by searching for a program's real file name instead of its long name when you want to run it. Here is a list of some of the most common. *iexplore* (Internet Explorer), *explorer* (File Explorer), *calc* (Calculator), *wmplayer* (Windows Media Player), *control* (Control Panel), *regedit* (Registry editor), *msconfig* (System Configuration Panel), and *gpedit.msc* (Group Policy Editor).

Windows Mobility Center

The Windows Mobility Center (see Figure 8-18) is designed to help keep you productive on devices such as laptops, ultrabooks, and tablets. The easiest way to find it is to type **mobile** or **mobility** at the Start screen; you'll find it in the search results. I want to discuss the areas of the Mobility Center by the type of tasks you want to perform.

Figure 8-18. *Windows Mobility Center*

■ **Tip**   You can access the Windows Mobility Center by right-clicking the battery button on the taskbar or through the Win+X administration menu.

Managing Battery Life on Laptops, Ultrabooks, and Tablets

Battery life is critical on laptops, ultrabooks, and tablets. Although many computer reviews and manufacturers now claim that some devices manage 8 hours of life on "light use," the definition of light use means not really using the machine the way you want to in an average day. There are several tools you can use in the mobility center to optimize your battery life:

- **Brightness** is a simple slider to adjust the brightness of your screen. Lower levels of brightness prolong battery life.

- **Battery Status** provides a quick indication of the amount of power your battery has remaining. It also provides a drop-down menu that includes a power-saving mode to prolong battery life.

For more information on battery power management in Windows 8.1, see Chapter 9.

Maintaining Productivity Without Electricity/Internet Access

If you have ever been in a workplace during a power outage or when the Internet connection fails, you know that it commonly results in work stoppage and card playing.

The absence of electricity or an Internet connection doesn't need to mean that you can't get any work done. There are ways around these problems. Most obviously, if you have a laptop, it can continue to run as long as its battery lasts, which is often long enough to wait out a power outage.

You can also install Uninterruptable Power Supplies (UPS) in your workplace, which keeps computers, and even the Internet connection, running smoothly. Remember that your broadband line comes through a phone cable that is on its own external power circuit. Having a UPS plugged into your router (and perhaps a switch box if required) keeps your Wi-Fi and network online.

PCs plugged into UPS boxes can keep running for an hour or more in the event of a power outage. This means that you should have plenty of power to continue working while you wait for the electricity to come back on.

Sharing a Mobile Broadband Connection

When your Internet connection goes down, you don't have to do without web access. If you have a laptop containing a mobile broadband (3G or 4G/LTE SIM card), you can share this connection through the laptop (or even an Intel-based tablet) and with other computers in the office.

There are two ways to share a mobile broadband connection in Windows 8.1, the simplest of which resides in PC Settings. To access it, open PC Settings, then click *Network*, click *Connections*, and finally click the name of the mobile broadband connection you want to share.

If your connection can be shared, a *Share your mobile broadband* button will be clickable. As shown in Figure 8-19, it isn't always the case because this facility can be disabled by your mobile network. Sharing a connection in this way sets up an *ad hoc* Wi-Fi network with its own name and access code to which you can connect up to ten devices of any type. By this I mean that you're not limited to connecting only other Windows 8.1 PCs. Any device that can connect to the Internet via Wi-Fi can share this connection.

Share this connection

We can't set up Internet connection sharing.

Share your mobile broadband Internet connection with other people. They'll need the network name and password to connect.

Off

Properties

Manufacturer:	Dell
Model:	DW5550
Firmware:	R2A07(R2A07)
Network type:	GSM
Data class:	HSPA+
IMEI:	3562
Mobile number:	0780
IMSI:	2343
SIM ICCID:	8944

Copy

Figure 8-19. *You can share a mobile broadband connection in PC Settings*

You can also share a mobile broadband connection in the Network and Sharing Centre, which you can access from the desktop.

■ **Tip** Many modern smartphones, including Windows Phones, can be set up as mobile Wi-Fi hotspots so that their connection can be shared with other computers and devices. This feature may be called *tethering* on your smartphone. You should check with your carrier to see whether this feature is supported on your tariff because not all carriers permit tethering, and you may incur additional data charges.

To share a mobile broadband connection from the desktop, perform the following steps:

1. In the Control Panel, open the Network and Sharing Center.

2. In the left pane, click Change Adapter Settings.

3. Right-click the Mobile Broadband connection and select Properties from the context menu.

4. Click the Sharing tab in the dialog (see Figure 8-20).

Figure 8-20. *Sharing a mobile broadband connection in Windows 8.1*

5. Select the check box to **Allow other network computers to connect through this computer's Internet connection**.

6. Set the Home Networking Connection type to Wi-Fi.

Other computers in the vicinity can now get online using the mobile broadband connection of the host laptop.

■ **Note**   Be aware that mobile data can be costly, and you should not use metered mobile broadband connections for Internet activities that are bandwidth-intensive.

Mobile operators sell 3G and 4G/LTE Wi-Fi mini routers that act in the same way as a standard DSL router in the home or workplace. Also, some standard DSK and cable routers include SIM card slots as a backup connection. They can usually be set to automatically switch the data connection if the main Internet connection stops working.

Working with Secondary Displays

When you are a road warrior, you are often working with projectors or secondary displays. You can normally access them in the Charms menu on the Start screen under Devices. But if you are presenting, perhaps using PowerPoint, you are using the desktop.

In the Mobility Center, you have options to connect to and manage an external display, as well as to rotate the orientation of your screen (perhaps if you are working on a tablet or a vertically aligned screen).

■ **Note**   What is Presentation mode? This option, found in the Presentation settings, disables all Windows, e-mail, and other notifications when you are using your computer for a presentation. It also disables Sleep mode during a presentation. This prevents the machine from switching itself off to save power (remember to have a main power adapter handy). It also prevents e-mail pop-ups from appearing so that your audience doesn't see that a friend just tagged you in a picture on Facebook.

Synchronizing Files with Other Computers and Devices

The Windows Mobility Center contains a quick link to the Windows Sync Center. It is here that you manage any ActiveSync devices that your computer or Windows Server domain account is linked to. These devices include smartphones and tablets. If you have a device managed through ActiveSync, it is commonly set up by your systems administrator through Microsoft Exchange.

The Sync Center allows you to manage your synced devices (see Figure 8-21). You may have a hardware device that you want to sync with your computer, but you can also use the Sync Center to keep an offline version of server files so that you can work on the move.

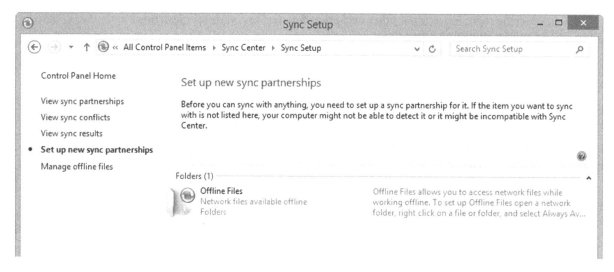

Figure 8-21. *Sync Center*

On the Sync Setup page, you can view your current sync partnerships and any conflicts that you might have. To check that everything is up to date, you can also get the current status of synchronization with devices.

Click **Set up new sync partnerships** to synchronize files with another device on Windows 8.1. Note that the other device needs to be connected to your computer to set up the partnership. When you select a sync partnership in the Sync Center, buttons to force a *Sync* and to set the sync *Schedule* appear across the top of the list of partnerships. You can click them to manage the partnership sync settings.

If you are using the Sync Center to keep offline copies of files from a Windows Server, click **Manage offline files** to control your settings for the sync partnership.

In the Offline Files dialog (see Figure 8-22), you can control the current state of the partnership, including the ability to specify the amount of hard disk space on your computer that is available for syncing. You do this on the Disk Usage tab. The more space you make available, the more files you can sync with your computer and store locally.

Figure 8-22. *Offline Files dialog*

This dialog also allows you to make sure that offline files are automatically encrypted. This option is very useful if you keep offline versions of files on a laptop that you travel with.

Setting Up and Using Work Folders

If your company uses the new *Work Folders* feature in the latest version of Windows Server, this is often a simpler and easier to manage system for maintaining offline versions of files for the user. You can find *Work Folders* in the Control Panel. Click *Set up Work Folders* to get started and you are asked for your work e-mail address or the URL of the work folder on the company server.

Once the first file sync has taken place, the Work Folders panel changes to display a status of the current file sync with the server (see Figure 8-23). This panel can then be used to control how the file sync works, such as whether files should also sync over mobile broadband connections. You also turn Work Folders off here.

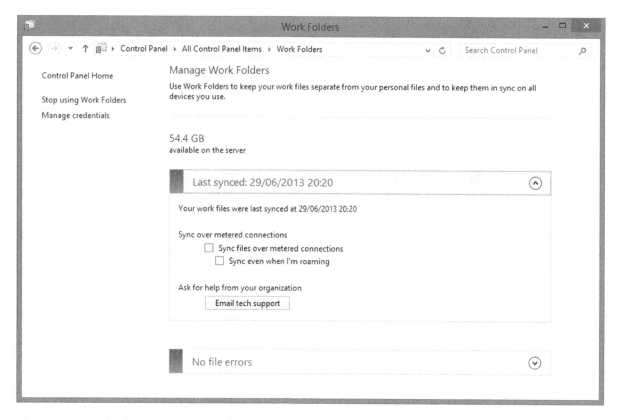

Figure 8-23. *Work Folders are new to Windows 8.1 and Windows Server*

The synced work folders then appear in the This PC view of File Explorer (see Figure 8-24), and can easily be opened and accessed from here. In many ways, this makes Work Folders a significantly more friendly and powerful alternative to the older ActiveSync feature, though it does require a specially configured server that ActiveSync does not require.

Figure 8-24. *Synced work folders appear in the This PC view of File Explorer*

Working with Multiple Screens and Desktops in Windows 8.1

Many people like to use multiple monitors with their computers. Laptops especially might have a secondary monitor, or you might work in a financial or design environment in which multiple displays are commonplace. In this section, I show you how to manage multiple displays in Windows 8.1, and how you can get the best from those displays through the use of multidesktop wallpapers and new taskbar options.

Managing Multiple Displays in Windows 8.1

You can manage multiple displays in Windows 8.1 in one of two ways. From the charms, you can select Devices; management of secondary displays is located here. If you are using multiple monitors, however, you will most likely use the Windows desktop.

To manage multiple displays from the desktop, right-click anywhere in free desktop space (see Figure 8-25). From the context menu, select Screen Resolution.

Figure 8-25. Managing multiple displays from the desktop

■ **Note** You can't span the Windows 8.1 Start screen across more than one display; it always appears on the primary display. The Start screen always displays on the monitor last used to display an app.

The Screen Resolution window shows each monitor connected to your computer. Here you can drag and drop the monitor displays to the left and right, and even up and down to organize them. You also have several other options, including whether to duplicate or extend the main display onto the secondary screen.

You can also select to make a screen your *main display* (I'll explain why you might want to do this shortly). Simply select the display icon that represents the one that you want to be your primary display and then check the box **Make this my main display**.

Several very useful new multimonitor tools in Windows include the ability to display the Start screen and the desktop on separate monitors simultaneously, though you can't stretch the Start screen across multiple displays.

■ **Tip** Many laptops now come with a new feature called Wi-Di (wireless display) or its companion technology Miracast, both of which allow you to project your screen to a compatible projector or screen that also supports the Wi-Di technology. If you use this feature, the wireless display may now appear on the Screen Resolution page. There are two ways to activate the wireless display: press Win+P (project to a second screen) or click *Project* in the Devices charm.

There are also some new tools for managing the taskbar in Windows 8.1. For example, on some screens there is no system tray shown; it is shown only on one screen. If you want to move the system tray to another screen, you can do this by right-clicking the taskbar on the target screen and from the context menu, click **Make this my main taskbar**.

You can also manage the taskbar in other ways when you have multiple monitors attached. By right-clicking the taskbar and selecting Properties, you see a dialog that shows additional multimonitor controls (see Figure 8-26).

Figure 8-26. *Managing the taskbar on multiple screens*

In taskbar properties, you can uncheck the box to automatically display the taskbar on all displays. If you do this, you see the taskbar only on your primary screen. Here are other options that you might find useful:

- Show taskbar buttons on **all taskbars** shows all your pinned buttons for both open and inactive programs on every screen.

- Show taskbar buttons on **main taskbar and taskbar where window is open** shows all the pinned application buttons on your main display, but only the buttons for open programs residing on the secondary display(s).

- Show taskbar buttons on **taskbar where window is open** shows all your pinned buttons, but open programs are indicated on the screen only where they are actually open.

You may want to show the taskbar only on a single display, however, because it enables you to use the whole of each secondary screen for programs without a (likely empty) taskbar getting in the way.

■ **Note**   You can take screen shots of multiple monitor displays in Windows 8.1 by pressing Win+PrntScrn (see Figure 8-27).

Figure 8-27. *Take multiple monitor screen shots in Windows 8.1*

Using Multimonitor Wallpapers in Windows 8.1

Windows 8.1 now supports widescreen desktop wallpapers that can be spanned across multiple displays. Windows 8.1 also allows you to set different wallpapers on different screens. You select your multiscreen wallpaper in the usual way: by right-clicking a blank space on the desktop and selecting Personalize, or by right-clicking an image and then selecting **Set as desktop wallpaper**.

It is in the Personalization options that you choose the new Span option. It sits in the Picture Position drop-down box (see Figure 8-28). Windows 8.1 now gives you the option to span your wallpaper across several different screens.

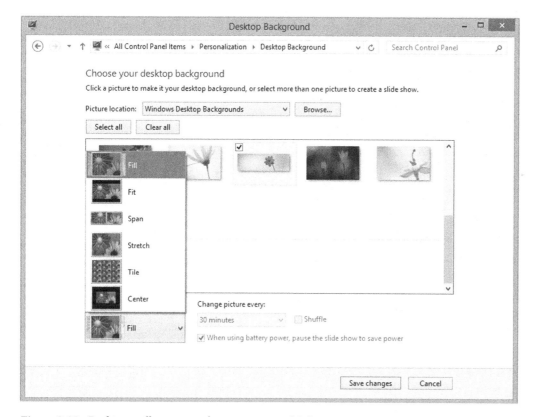

Figure 8-28. *Desktop wallpapers can be set to span multiple screens*

■ **Note** Spanned wallpapers really work only when all the attached screens are running at the same resolution. If they are not, you may see areas of black.

Creating a Windows To Go Drive Without Windows To Go

Windows To Go is a feature of Windows 8.1 Enterprise that allows system administrators to provide people with USB flash drives containing a copy of Windows 8.1 and required work software. You start any USB-bootable PC from this drive and be using your own copy of Windows 8.1 and your own software, anywhere, any time, and on any PC. I won't explain how to use Windows To Go here because as an enterprise feature, any Windows To Go drives you use are provided to you by your system administrator. However! It is still possible to create a Windows To Go drive yourself—after a fashion, anyway.

Creating a bootable USB flash drive in this way, although not the same as Windows To Go, also gets around the limitation that Windows To Go has of working with only a select few supported drives. This method works on any USB flash drive of 16 GB or more, though a larger capacity and fast USB 3.0 drive enables you to get the best experience.

■ **Note** Unlike when using Windows To Go, you need a spare and valid product key for the copy of Windows you want to install to the USB flash drive and also for any software you want to install onto it.

1. Plug your USB flash drive into the PC.

2. Press **Win+X** to open the Administration menu (you can also right-click the Start button on the desktop).

3. Open **Command Prompt (Admin)** and click through the UAC warning.

4. In the Command window, type **diskpart** and press Enter.

5. Type **list disk** and press Enter to display a list of available drives in your PC. Make a note of the number (0, 1, 2, etc.) for the USB flash drive which will be identifiable best through its capacity.

6. Type **select disk 2** where the number represents the disk number for the USB flash drive and press Enter.

7. Type **clean** and press Enter to prepare the drive for formatting.

8. Type **create partition primary** and press Enter.

9. Type **format fs=ntfs quick** to format the USB flash drive. This erases everything from it.

10. Type **active** and press Enter.

11. Type **assign letter=e** and press Enter. This assigns a drive letter to the USB flash drive. Make sure that the letter you want to use isn't already in use.

12. Type **exit** and press Enter.

13. Mount a Windows 8.1 ISO file on your computer by right-clicking it in File Explorer and clicking *mount* or inserting a Windows 8.1 installation DVD on your computer. Make a note of its drive letter; you will need it.

14. Back at the Command window, type **dism /apply-image /imagefile=f:\sources\install.
    wim /index:1 /applydir:e:** and press Enter, where *e* is the letter for your USB flash drive
    and *f* is the drive letter for your mounted ISO file or DVD. It copies the installation files
    from the Windows 8.1 installer to the USB flash drive.

15. Type **bcdboot.exe e:\windows /s e: /f ALL** and press Enter to set the USB flash drive as
    bootable.

You can now restart your PC and start it from the USB flash drive from the boot menu (usually F12 or Esc at
startup). The initial install can take some time, especially on slower USB 2.0 drives. It is also a good idea to run this
installation process, if possible, on the PC you will most often be using the drive with to ensure hardware driver
compatibility. This is because in my own tests the drive worked and identified itself as Windows To Go on two PCs
with the older BIOS motherboard software, but on two UEFI firmware machines it would start only on the PC for
which it has driver compatibility.

Once you have installed Windows (see Chapter 15 for full details on how to do this), you should then install on
the USB flash drive all the software you want to use on the flash drive because when you use it on other computers,
it identifies as Windows To Go and doesn't allow you to install software. Any and all software should be installed when
the USB flash drive is started on the same PC it was installed with.

Summary

Windows 8.1 contains volumes of productivity tools and ways to make the operating system, your programs, and
documents easier to use. The mobility features also help squeeze more life out of your laptop's battery.

There are other productivity tools that I discuss later in this book, including the new Hyper-V virtualization
software. As a guide to help you maximize your time with Windows 8.1, this chapter has covered what most people
need to know.

CHAPTER 9

■ ■ ■

Personalizing Your Windows Experience

Windows has always been one of the most customizable operating systems available, which is one of the things that has made it so popular over the years. Indeed, a whole industry of third-party products is well established with companies providing ever more imaginative ways for you to personalize your copy of Windows.

Windows Vista introduced the Aero Glass interface. Here was something that had a much nicer appearance than the Teletubby blue of XP or the battleship gray of Windows of old, so fewer people felt the need to customize their Windows installation.

When Aero Glass was further refined in Windows 7, changing the look of Windows to a metallic or movie-style theme, it became even less likely that people would personalize the desktop.

Windows 8.1 has the new Start screen and apparently fewer personalization options than the desktop. There are fewer wallpaper and color options, and a sea of colored squares and rectangles.

So how can you personalize your copy of Windows 8.1? What options exist to allow you to change the desktop in imaginative ways? What hacks and third-party software exist to change the look of Windows 8.1 by perhaps customizing the taskbar or even bringing back the Start menu?

You'll be pleased to hear that Windows 8.1 is just as customizable as its predecessors. In this chapter, I'll show you how to give it a look and feel that best suits you.

Personalizing Windows 8.1

Again, Microsoft doesn't really allow a great deal of personalization with the new user interface (UI). When you first install Windows 8.1, you're asked to choose a color for the background—but there are other ways you can make the Start screen your own.

The main personalization options for the Start screen are in the PC Settings' Personalize section. Here you have three tabs across the top of the page: Lock Screen, Start Screen, and Account Picture. In the following sections, you'll look at these primary options and other ways that you can personalize Windows 8.1.

Personalizing the Lock Screen

You personalize the lock screen in PC Settings by clicking *PC & Devices*, and the Lock Screen settings will be highlighted straight away. You might also see *Lock Screen* in the Top Settings section when you enter **PC Settings.** You can change the main background picture on the lock screen, but there's much more you can do with it besides, and I'll show you what else you can do shortly.

Figure 9-1 shows a selection of standard photographs you can choose from for your lock screen image. You can also click the Browse button to choose an image from your computer or network attached storage.

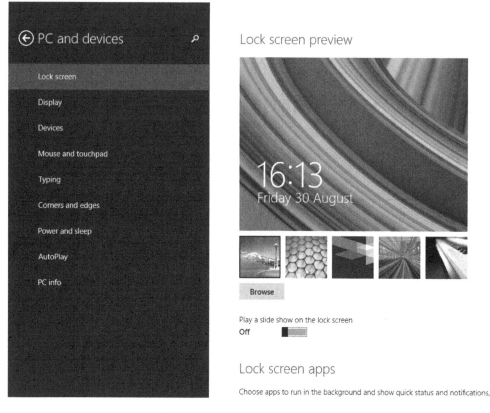

Figure 9-1. *Personalizing the Windows 8.1 lock screen*

You can also turn your lock screen into a picture slide show. To do this, activate the Slide Show switch and then you can add multiple picture folders to the slide show. The options here are quite comprehensive, allowing you to let Windows decide which pictures to display (sort of a shuffle mode), when the lock screen photo slide show appears, and whether it turns off. If you have a low-power PC such as a Surface, this option enables you to use the PC as a digital photo frame.

More interesting are the lock screen apps. You can choose from installed apps that are capable of displaying live information on the lock screen. Not every app is capable of this, but those that are greatly increase the functionality of the lock screen.

To examine just how useful this can be, let's have a look at earlier Windows versions and the way we use our computers. In every earlier version of Windows, the lock screen didn't provide any information except which user was logged on.

With Windows 8.1, the lock screen always provides the time and date. It can also show additional information, such as the number of unread e-mails, the number of instant messages you have received, the current weather, and much more. You can also have an alarm app shown on the lock screen, and Windows 8.1 ships with such an app. This makes low–power Windows RT devices suitable as alarm clocks as they will wake from sleep to sound your morning alarm.

■ **Tip**   At the bottom of the lock screen options is one to allow the camera to be used with a downward swipe on the screen (as opposed to the upward swipe to unlock the PC). This enables you to use the camera quickly without having to unlock the PC.

As I mentioned earlier, not every app is compatible with the lock screen, and some are capable of displaying only limited data. This includes the e-mail app because you don't necessarily want people who are walking past your computer to be able to read the names of the senders and the subjects of the e-mails you have waiting.

You can add up to seven apps to the lock screen in Windows 8.1. They always display in the bottom left of the screen under the date and time.

Some apps provide much more information, including the calendar. It is very useful for providing details about your afternoon schedule, seeing what your friends are doing on social networks, or informing others that you'll be at the dentist for the next hour—so that they can mess around with your computer.

You can only have one of the seven apps display additional information (this is optional). If you want to turn off this feature so that you see only the basic apps, click the Detailed Status app and select **Don't display detailed status on the lock screen**.

■ **Tip** You can remove any or all of the apps from the lock screen by clicking them in the Personalize page and selecting **Don't show quick status here** from the options.

Personalizing the Start Screen

There are a great many ways to personalize the Windows 8.1 Start screen. Changing the color and background picture are just two. Depending on how you use Windows, you may want to use the Start screen in one of several ways, so I'll show you how to configure it for different scenarios. Let's begin with the color and background.

To access the personalization options for the Start screen, open the Settings charm (see Figure 9-2). You see a personalization option near the top right of your screen; click it.

Figure 9-2. *You access the personalization options for the Start screen from the Settings charm*

The main options are to select a background image. In the top of the personalization panel are the background images from which you can choose; notice that the last of these is your desktop wallpaper. This option isn't quite as animated as some of the standard Start screen backgrounds, but it can make the transition between the Start screen and desktop less jarring. These images are specially designed to pan sideways as you scroll around a crowded Start screen, and some of them include animations. Beneath the images are the color options. As you change the background image and color options, a live display shows you exactly how the new image/color combination will look (see Figure 9-3).

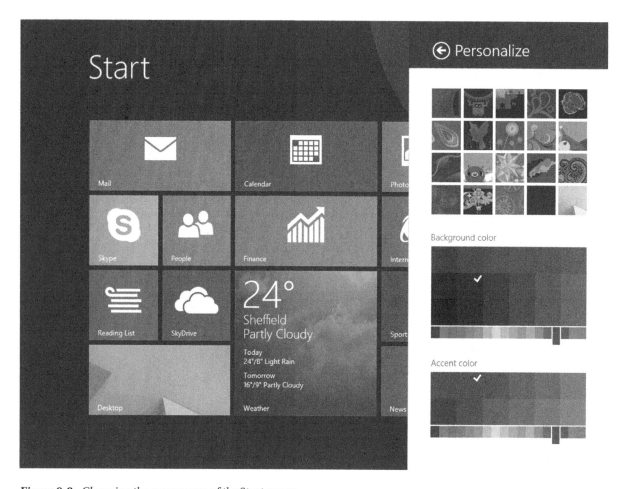

Figure 9-3. *Changing the appearance of the Start screen*

The Background color and Accent color options give you a tremendous amount of control over the way Windows 8.1 looks, and they can also make things very easy to see for people who need high-contrast color schemes. The accent color is the color that highlights items on your screen and in apps. There is no need to press an OK or Apply button—just clicking a background object and moving the color slider is enough to apply your selections.

So what are these mythical Start screen scenarios of which I spoke, and how can you personalize the Start screen to make it suitable for both app and hard-core desktop users? To examine this in greater detail, let's split it into specific scenarios. For this scenario, I assume that a person is happy to use both the apps and the Windows desktop, and to switch between them.

The Switcher

The Start screen offers compelling new ways to use Windows. If you have a touchscreen laptop or a professional-grade tablet, you might want to use both the apps and the desktop programs. This would make you a *switcher*, someone who wants to use both Windows 8.1 interface types equally.

The Start screen allows you to arrange your tiles and icons into groups that you can name. Tiles and icons can be moved around the Start screen by simply dragging and dropping. If you want to create a new group, move slowly when you are between two groups (or at the very left or right of the Start screen), and a vertical colored bar appears. If you drop an icon onto this bar, you create another group.

To name a group, you need to zoom out of the Start screen, either with a pinch-out touch gesture or by clicking the bottom right of the Start screen. In this zoomed-out view, you can right-click (or tap and drag downward) on a group; from the App bar, an option to name the group appears. Naming groups can prove handy, as seen in Figure 9-4.

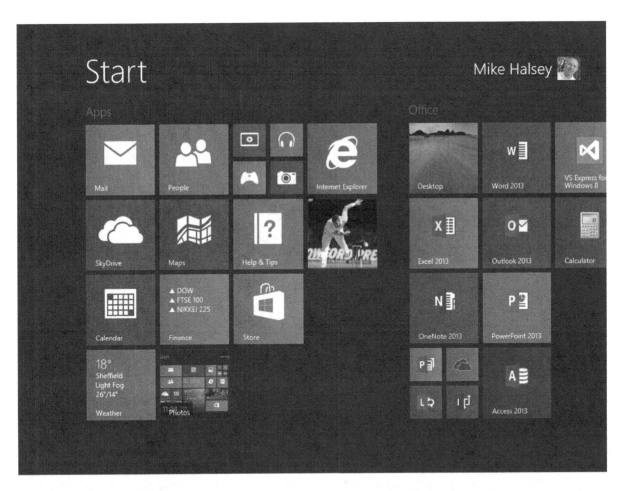

Figure 9-4. *The switcher's Start screen*

The Intensive Desktop User

Let's say you're not especially fussy about apps because you use your computer for work and you have enough desktop software anyway. In Windows 8.1, you can start the operating system directly to the desktop, and I will show you how to do this later in this chapter. However, the Start screen offers some advantages, not the least of which is being able to pin a great many more programs to it than you can to the taskbar and to group them more effectively and make them larger and easier to click. You can hide any app or program from the Start screen by right-clicking it or touching and holding it (you can select multiple apps this way, too). On the App bar, you will see an option to unpin the app from the Start screen.

■ **Tip**   Don't forget that you can bring up the All Apps view by clicking the small *down* arrow near the bottom left of the Start screen or touching and dragging upward anywhere in a blank space on the Start screen. From All Apps, you can repin apps and programs to the Start screen or just run software you don't use very often.

By unpinning your apps, you can turn the Start screen into a very organized alternative to the former Windows Start menu, with all your programs and software organized into groups (see Figure 9-5). You may also want to name these groups to make programs easier to find using the method I described for switchers.

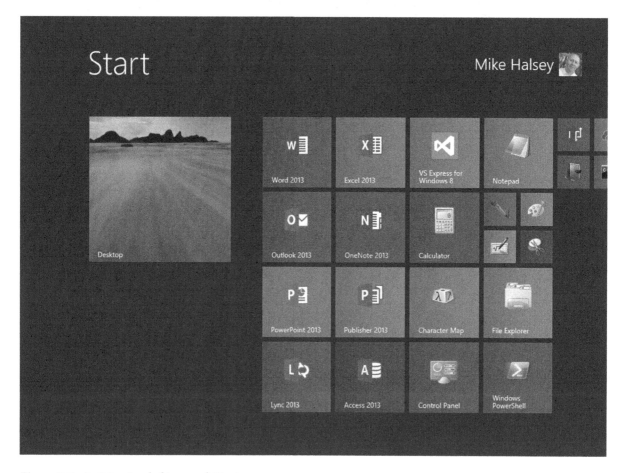

Figure 9-5. *An intensive desktop user's Start screen*

The Light Desktop User

Many people don't use very many desktop programs, so their Start screens might look quite barren and dark. If you are one of these people and you're not really interested in using apps, you can scale up everything on the Start screen to make things easier to see and click, and so that your desktop software icons take up more space.

To do this, you need to go into PC Settings and turn on one of the usability settings. Under the *PC's & Devices* and then *Display* controls, turn on the option to **Change the size of apps on displays that can support it** (see Figure 9-6). Note, however, that this option works only on screens with larger resolutions, such as full HD.

Figure 9-6. *Changing the size of tiles on the Start screen*

The advantage of this is that it affects only the Start screen, not your desktop, on which you scale up everything separately. As you can see from Figure 9-7, it has quite a profound effect on the Start screen.

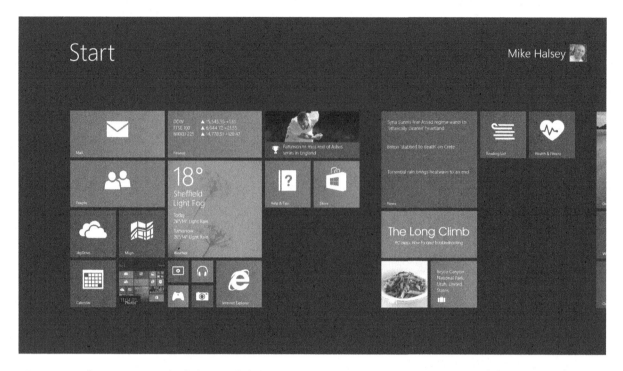

Figure 9-7. *The Start screen of a desktop-only light user*

The Work/Life Balance User

One of the most compelling things that the new Start screen offers people who use their computers for both home and work is a unique way to separate the two. By using the desktop for work and the Start screen for leisure time, you can completely ignore all your desktop programs, such as Microsoft Outlook and Microsoft Excel, and just use the app equivalents for play.

This makes sense in a lot of ways because apps are extremely different from their desktop equivalents—especially the Mail and Calendar apps, which can be set up for different e-mail accounts from your desktop e-mail software if you use an Exchange account for work.

You also have access to different photo viewers, video players, and music players. You might be surprised at how it feels as if you're using a completely different computer in the evening from what you're using during the day at work.

To set this up, you'll want to make the desktop tile the very last thing on your Start screen because you don't want to click it by accident when you're not at work (see Figure 9-8). It's fine at the far right of the Start screen anyway because it's extremely easy to remain working on the Windows 8.1 desktop all day without ever having to see the Start screen (something I will talk about later in this chapter).

Figure 9-8. *The work/life balance user*

The Widget Dashboard

There are those who really don't want to know about the new UI, don't want to use the apps, and aren't interested in the Start screen, but who are interested in some of the new features in Windows 8.1, such as Windows To Go or Hyper-V.

It's possible to turn the Start screen into a widget dashboard—reminiscent of the widget dashboard in Apple's OS X desktop operating system (see Figure 9-9).

Figure 9-9. *The widget dashboard*

To turn the Start screen into a widget dashboard, you first need to remove all the tiles and icons from the Start screen that you won't use or that can't give you live information. You can then scale up the Start screen using the display scaling feature that I described for light desktop users.

This will turn the Start screen into a dashboard with live widgets that can provide you with information on everything from e-mail and calendars, to foreign currency exchange rates, stock market figures, the local weather, and more.

■ **Tip**   Even if this type of user is unlikely to be much interested in apps, it's a good idea to look in the marketplace occasionally to see what new apps are available that have Live Tile displays.

Displaying Administrative Tools on the Start Screen

The Windows 8.1 Start screen doesn't show any of the administrative tools. Sure, you can access most of them by pressing Win+X to bring up a menu, but there is another way to display them on the Start screen.

To display the administrative tools on the Start screen, open the Settings charm from the Start screen (it doesn't work from the desktop). You see Tiles at the top right of the screen; click it.

You see an option to show the administrative tools (see Figure 9-10). Turning it on automatically displays a wide range of new icons to the All Apps view (see Figure 9-11), and if you don't want them all, you can still right-click individual tiles (and groups of tiles) to hide them. Here if you want any displayed on the Start screen you can select them. From the App bar, click Pin to Start.

Figure 9-10. *Displaying the administrative tools on the Start screen*

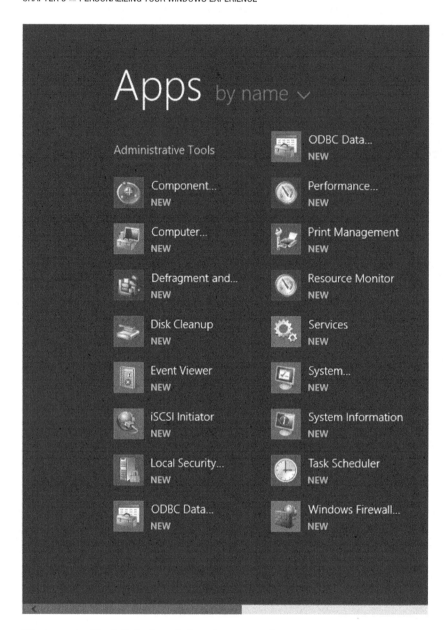

Figure 9-11. *The full display of administrative tools*

Managing Notification "Toasts"

Toasts in Windows 8.1 are the notifications that pop up in the top right of your screen. Depending how many apps you have installed, they can become intrusive, but there are several ways to manage them in Windows 8.1. The first method is to temporarily silence them. Open the Settings Charm and in the bottom right of the screen click the *Notifications* icon. Here you can hide toasts for 1, 3, or 8 hours.

If you want to silence some or all toasts completely, in PC Settings navigate to *Search & Apps* and then *Notifications*. Here you have several options (see Figure 9-12).

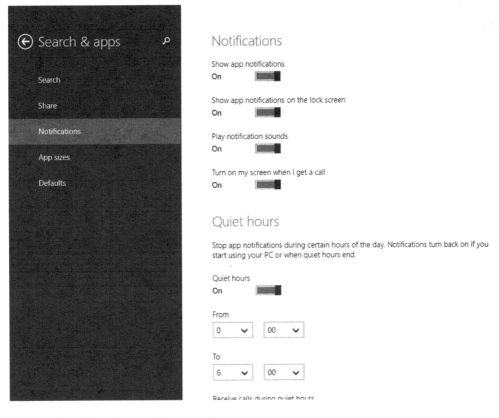

Figure 9-12. *There are several ways to silence toasts*

1. The first option, *Show app notifications*, allows you to silence all toasts altogether. If you don't want to do this, additional options exist such as turning off notification sounds and disabling notifications on the lock screen.

2. Perhaps of more interest is the Quiet Hours feature, which allows you to automatically silence all notifications between certain times of the day, such as at night if you use your PC as a bedside alarm or during work hours if you simply cannot afford to be disturbed (like I was when writing this book).

3. Below this is a list of all the apps you have installed; here you can disable toasts from individual apps one at a time, allowing you to very selectively decide from which apps you want to receive notifications.

That Syncing Feeling

Windows 8.1 includes a facility that can synchronize many of your settings, configuration options, and more besides. You need to be logged in to the PC with a Microsoft account for this to happen, and it's very controllable if you don't want settings to be synced (for example, to separate home and work PCs). You access these settings in PC Settings under *SkyDrive* and then *Sync Settings* (see Figure 9-13).

Figure 9-13. *You can syncronize lots of settings in Windows 8.1*

The different settings type that can be synced are as follows:

- **Personalization**, which are your settings for the look and feel of both the Start screen and the desktop, including the locations of live tiles—though not desktop and taskbar icons.

- **App settings**, which are the specific configuration options you have set for apps.

- **Other settings** including your Internet Explorer favorites and open tabs (more on this shortly), your passwords, ease of access, and other settings.

Each one can be individually turned on and off so you can, for example, choose not to synchronize your Start screen tiles layout between your Surface tablet, which has a low resolution screen and a three-row tile layout, and your new 4 KB display with considerably more rows of tiles.

Syncing Internet Explorer Tabs

I mentioned that you can synchronize your web browser tabs between different Windows 8.1 computers, but in use you might not notice this working because when you return to a PC, the tabs will be just as you left them and won't have changed. When you open the address bar and tabs view in Internet Explorer, you see the word *Tabs* on the left of your screen. Clicking it displays a drop-down menu of all your Windows 8.1 PCs and you can select another PC to work with the tabs from that PC (see Figure 9-14).

Figure 9-14. You can access browser tabs from other PCs

Personalizing the Windows 8.1 Desktop

If you've been using Windows 7, you're already familiar with the Windows 8.1 desktop personalization options because little has changed. The Start button is gone, but I'll talk about alternatives later in this chapter. Everything else is accessed in the same way.

The main desktop personalization options are accessed by right-clicking (or touching and holding) any empty space on the desktop and then selecting Personalize from the options that appear.

There have been a few changes, including the themes that change the color of your windows to complement your desktop wallpaper.

Personalizing the Desktop Wallpaper

As with Windows 7, you can choose themes with desktop backgrounds. You can also manually select several backgrounds and have Windows rotate them at a set frequency. Windows 8.1 can also change the color of the surrounding Windows furniture to match.

There are two ways to do this. The easiest way is to go to the Personalization page and click a theme that is overlaid by a color swatch (see Figure 9-15). A foldout card shows a range of colors overlaid onto the background image(s) of the theme.

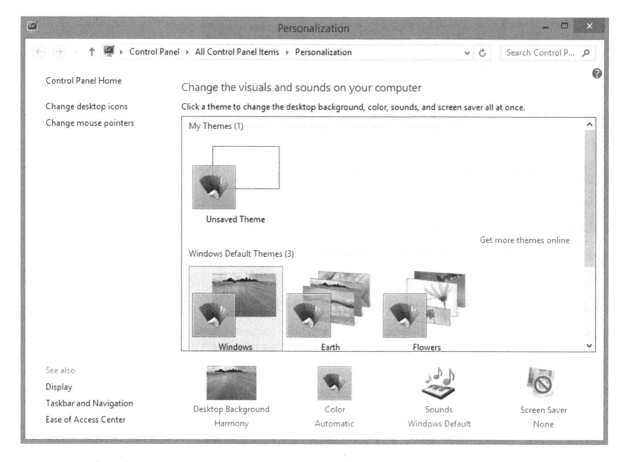

Figure 9-15. *The desktop Personalization options*

I'll come back to this automatic color-changer shortly, but first let's have a look at changing the background image.

You can change the desktop wallpaper by clicking Desktop Background at the bottom of the Personalization page. This brings up a new page that has several different elements to it.

In the main part of the window are the currently available wallpapers. By default, you see all the wallpapers that ship as standard with Windows 8.1, including those that are for dual-screen setups.

In the Picture Location section, you can choose from several commonly or recently used picture locations. You can also click the Browse button to search for any picture (or pictures) on your computer to use as wallpapers.

At the bottom of the window is an option that changes how the wallpaper fills your screen (see Figure 9-16). The default option is to have the wallpaper fill the screen so that you don't have any areas of black. There are other options to consider, however, especially if you are using a 4:3 ratio screen.

Figure 9-16. *Changing the desktop wallpaper*

If you have multiple wallpapers selected, you can decide how often you want Windows 8.1 to change the desktop wallpaper. The options range from every ten seconds to once per day. You can check the Change picture every: box to randomize the order in which they appear.

■ **Tip** Graphics can adversely affect your battery if you are using a laptop or other portable device. If you have your desktop wallpaper set to change regularly, there is an option at the bottom of the Desktop Background screen to pause the changing of the desktop when running on battery power.

Personalizing the Window Color

I mentioned that Windows 8.1 can automatically change the color of the windows on your desktop to complement the color of your desktop wallpaper. Clicking Window Color and Appearance on the Personalization page displays these options.

The Window Color and Appearance page features a color swatch and cards in various colors. This signifies that the window color will be changed and managed automatically by Windows 8.1.

Elsewhere in these options are 15 other window colors, each of which can be modified by sliding the color intensity slider. If you can't find the color you want (perhaps you are after a rich brown, for example), you can click **Show color mixer** to create your own custom color by setting hue, saturation, and brightness levels (see Figure 9-17).

Figure 9-17. *Changing the window color*

Personalizing Sounds in Windows 8.1

It's much less common for people to personalize the sounds in Windows. There are modifications you might like to make, however, especially if you've never been a fan of the critical-error "*donk!*" sound, or if you want to turn the Windows startup sound on or off.

You can most easily access the sounds in Windows 8.1 by right-clicking the volume icon on the far right of the desktop taskbar and selecting Sounds from the options. You can also go to the Personalization page to display the Sound dialog (see Figure 9-18).

Figure 9-18. *Changing the sound options*

You can easily and quickly turn off all Windows sounds by selecting No Sounds from the Sound Scheme drop-down list or you can modify any individual Windows sound in the list.

You can even use your own sounds in place of the standard sounds any type of playable sound file can be used, including MP3s. After you choose your sounds and create your own customized sound scheme, click the Save As button. You can share your personalized sound with friends and family as well as keep a copy as a backup.

Choosing a Screen Saver

The screen saver options are last on the Personalization page. Unlike earlier versions of Windows, Windows 8.1 does not use a screen saver as the default setting, but instead turns off the display after ten minutes (see Figure 9-19) because screen savers are necessary only for older CRT monitors (a fuller explanation follows).

Figure 9-19. *Choosing a screen saver*

Some screen savers come with additional settings. You can preview the screen saver before turning it on by clicking the Preview button.

There is also an option to control the amount of time the computer is inactive (i.e., not using the keyboard, mouse, or touchscreen) before the screen saver switches on.

By default, Windows 8.1 returns you to the desktop when you return to the PC, but for extra security, you can check the option to instead return you to the logon screen.

■ **Note** Do you need a screen saver? Screen savers are necessary for older cathode ray tube (CRT) monitors, in which a beam of electrons is fired at a phosphor layer inside the screen glass to display a picture. If a single electron beam fires for too long at the same patch of phosphor, the image could end up physically burned into the phosphor layer—an effect called *phosphor burn in*. Modern flat-panel monitors do not suffer from this because they use individual pixel lights instead of an electron gun, so Windows 8.1 is set by default to simply turn off the screen instead. This saves a considerable amount of power over the lifetime of your computer.

Changing the Desktop Icons

In the top left of the Personalization page is the option to Change desktop icons. To be honest, I love the argument about whether people have icons on their desktop or not. Many people like a desktop with icons and folders scattered over it, whereas other people, including myself, like a clean desktop. Frankly, this is why some of the arguments surrounding the new Start screen have been so intense.

So let me be fair here. The Desktop Icon Settings dialog is where you can both turn on *and* off desktop icons in Windows 8.1. You can turn on and off the icons for the computer, your user folder, your network, the recycle bin, and the Control Panel (see Figure 9-20).

Figure 9-20. *Changing the desktop icons*

You can also restore default icons or prevent desktop themes from automatically changing the icons to custom icons.

Changing the Mouse Pointer

Also in the Personalization page is the option to Change mouse pointers, which opens the Mouse Properties dialog. The mouse properties options, including those for mouse pointers (see Figure 9-21), are much more useful than you might think. I want to look at each tab in this window to explain what it does.

Figure 9-21. *Changing the mouse options*

- **Buttons tab:** Used for left-handed people to switch the left and right mouse buttons. It also swaps the buttons on a laptop trackpad. You can slow down or speed up the double-click speed, which is extremely useful for people who can't click as quickly. ClickLock allows you to avoid having to hold down the mouse button to drag items around the screen. These last two features are excellent for people with weaker motor skills.

- **Pointers tab:** Includes options to change the mouse pointer to a variety of high-visibility options, which is excellent for people who have difficulty seeing or reading the computer screen. There is more information about this in Chapter 10, in which I show you how to change the mouse and keyboard options in detail.

- **Pointer options:** Allow you to turn on useful features such as mouse trail so that you can see the mouse moving across the screen more easily. You can also display the position of the mouse by pressing the Ctrl key on your keyboard. You can slow down the mouse speed (or speed it up for gaming). You also set the mouse to automatically snap to the closest button. This is a great feature for those with weaker motor skills.

- **Wheel tab:** Contains the vertical and (if your mouse supports it) horizontal scrolling options for Windows 8.1. If you do not have a wheel on your mouse, you might not see this tab.

- **Hardware tab:** Allows you to view information on the hardware driver and driver settings for your mouse.

■ **Tip** If you find Windows 8.1 difficult to use because of challenges with eyesight or motor skills, changing your mouse settings can help make Windows 8.1 more accessible and usable.

Personalizing the Taskbar

I would imagine your biggest question about the taskbar is how to get the Start menu back. Okay, I'll get to that, but I want to talk about other ways to personalize the taskbar first.

Access the taskbar personalization options (see Figure 9-22) by right-clicking the taskbar and selecting Properties from the options.

Figure 9-22. *The Taskbar and Navigation properties dialog*

The options allow you to automatically hide the taskbar so that you can take full advantage of your screen when running programs. You can also lock the taskbar to prevent toolbars (if you use any) from being moved around, and you can change how icons appear on the taskbar.

The Navigation tab includes options for changing the Windows 8.1 startup behavior and more. I will explain these features later in this chapter.

■ **Tip**   Aero Peek was a feature in Windows 7 that would hide all your windows when you moved your mouse to the bottom right of your desktop. This feature is turned off by default in Windows 8.1, but you can turn it back on in the Taskbar and Navigation properties dialog.

Tweaking the Taskbar

The three views available of the taskbar are useful, but I've always felt there was something missing—the ability to have separate buttons for running instances of a program without the text labeling (see Figures 9-23 and 9-24). It's possible to add this feature, however, with a simple registry change.

Figure 9-23. *Combining buttons into stacks (with labels hidden)*

Figure 9-24. *Never combining buttons*

One thing to note is that whenever you make a change to the Windows registry, you should create a backup copy of the registry first. You can do this in the registry (from the File menu) by clicking the Export option. If a problem occurs, you can later restore this backup by clicking Import from the File menu in the Registry Editor.

1. Right-click the taskbar and select Properties.

2. In the pane that appears, make sure the Taskbar buttons option is set to **Never combine** and then click OK.

3. Open the Registry Editor by searching for **regedit** at the Start screen.

4. Navigate to Computer ➤ HKEY_CURRENT_USER Control Panel ➤ Desktop ➤ WindowMetrics (see Figure 9-25).

Figure 9-25. *Personalizing the taskbar using the Registry Editor*

5. Right-click in the right pane. From the options that appear, click New.

6. Click *String Value.*

7. Name the string value **MinWidth** and press Enter.

8. Right-click MinWidth. From the options, select Modify.

9. Change the value data to **54** and press OK.

10. Close the Registry Editor.

You should restart the computer. Your taskbar buttons are now separated for different instances of a program, and the text labels are gone.

Personalizing Jump Lists

If you click the Jump Lists tab in the Taskbar and Navigation properties dialog, you can change the number of recent items that appear in Jump Lists for taskbar buttons. This is useful if you share your computer (and the same user account) with others and you want your file activity to remain private.

Personalizing the System Tray

By default, Windows 8.1 hides all your system tray icons and their notifications. Some people want to be able to see the tray icons, however, and you can turn them on or further hide icons. Click the small white up arrow to open the system tray. Click Customize (you can also click Notification Area Icons in the Control Panel). You can also right-click near the system tray or on the clock and select **Customize notification icons** from the options.

In the Notification Area Icons window (see Figure 9-26), you can change the options for all the installed software for which a system tray icon already appears. The options are these:

- Show icon and notification

- Hide icon and notifications

- Only show notifications

Figure 9-26. *Customizing the system tray*

Completely hiding icons and notifications is useful if you find a particular piece of software annoying, but showing icons and notifications makes the system tray more like the one in Windows XP (if you like that sort of thing).

Perhaps you really want to minimize things on the desktop and don't want to even see the standard notification icons or the clock. You can turn these icons off completely by right-clicking in the notifications area or on the clock and selecting Properties from the options. The System Icons screen shown in Figure 9-27 appears.

Figure 9-27. *Turning the system icons on or off*

Bear in mind, however, that if you turn off the icon for the Action Center, you won't be alerted when security issues arise. Also, turning off the laptop battery indicator could leave you running low and needing a recharge without realizing it.

■ **Tip** You can rearrange the order icons appear in the system tray by simply dragging and dropping them.

Setting the Date and Time

In the Date and Time dialog, you can quickly change the time and date on your computer, use time-syncing services on the Internet to automatically keep your time and date correct, change your time zone, and control automatic adjustment for daylight saving time (see Figure 9-28). You can also get to the Date and Time dialog by right-clicking the clock on the taskbar.

Figure 9-28. *Changing the date and time*

You also have the ability to add extra clocks to Windows! They appear when you click the date and time on the Windows taskbar. You can add up to two for different time zones, each with a custom name (see Figure 9-29).

Figure 9-29. *Adding clocks to Windows 8.1*

Enabling Recycle Bin Warnings

When you delete a file in Windows 8.1 you don't get the "do you *really* want to delete this file" warning of Windows versions of old. This is because with the recycle bin combined with the File History feature (which I shall show you how to use in Chapter 12), it's very easy to recover accidentally deleted files. You can turn this feature back on if you want to, though, by *right-clicking* the recycle bin icon on your desktop and selecting *Properties* from the menu that appears.

The Recycle Bin Properties panel includes some simple controls, including being able to bypass the recycle bin altogether and just permanently delete everything. At the bottom of this dialog (see Figure 9-30) is a check box for *Display delete confirmation dialog*; you can turn this back on if you want these warnings re-enabled.

Figure 9-30. *You can re-enable recycle bin warnings*

Start Windows 8.1 Directly to the Desktop

Earlier in this chapter, I wrote about how you can modify the taskbar, unless you've skipped all of the book so far and turned directly to this page in excitement, and something that's changed from the first release of Windows 8.1 is the addition in the Taskbar properties of a *Navigation* tab. If you're a serious desktop user, there are controls in here aplenty that are really very clever and powerful.

You access these controls by right-clicking on the taskbar and then clicking *Properties* from the menu that appears. When the Taskbar and Navigation properties panel pops up on your screen, click the *Navigation* tab quickly because it's exciting!

The controls you have under the Navigation tab, see Figure 9-31, are the following:

- **Corner Navigation** includes
  - A control for turning off the charms when you move your mouse to the top-right corner of your screen (you need to open them with the Win+C control instead)
  - The ability to switch between running apps when you click the top-left corner of your screen
  - Replacing the Command Prompt in the Win+X menu with Windows PowerShell

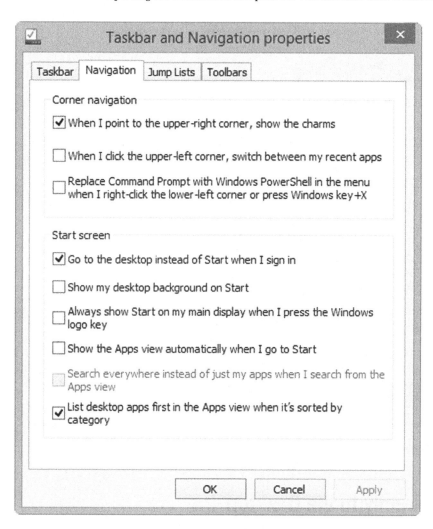

Figure 9-31. *You can now start Windows 8.1 directly to the desktop*

■ **Tip**   Windows PowerShell is a powerful scripting language and an excellent alternative to the old DOS command language if you want to learn it. Although people have become used to using DOS over the last 30 years, you can replace the Command Prompt link in the Win+X menu with PowerShell.

- The **Start screen** navigation includes the following:

  - **Boot to the desktop!** If you want your PC to always start directly to the desktop, check the *Go to the desktop* box.

  - **Show my desktop background on Start** is another way to force that Start screen to use the desktop wallpaper, in addition to the method in the Personalization options I mentioned at the beginning of this chapter

  - If you are using multiple monitors the **Always show Start on my main display when I press the Windows logo key** if checked will force the Start screen to display on the screen with the currently selected window, instead of the default behavior which is the primary display.

  - **Show the Apps view automatically when I go to Start** forces the Start button and Windows key to take you to the All Apps view by default. You can swipe downward from this view to display the Start screen if you want it.

  - **Search everywhere instead of just my apps** appears if you check the *Show the apps view automatically*. This changes the behavior of the Search charm on the All Apps view to match that of the Start screen

  - **List desktop apps first in the apps view when it's sorted by category** displays your desktop programs *before* your apps in the All Apps view. To enable this, you also need to change how the All Apps view is organized and you can do this by clicking the *by name* link in the top left of the screen, see Figure 9-32.

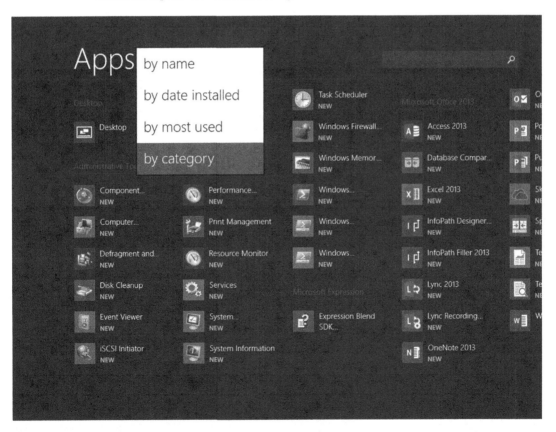

Figure 9-32. *You can change how the All Apps view displays programs and apps*

Changing the Default File Explorer View

If you activate the Libraries in Windows 8.1 (see Chapter 5 for how to do this), opening File Explorer always then takes you to your Libraries. But what if you don't want this and instead want File Explorer to default to the new This PC view?

You can do this by creating a new shortcut for File Explorer on the Windows 8.1 taskbar:

1. Right-click in a blank space on the desktop and from the context menu that appears, click *New* and then click *Shortcut*.

2. In the *Type location of the item* box to **%SystemRoot%\explorer.exe /e,::{20D04FE0-3AEA-1069-A2D8-08002B30309D}** and click Next.

3. Name the shortcut **This PC** and press Enter.

4. Drag the shortcut from your desktop onto the taskbar to pin it there.

5. Delete the shortcut from your desktop (if you want to). You can then optionally unpin the original File Explorer icon.

You can also change this target to anything you like; for example, you can put a folder location in there instead. If you click the icon on the far left of the address bar, the text in the address bar changes to display the current folder location. It can be copied and pasted into the Target box (see Figure 9-33).

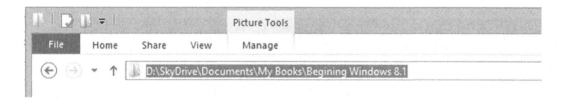

Figure 9-33. *Copying the current folder location from the address bar*

Changing and Customizing Your Region Settings

The Region settings in both PC Settings (available in the *Time & Language* section) and the Control Panel allow you to do much more than tell Windows the country in which you are located. You can customize the time, date, and numerical systems in Windows so that, for example, you can change the digit grouping symbol from a Western comma (,) to an Arabic point (.) or change the negative number format from a minus sign (–) to having the digit appearing in parentheses (). You can control these options by clicking the Additional Settings button.

Perhaps of more use is the ability to change the default date and time display options. These are two options I always change. I set the time to h:mm tt (single-digit hour:minutes seconds) and make the AM and PM labels lowercase text.

Additionally, you can display the full day of the week by adding dddd to the date options or the first three letters of the day of the week (see Figures 9-34 and 9-35).

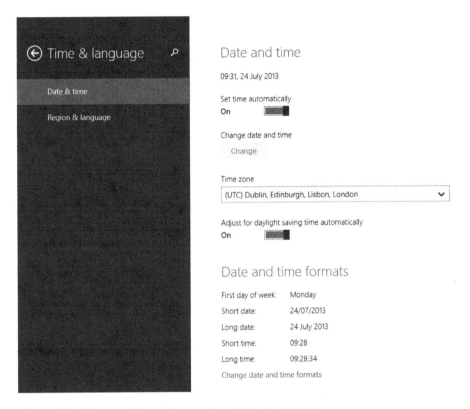

Figure 9-34. You can change some region settings in PC Settings

Figure 9-35. *Customizing region options*

Working with Multiple Languages in Windows 8.1

If people who speak different languages use your computer, or if you are an interpreter or language student, you can add additional languages to Windows 8.1 by opening Time & Language in PC Settings and then clicking the Region *and* Language options, or by clicking Language from the Control Panel (see Figures 9-36 and 9-37). You can click Add a Language on the main Language page to add languages to Windows, as well as change other regional settings, such as number and date formats, which may be applicable to a certain language. The options link appears when you select a language.

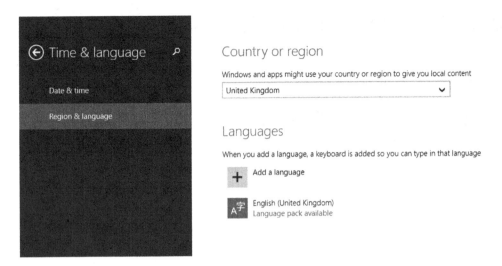

Figure 9-36. You can manage languages in Windows 8.1 from PC Settings

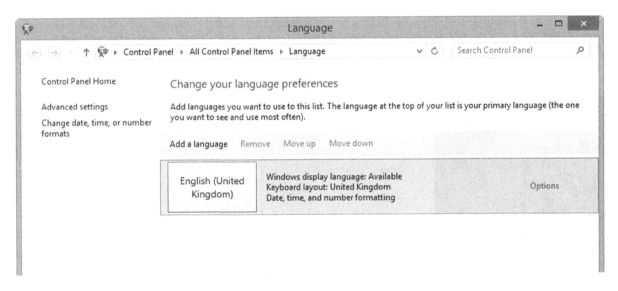

Figure 9-37. Adding languages to Windows 8.1

If you click Advanced Settings in the left pane of the main Language page, you find additional options, including the option to turn on or off the *language bar*. This helpful tool, which can be docked to the taskbar, enables you to quickly and easily swap between installed languages on your computer.

■ **Tip**   Clicking the options for a language allows you to change the handwriting recognition options from freehand to single characters. This is useful for pictographic languages such as Chinese.

Personalizing the Power Management Options

It doesn't matter if you're using a laptop, ultrabook, tablet, or even a powerful desktop computer, you still probably want to customize the power options for your Windows 8.1 computer. So why would desktop users want or need to change the default power settings? After all, the default settings of turning off the display after 10 minutes and putting the computer to sleep after 30 minutes must be pretty perfect, right?

Well, by default, when Windows 8.1 turns off the display, touching the keyboard or mouse returns you to the workspace you were at when you left the computer. Instead, you might want Windows 8.1 to return to the logon screen. This is especially useful if you are using your computer for work or perhaps don't want other people easily seeing your e-mail correspondence or your social networking (especially if they're mischievous like *my* friends are).

When you put your computer to sleep, it also keeps drawing power. Many people say that the average power draw for a Windows 8.1 PC in sleep is tiny. Multiply that by millions of machines, however, and you quickly see how this can balloon into a very considerable sum. When Windows 8.1 is capable of booting to the logon screen from a cold start in just 10 seconds, do we still need sleep at all?

In this section, I want to look at the power options thoroughly and holistically, so that you can select the best options for you.

Changing the Power Plan

You can access the main power settings by clicking Power Options in the Control Panel. You get quick and easy access to the power plans, which are preconfigured options for your screen, shut down, sleep, and more; as well as the default plans added by PC manufacturers. Basic power plan options are available in PC Settings in the *PC & Devices* section and then by clicking *Power & Sleep* (see Figure 9-38).

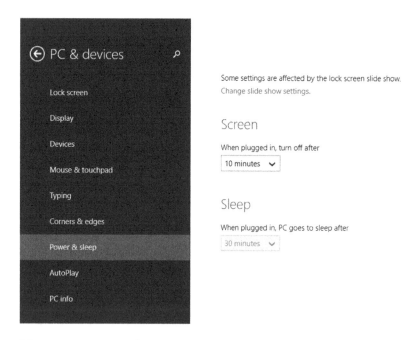

Figure 9-38. *You can change some power settings in PC Settings*

Figure 9-39 shows a Dell laptop—on which this book was written—that has two default power plans; three is the normal standard for Windows. Your laptop or tablet may come with more, however, because hardware manufacturers may add their own power plans.

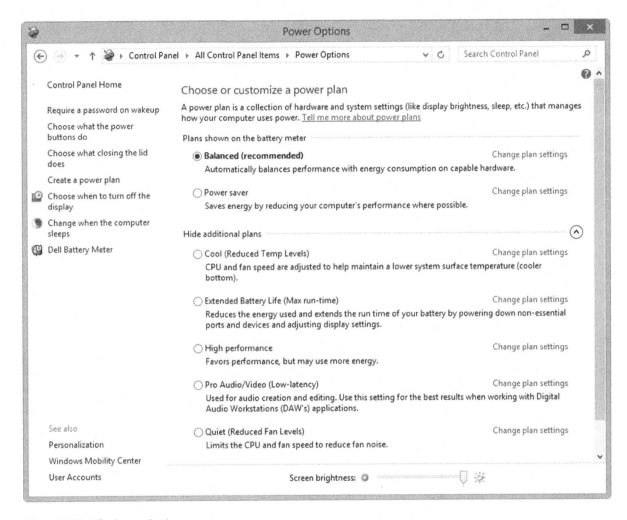

Figure 9-39. *The Power Options page*

The following are the default power plans:

- **Balanced:** The computer balances performance with energy consumption.

- **Power Saver:** Energy consumption is given top priority to extend battery life.

- **High Performance:** Battery life isn't an issue and you want the maximum performance from your PC (shown as an optional setting in the figure).

You may have additional power plans, such as Quiet or Cool. In the pane on the left of the page is the option to create your own power plan. It displays a wizard from which you can base your plan on one of the three default plans, but you can also choose from four more options: dimming or turning off the display, putting the computer to sleep, and the overall screen brightness.

You can choose a plan by clicking it. Each one can be modified by clicking **Change plan settings**.

Controlling the Power Button, Power Options, and Password Wakeup

You might want more control over the power options. Click **Require a password on wakeup** to take you to the System Settings screen (see Figure 9-40).

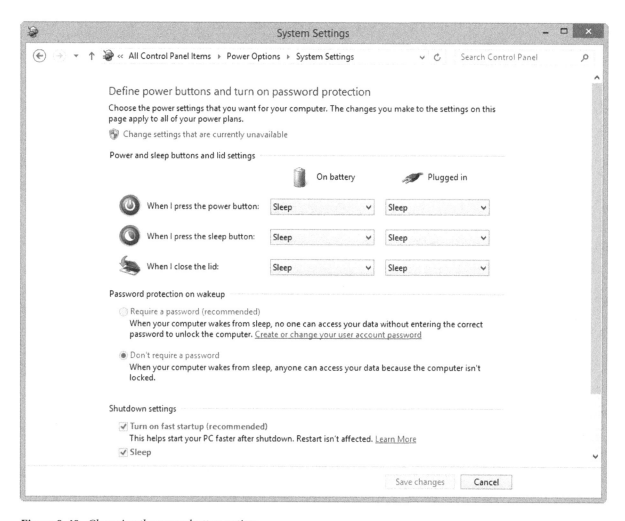

Figure 9-40. *Changing the power button options*

You can determine what the physical power and sleep (if you have one) buttons on your PC's case and keyboard do, as well as any actions that happen when you close the laptop lid. For example, if you set the close-the-lid action to Sleep, but the battery dies because you thought the computer was actually turned off, you will lose unsaved work.

On the main Power Options page, you can also click **Choose when to turn off the display** or **Choose when the computer sleeps** in the left pane and you are shown the Edit Plan Settings options, which control the amount of time the computer remains idle before turning off the screen or putting the computer to sleep (see Figure 9-41). Note that if you have a desktop computer that does not have a battery, you will see a slightly different screen.

Figure 9-41. *Changing the display and sleep options*

If the computer is sleeping and Windows detects that the battery is very low, it will change to hibernate mode, in which the contents of memory are saved to the disc. This can prevent unsaved work from being lost, but it is always wise to check that your work is saved before you step away from your computer.

Alternatively, if you use your laptop with an external keyboard, mouse, and monitor, you may not want it to sleep when you close the lid. You can change this setting. I do not personally recommend that you use a laptop with the lid closed, however, because this can cause some models to overheat.

■ **Caution**   Remember that if you set a PC to shut down instead of sleep, you lose any work that hasn't been saved.

Many of the options on this screen are grayed-out and you cannot change them. To change these options, click **Change settings that are currently unavailable** at the top of the screen. Some of the additional options can be extremely useful:

- **[Don't] Require a password** has Windows 8.1 return automatically to the logon screen after returning from sleep or hibernation, or if the screen saver is on or the screen is turned off. If you share your computer or keep it in a room shared by other people, you might want to leave this setting turned on. But if the computer is not physically accessible to others, you may find this setting unnecessary.

- **The shutdown settings** allow you to turn on and off the sleep and hibernate functions on your computer. It also permits you to turn off the new Fast Startup feature of Windows 8.1, which allows Windows 8.1 to boot to the lock screen from a cold start in just 10 seconds. It does so by hibernating the kernel (the core OS) so that it doesn't have to load everything from scratch; it just opens the hibernation file and reads it back into memory.

    Some computers, especially older machines, have trouble with sleep and/or hibernation, and some don't support these features at all. If you are having trouble getting Windows to sleep, hibernate, or start quickly, you can turn off these settings.

■ **Tip** There was a proof-of-concept attack on Microsoft's BitLocker security system a few years ago, when it was proven that the encryption key could be retrieved from a hibernating (or sleeping) computer because Windows keeps the key in memory while you are working. This key is readable from a hacked computer in sleep or from an extracted hibernation file. It can be used to gain access to BitLocker-encrypted computers. At the time of writing, there is no word on whether this vulnerability has been fixed with Windows 8.1. So it is best to assume that it still exists.

You can also turn off the display of your logon picture on the lock screen. This is most useful if you have chosen a really embarrassing photo of yourself.

Controlling Sleep and Hibernation

You can choose the sleep and hibernation options for your computer by clicking either **Choose when to turn off the display** or **Change when the computer sleeps** on the Power Options page. You probably have seen these options available in other sections of Power Options; they remain the same.

What is the difference between sleep and hibernation? When you put your computer to *sleep*, it retains its memory by drawing a very small electric charge. This means that when you turn the computer back on, you are up and running extremely quickly at exactly the point at which you put the computer to sleep because nothing needs to be read into memory. It's already there.

Hibernation writes the contents of memory to a file on the hard disk. This means the computer can be shut down without requiring any power to keep the memory live, but it won't restart quite as quickly.

■ **Tip** You can restore the Hibernate command to the main power menu in Windows 8.1 by clicking *Change what the power buttons do* at the main Power Options screen and then clicking *Change settings that are currently unavailable*. At the bottom of the screen, you now see a Shutdown Settings section, and *Hibernate* now displays as an option that can be checked. Doing this restores the Hibernate function to the main PC shutdown controls and also to the Win+X menu.

Changing the Advanced Power Settings

When you are viewing the sleep options, you see the option to **Change the advanced power settings**. Here you have many more options (click **Change settings that are currently unavailable** to edit them all). Figure 9-42 shows the advanced power settings.

Figure 9-42. *Changing the advanced power settings*

I want to talk about some of these settings and look at how they can be useful.

- **Hard disk:** Why might you want to turn off the hard disk? Hard disks unnecessarily consume a lot of energy when not in use. Perhaps you have multiple hard disks on your computer, and most of the time they are used only for file storage (perhaps files you don't often access) or for backups. Setting Windows 8.1 to turn off the hard disks on drives you are not using reduces overall power consumption on your computer. On any hard disk in use, the power remains. Remember that when you want to access a mechanical hard disk that is powered down, there is a slight delay as the disc spins up.

■ **Tip** If you want to set any timings in the advanced power settings to Never, change the default time to 0 (zero).

- **Wireless Adapter Settings:** Wi-Fi and mobile broadband are a huge power drain for a laptop, ultrabook, or tablet because they turn your computer into a radio transmitter and receiver. If you change the default setting for locations in which you have a strong signal, you still get a good signal, which means that the computer uses less electricity to power the Wi-Fi system.

- **Sleep:** You can turn sleep and hibernate off completely if they cause problems on your computer.

- **USB Settings:** If your computer is connected to USB devices that draw power from the PC—perhaps an external hard disk or optical drive—you can enable a setting that will cut power to the devices when they are not in use. This can dramatically extend the life of a portable computer such as an ultrabook.

- **Display:** While the main power options allow you to choose when to dim your computer's display to save power, these options give you finer control over exactly how much the display dims and how bright it is when plugged in. If your computer comes with a built-in light-meter, you can turn on the Adaptive Brightness, which automatically changes the brightness to match the available lighting.

- **Battery:** The battery options allow you to control what Windows 8.1 sees as low and critical battery levels. If you know that your battery is generally excellent and you don't want to be nagged, you could lower the low battery alert by 10 percent. If you often step away from your computer while it is running on batteries, however, you might want to set Windows 8.1 to automatically hibernate when the battery runs low.

Maximizing Battery Life on Mobile Devices

If you are using a laptop, ultrabook, or tablet on the go and want to maximize your battery life, there are certain things you can do that will help.

1. Dim your screen brightness as much as you can. The less power needed to display an image, the longer your battery will last. Your screen is a real power hog.

2. Turn off your backlit keyboard (if you have one) because this will save power as well.

3. Set the screen to turn off after two minutes of inactivity and perhaps set the computer to sleep after 10 minutes.

4. Turn off your Wi-Fi, cellular (3G/4G/LTE) or Bluetooth connections if they're not needed.

On a laptop or tablet, you might want to set the screen to turn off after only a couple of minutes—until you touch the screen, keyboard, or mouse to wake it up. The screen on a mobile device is the most power-hungry component. Having the screen switch off when not in use greatly extends battery life.

You might also want to turn off features such as 3G and GPS, both of which consume power through broadcasting and receiving radio signals.

Also, have Windows 8.1 cut power to any attached USB devices that can also drain the battery on your computer.

Adding Power Buttons to the Start Screen and Taskbar

Although the main Shut down, Restart, and Sleep options for Windows 8.1 might be hidden away in the Settings charm, it's still possible to add them to the Start screen and the taskbar.

1. Right-click a blank space on the desktop and from the options that appear, click New ➤ Shortcut (see Figure 9-43).

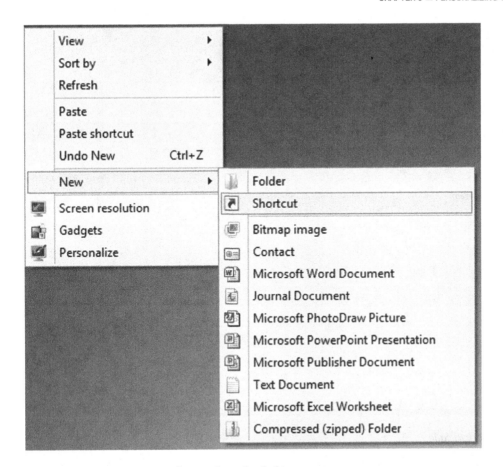

Figure 9-43. *Creating a new shortcut from the desktop*

2. In the window that appears, type **shutdown.exe –s –t 00** and then click Next
(see Figure 9-44).

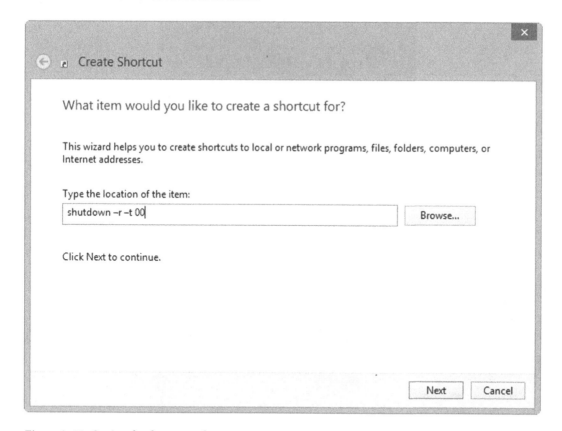

Figure 9-44. *Setting the shortcut code*

■ **Tip**   To create a Restart shortcut, type **shutdown –r –t 00**. To create a Sleep shortcut, type **rundll32.exe powrProf.
dll,SetSuspendState 0,1,0**. To create a Hibernate shortcut, type **rundll32.exe powrProf.dll,SetSuspendState**. To create
a Lock Computer shortcut, type **rundll32.exe powrProf.dll,LockWorkStation**.

To enable sleep from a RUNDLL32 command, you also need to disable hibernation on the computer. To do this, open
a Command Prompt (Admin) window and run (type) the **powercfg.exe /hibernate off** command. You can use the
powercfg.exe /hibernate on command to switch it back on. Note that disabling hibernation on a laptop or tablet can
result in the battery running to empty, and you will lose work on unsaved files and documents.

---

3.   Give the shortcut an appropriate name and then click Finish (see Figure 9-45).

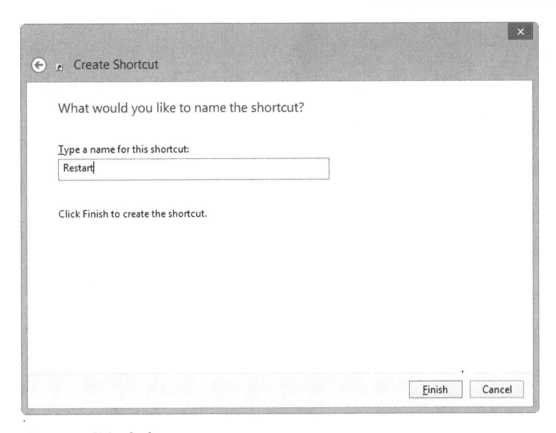

Figure 9-45. Giving the shortcut a name

4. Right-click the newly created shortcut and then select Properties from the options.

5. In the Shutdown Properties dialog, under the Shortcut tab, click the Change Icon button (see Figure 9-46). You are told that icons for this shortcut don't exist. This is fine—just click through it.

Figure 9-46. *The properties for the shortcut*

6. Choose an icon from the Change Icon dialog, and then click OK (see Figure 9-47).

Figure 9-47. *Adding an icon to a shortcut*

■ **Note**   If you add an icon to a Sleep, Hibernate, or Lock icon, double-click the Shell32.dll file at the next view to display icons.

---

7.   Right-click your new power shortcut icon in File Explorer. Select Cut from the options.

8.   In File Explorer, click the icon to the left of the address bar. Navigate to C:\ProgramData\ Microsoft\Windows\Start Menu\Programs (see Figure 9-48).

Figure 9-48. *The C:\ProgramData\Microsoft\Windows\Start Menu\Programs folder*

■ **Note** You can also use your own .ico icon files. Many custom icons can be created from web sites, including the excellent www.iconarchive.com, which I used for the icons in the screen shots here.

---

9. Paste the shortcuts into this folder.

10. At the Start screen, open the All Apps view.

11. In the All Apps view, find the shortcut(s) you have created. Right-click it/them to open the app options for each shortcut. Here you can pin it/them to the Start screen (if they are not already pinned there) and to the taskbar (see Figure 9-49).

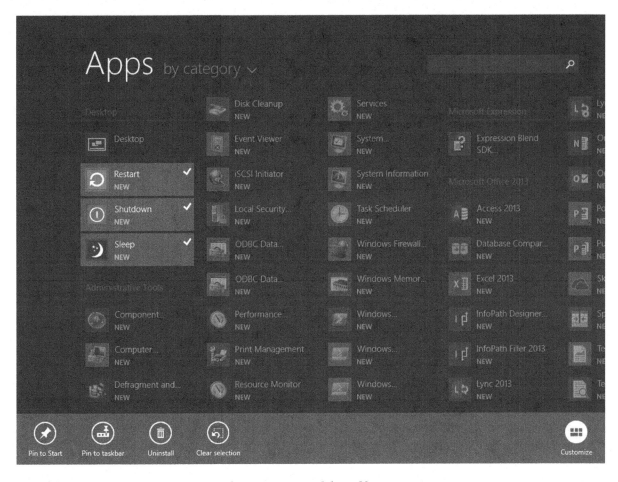

Figure 9-49. Pinning your power icons to the Start screen and the taskbar

■ **Note** Sometimes these shortcut links won't work because of security that Windows 8.1 puts in place to prevent malware from shutting down your computer. If this happens, reopen the C:\ProgramData\Microsoft\Windows\Start Menu\ Programs folder and right-click each shortcut, selecting its properties. With each shortcut, re-paste the command (e.g., **shutdown.exe –s –t 00**) into the Target field and then click OK. The shortcut should now work.

Creating a Power Buttons Toolbar

If you pin the power buttons to your taskbar, you probably don't want them right next to your program buttons, where they're far too easy to click by mistake. You can create a custom toolbar for the taskbar to keep the buttons on the far right of the screen, next to the system tray.

1. Right-click in a blank space on the taskbar and then uncheck **Lock the taskbar** in the options.

2. Right-click the taskbar again and then select Toolbars ➤ New Toolbar (see Figure 9-50).

Figure 9-50. *Creating a new toolbar on the taskbar*

3. Create a new folder for the toolbar. Copy your power shortcut files into it. When you create your folder, select it and then click the Select Folder button (see Figure 9-51).

Figure 9-51. *Creating a folder for the toolbar*

4. Your toolbar now appears on the taskbar. Drag the vertical bars to the left of it to resize it.

5. You can also right-click within the new toolbar to select different options (see Figure 9-52). They include turning off the toolbar's text title and labels, and changing the View options so that it displays large buttons.

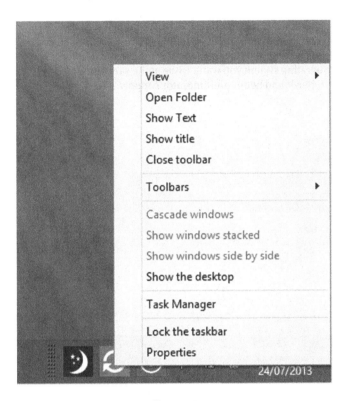

Figure 9-52. Changing toolbar options

Your finished toolbar displays on the right of the taskbar, keeping the power buttons safely away from your program buttons (see Figure 9-53).

Figure 9-53. A power toolbar on the taskbar

Summary

Despite many of the initial reactions to Windows 8.1 when it was unveiled to the public and press, this operating system is extremely customizable. Even the new Start screen can be customized in a variety of ways to suit many types of users. This includes turning the Start screen into a very useful widget view. You can turn the Start screen off completely with third-party software, if you choose.

Being able to personalize your computer is important to many computer users and it is a mainstay of the Windows operating system. Personalization options go far beyond what is included in this chapter. Chapter 10 shows how these options can be configured further to assist people who have difficulty using computers.

This all helps make Windows 8.1 the customizable operating system you want, while at the same time still affording you all the cool new features it brings, such as Hyper-V and better multimonitor support.

■ ■ ■

Making Windows 8.1 More Accessible and Easier to Use

User accessibility is one of the biggest challenges facing companies that make computers, operating systems, and software. Accessibility is particularly important for touch-controlled systems, which improve computer use for people who have difficulty using a keyboard and mouse.

Who are Windows' accessibility features for? People of all ages, from all walks of life, and of all abilities can benefit from them. Perhaps you need text to be larger, perhaps you've never used a computer, perhaps you're left-handed, or perhaps you find it difficult to stare at a screen for a long period of time.

There are several ways to access the settings that can make Windows 8.1 considerably easier to use. The options available on each page vary, depending on what is likely to be required for the interface, Start screen, or desktop.

Making Windows 8.1 Easier to Use

You can access the Windows 8.1 Ease of Access settings through the charms by selecting Settings ➤ Change PC Settings and then clicking *Ease of Access* (see Figure 10-1). Most of the settings for making Windows easier to use can be found here, and most people find that there's no need to visit the full Ease of Access Center on the desktop (more on this in a moment).

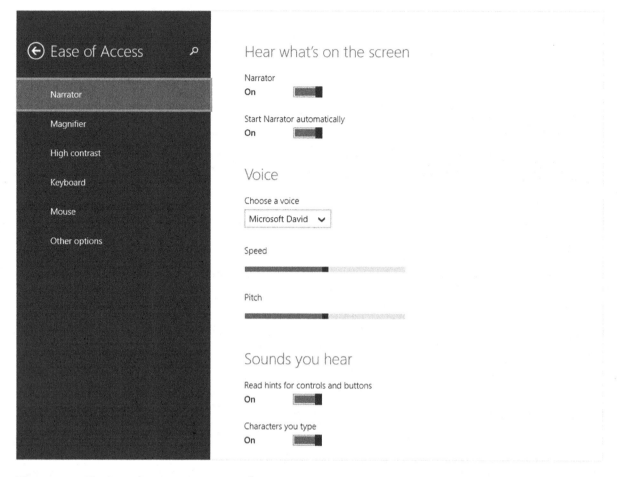

Figure 10-1. *The Ease of Access settings in Windows 8.1*

■ **Note**   You can launch and switch to programs on the taskbar by pressing the Windows key + a number (1 to 0), where the number corresponds to the position of the icon on the taskbar.

The following lists the options listed in Ease of Access.

- **Narrator** turns on a facility whereby items onscreen are read to you by your PC.

- **Magnifier** makes the entire screen much larger and treats your monitor (and mouse) as a magnifying glass that moves across it.

- **High contrast** changes the default Windows color scheme to make the difference between background and foreground items much clearer and easier to see.

- **Keyboard** and **Mouse** include controls for making your keyboard and mouse easier to use.

- **Other options** includes additional controls such as the cursor thickness and whether the background wallpaper is displayed.

The Ease of Access Center

So far, I've discussed how the Ease of Access options affect the way you interact with Windows 8.1. If you use the desktop, however, there are many more options available to you. This is because of the differences between the desktop and standard Windows 8.1 interfaces, and the added complexity of desktop software.

You can access the full Ease of Access Center through the Control Panel on the desktop. In the main part of the page are clear and large controls for turning on the Magnifier, Narrator, onscreen keyboard, and high-contrast color scheme (see Figure 10-2).

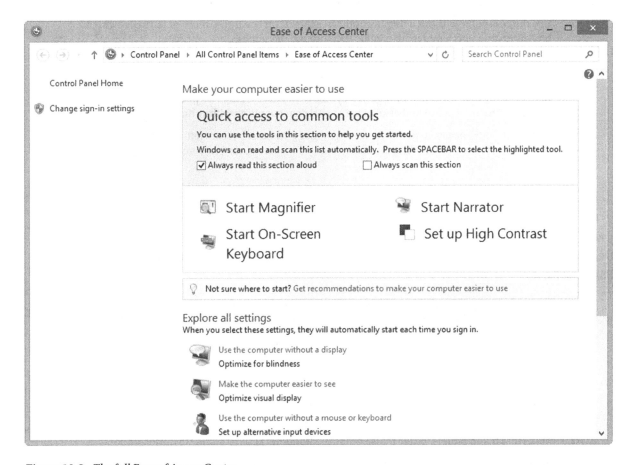

Figure 10-2. *The full Ease of Access Center*

Below this, you see **Not sure where to start? Get recommendations to make your computer easier to use**. This option activates a wizard that asks you simple questions. The wizard automatically sets the Ease of Access Center settings according to the answers that you provide.

▪ **Tip** If you have motor problems, you can turn off the snap and shake effects on the desktop, which snap windows to the sides of your screen and minimize all your programs when you shake the mouse, by searching the Start screen for **shake** and clicking *Turn off automatic windows arrangement.* At the bottom of the window that appears check *Prevent windows from being automatically arranged when moved to the edge of the screen.*

The following are the full Ease of Access Center options:

- **Use the computer without a display** optimizes the PC for use by the blind or partially sighted. It reads instructions aloud to help guide you through the settings.

- **Make the computer easier to see** contains many options, including turning on a high-contrast color scheme, making the cursor thicker, and turning on the Magnifier.

- **Use the computer without a mouse or keyboard** includes settings for permanently turning on the onscreen keyboard and also for using speech recognition with your computer.

- **Make the mouse easier to use** switches the mouse buttons (if you are left-handed). It also offers other functions, including the ability to use the numeric pad on your keyboard as a mouse substitute.

▪ **Tip** As muscular problems such as repetitive stress syndrome (sometimes known as repetitive strain injury [RSI]) become more commonplace, it is becoming easier to find and purchase mice designed to help people continue to use their computer when a standard mouse and keyboard are uncomfortable to use. To find these devices, search online for **RSI** or **RSI mouse**.

- **Make the keyboard easier to use** turns on sticky keys so that you don't have to press two keys simultaneously when performing Ctrl+ actions, among other functions.

- **Use text or visual alternatives for sounds** activates visual clues, such as flashing the desktop, on occasions when Windows 8.1 would ordinarily play a warning sound.

- **Make it easier to focus on tasks** turns off background images and animations. This option is useful for people who find background images distracting.

- **Make touch and tablets easier to use** offers the Windows key + Volume Up button options.

In the left navigation pane of the Ease of Access Center is an option to Change Sign-in Settings. It is here that you find additional options to automatically turn on Ease of Access features at Windows logon. This includes the onscreen keyboard, the Magnifier (so that you can see where to enter your password), and the Narrator (see Figure 10-3).

Figure 10-3. *Changing the Ease of Access sign-in settings*

Making Text and Windows Easier to Read

If you find the Windows desktop text and buttons difficult to see and read, there are several options you can select and features you can activate to help. These include the ability to scale up everything on the desktop to a maximum of 150 percent its normal size. Windows can do this without distorting anything on the screen.

To access this feature, right-click anywhere in a blank space on the desktop. From the context menu, select Screen Resolution. Next, click **Make text and other items larger or smaller** for scaling options (see Figure 10-4).

Figure 10-4. *Scale items on your desktop to make them larger*

This option makes everything on the screen proportionally larger without causing blurring, which is a common side effect of lowering the PC's screen resolution. You may want to scale up only certain types of text, however; perhaps even greater than the 150 percent offered. If you use multiple monitors you can choose the scaling for your current screen by using the slider control or you can set the scaling options for all your screens by checking the *Let me choose one scaling level for all my displays.*

Below the main scaling options is an additional option to individually specify the size of a variety of text items on the screen. You can change the Title bars on windows, menus, message boxes, palette titles, items, and tooltips. What this option doesn't allow you to do is further scale up the main text within windows and programs; but many software packages—including Internet Explorer and Microsoft Office—allow you to do this anyway, as I will detail shortly. Also with this option, you can specify that items always appear in bold to help them stand out.

In the left navigation pane, you see an option to Adjust ClearType Text. ClearType is a system that Windows uses to make text more legible onscreen. There are many different types of screens, however, and people see in different ways, so the default settings may not be best suited for an individual user.

Clicking Adjust ClearType Text displays a wizard in which Windows shows you different blocks of text. At each stage, you click the one that is most legible, and Windows automatically adjusts the ClearType settings accordingly, so that the text onscreen is at its most legible for you.

It is also possible to scale web pages and some document types. Not only does this make text easier to read but it also makes some web sites easier to navigate because buttons and links become larger.

In Internet Explorer 11, you can zoom in and out of web sites by pressing the Ctrl++ and Ctrl+- keys and also by holding down the Ctrl key and moving the mouse scroll wheel. These controls are also found in IE10 settings (see Figure 10-5). When you are using IE11 with touch, you can zoom in and out with pinch zoom gestures.

Figure 10-5. *Zooming web pages*

Some document types allow zooming. For many years, Microsoft Office has offered a tool that is located on the bottom right of the Open window (see Figure 10-6). With this tool, you can zoom in and out of a document by using the slider or clicking the current percentage.

Figure 10-6. *Scaling documents*

Many Windows 8.1 apps support pinch-touch gestures to zoom in and out. You can take advantage of them if you have a touchscreen on your computer.

■ **Tip** You can zoom in and out of many apps and desktop programs in Windows 8.1 by pinch-zooming outward with a touch gesture. Some laptops come equipped with multitouch trackpads that support pinch-zoom gestures if you do not have a touchscreen.

Zooming in and out of documents and the desktop may not be sufficient enough. A high-contrast color scheme may be required if you are colorblind or visually impaired. To access this option from the desktop, right-click anywhere in a blank space on the desktop and from the context menu, click Personalization (see Figure 10-7). You can also turn on high-contrast color schemes from the Ease of Access options in PC Settings.

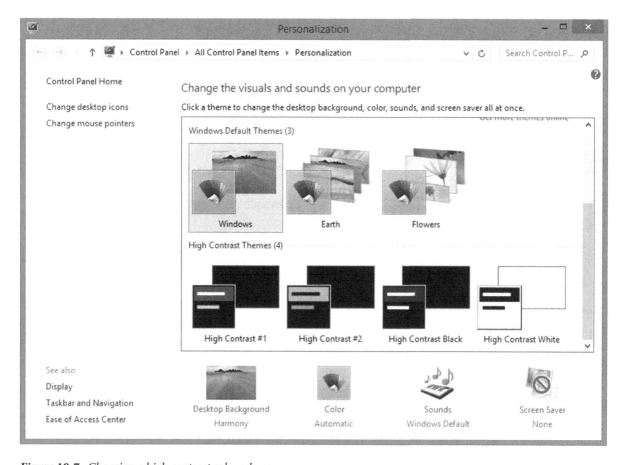

Figure 10-7. *Choosing a high-contrast color scheme*

In the Personalization window, there are several high-contrast color schemes for you to choose from. Alternatively, if you don't need a high-contrast scheme but have trouble with the look of Windows, you can switch to a different Windows color scheme, which makes some parts of the window furniture—such as the Minimize, Maximize, and Close buttons—much easier to see.

There are also high-contrast desktop themes available to help with issues varying from poor eyesight to colorblindness. These are also from the main Personalization page. Some public and charitable organizations provide additional themes for Windows. They can advise on the best combination of options for your specific circumstances.

If the scaling options and high-contrast themes don't make it easier for you to see in Windows 8.1, you can turn on the Magnifier from the Ease of Access Center. By default, this tool zooms everything on your screen. You can click the magnifying glass icon near the top left of the screen to access additional Magnifier controls (see Figure 10-8).

Figure 10-8. *The Magnifier displays a magnifying glass that you can click for more control*

The main controls for the Magnifier allow you to zoom in and out, as well as display the Magnifier in different ways:

- The Magnifier can be **Docked** to the top of the screen to display a larger version of the portion of the screen where your cursor is located.

- A **Lens** follows your cursor around the screen, zooming in on that small portion of the screen.

All options are selected by clicking the magnifying glass icon to reveal the full Magnifier options (see Figure 10-9).

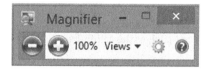

Figure 10-9. *Clicking in the magnifying glass reveals the full Magnifier controls*

■ **Tip** If you are stuck in Magnifier view and are unsure how to disable it, look for the magnifying glass and click it (see Figure 10-8). It changes to the panel shown in Figure 10-9, in which you can click the close button.

Clicking the Cog button displays a menu of options for the Magnifier, including inverting screen colors to improve contrast and automatically jumping to text input boxes.

You can make the mouse cursor easier to see independently of the desktop theme as well. In the Ease of Access Center, click Make the Mouse Easier to Use. It displays some high-contrast options for the mouse, complete with images of what the cursor will look like with each option selected (see Figure 10-10).

Figure 10-10. *Making the mouse easier to use*

By turning on Mouse Keys, you can also use the keyboard as a mouse, either as a replacement to or in conjunction with your regular mouse. This feature allows you to use the arrow keys on your computer's number pad (if your keyboard has one) to move the mouse cursor. It can also be useful if you have trouble using the mouse for long periods of time.

Other useful features include making a window active simply by hovering over it with your mouse. If you have difficulty with mouse buttons, you might find this option helpful.

Using the Narrator to Read Text Aloud

The Narrator tool assists those who are blind, are partially sighted, or simply have trouble reading the computer screen. This feature reads out text and other items on your screen as you mouse over, touch, or click it. It also reads text in panels, such as web sites and Windows alert messages. As an item onscreen is read, it is highlighted by a blue box. This helps people who are partially sighted track what is being read. The Narrator is most easily switched on by pressing the Windows key to return to the Start screen, typing **narrator**, and pressing the Enter key.

Controls are available both from **Control whether Narrator starts when I sign in** and from the sign-in screen (in the bottom-left corner) to make sure the Narrator is automatically turned on when you sign in to your computer.

There are also a significant number of keyboard shortcuts that you can use to control the Narrator. You can display a complete list of them at any time by pressing the Caps Lock+F1 key combination. Most of the Narrator commands use the Caps Lock key because it isn't used for any other purpose. While the Narrator is on, you need to use the Shift key for capital letters.

Windows 8.1 enhancements to the Narrator include the welcome ability to speed up and slow down the narrator's voice. In the Voice section of the Narrator Settings window, there are slider controls that adjust the speed of the voice, which by default is set at 50 percent; the volume of the voice, which is set at maximum by default; and the pitch of the voice, which is set at 50 percent. There are also a variety of voices that you can select. The commands available for reading web sites have also been expanded to ensure that more items on a web page can be read aloud.

The main Narrator Settings window is shown in Figure 10-11.

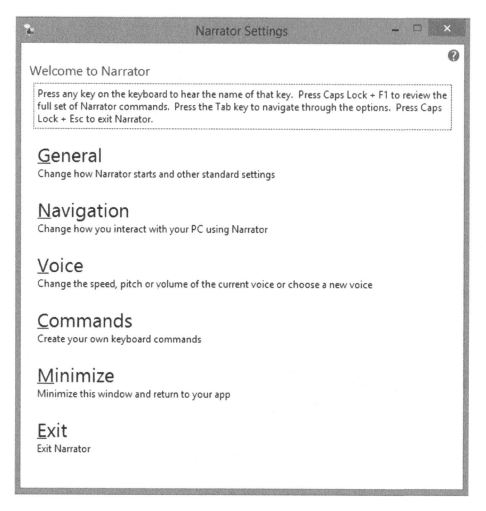

Figure 10-11. *The Narrator in Windows 8.1X*

Windows 8.1 Narrator enhancements include ways to assist people with using touchscreen devices, including sounds to accompany actions that are performed with touch. These actions audibly confirm that your touch gesture was successful. The Narrator can also read text under your finger as you move it across the computer's screen.

It is important to note that if you want to use the Narrator with a touchscreen, the screen needs to support four or more touch points because some of the Narrator touch gestures use three or four fingers. If you are buying a new touchscreen computer on which you want to use the Narrator, it is important to be aware of this.

Controlling the Narrator with Touch

When you use the narrator with a touchscreen, it reads aloud anything that you swipe your finger over, or you can tap an item to have it read individually. There are additional controls you can use, however, that directly control the Narrator (see Table 10-1).

Table 10-1. *Narrator touch gestures*

Effect	Action
Stop Narrator	Single, two-finger tap
Read all current window	Swipe up with three fingers
Click	Double-tap
Double-click	Triple-tap
Show or hide Narrator window	Tap with four fingers
Move to next or previous item	Flick left or right with one finger
Drag an item	Tap with three fingers
Scroll the window	Swipe up, down, left, or right with two fingers
Tab forward and backward	Swipe left or right with three fingers

When you are using the Narrator on a web site, additional controls are available, and as you flick up and down you will hear the PC read the following phrases. This is what they mean:

- **Heading view** speaks the headline and then highlights the previous/next one with a left/right swipe.

- **Item view** speaks and highlights the previous or next item on a page with a left/right swipe.

- **Paragraph view** speaks and highlights the previous or next paragraph with a left/right swipe.

- **Line view** speaks and highlights the previous or next line to text with a left/right swipe.

- **Word view** speaks and highlights the previous or next work with a left/right swipe.

- **Character view** speaks and highlights the previous or next character of text with a left/right swipe.

- **Table view** highlights and reads the previous or next table on the web site with a left/right swipe.

- **Link view** highlights and read the previous or next link of the page with a left/right swipe. It can then be activated with a double-tap.

Controlling the Narrator with the Keyboard

If you are using the Narrator with a keyboard, there are controls that you can use (see Table 10-2).

Table 10-2. *Narrator keyboard commands*

Effect	Action
Click the selected item	Spacebar or Enter
Move the cursor around the screen	Tab + cursor keys
Read item	Caps Lock + D
Read entire document	Caps Lock + H

(continued)

Table 10-2. (*continued*)

Effect	Action
Read last read item	Caps Lock + V
Read entire window	Caps Lock + W
Move to previous/next item	Caps Lock + left or right cursor
Adjust volume	Caps Lock + Page Up or Page Down
Adjust reading speed	Caps Lock + Plus (+) or minus (-)
Turn Caps lock on or off	Press Caps Lock twice quickly
Stop reading	Ctrl
Exit Narrator	Caps Lock + Esc

Making Your Keyboard and Mouse Easier to Use

It is common for people to have trouble using devices like the mouse. Windows features such as Shake, although perhaps very useful for some people, might prove to be hugely irritating for others. Shake is a desktop feature that minimizes all the windows on the screen when you shake the mouse; it is not very useful if you have difficulty in using a mouse.

To turn off Shake and Snap (they can only be switched off together), follow these instructions:

1. Open the Ease of Access Center from the Control Panel.

2. Click **Make the mouse easier to use**.

3. Check the box **Prevent windows from being automatically arranged when moved to the edge of the screen**.

Additional settings for the mouse are located in the Control Panel or by searching for **mouse** at the Start screen. Some of these functions are extremely useful (see Figure 10-12).

Figure 10-12. *The Mouse Properties dialog box*

- The **Double-Click Speed** of the mouse can be modified to suit you. If you find that you can't double-click the mouse at the speed Windows wants, you can slow it down.

- **ClickLock** is a feature that makes it easier to drag items on the screen. With this feature activated, you don't need to hold down the mouse button to drag. Click the mouse button once to select an item and then click it again to drop it. This feature works with both the mouse and the trackpad.

- Windows 8.1 includes several different schemes to modify the mouse **Pointers,** including the option for large and high-visibility pointers.

- The **Pointer Speed** can be modified in Windows so that the mouse moves more slowly.

- **Snap To** is a useful feature that moves the mouse pointer automatically onto a button when you get close to it.

- **Pointer Trails** can be displayed so that you can more easily see where the mouse is on the screen.

- The ability to **highlight the location** of your mouse pointer on the screen is particularly useful. It is made available when you press the Ctrl key on your keyboard.

> ■ **Tip** Left-handed computer users can switch the mouse buttons in the Mouse Properties settings.

In the Ease of Access Center, you can turn on various additional features for the computer's keyboard by clicking **Make the keyboard easier to use**. A feature called Sticky Keys is particularly useful.

Sticky Keys allows you to use the keyboard one key at a time. If you need to press a keyboard combination involving the Shift, Ctrl, Alt, or even the Windows key (it is supported even though the Sticky Keys options don't specify it), just press one of these keys, wait to hear a tone while pressing the key, and then press the letter associated with that keystroke (for example Ctrl+C).

Filter Keys is a useful feature that prevents repeated instances of a letter, number, or other character when a particular key is pressed.

Using Text or Visual Alternatives for Sounds

There may be times when you can't hear an alert or other sound on your computer; or to hear, you need the volume turned up to a level where other people complain about it. To help with these issues, Windows 8.1 offers visual cues to alert you when it would normally use a sound.

From the Ease of Access Center, click Use Text or Visual Alternatives for Sounds. The options include a flashing caption on the screen or flashing the whole desktop to alert you that something needs your attention. Alternatively, Windows can speak the caption (this is useful if you hear voices well but have difficulty with other sounds).

Making It Easier to Focus on Tasks

To help navigate through the many and varied options in the Ease of Access Center, there is a clickable option to Make It Easier to Focus on Tasks. This page includes many of the common accessibility controls, such as Sticky Keys, the Narrator, and Filter Keys. You can also turn off the desktop background image in this option.

Training Windows 8.1's Handwriting Recognition

Windows 8.1's handwriting recognition is pretty good but you might find that for you it could use some extra training. You can do this by opening the *Language* options from the Control Panel, highlighting the language you want to train, and clicking the *Options* link to its right.

In the window that next appears, click the *Personalize handwriting recognition* link (see Figure 10-13).

Figure 10-13. Accessing the handwriting recognition training

The training window now appears (see Figure 10-14). Here you can choose whether to retrain Windows where it makes specific errors with your handwriting or to train it more generally. Note that this second option can take some time to complete.

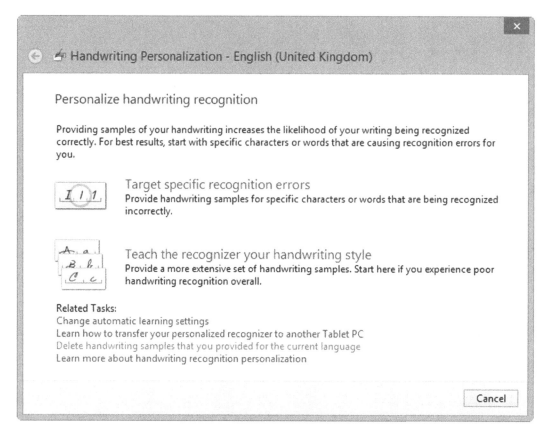

Figure 10-14. *You can traing Windows 8.1's handwriting recognition*

Using Speech Recognition with Windows 8.1

Windows 8.1 allows you to control your PC using speech, either through a microphone built into a tablet, laptop, or ultrabook; or through a headset. You can access the speech recognition by searching for **speech** from the Start screen and when you run it, you will be asked which audio device you want to use.

You are asked a series of questions, after which you are invited to take a tutorial. Doing so helps train the speech recognition software, and it is always advisable to spend some time training Windows 8.1 to understand your voice.

There is a reference card that you are invited to view; printing this card can be extremely helpful for remembering the different voice commands for the speech recognition software. When it's running, the speech recognizer floats on your desktop and can be docked to the top or bottom of the screen (see Figure 10-15).

Figure 10-15. *The speech recognizer floats on your desktop*

Generally speaking, the speech recognition software in Windows 8.1 is excellent; indeed this section of the book was written by using it, which was rather handy as I had a fractured wrist at the time.

Full controls for his speech recognizer can be accessed easily by right-clicking the speech recognizer window. These controls include options to continue the speech recognition training and to configure both the speech recognizer and your microphone.

Common Speech Recognition Controls

Although it is a good idea to keep a copy of the reference card handy there are some commands that you will often use:

- **Start** and the name of a program, for example *Calculator, Word*, or *Excel*, starts the program

- **Switch to** and the name of a program switches to that program if is already running.

- You can control programs that have drop-down menus by speaking the name of that menu and then speaking the name of the option you want to select from it. This also works for Ribbon controls in Windows 8.1, Microsoft Office, and other programs that use it.

- **Show numbers** displays numbers overlaid on a program's controls that can then be spoken to activate that control (see Figure 10-16).

Figure 10-16. *You can activate a program's controls with the speech recognizer*

- On a web page, you can select links by saying their name; for example, *Contact us*.

- You can activate clicks on an item by saying *double-click* or *right-click* for a specific item; for example, *Double click Recycle bin*.

- **Start Listening/Stop Listening** turns the speech recognition system on or off.

- **What can I say?** Will display help prevent the speech recognition system.

- **Show speech options** displays the list of options for the speech recognizer; it is also available via a right-click.

- **Show speech recognition/Hide speech recognition** minimizes the speech recognizer to the system tray or returns it to the desktop.

If at any time the speech recognizer does not recognize something you have said, it displays an **Alternatives Panel** that contains its best guesses for what it was you said (see Figure 10-17). You can make a choice from this panel by saying the number to the left of the correct item. This also has the added benefit of helping to train the Windows 8.1 speech recognition system.

Figure 10-17. *The speech recognition system lets you know if it is unsure of what you say*

Finding Accessible Apps in Windows 8.1

With the new Windows Store, Microsoft is making it easier for customers to find accessible apps and for developers to write apps that are accessible. The tools for creating apps that support Windows accessibility are now much simpler for app developers to use.

To find accessible apps, open the Windows Store. Then open the charms to click the Settings charm. In the top right of the screen, a *Preferences* option, when clicked, displays a switch to *make it easier to find accessible apps*. With this selected, the Windows Store displays only apps that support accessibility features.

Where to Find Accessibility Help and Support

Many of the option pages in the Ease of Access Center offer you the option to **Learn about additional assistive technologies online**. Clicking this link directs you to the Microsoft web site at www.microsoft.com/enable. Here you can read more about the accessibility features in Windows 8.1, as well as view video and other tutorials on their use.

This web site also contains links to third-party help, support, and commercial web sites where you can find advice and products designed to help make your computer more accessible and easier to use.

Summary

The accessibility features in Windows 8.1 are extensive and make Windows 8.1 the most accessible operating system available today. I recommend starting at the desktop Ease of Access Center Wizard. Run it by clicking **Get recommendations to make your computer easier to use**. The wizard asks you a series of questions about how you use your computer and where you find it difficult to use. It then makes recommendations for settings that you can select to make Windows 8.1 easier to use.

■ ■ ■

CHAPTER 11

Keeping You, Your Files, and Your Computer Safe

Despite Windows' history of being very insecure and a hotbed for malware and viruses, this really isn't true any more. It's also not true that the security systems in Windows 8.1 are annoying, or lacking in flexibility, or difficult to use.

By default, Windows 8.1 is actually very good at taking care of itself. It needs to be. Most users don't want to worry about updates to Windows and antivirus software. They certainly don't want to have to change firewall settings to allow a game through a port.

If anything, the default settings for security in Windows 8.1 really are perfectly all right for general computer usage. If anything will be exploited, it's the soft, squidgy thing sitting at the keyboard, vulnerable to criminals who get them to click something that allows malware through the already excellent security in Windows 8.1.

Windows 8.1 includes more than just antivirus software and security features, though, because there are also government-level file and disk encryption technologies that can be as simple to set up and use as a fresh user account.

In this chapter, I'll talk you through all the security features in the operating system, explain what they do, and show you how you can customize them to meet your own individual needs.

How Secure Is Windows 8.1 Really?

Windows 8.1 is arguably the most secure version of Windows in the history of the operating system due to the inclusion of antivirus security software. It builds on previous security features, including User Account Control (UAC), which was first introduced in Windows Vista.

Some security researchers claimed that Windows 7 is even more secure than some UNIX-based operating systems; they will no doubt applaud Windows 8.1 as well. This is security is primarily due to the proactive approach that Microsoft takes to patching security flaws as they are discovered.

However, you cannot rely on an operating system to be secure on its own. Every time you install a program or app, you open the possibility of compromising your security. When you go online or check your e-mail, you open the possibility that someone, somewhere might attempt to trick you into installing malware.

It is important to look at Windows 8.1 security in a holistic way, not in isolation. In this chapter, I'll show you how to make sure that Windows 8.1 is completely secure. This chapter also sometimes refers to Chapter 3, in which I showed you how to stay safe when you are connected to the Internet.

Maintaining Security When Using Windows 8.1 with Other Windows Versions

Windows 8.1 is secure, and Windows 7 and Windows Vista are also secure, at least when all precautions and safeguards are put in place and when features such as UAC remain turned on at their default setting.

Computers are commonly used in a networked environment with other Windows PCs, not all of which run the same version of Windows. It is possible that some of these PCs are running Windows XP. All security and update support ends (or ended, depending on when you are reading this) for Windows XP in April 2014. This means that after this date, there will no longer be updates or patches to fix security or other vulnerabilities. If you are using your Windows 8.1 computer in an environment in which there is an XP machine, you should not share files and folders with it.

The reason for this is that Windows XP is still widely used in the developing world and some countries in Asia. The arrival of Windows 8.1 is unlikely to change this situation much in the near future, so after April 2014, the Windows XP operating system will be a huge target for malware writers and hackers. After 12 years of patches and updates, there really shouldn't be any security flaws left, but you can be certain that some will still exist and be the targets of criminals.

You should also be wary of sharing files and folders with Windows 7 and Windows Vista, which is the main way that malware spreads on a home or work network. This is because you may not know how the other computers on that network are managed or what their security is like. You may be using your Windows 8.1 computer in a workplace in which all computers are managed the same way. Here you can be confident that the environment is enclosed with an SEP field[1] and is the responsibility of the IT department.

Maintaining Security When Using Windows 8.1 with Non-Windows Operating Systems

If you are using Windows 8.1 in an environment in which there are other operating systems, people's views might differ. If the other computers were Apple iMacs, for example, then some would argue that they're more secure than Windows. In fact, I would argue that the opposite is true because Apple doesn't adopt the same stringent policy for maintaining security that Microsoft does. As a result, Apple can be slow to respond to threats such as the malware attack in early 2012 that infected some 600,000 Apple Mac computers.

Computers running Linux are unlikely to pose a threat to your own computer security because the overall market share for this operating system isn't large enough to get the attention of malware writers.

This brings us to tablets, where Apple's iOS operating system and Windows 8.1 are perfectly secure—but Google's Android is anything but. This is because Google does not vet programs submitted to its app store in the same way that Apple and Microsoft do. As a result, any tablets or computers running Android should always be treated with caution.

---

[1]In the comedy science-fiction book, *Life, the Universe and Everything* by Douglas Adams (Pan Macmillan, 1982), an SEP field is described as "something we can't see, or don't see, or our brain doesn't let us see, because we think that it's somebody else's problem ... The brain just edits it out, it's like a blind spot. If you look at it directly you won't see it unless you know precisely what it is. Your only hope is to catch it by surprise out of the corner of your eye."

The technology involved in making something properly invisible is so mind-bogglingly complex that 999,999,999 times out of a billion it's simpler just to take the thing away and do without it. The "Somebody Else's Problem field" is much simpler, more effective, and "can be run for over a hundred years on a single torch battery."

This is because it relies on people's natural predisposition not to see anything they don't want to, weren't expecting, or can't explain.

■ **The Myth of Mac and iOS Security**   Although it's true that, historically, Apple's Mac computers have been *almost* invulnerable to virus attacks due to the way the security of the operating system's UNIX-base was designed, this is sadly no longer the case. In recent years, malware writers, primarily in response to improved security in Windows but also because of the popularity of the iPhone and iPad, which share the same core OS, have focused more on tricking the Mac user into installing and permitting malware. This—along with Apple's slow response to some malware threats, as well as the rapid market growth for Apple computers—has greatly increased the threat to the platform.

Windows Defender

I started this chapter by saying that Windows 8.1 is the first version of Windows to come with built-in security software. Some of you may balk at the suggestion that Windows Defender, a rebadged version of Microsoft's free antivirus solution, Security Essentials, is actually effective at defending against malware at all.

In truth though, so long as you're aware of the online threats, Windows Defender is a perfectly good antivirus package and is all the malware protection you need on your computer.

It is based on Microsoft's award-winning Forefront antivirus package for Windows Server and it is very effective. When you look at the quarterly reports for the effectiveness of all the major antivirus packages, there is always some fluctuation in the brand rankings, depending on the threats that have been found in the previous 6 months and how effectively the manufacturers dealt with them.

There is no reason not to use Windows Defender, however. I never recommend installing any software that duplicates functionality that's already in Windows because this adds layers of complexity that can lead to problems. Shortly, I will detail some of my recommended alternatives if you want to use something else.

Configuring and Updating Windows Defender

One of the problems for Windows 8.1 users is that Windows Defender (see Figure 11-1) is very difficult for casual users to find. It doesn't appear in the PC Settings window; it is hidden on the desktop. You can most easily find it by searching for **defender** at the Start screen.

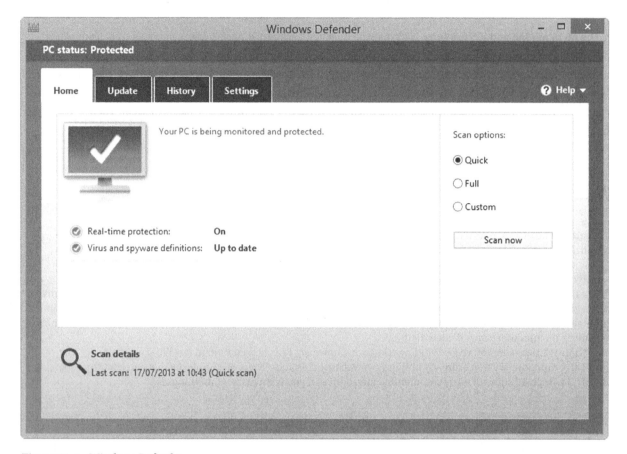

Figure 11-1. *Windows Defender*

■ **Note**   Never assume that because you have antivirus software, SmartScreen, and a firewall on your PC that you're immune from malware. The people who write and distribute malware know that PCs are quite safe these days and use all manner of trickery, from fake web sites to telephone calls, to exploit the inexperience and ignorance of users and to convince them to install the malware themselves, with the user authorizing the install through security features such as UAC.

Windows Defender has quite a simple interface with just four tabs: Home, Update, History, and Settings.

- The **Home tab** provides details on the current update and scanning status of the software. It allows access to perform quick, full, and custom scans. A custom scan includes scanning an external hard disk, for example.

- The **Update tab** provides information on when the software was last updated. The large Update button updates the software. It really is that simple.

- The **History tab** allows you to view reports of any suspicious or dangerous files.

- The **Settings tab** contains advanced settings for the program. It is here that you can exclude certain files (perhaps a program is being reported as malware when you know it isn't) and you can also join the Microsoft Active Protection Service and report details of suspicious files back to Microsoft.

■ **Note** Real Time Protection should remain switched on. If you deactivate it, Windows Defender can't scan new files or web sites as you open them.

This does mean that Windows Defender isn't as configurable as some other packages, but why do we need antivirus software to be configurable anyway? I would argue that the whole point of antivirus software is to always provide complete protection while staying out of the way.

Staying out of the way is something that Windows Defender does extremely well because it runs scans and downloads updates only when you're not using the computer. This means that if you're working, gaming, or doing some other intensive job on your PC, Windows Defender doesn't hog processor cycles or memory trying to update itself or run a full scan.

■ **Note** Windows Defender is updated through Windows Update, so it is extremely important not to switch this service off.

You can configure Windows Defender in the options under the Settings tab. Here you can exclude certain file locations. For example, perhaps you work in computer security or for a computer magazine and have a drive containing viruses so that you can test antivirus products (in which case, you made a good choice using Windows Defender, I might add). You can also exclude certain file types.

■ **Note** You can set Windows Defender to automatically create a Restore Point when it scans. This can slow your computer slightly, but if you have a fast PC, you won't notice. It can improve resiliency if virus removal causes Windows to become unstable. Using System Restore might also risk restoring the virus!

To be honest, I wouldn't recommend using either of these two settings unless it is absolutely necessary. The next setting, which excludes certain processes, is of much more use. You can use this feature to exclude some programs from scans if they cause conflicts or report as malware (see Figure 11-2).

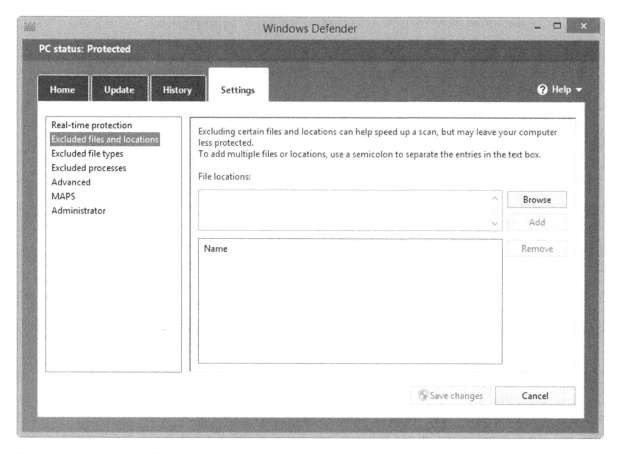

Figure 11-2. *Configuring Windows Defender*

It is actually more common than you might believe for programs to register as malware when they're not. These are called *false-positives*. It might be because the software has to perform the same type of actions on your computer that malware would, perhaps as a diagnostic tool. If you have software installed that registers as malware when it is not, you can exclude it here.

The Advanced settings (shown in Figure 11-3) offer some excellent features that you may want to turn on. They include the full scanning of USB-attached drives when a scan is in operation (remember that malware loves to infect USB flash drives because it's a great way to propagate). You can also set Windows Defender to automatically create a Restore Point when removing a virus. I thoroughly recommend this in case something does indeed go wrong.

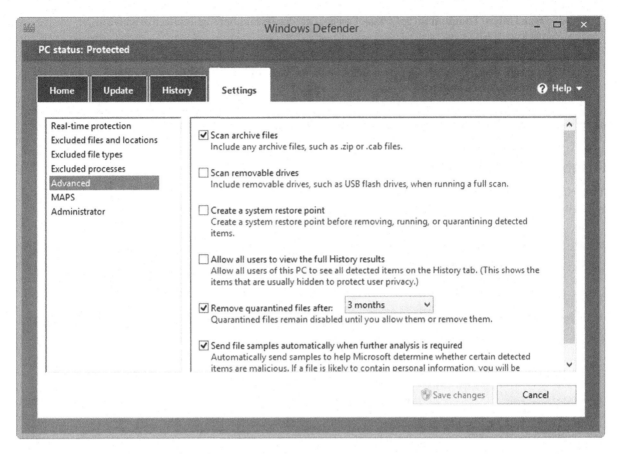

Figure 11-3. *Windows Defender advanced settings*

■ **Tip** It is well worth turning on the Scan Removable Drives and Create a System Restore Point options in Windows Defender. They provide extra security and reliability.

Finding and Installing Third-Party Antivirus Software

So what other antivirus packages are available? Which should you choose? I recommend four that I believe are worthy of consideration because they have consistently scored highly in antivirus scanning tests over the last few years:

- **AVG Anti-Virus Free** (http://free.avg.com) has long been considered one of the best packages available. There is a free version, though in recent years it's become rather obtrusive with annoying ads encouraging you to upgrade to the full paid suite.

- **Norton AntiVirus** and **Norton 360** (http://www.symantec.com) provide some of the finest malware scanning available. It isn't free, but is well worth considering. It has a friendly, simple interface and is extremely effective at protecting your computer.

- **Trend Micro Titanium** (http://www.trendmicro.com) is another highly effective antivirus package. It isn't free.

- **Kaspersky Anti-Virus** (http://usa.kaspersky.com) is an extremely configurable security package. For the power user who wants a fine level of control, it is a very suitable option. This is not a free product.

It is not as easy to recommend McAfee's antivirus products because they have been known to cause problems in recent years. Also, McAfee's scanning and protection capabilities are not anywhere near as good as they used to be.

Disabling Windows Defender

If you choose not to use Windows Defender because you are using third-party antivirus software instead, you can switch it off. This is done under the Settings tab, in the Administrator section (see Figure 11-4).

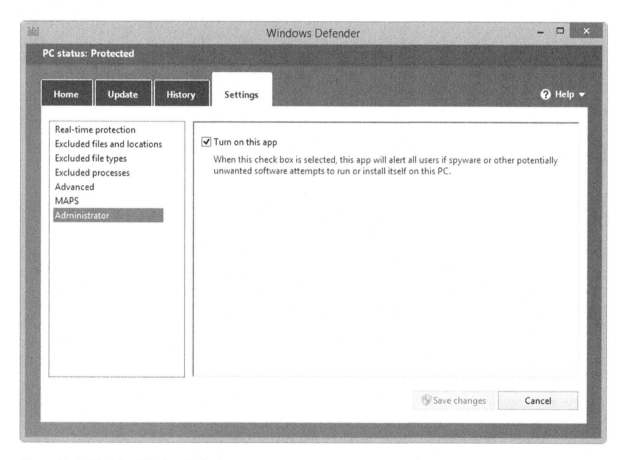

Figure 11-4. *Disabling Windows Defender*

If you are using a third-party antivirus product, you should turn Windows Defender off. I never recommend having two antivirus packages running concurrently because one can interfere with the operation of the other.

Offline Antivirus Scanners

There are some very effective offline virus scanners that start your computer from a USB flash drive to scan for and remove malware.

Regardless of what I said earlier about McAfee, it is difficult to criticize the quality of its offline offerings (www.mcafee.com/us/downloads/free-tools), which include the malware removal tools GetSusp and Stinger.

Microsoft also has an offline antivirus package called Microsoft Safety Scanner (http://www.microsoft.com/security/scanner), which scans your computer for malware and remove it.

You should download these tools only as required. Do not use older versions. This ensures that the software version you use includes the most up-to-date malware data.

Using the Windows Firewall

Unlike Windows Defender, the Windows Firewall could be described as having a split personality. On initial examination, it's no more complicated to use than its antivirus brother is, but the number of configuration options are huge under the surface.

Configuring and Maintaining the Windows Firewall

The basic Windows 8.1 Firewall window, which you can open by searching for **firewall** at the Start screen, doesn't offer many features and certainly doesn't offer a large Turn the Firewall Off button. It gives you information about the network you are currently connected to and shows you the current state of the firewall as it pertains to that network (see Figure 11-5).

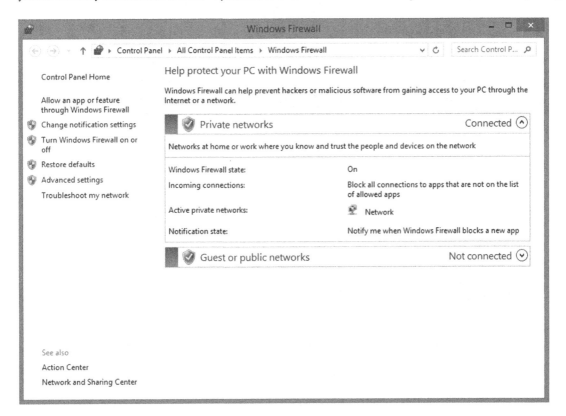

Figure 11-5. *The basic Windows 8.1 firewall*

There are many additional options, however, even for the basic firewall. You access these options through the left navigation. I want to talk you through each of them individually.

Allow an app or feature through Windows Firewall allows a program that has been blocked by Windows 8.1 because of suspicious activity (which is known to happen with older programs especially) or because you accidentally denied it permission.

It's not just simply allowing a program or app to install, however. You first have to click the Change Settings button to confirm to Windows that this is something you really want to do. This prevents malware from automatically coming through if you have inadvertently allowed it to install through UAC.

If a program or app doesn't appear in the list, you can click the Allow Another App button to manually browse for and permit a program or app (see Figure 11-6).

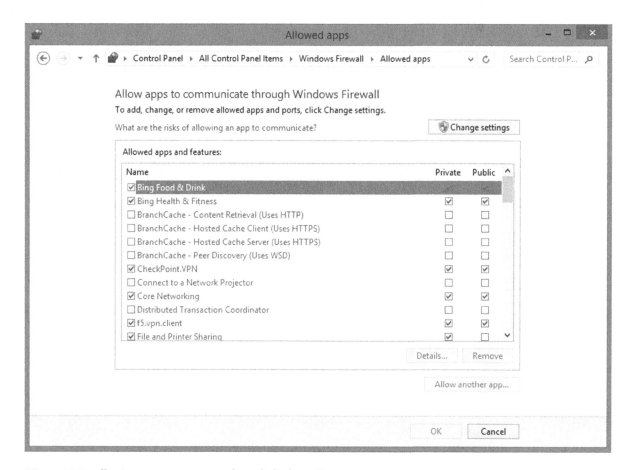

Figure 11-6. *Allowing a program or app through the firewall*

■ **Tip**   If you are having trouble with your firewall, you can click Restore Defaults in the Windows Firewall window to reset it to its default configuration.

Click the *Change settings* button in the top right of the window to allow or block a program or app through the firewall. Doing so allows you to check and uncheck the *Private* (such as home and work) and *Public* (such as cafes and libraries) network settings. You might want to set these individually if, for example, you have a file sync program such as SkyDrive or Dropbox that you want to block when connected to Public networks to minimize the risk of any transferred files being intercepted by hackers.

If you do not see the program that you want to let through the firewall listed, you can add it manually. Click the *Allow another app* button, and a new window appears again with a complete list of your apps and installed programs (see Figure 11-7). This shouldn't be any different from the main Allowed apps screen list, but there might be changes, depending on whether you have any custom software installed.

Figure 11-7. *You can manually allow a program through the firewall*

You can click the *Browse* button to add any desktop software that isn't included in this list. You can't add apps this way because they are stored in a hidden and protected folder on the PC to which even full Administrators can't get access.

When you select the program to add, click the *Network types* button to select which networks (Public and Private) you want to allow the program to connect to and finish by clicking the *Add* button.

In the main Windows Firewall window, the **Change notification settings** and **Turn Windows Firewall on or off** links allow you to turn off the firewall if you *really* want to. Both links take you to the same place (see Figure 11-8). I recommend using these options only if you are using a third-party firewall that you're happy with.

Figure 11-8. *You can turn off the Windows Firewall*

What's more, you can choose to have the firewall switched off in private networks, but remain on in public networks. But why would you want to do this? You might be a gamer and the firewall interferes with your online gaming at home, or you might be an office worker whose IT department asks you to switch off Windows Firewall because it conflicts with something on its system.

On a laptop, however, you still want to have the protection of the firewall when you're out and about. This is where you can leave the firewall turned on for public networks.

There is also a check box for blocking all incoming connections, which provides better security, especially on public networks, but you might find that some programs or apps don't work because they require this feature to be switched off.

Restore defaults resets Windows Firewall to its default setting. This option is very useful if you made advanced changes and can't remember what they were to undo them.

Using the Advanced Firewall

From the main firewall window, clicking Advanced Settings takes you to a different management console (see Figure 11-9), in which you can set specific rules for both inbound and outbound traffic; and perform other operations, such as opening and blocking specific connection ports.

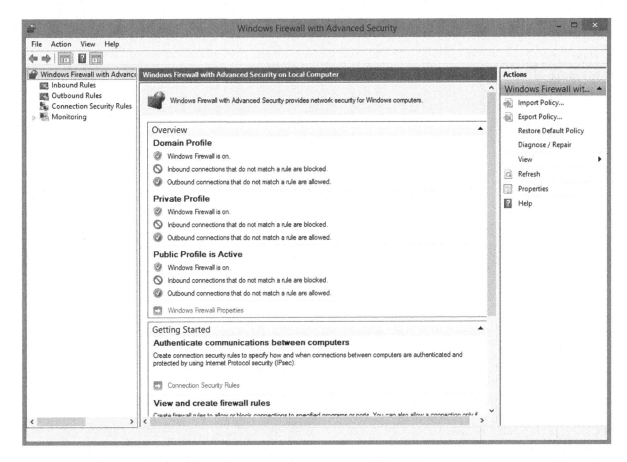

Figure 11-9. *The advanced firewall settings in Windows 8.1*

The main pane in the center displays the current firewall status, but there are two other panes here that you need to be familiar with. On the left side is a tree showing different options within the firewall: inbound and outbound rules, connection security rules, and firewall monitoring. (I will discuss each of these shortly.) On the right side are controls, including options to create and manage rules for the firewall.

To create a new firewall, first click Inbound Rules, Outbound Rules, or Connection Security Rules in the left pane; then click New Rule in the right pane to open the New Rule Wizard (see Figure 11-10).

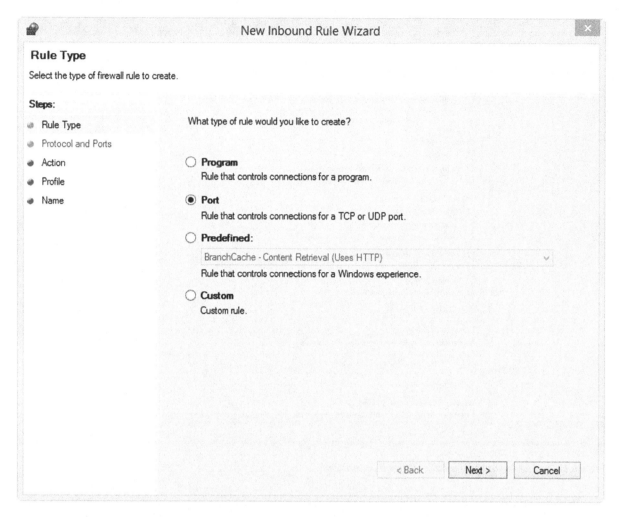

Figure 11-10. *All rules settings are done through helpful wizards*

Inbound Rules and **Outbound Rules** allow you to monitor and set rules for individual programs. You can click New Rule in the right pane to create a new rule for a program, or to allow or block a port on your computer. Table 11-1 shows a list of the common ports on your PC.

Table 11-1. *What Port Does What on Your PC*

Port	Service
7	Echo
21	FTP
22	SSH
23	Telnet
25	SMTP
42	Name Servers/WINS
43	Who is/Nickname
53	DNS
79	Finger
80 (also 8080)	HTTP
81	Kerberos
101	Hostname
110	POP3 (email)
119	NNTP
143	IMAP (email)
161	SNMP
162	SNMP Trap
3389	Remote Desktop
5631	PCAnywhere
5632	PCAnywhere
5900 and above	VNC
6881 to 6990	Torrents

Port opening and blocking is common with applications such as gaming and file sharing, in which communications ports that are not normally used are blocked by firewalls by default.

Here you can set, for example, certain programs or ports to operate only if the data connection is secure. If you use your computer for work and perhaps work in an industry such as security, government, research, or pharmaceuticals, you might want your work applications to transmit and receive data only when you are connected to a secured and properly encrypted network. Here you can set specific programs or apps to operate only under these circumstances (see Figure 11-11).

Figure 11-11. *Setting connection rules*

On the issue of secure connections, even if you only connect to your company through a virtual private network (VPN), you might be asked to set specific connection security rules so that your computer can be authenticated. You do this in the Connection Security Rules section, which specifies the type of connection you want (there are descriptions to assist you) and the type of authentication required by both computers before the connection is allowed.

When setting this up, you will likely have specific settings to input from your company or organization, and they will be specific to them alone.

One very useful feature is to create a custom connection rule whereby you can set—either with or without encryption or authentication—connections between two or several specific computers on specific IP addresses (see Figure 11-12).

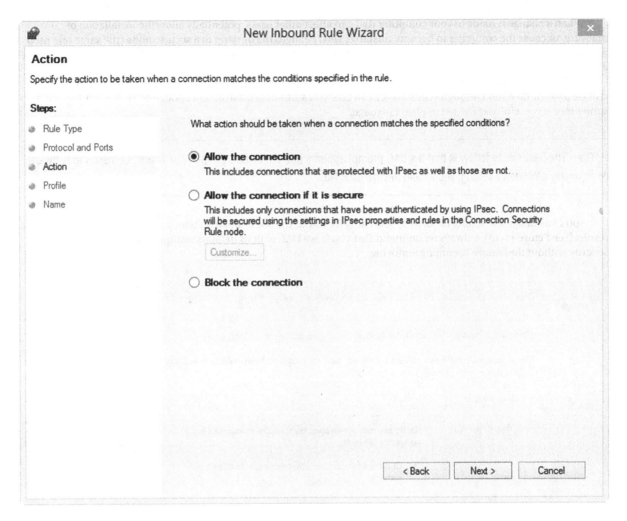

Figure 11-12. *The rules options are easy to follow*

If you have a closed connection in an office and only want computers in the payroll department (for example) to be able to see and connect to other payroll computers, you can set their IP addresses here. However, you need to set both inbound and outbound rules, as well as rules to clock all other IP address connections to the computer.

■ **Note** If you are only allowing connections from your computer, you need to make sure that the permitted computers have static IP addresses set in your router.

User Account Control

First introduced with Windows Vista, UAC is your main line of defense against unwanted software being installed on your computer, or unwanted changes being made to your copy of Windows or your computer's settings.

When a change is made to your computer that can affect other users, potentially allow the installation of malware, or cause the computer to become unstable, UAC changes the desktop to a secure mode (the same one used when you log on to your computer) and displays only the UAC prompt on the screen. Unlike Windows 7, you don't see anything else.

In this mode, no software is permitted to act, so malware can't automatically click itself through. You have to choose a yes or no option, though Windows 8.1 can give you additional information about what is happening—and sometimes it is useful and written in plain language.

■ **Tip** The best rule to follow is that if a UAC prompt appears at a time when you personally are not installing software or changing a Windows setting, you should *always* click **No**.

You can change the setting for UAC by searching for **uac** at the Start screen, in which you will find it in the settings results (see Figure 11-13). I always recommend that you leave UAC with its defaults setting because it offers the best security without the feature becoming annoying.

Figure 11-13. Changing the UAC settings

There are four settings for UAC that vary from off to annoying.

- **Never notify me** turns UAC off completely. I recommend never using this setting.

- **Notify me only when apps try to make changes to my computer (do not dim my desktop)** is another setting I don't recommend. Although this setting allows you to make whatever settings changes you want to Windows 8.1 without being bothered by UAC, it doesn't switch to the secure desktop mode when software is installed. This may permit malware to autoclick the UAC prompt for you.

- **Notify me only when apps try to make changes to my computer** is the default setting. I strongly recommend you leave it as is.

- **Always notify me** is otherwise known as "annoying mode."

So what is the difference between the default and the annoying modes? Some Windows 8.1 controls have a UAC shield icon next to them. This is to alert you that whatever you're doing here can affect other users or how the computer behaves.

In the default mode, Windows allows you to make changes that only affect your own user account, without popping up a UAC prompt. It is only when you're installing software or making changes that can affect other users (if you have only a single-user account, it assumes that more could be added later) that a UAC prompt appears.

Conversely, when in annoying mode, UAC gives you a security prompt for everything that can affect your own user account as well. This is much more secure but ... well, it is plain annoying.

Encrypting Files, Folders, and Drives

On your Windows 8.1 computer—be it a desktop, laptop, or tablet—you can encrypt your data and the entire hard disk. But should you? I want to carefully look at and consider the usefulness of each of the three encryption technologies in Windows 8.1.

Encrypting Files and Folders Using the Encrypting File System

The question of whether to use a Windows encryption technology applies especially to the Encrypting File System (EFS). This system can be used to encrypt individual files or folders in Windows. It has been with us since Windows 2000. It uses 256-bit keys and a mix of several encryption systems based around Advanced Encryption Standard (AES) to provide overall security.

You can encrypt an individual file or folder (or a selected group) by following these instructions:

1. Right-click the item(s) to be encrypted. Select Properties from the options that appear.

2. Click the Advanced button in the Attributes section.

3. Check the **Encrypt contents to secure data** box (see Figure 11-14).

Figure 11-14. Encrypting files and folders using EFS

4. Click OK to begin the encryption.

The encryption process could take some time, depending on the number of files and folders that you are encrypting. You should not cancel the dialog box that appears onscreen because it cancels the encryption process.

You can *decrypt* files in the same way by following the same instructions and unchecking the **Encrypt contents** box.

How EFS Works

EFS is tied to your Windows user account. Whenever you log on to Windows using this account, you can automatically read, write, and modify EFS-protected files. If you log on to your computer using another account, however, or even if you have to reinstall Windows 8.1 and then log on using the same username and password you used before, you can't access these files until you import your EFS key. After you import the appropriate EFS key, you can read the files again.

Backing Up and Restoring Your EFS Key

When you have encrypted files or folders using EFS Windows, a desktop Taskbar alert will prompt you to back up your EFS key. It is extremely important that you back up this key and keep it in a safe location *away* from the computer.

You are asked to set a password for your key, which prevents anyone from importing it onto their computer or user account and opening your files.

You can manually back up and restore EFS keys in Windows 8.1 by searching for **encrypt** at the Start screen and then clicking **Manage file encryption certificates** in the Encrypting File System window that starts the wizard (see Figure 11-15).

Figure 11-15. Backing up and restoring an EFS key

This is a wizard-based tool and it's extremely simple and easy to use. You can also set the EFS system to grant access to files only if used in conjunction with a smart card (assuming that your computer has a reader).

If you change your EFS key—let's say you've moved to a different computer—you can update the cipher used to encrypt the files to the new key on the new computer as well.

Working with EFS-Encrypted Files

In practice, there are several reasons why I can't recommend using EFS. The first and probably the most important is that although it encrypts the contents of files, it still allows people to drill down into your files and folders and view all the file names, which can give away important information (e.g., P. Grant Disciplinary 2012-08-21.docx).

EFS also has what I personally consider a significant flaw. It lost my files on both occasions that I've used it. Because it encrypts individual files and folders, not a whole disk, those files and folders are *still* encrypted when you copy them elsewhere.

If you have an automated backup solution that copies your files to an external hard disk or network attached storage (NAS) drive, the backed-up files will also be encrypted. "Great!" you say. This is exactly what you want.

Unfortunately, EFS requires NTFS-formatted hard drives in order to work, but some external hard disks, especially NAS appliances, are often formatted using different methods. In such cases, you may find that your backups are completely scrambled and unreadable when you try to restore them.

Using EFS from the Command Line

If you're a command-line user in Windows, it's possible to manage the EFS there as well. This uses the **cipher** command in the format **cipher [/switch] [\folder-or-file-1] [\folder-or-file-2]**.

What follows is a list of the more common cipher switches, though more are available with the /? Switch.

Table 11-2. *Switches for the cipher Command*

Switch	Action
/D	Decrypts the specified file or folder.
/E	Encrypts the specified file or folder.
/H	Displays a list of all files in a folder including hidden and system files.
/K	Creates a new encryption certificate for the currently logged-in user. This switch must be used on its own.
/N	Can only be used with /U. Lists every encrypted file without updating the user's encryption key.
/R	Generates an EFS recovery key and certificate in the form of a .pfx file and a .cer file containing only the certificate.
/S	Performs the operation on all files and subfolders subordinate to the specified folder.
/U	Updates the currently logged-in user's encryption key on every encrypted file.
/W	Wipes any unused space on the drive.
/X *filename*	Backs up the currently logged-in users' certificate and encryption keys.
/ADDUSER *username*	Adds a specified user to an encrypted file.
/REMOVEUSER *username*	Removes a specified user from an encrypted file.
/REKEY	Updates files to use your current EFS key.

Encrypting Drives with BitLocker

A much better encryption solution is BitLocker, which is a full-drive encryption system that was first introduced with Windows Vista. It uses a 128-bit AES cipher and can combine a Trusted Platform Module (TPM) chip on your motherboard with a pin and/or a USB flash drive to enhance security.

The main advantage of this method is that the encryption is tied to a chip on your motherboard, which contains the decryption cipher; not even the removal of the hard disk allows people to read your encrypted files. The downside is that you need a TPM chip on your motherboard for BitLocker to work on your computer's hard drive(s), and it's uncommon for desktops to come with one fitted.

TPM chips are much more common on laptops, but they can push up the price, so they are most commonly found only on high-end business and workstation laptops.

This is disappointing because modern data protection regulations around the world demand that data is protected securely—and BitLocker is an absolutely brilliant way of achieving it.

■ **Note** BitLocker is available only in Windows 8.1 Pro and Enterprise and Windows RT.

Because BitLocker provides full disk encryption, any files that you copy from your computer are decrypted automatically. Although this might sound like a disaster, it does mean that backups are always readable (you do need to keep them safe, however) and that nobody can read any of the file names on your computer without unlocking the drive(s) with the appropriate key.

Preparing Your TPM Chip

Before you can use Bitlocker on your computer with a TPM chip, you need to activate the chip. You can do this by clicking the *TPM Administration* link in the bottom left of the main BitLocker window (see Figure 11-16). The main TPM administration page (see Figure 11-15) shows the status of your Trusted Platform Module chip. Before you can use BitLocker, however, you need to turn on the TPM chip on your motherboard.

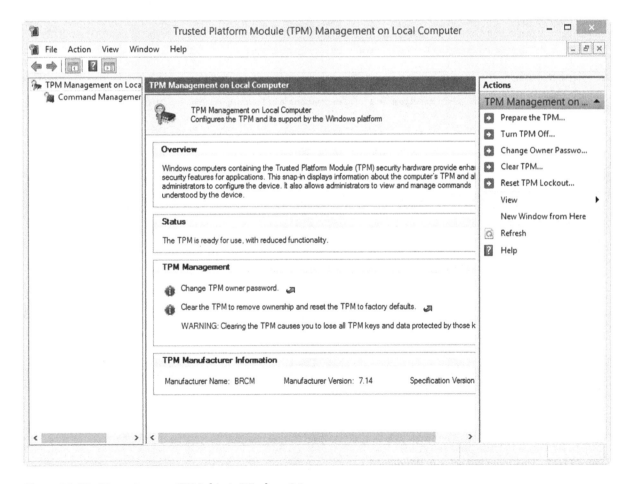

Figure 11-16. Managing your TPM chip in Windows 8.1

If you do not have a TPM-enabled computer, you can't encrypt your hard disk. If your computer is TPM-enabled, however, you will see options to prepare the TPM and more. For example, you can turn off TPM (be certain that you have no encrypted drives when you do this—see "When to Decrypt Your Hard Disks" later in the chapter) or clear the TPM of all its stored ciphers completely. If the TPM chip has locked you out of your computer (more on this later), you can reset a lockout after you gain access.

To use BitLocker, you need to prepare the TPM, which requires rebooting your computer because settings are changed in the BIOS or UEFI firmware (you can also turn it on there). If you need to manage the TPM later on, this page provides all the controls to do so.

Activating BitLocker

Once your TPM chip is enabled, use the main BitLocker page to turn the feature on (see Figure 11-17), which you access from the Control Panel. You can encrypt all the hard drives on your computer, but you must complete the encryption of the drive on which you have Windows 8.1 installed. In order to encrypt any extra drives with BitLocker, your Windows 8.1 drive *must also* be encrypted.

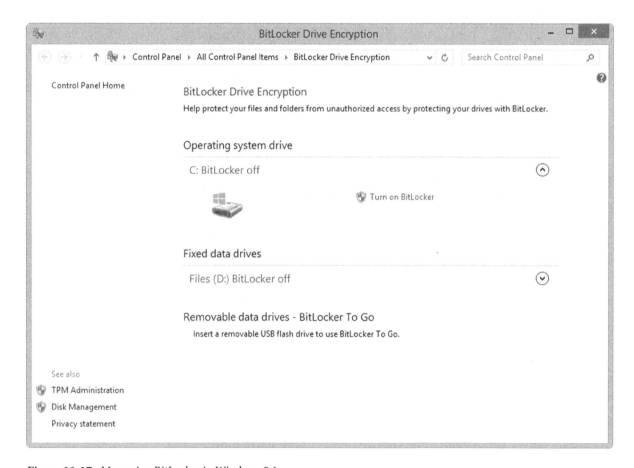

Figure 11-17. Managing BitLocker in Windows 8.1

■ **Note**   BitLocker does *not* work with dual-boot systems! If you have or are planning to have a dual-boot system on your computer, BitLocker locks you out of your computer each time you try to start it.

Unlike EFS, BitLocker encrypts your hard drive in the background, and it is perfectly fine for you to shut down your computer during the process because BitLocker simply continues when you next log on. This is useful because it can take many hours to encrypt a large hard disk that is already full of files and folders.

You can also turn off BitLocker on protected drives. This is where decrypting drives is slightly easier than encrypting them. If, for example, you have two or more physical hard disks or partitions on your computer and you want to encrypt several of them, you must first complete the encryption of your Windows 8.1 drive before you can manually start encryption of the others. When decrypting drives, however, you can start all the jobs at the same time—and Windows 8.1 happily continues if you shut down the computer occasionally.

Backing Up and Restoring Your BitLocker Keys

When BitLocker has encrypted your hard drive, you are automatically prompted to back up your BitLocker key. There are three locations where you can do this:

- **A file on your computer?:** Do *not* save the key to a drive that has been encrypted with BitLocker, or else you might not be able to read it again.

- **A USB flash drive:** I strongly recommend you save your key. I will explain the reasons in the next section.

- **Microsoft SkyDrive:** This cloud service is a secure location. I recommend that you store a copy of your key on a cloud service like this, but it's no good for your main backup.

Starting a BitLocker-Encrypted Computer

The reason I recommend you keep a copy of your BitLocker encryption key on a USB flash drive is because if something happens to make BitLocker unhappy, such as boot change, you will be completely locked out of your computer until you can input the key.

You can type the encryption key, but it is a very long and complex string of characters. You can insert a USB flash drive containing the key, however, and the Windows boot loader will recognize it and grant you access again.

Surely, you say, this defeats the purpose of having an encrypted computer. I argue that if you never keep your computer *and* the USB drive containing the unlock key in the same place (there is a separate key for each encrypted hard disk or partition). If you are traveling, however, you don't need BitLocker locking you out. It might be some time before you can get to another Internet-connected computer to download the backup.

Therefore, I always recommend that you keep a copy of the backup key(s) on a USB flash drive in a safe location—because you never know when you might need it.

Using BitLocker After a Reinstall of Windows 8.1

If you are using BitLocker on a computer in which it has been used before—perhaps because you reinstalled Windows 8.1 or performed a clean install to upgrade from Windows 7 (you should never upgrade an operating system encrypted with BitLocker), you will probably be asked to enter the owner password for your TPM chip (see Figure 11-18). This is set when you activate BitLocker. It is stored in the chip.

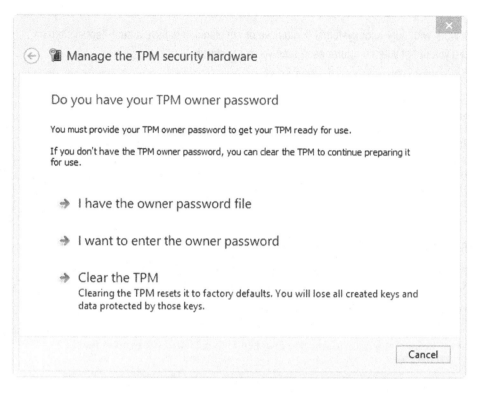

Figure 11-18. *Clearing the TPM*

You need to do this only if you still have BitLocker-protected drives on the computer, which I don't recommend because you never know what might go wrong, such as electricity surges or laptop drops that cause hard disk corruption. What you can do, however, is clear the TPM chip completely and start afresh, which is the best option if you have no BitLocker-encrypted drives in the computer.

You might be prompted to enter the owner password when restoring from a backup—if that backup was made before you encrypted your hard drives with BitLocker. Which brings me to the next section.

When to Decrypt Your Hard Disks

There are times when you should turn off BitLocker—purely to prevent disasters from occurring, as always happens with security technologies. These times include the following:

- When upgrading your copy of Windows or when installing a new operating system, such as migrating from Windows 7 to Windows 8.1

- When moving a hard disk from one computer to another

- When sending a computer out for repair (I always recommend wiping the data drive in this case)

When you restore your computer from a backup, your drives won't be encrypted. You will have to re-encrypt them.

Using BitLocker To Go

The BitLocker To Go feature doesn't require a TPM chip. This is a full-disk encryption system for USB and other attached flash drives and external hard disks. Unlike BitLocker, it is compatible with a variety of drive formats, including FAT32, exFAT, and NTFS—making it perfect for USB drives.

You encrypt an attached USB or other device with BitLocker To Go through the main BitLocker window. Again, there is the same on/off control as there is for your internal hard disks (see Figure 11-19). BitLocker To Go only requires that you set a password, which is entered when you want to read or access the disk on another computer.

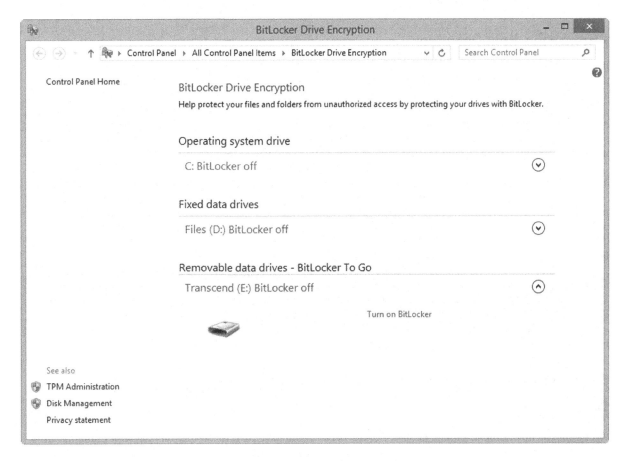

Figure 11-19. *Using BitLocker To Go*

■ **Note**   You cannot create Bitlocker To Go Drives in Windows RT.

When using a BitLocker To Go encrypted drive on another computer, there are limits to what you can do. For example, in versions of Windows that support the same version of BitLocker, namely Windows 7, you can get full access to the drive.

On Windows Vista and Windows XP, however, you have the BitLocker To Go Reader, which is software that, when you enter your password, allows you to read the contents of the protected drive, but doesn't allow you to write files back to it.

This is an important consideration when using BitLocker To Go. You should ask yourself, "Am I going to want to edit these files on another computer?" If the answer is yes, as long as the computer is running Windows 7 or Windows 8.1, you will be fine. If not, then you will have more difficulty.

Because you can open and read files, however, there is nothing to stop you from saving a copy of that file locally and e-mailing the modified file to yourself once you have edited it. This is really the only way to edit files on a protected drive in Windows Vista or Windows XP.

Encryption Best Practice

BitLocker is an incredibly useful technology, and there are many situations in which you will want to use it. Having a password on your computer is not normally enough protection because a hard disk can be removed from a computer and read on another device.

If you are using a tablet or an ultrabook, you *do* have an advantage because the hard disk is a slim sliver of circuit board that requires specialized equipment to read it if it is removed. Even so, unless you store all your documents and files on a cloud service such as SkyDrive or Dropbox and access them only over a live Internet connection, you probably have files on your computer that contain personally identifiable information (PII) about yourself or others.

Even the contacts database in your e-mail account is valuable because it can contain not only names, addresses, and e-mail addresses but also dates of birth and other information that can be used to clone a person's identity.

If you are using an office laptop for work, you have tougher data protection rules governing how you use and protect the data of individuals. If you lose your laptop or it is stolen, you can face considerable fines or jail time if the laptop contains unencrypted data on individuals. This is on top of the damage done to your reputation or business, if it is discovered that you have lost sensitive and important information. If you travel abroad on business, you can also face penalties from data protection authorities in the country that you are in.

For these reasons, I recommend that you buy a laptop that comes equipped with a TPM chip, if you can afford it, so that you can take advantage of BitLocker. It is true that it is commonly just the high-end laptops that come with TPM chips, but if you shop around, you can normally find other laptops, ultrabooks, and tablets containing the chip. For businesses, a TPM chip is an essential business expense. For consumers, it can be a very worthwhile addition.

If you are on the road, it is a good idea to carry—separate from your laptop—a USB flash drive containing the BitLocker keys for your computer. The system has been known to lock users out at the most inopportune moments.

Permitting and Blocking File and Folder Access with NTFS Permissions

Whenever you open a file or a folder on your PC, it is because you have permission to do so. These permissions are managed on a file and folder level and can be controlled to allow (or prevent) specific users or groups of users from being able to open them.

To change the permissions on a file or a folder, right-click it; from the menu that appears, click *Properties* (see Figure 11-20).

Figure 11-20. *You can change permissions for individual files and folders*

In the dialog that appears, click the *Security* tab and you will see the users and user groups who currently have permission to use the file or folder and, in the bottom part of the dialog, the individual permissions they have. These permissions are easy to understand: Full Control, Modify, Read & Execute, List Folder Contents, Read, and Write.

You can edit the permissions for any of the users or groups listed by clicking that user or group and then clicking the *Edit* button. The check boxes in the lower part of the window then become editable. If you do not see a user or group already listed, however, click *Edit*. In the next dialog, click the *Add* button.

A new dialog displays in which you can type a username (or just a partial name) and click the *Check name* button to search for a specific user or group of users (see Figure 11-21).

Figure 11-21. *You can add user permissions to files and folders*

After you add users or groups in this way, they will be added to the main options (refer to Figure 11-20).

Clicking the *Advanced* button in the security properties dialog for a file or folder displays additional controls (see Figure 11-22). This includes the place from which permissions are inherited. Let's say, for example, that you give somebody access to your Documents folder. Every folder under this will also be open to them, and the permissions will have been inherited from the parent, the main Documents folder. At the bottom left of the dialog is a *Disable inheritance* button that is used to prevent the automatic inheritance of security and other sharing properties from the parent for the currently selected file or folder.

Figure 11-22. *Advanced permissions options are also available*

If you want to view in a verbose manner the full permissions a user or group of users has for the currently selected file or folder you can click the *Effective Access* tab. This will display a clear list of all the permissions that the chosen user or group has for that item, see Figure 11-23.

Figure 11-23. *You can view full permissions information under the Effective Access tab*

Using Biometric Devices with Windows 8.1

Encryption isn't the only way to secure your computer. There are a variety of biometric devices available for computers. They require third-party tools because they are not normally controlled by Windows, but Windows 8.1 does contain controls, which you access through the Control Panel, for working with biometric devices installed on your computer (see Figure 11-24). This is a central location from which you can manage devices such as smart card readers and fingerprint scanners.

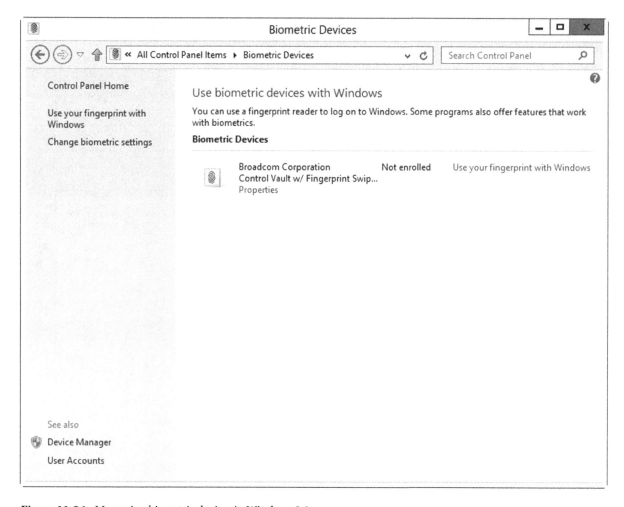

Figure 11-24. *Managing biometric devices in Windows 8.1*

You will probably find that when you open the management options for a particular biometric device from the Control Panel, it starts a third-party security utility rather than a Windows 8.1 wizard.

This is very common for biometric devices, but it is useful for Windows 8.1 to have a central location to manage them.

■ **Note**　Biometric devices use features unique to human physiology to identify a user. This commonly includes fingerprints, but can also include retinal scanners, voice and facial recognition, handwriting, and anything else that's noninvasive for the user.

Some companies offer software with webcams (or the Kinect controller) that use technologies such as facial recognition to lock and unlock your computer. One example is a webcam that automatically locks the computer when it can no longer see your face.

Unless these security devices appear in the Biometrics page in the Control Panel or are listed as security devices in the Device manager, you should treat the actual security they offer with caution. For example, software that comes with a webcam is unlikely to prevent anyone who wants to hack into your computer from doing so (your photograph might be enough to fool a webcam, which can see only in two dimensions anyway).

Don't assume that because your computer comes with a facility like this that it is secure. It doesn't necessarily work that way.

If you have a fingerprint sensor in your PC, an easy way to use your fingerprint with Windows 8.1 is directly through PC Settings, which now allows you to use your fingerprint to log in to Windows. You can find this setting in *Accounts* and then *Sign in Options* under the *Fingerprint* section. Clicking the *Add [fingerprint]* button opens an easy-to-use wizard that will scan your fingerprint (see Figure 11-25). A fingerprint option then appears on the Windows 8.1 login screen.

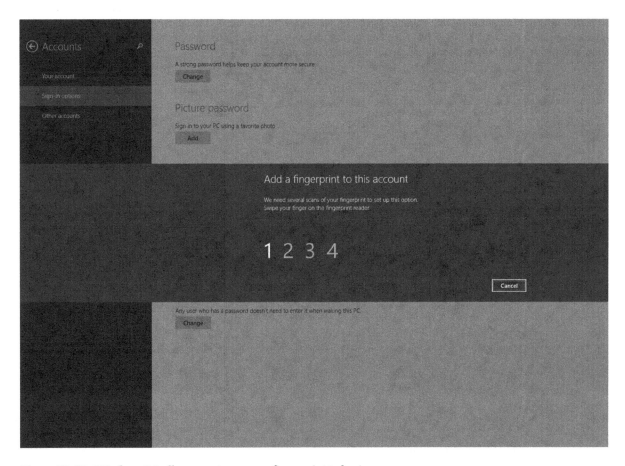

Figure 11-25. *Windows 8.1 allows you to use your fingerprint to log in*

Summary

When it comes to security, Windows 8.1 is very good at taking care of itself. With the default settings left unchanged for Windows Defender, User Account Control, and Windows Update, the operating system installs all the updates it requires as they become available.

Sometimes you may want to customize settings, perhaps to hide updates or to custom-configure the firewall. Some third-party antivirus vendors will tell you that in order to get full and flexible control of antivirus software and a firewall, you need their software. This simply isn't the case. Windows Defender is really quite flexible for a small lightweight package, and Windows Firewall is very powerful and flexible, indeed.

I never recommend changing the default settings in Windows. Making them tougher only makes life difficult for you, and turning them down takes away the protection that you need. These are parts of Windows 8.1 that you are wise to leave well alone.

When it comes to encryption, you have several options, and if you carry personal or sensitive files on your laptop or tablet, I strongly recommend that you purchase a device with a built-in TPM chip, allowing you to use BitLocker. If you are using a Windows RT device, device encryption technology is built into the operating system. It works in the same way as BitLocker and is just as secure, but it doesn't require the TPM.

Maintaining and Backing Up Your Computer and Files

Once you are using your new Windows 8.1 computer, the most important consideration is keeping it running smoothly to avoid downtime. Sometimes, despite all your best efforts, problems arise. If they do, visit my web site (http://www.theLongClimb.com), which has articles and videos to help you through problems.

So how can you set up Windows to maintain trouble-free use? And how can you set up backups to help you return to work quickly and easily if something goes wrong?

Maintaining a Healthy Computer

Why is it important to maintain a healthy operating system and have backups in place? Surely, Windows 8.1 is the most reliable and robust version of the operating system Microsoft has ever released. It comes with more tools for diagnosing and mitigating problems than any version of Windows before it.

I have long found it ironic that as Windows becomes increasingly stable and reliable, the number of diagnostic and repair tools provided as part of the operating system also increases.

The simple fact remains, however, that your computer is not a domestic appliance, and with the exception of Windows ARM–powered tablets, which have the operating system embedded on a chip, every single file that makes up Windows can potentially be changed, deleted, or become corrupt.

What Causes Computers to Become Unstable

I want to talk about why computers become unstable, crash, and fail to boot. There are actually many causes for these problems including the following:

- **Spikes, surges and interruptions to the electricity supply** can cause Windows files to become corrupt. You should always have your computer plugged in to a surge protector (as well as an uninterruptable power supply if you live in an area with an unreliable electrical supply). The power lead coming loose in the computer and the dog leaning against the power button are also causes. (I've suffered this many times, though it is very amusing when he switches on the Xbox and can't figure out why the floor makes a noise when he lies down.)

  Any interruption in the electrical supply can come at a time when a Windows file is being amended; it happens quite a bit. This problem can also cause the partition table—the database listing the physical location of each file on your hard disk—to become scrambled if the power is cut when it's being written to.

- **Poorly written software and drivers** are a very common cause of Windows failures. Don't assume for a moment that drivers delivered through Windows Update will always give you trouble-free operation; I've seen many a Blue Screen of Death happen this way. The problem here is that there is no way to predict or accommodate for the truly limitless variations in hardware and software on a specific machine.

  This is one of the reasons why Apple computers are reliable. As the manufacturer of both their operating system and all their hardware, they have complete and very tight control over the quality of drivers for the platform. It is the same with the App Store. Don't think that these app stores are just money-making schemes for Apple or Microsoft—they are, in fact, ways to ensure that the correct development tools are used, which encourages apps to be written in the right way.

  With the anticipated withdrawal of the x86 versions of Windows in Windows 9 (expected in 2015), Microsoft is expected to move to a strict signed-driver model in which all hardware drivers must be officially tested and signed off by Microsoft. At the moment, it is recommended but isn't mandatory, and because it can be expensive, many hardware manufacturers choose not to pay for it.

- **Malware and viruses** sneak onto the computer by taking advantage of the user. These malicious programs can cause all manner of havoc on a machine before you even know what's happened.

- **Installing too many programs and temporary files** causes a computer to fail over time. The more you try to do with your computer, the greater the risk that something will go wrong; and the more unnecessary files you have, the slower the computer will become over time.

How is Windows RT Different?

Windows tablets with ARM processors run a modified version of the Windows 8.1 operating system—called Windows RT—written onto a silicon chip instead of written file-by-file onto a hard disk. This offers greater speed because operating system files can load as quickly as they can from the fastest solid-state drive (SSD) in a desktop or laptop PC, and it's far less likely that a sudden power surge will corrupt any files (and the fact that tablets are much less likely to be in use when plugged into main electricity).

You also cannot install desktop software on Windows RT tablets; you can only download apps from the Windows Store. This reduces the chance of poorly written software causing problems and is because desktop apps are incompatible with the different processor architecture of ARM chips.

However, this does not extend to hardware because Microsoft has done an excellent job of making sure that you can still use existing USB and other hardware on these tablets in the way that you can with desktop PCs, laptops, and professional-grade tablets.

Using the Windows 8.1 Action Center

The Action Center (see Figure 12-1) is the central location in Windows for all important system messages and help tools. You access it by clicking the white flag icon on the far right of the Windows taskbar.

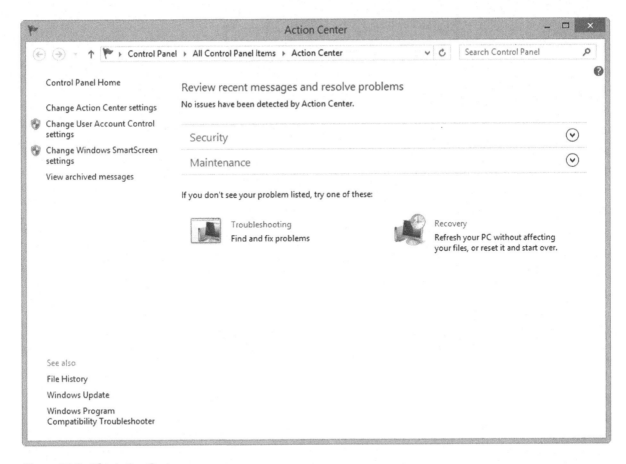

Figure 12-1. *The Action Center*

The Action Center is split into categories for Security and Maintenance, and warnings and alerts are automatically highlighted in amber or red.

Although the collapsible Security and Maintenance lists provide you with a great deal of useful and helpful information about Windows 8.1, you may want to customize the messages that you receive. The reason for this is that the Action Center will still alert you about backing up your files, for example, even if you have a third-party backup solution installed on your PC.

Managing Action Center Messages

To customize the messages you receive in the Action Center, click Change Action Center Settings in the top of the left pane. This opens a settings window with check boxes that allow you to turn on or off messages for all the alerts in the Action Center (see Figure 12-2).

Figure 12-2. *Changing the Action Center settings*

■ **Tip** I do not recommend turning off any of the alerts for Security Messages in the Action Center.

Using the Automatic Maintenance System in Windows 8.1

Windows 8.1 includes an automatic maintenance system that helps keep your computer running happily and healthily. These settings are in the Maintenance section of the Action Center. Click **Change maintenance settings** or search for **maintenance** at the Start screen.

The automatic maintenance includes deleting temporary and other unwanted files (such as those used by Windows Update), defragmenting of your hard disks, and checking for and installing updates for the operating system.

You can configure how and when you want this tool to run (see Figure 12-3) by choosing the time of day you want it to run or whether you want it to run at all. The time of day selection is important because if you are using a laptop or a tablet, Windows 8.1 will wake from sleep to perform the maintenance. It doesn't wake the computer if it is switched off, however.

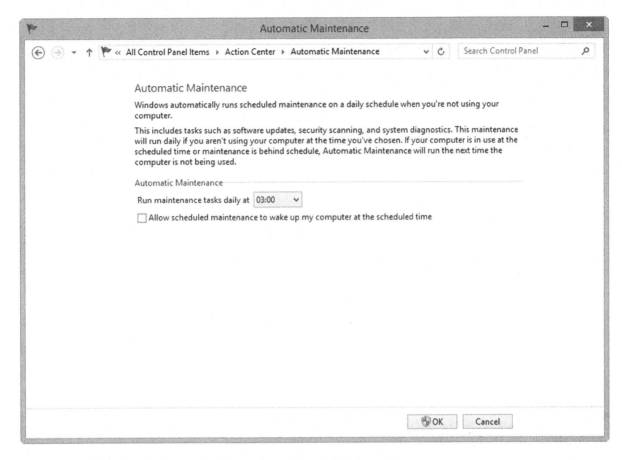

Figure 12-3. Changing the Automatic Maintenance settings in Windows 8.1

If you think your computer will be switched off at the time maintenance is due to be performed, you can choose the time that maintenance is performed.

You can run these tools independently as Disk Cleanup and Defragmenter, both of which are available by searches from the Start screen. I will show you how to use these tools and the additional options they provide in Chapter 13 if you want finer control over the automatic and manual maintenance options in Windows 8.1.

Using the Automated Troubleshooters

In the Action Center, you can run Windows 8.1's automated troubleshooters by clicking Troubleshooting (see Figure 12-4). There are many troubleshooters for almost every aspect of Windows, including networking and drivers.

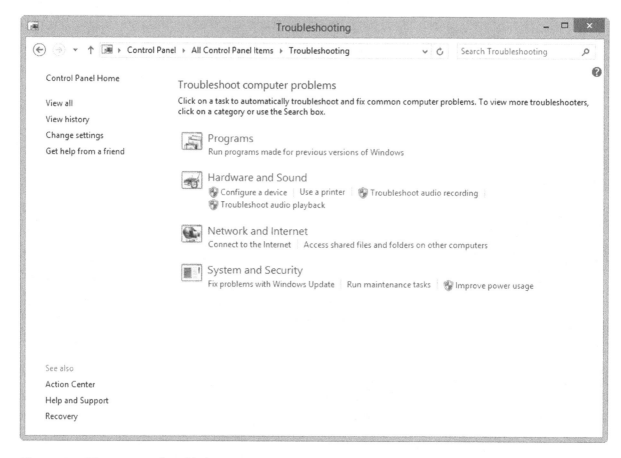

Figure 12-4. *The automated troubleshooters*

■ Note The automated troubleshooters resets Windows components and drivers to their default state. This is often enough to fix many problems, but if the issue is caused by a conflict with another driver or software package, the troubleshooters are unlikely to fix the problem. You can visit my web site (`http://www.theLongClimb.com`) for more troubleshooting help.

The troubleshooters are wizard-based and give clear information. They can be run easily by users of any technical ability. They are split into handy categories covering Programs, Hardware and Sound, Network and Internet, and System and Security. Each troubleshooter is explained in plain language.

■ Tip You can also access the automated troubleshooters by clicking Troubleshooting in the Control Panel.

You can change settings for the troubleshooters by clicking Change Settings in the left pane (see Figure 12-5). I do not recommend changing any of these settings, however.

Figure 12-5. *Changing the troubleshooting settings*

The Windows 8.1 Task Manager

The Windows Task Manager has been given its first significant overhaul in 20 years, and the new look provides more helpful information about Windows than we've seen before. By default, you just see a list of running programs with an *End Task* button in the bottom right of the window. It can be used to forcibly close troublesome programs and apps, but clicking the More Details button expands the window (see Figure 12-6).

Figure 12-6. *The simplified Task Manager in Windows 8.1 with a More Details button*

When you click the More Details button, the Task Manager expands to display not just more information but also a wealth of data about your running programs, apps, services, processes, hardware, and connections. The first thing you see is the Processes tab, which provides a heat-mapped display of the current processor, memory, disk, and network usage for all your running apps and desktop programs. This means that if something is hogging huge amounts of memory, for example, you can see it straightaway (see Figure 12-7).

Figure 12-7. *Monitoring software in the Task Manager*

To close a program in the Task Manager, highlight the program and click the End Task button in the bottom right of the window.

■ **Tip** If you are unsure about which programs and processes you can shut down, the Task Manager offers several ways to find out. If you right-click a process, you can select options to view its Properties or open its File Location. Both reveal information about the process. You can also search online for this process from the context menu, which provides even more detailed information about the process.

There is a great deal you can now do with the Task Manager in Windows 8.1. The Performance tab now provides live graphs similar to the Performance Monitor, but with general overviews of performance information rather than the extremely detailed metrics offered by its big brother.

The App History tab is a great way to determine if the apps you are using in Windows 8.1 are well written and fit for purpose. Let's say, for example, that you are finding that something is chewing through your mobile broadband allowance. On the App History tab, you can see the total amount of data that your apps have used, even when those apps are not running (see Figure 12-8).

Name	CPU time	Network	Metered network	Tile updates
Alarms	0:00:04	0 MB	0 MB	0 MB
Calculator	0:00:01	0 MB	0 MB	0 MB
Camera	0:00:00	0 MB	0 MB	0 MB
Finance	0:00:13	17.4 MB	0 MB	0.4 MB
Food & Drink	0:00:08	2.3 MB	0 MB	0.1 MB
Games	0:00:00	0 MB	0 MB	0 MB
Health & Fitness	0:00:00	0 MB	0 MB	0 MB
Help & Tips	0:00:00	0 MB	0 MB	0 MB
Internet Explorer	0:00:52	10.7 MB	0 MB	0 MB
Mail, Calendar and Peopl...	0:00:01	0.1 MB	0 MB	0 MB
Maps	0:00:00	0 MB	0 MB	0 MB
Music	0:00:00	0 MB	0 MB	0 MB
News	0:00:35	91.9 MB	0 MB	0.7 MB

Figure 12-8. The App History tab

It includes the ability to see the amount of data consumed by the Live Tile for an app, if appropriate. Probably less useful is the processor time taken by an app. This chart doesn't take into account how much you use one app compared to another. Metrics that are more relevant are gained through the Processes tab when an app is running or through the Performance Information and Tools page.

■ **Tip** You can open the Task Manager by pressing Ctrl+Alt+Del on your keyboard and selecting Task Manager from the options, by right-clicking the taskbar, or from the Win+X administration menu.

The Details tab is more like the traditional Task Manager, if you prefer that look and usage (see Figure 12-9). Here you see a complete list of every program, app, and process running in Windows 8.1. It works the same way as the old Task Manager in that you can right-click a program to shut it down.

Name	PID	Status	User name	CPU	Memory (p...	Description
armsvc.exe	2128	Running	SYSTEM	00	676 K	Adobe Acrobat Upd...
audiodg.exe	4240	Running	LOCAL SE...	00	4,212 K	Windows Audio Dev...
BtwRSupportService....	2148	Running	SYSTEM	00	896 K	Bluetooth Radio Ma...
csrss.exe	572	Running	SYSTEM	00	1,044 K	Client Server Runtim...
csrss.exe	684	Running	SYSTEM	00	1,260 K	Client Server Runtim...
dasHost.exe	2208	Running	LOCAL SE...	00	4,652 K	Device Association F...
DCPSysMgr.exe	5092	Running	Mike	00	1,764 K	Dell System Manager
DCPSysMgrSvc.exe	2488	Running	SYSTEM	00	1,692 K	Dell - System Mana...
dwm.exe	996	Running	DWM-1	00	41,564 K	Desktop Window M...
explorer.exe	1464	Running	Mike	00	52,368 K	Windows Explorer
FlashUtil_ActiveX.exe	3872	Running	Mike	00	1,988 K	Adobe® Flash® Pla...
GoogleCrashHandler...	1416	Running	SYSTEM	00	492 K	Google Crash Handler
GoogleCrashHandler...	2724	Running	SYSTEM	00	472 K	Google Crash Handler
iexplore.exe	5004	Running	Mike	00	13,624 K	Internet Explorer
iexplore.exe	4528	Running	Mike	00	82,208 K	Internet Explorer
iexplore.exe	5208	Running	Mike	00	171,544 K	Internet Explorer
jusched.exe	5116	Running	Mike	00	664 K	Java(TM) Update Sc...
lsass.exe	792	Running	SYSTEM	00	6,180 K	Local Security Auth...
minibin.exe	944	Running	Mike	00	892 K	The free recycle bin ...
mobsync.exe	4300	Running	Mike	00	1,428 K	Microsoft Sync Center
MsMpEng.exe	2312	Running	SYSTEM	00	45,084 K	Antimalware Service...
NisSrv.exe	3316	Running	LOCAL SE...	00	716 K	Microsoft Network ...
nvSCPAPISvr.exe	592	Running	SYSTEM	00	1,900 K	Stereo Vision Contro...

Figure 12-9. The Details tab gives very detailed information

It is interesting that only through the Details tab can you shut all the dependencies for a program. This means that when you shut down the program, all the processes and other programs that rely on it are also shut down automatically.

■ **Tip** You can shut down all the dependencies for a program under the Details tab by right-clicking the program or process and selecting *End Process Tree* from the options.

Customizing the Task Manager

When you click the *Performance* tab in the Task Manager, you are presented with a series of live graphs displaying the current status of your PC's processor (CPU), memory, hard disk(s), networking (Ethernet) and Wi-Fi, and other network connections if applicable. This view can be customized in a great many ways, just some of which can be seen in Figure 12-10.

Figure 12-10. *You can customize the Task Manager's Performance data in many ways*

You customize these views by right-clicking any of the graphs, both in the left pane and in the main view, and it's worth spending a few minutes playing with these views because they not only provide a great deal of valuable (and additional) information but they can also become useful widgets for leaving on your screen if you are troubleshooting a problem and want to keep one eye on something such as your network connection. These miniwindows can also be resized to make then smaller (or larger), making them even easier to leave running on your desktop, though you can only have only one open at a time.

Managing Startup Programs

The Task Manager is where you manage the programs that run at Windows startup. Not only does it make this feature simpler for nontechnical users but it also adds a very helpful Startup Impact column, which tells you—in simple *low, medium,* and *high* terms—how long the program slows down your computer when you turn it on (see Figure 12-11).

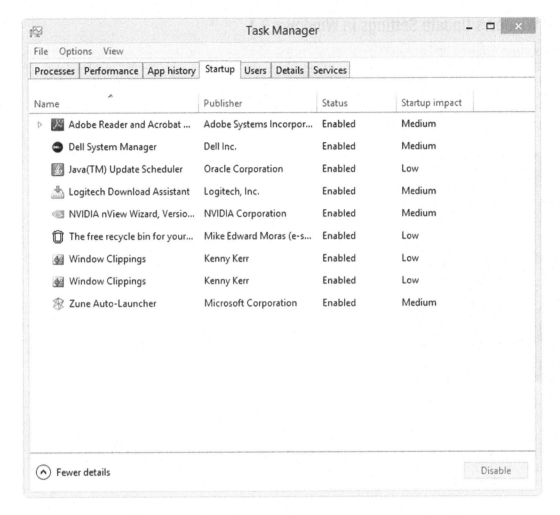

Figure 12-11. *Managing startup programs*

You can disable programs by highlighting them and then clicking the *Disable* button in the bottom right of the window. You can also re-enable programs the same way because disabled programs are not removed from the list.

You don't see Windows 8.1 apps here because they can't be set to run at startup, and any Live Tiles are automatically enabled unless you disable them by right-clicking the tile and selecting Disable Live Tile from the App bar.

Using Windows Update

Like Windows Firewall, Windows Update in Windows 8.1 has a split personality that is controllable through PC Settings and from the full Control Panel. Windows Update keeps your PC up to date with not just the latest security and stability patches and updates but also includes updates and improvements for both Windows and other Microsoft software you have installed, such as the Windows Essentials Suite and Microsoft Office.

Managing Windows Update Settings in Windows 8.1

The easiest way to use Windows Update is in PC Settings, where it can be found in the *Update & Recovery* section. It is a very simple affair. Windows Update automatically installs all critical, important, and recommended updates for a computer. There's very little the user has to do. In many ways, especially with regard to safeguarding people's personal privacy and security, it's exactly what the average nontechnical computer user needs (see Figure 12-12). More-technically savvy users, however, may prefer the added control that comes with the full Windows Update desktop settings, which are covered in the following section.

Figure 12-12. *Windows Update basic settings*

You can also use PC Settings to configure Windows Update: from the Start screen, search for *update* and then click *Choose whether to automatically install Windows updates*. The options display (see Figure 12-13) that allow you to configure Windows Update without having to visit the desktop. The settings include how Windows Update gets updates and whether additional and updates are included.

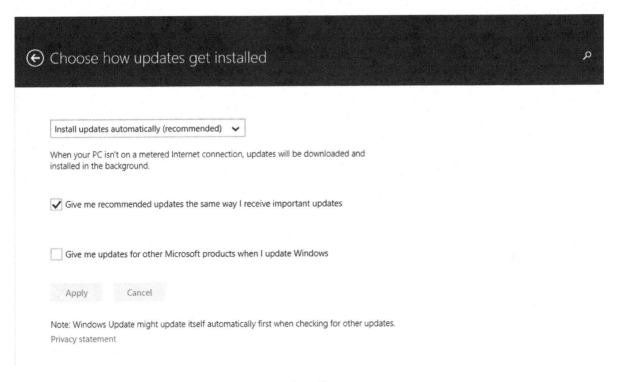

Figure 12-13. *You can configure Windows Update in a friendly way*

Managing Windows Update on the Desktop

If you want to control Windows Update from the desktop, access is on the desktop through the Control Panel. The features here are instantly recognizable to anyone who has used Windows Vista or Windows 7 and do include features not available in PC Settings.

The main control (see Figure 12-14) is color-coded to show at a glance your computer's current update status. There is a large green, amber, or red icon to alert you.

Figure 12-14. *Windows Update on the desktop*

Beneath this are details on when you or Windows 8.1 last checked online for updates, the updates received, and when they were installed.

■ **Tip** Windows Update on the desktop can check for updates to other Microsoft software, including Office and the Windows Essentials suite. You can turn this feature on from the main Windows Update screen.

When you are looking at the list of updates for your PC, if you're not sure what an update is, or what it will mean for your PC and your software, you can click it; and further information, including support links, appear in the right panel of the window (see Figure 12-15). This information also informs you if your PC is likely to need restarting after the update is installed, though it won't be required for two days.

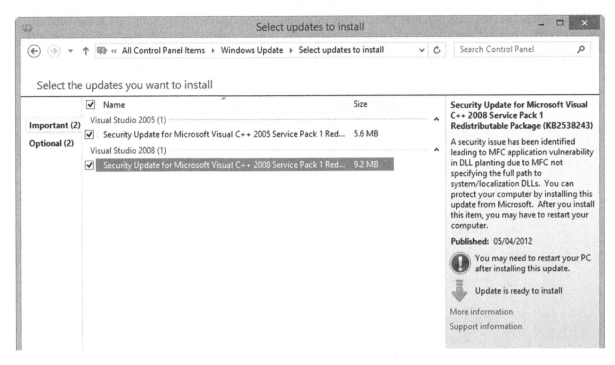

Figure 12-15. *You can get additional information about updates*

When you install an update that requires a restart, you will be prompted when you log into your PC and also when you put it to sleep and shut it down (see Figure 12-16). Please note, however, that just because an update has been downloaded, it will not be installed until you restart your PC.

Figure 12-16. *Windows notifies you politely if it needs to restart to install an update*

In the left pane of the main Windows Update page are the options you may want to change. In Change Settings, you can decide when and how Windows 8.1 installs updates. First, it's important to note that Windows 8.1 has many fewer restarts than earlier versions of the operating system, waiting a good two days before forcing a restart in the hopes that during that time you'll shut your computer down anyway. This means that there is less of a requirement to change the autoinstall settings in Windows 8.1 by clicking Change Settings in the left navigation pane to open the full Windows Update controls (see Figure 12-17), though I personally recommend that they be left in the default state.

Figure 12-17. *Changing the settings for Windows Update*

The following are the four Change Settings options for Windows Update:

- **Install updates automatically** (recommended by both Microsoft and me)

- **Download updates**, but let me choose whether to install them

- **Check for updates**, but let me choose whether to download and install them

- **Never check for updates**

Additionally, you have controls to allow Windows 8.1 to install recommended updates in the same way as it receives important updates. Recommended updates can include new features to the operating system.

You can also choose if you want to receive more updates through Windows update, including the following:

- **Recommended updates:** Include stability and feature updates that aren't deemed critical

- **Microsoft Product Updates:** Include software such as Microsoft Office, the Windows Essentials suite, and the Bing Bar for Internet Explorer

Hiding and Restoring Updates

On occasion, you may want to hide certain updates so that they don't appear and don't install. You might want to do this, for example, when Microsoft offers additional language packs that you don't want or need, or if a hardware driver issued through Windows Update is causing your computer to crash or the hardware to misbehave.

You can hide any update by right-clicking it in the main updates screen and then selecting Hide Update from the options. This process prevents the update from appearing again (see Figure 12-18).

Figure 12-18. *Hiding Windows Updates*

■ **Note** If you restore Windows 8.1 from an image backup or by using the Refresh option, all the hidden updates in Windows Update are visible once again. You have to re-hide them.

You can also select a group of updates to hide. To select multiple consecutive updates, click the first one and then hold the Shift key while clicking the last update in the series. To select nonconsecutive updates, hold the Ctrl key while clicking the updates you want to select.

To unhide all the updates you have hidden (you can't do just a few), click Restore Hidden Updates in the left pane of the main Windows Update screen.

Managing Hardware Drivers and Rolling Back Windows Update

I mentioned that some updates, especially drivers, occasionally cause Windows to become unstable. If this happens to you, be aware that Windows 8.1 creates a System Restore point whenever it runs Windows Update, so you can roll back to the last restore point to undo the driver change.

To do this from the Start screen, search for **system restore** and (though this might seem odd) select Create a Restore Point from the settings results. In the dialog, click the System Restore button.

You can now restore Windows to the way it was before the update was installed, and when you run Windows Update again, you can hide the offending update so that it doesn't bother you (see Figure 12-19).

Figure 12-19. *Using System Restore to roll back Windows Update*

Getting Updates from the Windows Store

Updates for your purchased and downloaded apps don't come through Windows Update, even if you have Microsoft Update turned on and the apps are written by Microsoft. All updates for anything downloaded from the Windows Store come *through* the Windows Store.

When you install Windows 8.1, all apps from then on are automatically updated when new versions become available and you won't be notified. You can control this, however, and turn it off by opening the Settings charm from within the Store app and then clicking the *App update* link near the top right of your screen. This displays the updates panel (see Figure 12-20), which includes the update controls.

Automatically update my apps

Yes

Automatic app updates isn't available when using a metered Internet connection.

Check for updates

App licenses

If you're not seeing up-to-date info for the apps you own, try syncing app licenses.

Sync licenses

Figure 12-20. *You can disable automatic updating of apps*

Major updates to Windows now also come from the store, and if you upgrade from Windows 8 to Windows 8.1, this is how the update is delivered. For more detailed information on how you get the Windows 8.1 update, see Chapter 15.

Installing Major Windows 8 Updates and Service Packs

About once per year, Microsoft releases a Windows service pack or a major update, such as Windows 8.1. Back in the days of Windows XP, some service packs, including the now famous XP SP2, included many new features for the operating system. For example, XP SP2 brought with it the new security center and many new security features. Indeed, there was so much in it that some commentators said that Microsoft could have sold it as a completely new version of Windows. Windows 8.1 picks this up again with a major overhaul of the operating system and the inclusion of many new features.

This makes some power users quite excited about these major updates, with some even wanting to download and install the beta of the service pack.

Depending on the type of update, they could come either through Windows Update or through the Windows Store, and it's too early yet to tell what Microsoft's long-term strategy will be (though I would guess that eventually all updates will be delivered through the Store, and Windows Update will be retired).Windows does a good job of notifying you when a major update is available (see Figure 12-21), and although the methods for informing you might vary, you are likely to be informed by a pop-up toast on your screen.

Updates (13) Installing 26...

Store

Update Windows

Spotlight

Figure 12-21. *Major updates are now beginning to be delivered through the Windows Store*

Protecting and Repairing Windows

Although it is simple and straightforward to keep your copy of Windows 8.1 running smoothly and in a healthy state, it can also be simple and straightforward to rescue the OS in the event something goes wrong. In this section, I'll show you what the various options are and how they work.

Creating a Recovery Drive

A *recovery drive* is a USB flash drive containing the tools required to repair Windows and get to options such as Startup Repair, Refresh, Reset, and System Restore if your copy of Windows 8.1 can't start.

You create a recovery drive from the Control Panel by clicking Recovery (in the large or small icons view, it will not appear in the Category view of the Control Panel). You initially see options to refresh and reset the PC, but if you click Advanced Tools, an option to **Create a recovery drive** will appear (see Figure 12-22).

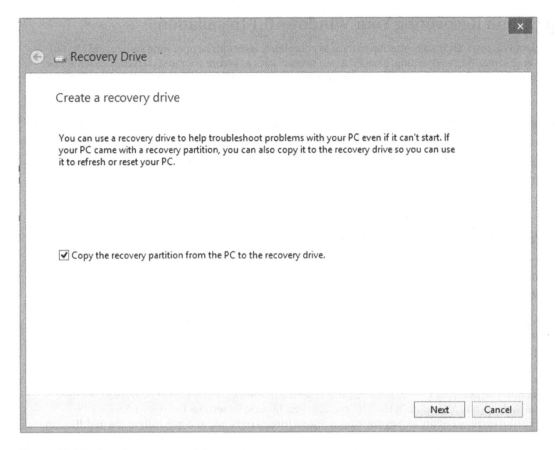

Figure 12-22. *Creating a recovery drive*

■ **Tip** If you have a recovery partition on your computer that was preconfigured by the manufacturer, you can check a box to add this image to the recovery drive. This substantially increases the size of the recovery drive files, however, and is suitable only for USB flash drives of 32 GB capacity and higher, but it gives you a valuable extra option for rescuing Windows if a disaster occurs.

Once the recovery drive is created, you can start your computer from it to access the recovery options. Note, however, that booting from USB needs to be turned on in the BIOS or UEFI firmware on your motherboard.

■ **Caution** If you are using a Windows RT tablet such as Microsoft Surface, you should *always* create a recovery drive containing a backup copy of the system image. There is no way to reinstall Windows RT other than from a recovery drive, so if complete disaster strikes, the only other option available to you would be to return the PC to the manufacturer for reimaging, which can take time and could incur a charge. You can create a recovery drive with a full system image of Windows RT on a USB flash drive as small as 4 GB in size.

Backing Up and Recovering Your Windows 8.1 Installation

Back in the days of Windows XP, it was common to have to completely reinstall the operating system and all your software every time something went wrong. Now there are several ways to secure your installed copy of Windows and restore it in the event of a crisis. In this section, I will show you how to do just that.

▪ **Note** Windows 8 included a full system image backup facility that could be found in the *Windows 7 File Recovery* option in the Control Panel. This feature has been removed in Windows 8.1, as has the ability to restore one of these images. The alternative is Windows 8.1's Refresh feature, and I will show you how to get the best out of this and create custom Refresh images in the next section.

Repairing Windows 8.1 Quickly Using Refresh

With Windows 8.1, Microsoft has introduced a new way to create a backup image that, unlike its System Image Backup, is implemented so simply that users of any technical ability can use it. This new Refresh option creates a backup of the operating system that is easily and quickly restored from PC Settings or from the startup settings for the OS such as seen when you start your PC from a Recovery Drive.

There is one critical difference between the older System Image Backup and Refresh that affects power users, IT pros, and system administrators. Although you can create a custom Refresh image that will restore all your installed desktop software, it doesn't back up any of your settings for those programs. This means that software such as Microsoft Outlook will be returned to its *installation* settings and you will need to reconfigure e-mail accounts in it, and the settings and preferences in all your other desktop software.

Many users won't be bothered by this, however, and indeed Windows 8.1 syncs a great many of its settings, including for the desktop, and Microsoft Office 2013 can also synchronize its settings between different PCs.

Refresh is also an excellent utility for anyone who supports friends or family and gets calls in the middle of the afternoon about a problem "that will only take a minute."

You can access the Refresh from PC Settings by selecting *Update and Recovery* and then clicking the *Recovery* option in the left navigation pane (see Figure 12-23).

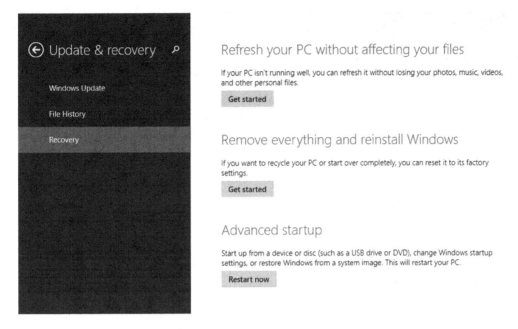

Figure 12-23. Activating Refresh from PC Settings

Refresh is the first option at the top of your screen and there is an explanation of what it will do. When you are ready to refresh your computer, click the *Get Started* button. The process is completely automated from that point. You will need to restart your computer several times.

When you want to refresh your copy of Windows, Windows 8.1 explains what the Refresh process will do and asks you to confirm that you want to refresh the computer. Click OK when you are ready to begin the process, which can take between 15 and 60 minutes, depending on whether you have created a custom Refresh image or not (see the next section).

You can also refresh your PC from Windows 8.1 Startup, and the details for how to this works can be found in the "Understanding Windows 8.1 Startup Menus" section a little later in this chapter. There are several ways to get to this:

1. If your PC doesn't start three times, Startup Repair runs. If this can't repair your computer, it offers you advanced repair options that include Refresh. (For more on this, see "Using Startup Repair" later in this chapter.)

2. You can start your PC using a recovery drive; note that you may need to access the boot device options on your PC (usually F12 or Del) to tell the PC to boot from a USB flash drive.

3. You can start your PC from a Windows 8.1 installation DVD. At the Install screen, click the *Repair your PC* link instead to take you to the repair options.

Creating a Custom Refresh Image

You can create a custom Refresh image. You may want to do this because, by default, this feature refreshes your copy of Windows 8.1 while keeping your files and apps intact, but it will wipe out all your desktop software.

Creating a custom Refresh image turns this into a snapshot of your PC as it is *then*, complete with all your desktop software installed.

■ **Note**   Remember that restoring from a custom Refresh image resets all your desktop software, so you will need to set up programs again unless their settings are automatically synced between PCs, such as can be done with Microsoft Office 2013.

Perform the following steps to create a custom Refresh image:

1. Press Win+X to open the Administration menu.

2. Select *Command Prompt (Admin)* to run the command prompt as an administrator.

3. Type **recimg -CreateImage C:\Folder**, where C:\Folder is the location in which you want the backup to be stored. This backup location can also be on a different partition or hard disk in your PC, and creating a Refresh image away from your Windows installation can add extra resiliency if your copy of Windows 8.1 becomes scrambled or wiped.

Windows 8.1 creates your custom Refresh image, which is restored using the Refresh feature.

Creating an Image Backup of Windows 8

Windows Vista was the first version of Microsoft's operating system to include image backup functionality. Windows 7 brought this excellent and very useful feature to all editions of the operating system. It remains in Windows 8 largely unchanged, though there is a new interface for restoring an image backup.

I always recommend that the backup image be from a relatively clean installation in which you have only made essential changes and all temporary files have been deleted. It's a good idea to run Windows utilities such as the Disk Cleanup Wizard, which you can find by searching **clean** at the Start screen, and clicking **Free up disk space by deleting unnecessary files** in the Settings search results.

Access the Windows Image Backup creation utility by clicking File History in the Control Panel, where you have the option to Create a System Image Backup in the bottom left corner of the window (see Figure 12-24).

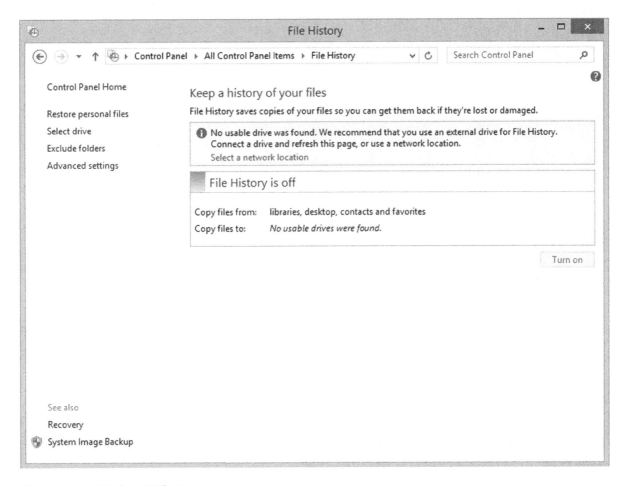

Figure 12-24. *Windows 7 File Recovery page*

Click System Image Backup to start the wizard, which guides you through creating a backup image of Windows 8. The backup image will be a complete snapshot of your PC at that time, including all of your installed software, their configuration settings and customized Windows settings, and all of your user accounts.

You will be asked where you want to store the image backup (see Figure 12-25). You can choose another hard disk or partition in your computer, one or more DVDs (though bear in mind these can degrade over time), or a network location.

Figure 12-25. *You can save your backup in different locations*

If your computer always connects to your network via Wi-Fi, you should not choose a network location. This is because the image is restored from the Windows boot menu where no Wi-Fi drivers are loaded. When restoring from a network location, the computer needs to be connected to the network via a physical cable.

■ **Note**   If you have several hard disks or partitions in your computer, you will be asked if you want to add any of them to the image backup.

Before creating the backup, Windows 8 shows you what you're backing up and where the backup will be stored (see Figure 12-26). Click the Start Backup button when you are ready to begin.

Figure 12-26. *Windows shows you the drives it will back up*

You cannot restore a System Image Backup from within Windows 8.1 in the way you can with a Refresh image, you need to start your computer from the F8 boot menu, a USB Recovery Drive or the Windows 8.1 installation DVD. When you do this the options to restore the System Image Recovery can be found in the Advanced Options menu in Startup Repair, and I will show you how to access this shortly.

■ **Tip**   While you can create a System Image Backup in File History you can also create one from the Command Line using the Windows PowerShell Utility. You create it by opening a *PowerShell (Admin)* window and using the command **wbAdmin start backup -backupTarget:D: -include:C: -allCritical –quiet**, where –backupTarget is the hard disk (or network location) in which the image is to be stored and where –include is the drive letter of the disk on which Windows 8.1 is installed.

For network locations, you might optionally need to insert the commands **-user:username -password:userPassword** just before the –allCritical switch. You can also specify more than one hard disk to be stored in the backup with the switch –include:C:,D:,E:.

This image backup can then be restored using a recovery drive or installation disc for Windows 8.1, and you find a *System Image Recovery* option in the *Troubleshoot ➤ Advanced* page. Although it is technically possible to create a system image backup in Windows RT, the restore option is not available in that version of Windows.

Safe Mode and Diagnostic Startup Mode

With Safe Mode removed from the new boot menu, how do you get to it? You can see the older boot menu by pressing Shift+F8 when starting Windows. Here you have the same familiar options, including Safe Mode and Safe Mode with Networking (see Figure 12-27). You can access these settings from the boot options by clicking *Troubleshoot*, then clicking *Advanced Options*, and then clicking *Startup Settings*. You are prompted to restart your PC, and the Safe Mode option is then available.

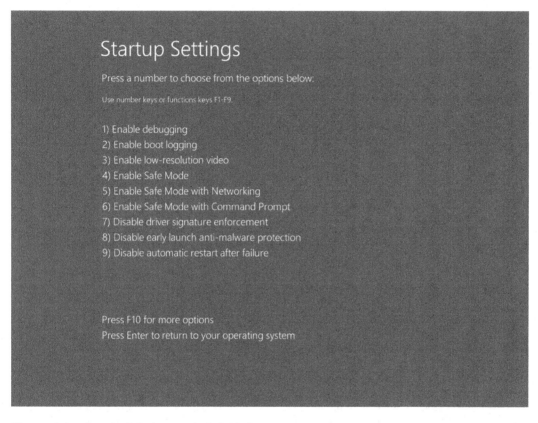

Startup Settings

Press a number to choose from the options below:

Use number keys or functions keys F1-F9.

1) Enable debugging
2) Enable boot logging
3) Enable low-resolution video
4) Enable Safe Mode
5) Enable Safe Mode with Networking
6) Enable Safe Mode with Command Prompt
7) Disable driver signature enforcement
8) Disable early launch anti-malware protection
9) Disable automatic restart after failure

Press F10 for more options
Press Enter to return to your operating system

Figure 12-27. *Starting Windows 8.1 in Safe Mode*

■ **Note**   Safe Mode is not available from the boot menu in Windows RT.

Not all computers allow you to press F8 or Shift+F8, however, especially ones that start up really quickly. If you need to get into Safe Mode in this case, you can do so from the Windows System Configuration page, in which Safe Mode comes with a whole variety of additional and useful options.

You access the System Configuration dialog by searching for **msconfig** at the Start screen. Under the Boot tab, there is an option to turn the computer on in Safe Mode the next time it starts.

The most interesting option is under the General tab. Although Safe Mode is very useful, it is also extremely limiting and doesn't allow you to perform many actions.

Under the General tab, there is the option to turn on a diagnostic startup (see Figure 12-28). It is equivalent to Safe Mode+ in that, in addition to loading the bare operating system, it also loads some system drivers, such as for your graphics, and it allows you to perform the full range of Windows 8.1 configuration operations.

Figure 12-28. *Turning on diagnostic startup mode*

■ **Note**   When you switch these options on in the System Configuration dialog, they remain on until you run `msconfig` again and switch them off.

Using Startup Repair

If Windows 8.1 fails to start three times, and the System Reserved partition isn't damaged, Windows launches Startup Repair. This is an automated system that resets Windows components to their default settings in an attempt to get things working again.

If Startup Repair can't repair Windows, it offers you advanced repair options, which are the menus shown in Figures 12-29 through 12-32. A refresh might be the best option to get Windows 8.1 working again.

Figure 12-29. *Windows 8.1 can self-repair when it can't start*

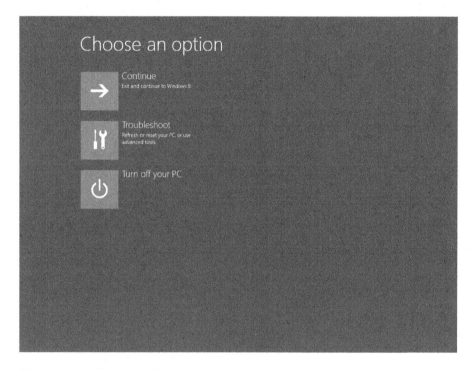

Figure 12-30. *The main Windows 8.1 startup menu*

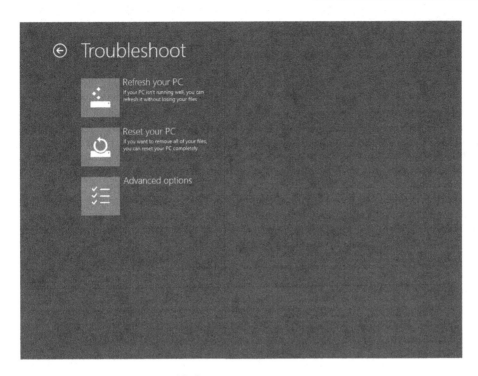

Figure 12-31. *The startup troubleshooting menu*

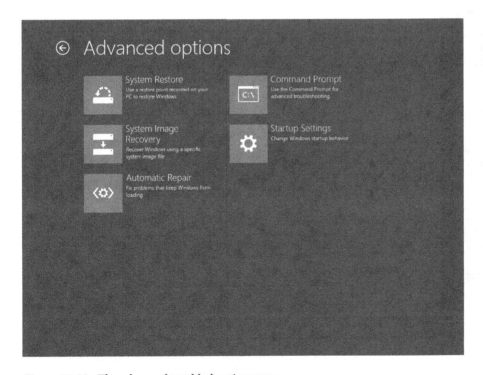

Figure 12-32. *The advanced troubleshooting menu*

Understanding the Windows 8.1 Startup Menus

The startup menus in Windows 8.1 have changed considerably to accommodate the mouse and graphical systems that were not supported on older computer systems.

This isn't to say that you can't access the previous DOS–type startup menu (it is still available with the Shift+F8 key press at startup), but the standard F8 key now takes you to the new graphical system if your hardware supports it.

At the first screen, you have three options: continue to start Windows 8.1, turn off your computer, or troubleshoot the machine (see Figure 12-30). Note that on some devices, you might also see a *Use device* option here. It allows you to restore a Refresh image from a USB flash drive on which you have created a recovery drive image if you need to.

The Troubleshooting options are quite basic, offering only the new options to refresh and reset your computer. You might expect to find the Startup Repair option here, for example, but it has been moved into the Advanced Options (see Figure 12-31).

All the remaining options are found in the Advanced Options. Here you have access to the command prompt, in which you can perform actions such as manually repairing the boot options, performing a CHKDSK (check disk), and more. You can also change the Windows Startup Settings, which allows you to turn off the new graphical menu and have Windows 8.1 use the traditional DOS menu instead (see Figure 12-32).

Restoring Windows 8.1 to Factory Settings

If you are selling your computer or giving it away, you can use the Reset option to restore Windows 8.1 to its factory settings. Doing this wipes out all your user accounts, files, settings, apps, and programs.

Remove Everything and Reinstall Windows is in PC Settings under *Update & Recovery* and then *Recovery* (see Figure 12-33). Make sure that you have backed up all your files before performing a reset because they will be deleted from the PC.

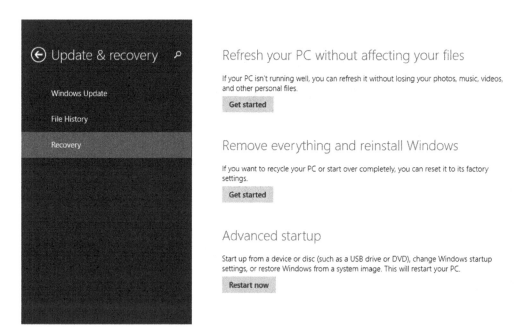

Figure 12-33. *You can retsore your PC to factory settings using Reset*

■ **Tip**   Reset does not securely erase your files, so they can be recovered later on using a file recovery program. If you want to securely erase deleted files and data on your hard disk, there are many third-party utilities that can do this, but the excellent—and free—CCleaner (`http://www.piriform.com/ccleaner`) does this job along, with providing other useful cleanup and maintenance tools for Windows.

Backing Up Files and Folders

Nothing is more important on your computer than your files and documents. Once you lose those precious family photographs of baby Gilbert's birth or last year's vacation in the Maldives, they're gone forever—and you have nothing but your memories from then on.

It is critical that you safeguard your files on your computer. I'll show you how to do this later in this chapter. It is very important that you make backups and keep them in safe and sensible places.

Where to Store Backups

Choosing where to store backups of your files is critical because choosing to store your backups in the wrong location can often be as bad as having no backups at all. So where can you store your backups, and what are the pros and cons?

■ **Tip**   Many Internet routers allow you to plug a USB hard disk into them to share on the network as storage. This can be an excellent local backup location.

- **A second hard disk on your PC** is the fastest and least difficult way to store backups because an automated system can update the backup every time you change a file. However, an electrical spike through the PC could fry the original data and the backup. A theft or a fire will destroy both copies.

- **Network attached storage** (NAS) is a great way to store backups in your home or workplace. NAS drives are hidden in inaccessible places. They are still vulnerable to fire, however.

- **CD/DVD/Blu-ray discs** aren't advisable for backups any more. Partly because, with the exception of Blu-ray, the discs don't have large enough capacities for our ever-growing collections of digital photographs and home videos. Also, these discs degrade—and there's little way to tell whether it will be 3 months or 30 years before they become unreadable.

- **USB hard disks** are probably the best option because they can be stored offsite in the home of a friend or family member, or at the home of the person responsible for backing up your vital business data.

- **USB flash drives** are of a size and price that you can consider storing backups on them. Bear in mind, however, that they are relatively easily broken (e.g., sat on, put in the washing machine, or chewed by the dog). If you store one on your key chain, you might never find it again.

- **Cloud storage** is becoming ever more popular and there are a lot of services to choose from, including Microsoft's SkyDrive, Google Drive, Carbonite, Mozy, Amazon S3, and many more. The problem here is the initial upload can be tens if not hundreds of gigabytes, and unless you are on a super-fast broadband connection, it can take weeks or even months to upload.

■ **Tip** I always recommend using two backup solutions. I store backups locally on a NAS drive for quick restoration, but I also use Microsoft's SkyDrive service for cloud backup.

Remember to Encrypt Business Backups

You can normally consider your workplace relatively secure. You control who has keys and access to the building and the room(s) containing your computers. If you store business backups offsite, however, which is highly recommended, you should make sure that those backups are either encrypted or kept in a very safe location.

Sending unencrypted backups home with a senior staff member is one thing, but given that you have no control over this person's home security presents a data protection risk. The only safe strategy with business data—and the one the data protection regulators are most likely to endorse—is a virtual private network (VPN) or cloud-based encrypted solution designed specifically for business.

■ **Caution** Beware of synced network and cloud backups! If you use a service such as SkyDrive that syncs the files on your computer with those in the cloud or a backup solution that keeps files in sync by *deleting the file on the backup destination when that file is removed from the computer*, you could find that your backup is wiped completely if you accidentally delete the files from your computer. To avoid this problem, stop your backup software from running until you can restore the files.

Backing Up Your Files in Windows 8.1

There are two ways to back up your files in Windows 8.1. The first method is to use Microsoft's SkyDrive cloud sync and backup service. You can set this up in PC Settings in the *SkyDrive* section, and it lets you know how much space you have available for file backups and make it easy for you to purchase additional space (see Figure 12-34).

Figure 12-34. *Microsoft's SkyDrive service is built into Windows 8.1*

You set up the SkyDrive file backup in the *Files* section of the SkyDrive controls and then, assuming that you have enough space in the cloud to accommodate all your files, they will be backed up (although the first backup could take several days or even weeks, depending on the speed of your Internet connection).

If you want to keep a local backup copy of your files, Windows 8.1 comes with a new file backup and versioning tool called File History, which keeps backup copies of files as you make changes to them so that if you accidentally make a change to a file that you didn't intend to make, the file can be restored.

File History can be incredibly useful if you use your computer for work and change files (such as Office documents) frequently. It can roll back accidental or unapproved changes.

File History is accessed from both PC Settings and the Control Panel. You can use local internal hard disks, USB attached drives, and network attached drives (though the latter two don't work if they're not plugged in or are inaccessible). Figure 12-35 shows the File History options in PC Settings.

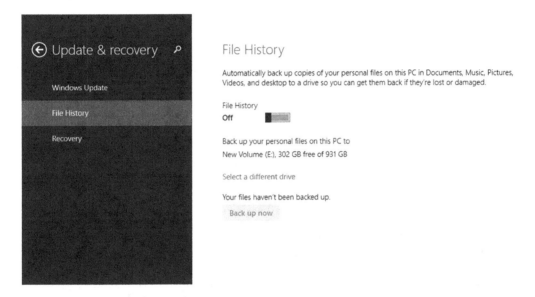

Figure 12-35. *Windows 8.1 File History*

The File History options in PC Settings automatically detects any USB attached hard disks or additional internal hard disks on your PC, but (as I mentioned earlier in this section), you can use networked locations as well. They include NAS drives and USB hard disks that are plugged into your Internet router. If you want to select one of these locations as the storage for your backups click the *Select a different drive* link.

You can get considerably more control over File History by accessing it from the Control Panel. It provides much finer control over the feature, such as drilling down into network locations or hard disks so that you can store your backup in a specific folder rather than just the root of the drive (see Figure 12-36).

Figure 12-36. *You can get finer File History options in the Control Panel*

■ **Tip**   If you use a USB hard disk plugged into your Internet router for backups, why not use it for File History as well?

The first time you run File History, it creates a full and complete backup of your Libraries (Document, Music, Pictures, and Video), and if you want to back up additional files you should add them to your Libraries. This initial backup can also take some time, depending on how many files you are backing up and your connection speed. You don't need to worry about leaving the PC on, however, because if you need to put the PC to sleep or shut it down, the backup pauses and resumes when you switch it on next.

File History also keeps copies of files that have been deleted and changed, helping you recover older copies of documents that were accidentally deleted or modified when they shouldn't have been. It also includes every minor change that's made to a file when it is opened. Every time you open a file such as a picture or an MP3, the file is changed to update the Last Accessed timestamp. You could find that your File History is full of MP3s and nothing else.

■ **Note**   When you use File History, both PC Settings and the File History controls in the Control Panel display the status of your backup.

You can rectify this from the File History pane by clicking Exclude Folders on the left of the page. Here you can exclude the drives containing file types that are likely to change only when the Last Accessed marker is set (see Figure 12-37). These file types include music, pictures, and video. Bear in mind, however, that this also excludes these files and folders from the backup, so you need to ensure that you have a backup copy of them elsewhere.

Figure 12-37. *You can exclude files and folders from File History*

If you want to change the location of the File History drive, you can do it in the left pane by clicking Change Drive. File History then moves all its backed-up files to the new location. Clicking Advanced Settings in the left pane gives you more control over how File History operates (see Figure 12-38):

- You can choose how often it saves copies of files. Remember that it doesn't do it automatically when a file is saved. You can also choose from periods as low as 10 minutes. If you use your Windows 8.1 computer for work, a shorter period may offer you more reassurance if you work on files that change regularly, such as Word documents.

- You can also select how much of the available hard disk space is reserved for an offline copy of your documents. This is a local copy of changed and deleted files that's kept on your own PC so that they can be restored even when you are separated from USB-attached or NAS File History backups.

- You can also choose the amount of time a version is kept. The Forever option is a little misleading because it is the same as the Until Space Is Needed option. Keeping files until space is needed is probably the best option, however.

Figure 12-38. *The advanced file versioning options*

■ **Tip**   If you are running short of hard disk space on the drive in which you keep your File History or if you just have too many old versions of files stored, you can click Clean Up Versions to delete older versions of files from the disk.

■ **Note**   If you are using a laptop or tablet that has only a single hard disk, you might not be able to keep File History versions locally on the computer because Windows 8.1 doesn't support keeping versions in the same location as the original files. Many Internet routers have USB ports so that you can plug in a hard disk to use as network storage. This is an excellent location for backups and File History versioning.

You can restore earlier versions of files using Restore Personal Files in the left pane of the File History page. It brings up a window showing you all the previous versions of documents that have been saved, along with their time and date. You can restore individual files or groups of files.

Restoring Backed up and Deleted Files with File History

File History is used to restore your files under four different circumstances: you had to reinstall Windows on your PC; you need to move your files to a new PC; you accidentally deleted a file or files and you need to recover them; or you accidentally made a change to a file that you didn't intend to make.

It is these last two scenarios I want to show you first. When you are in File Explorer and are looking at a specific folder, or indeed have a file highlighted, you will see a *History* button under the *Home* tab on the ribbon (see Figure 12-39). Click this to open the full File History restore window.

Figure 12-39. *You can restore files from File Explorer*

In the window that opens, you have several different sets of controls (see Figure 12-40). The back button and address bar at the top of the window operate in exactly the same way as they do in File Explorer, and typing a folder location into the address bar takes you to the corresponding backup.

Figure 12-40. *The main File History restore window*

At the bottom of the window are back and forward (in time) buttons that move backward and forward through the different dates and times that changes were made to files. These buttons help you find the right version of a file to restore. Between these buttons is a large, green Restore button.

To restore files, select the file (or files) you want to restore and then click the green Restore button. It really couldn't be simpler to restore your files.

In the main File History controls, accessed from the Control Panel, there is a *Restore personal files* link in the top left of the window (see Figure 12-41). Click it to open the File History restore window (see Figure 12-40).

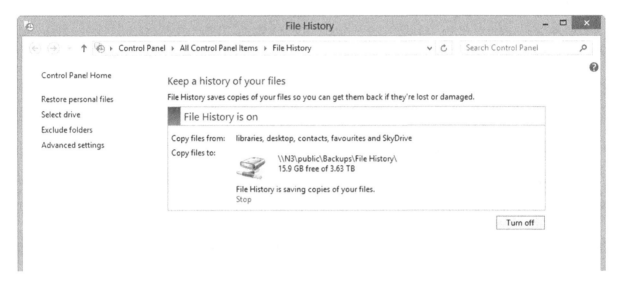

Figure 12-41. *Restoring files from the main File History window*

▪ **Note** If you are restoring your files from File History after reinstalling Windows, you need to set up File History again and point it at the same backup location you used before. You can then restore all your files to your PC.

Safeguarding Your Personal Files and Folders

One of the problems with Libraries is the uncertainty of where files are stored. If your files and data are stored on the same partition as your Windows installation, and you are forced to reformat the hard disk and reinstall the operating system from scratch, you could lose everything.

Although changing the default save location for Libraries is one way to do this, I prefer to move the user folders wholesale over to a new partition or hard disk in the computer.

A hard disk is a physical storage area in which everything is put in the same place, including your copy of Windows and all your files (see the left image in Figure 12-42). This means that if something goes wrong with Windows, you can face the possibility of losing all your files as well.

Figure 12-42. *An unpartitioned disk and a partitioned disk*

If you split your hard disk into several partitions, you are splitting that *physical* hard disk into several *logical* ones. File Explorer sees each partition as a different disk drive.

The image on the right in Figure 12-42 is my recommended setup. It has three partitions: one for Windows 8.1, a big one for files, and a third one for a backup copy of the operating system.

If you have a second hard disk in your computer, you might want to use it for files and backups. If something goes wrong with the hard disk on which Windows is installed, and this hard disk will see the most mechanical activity, your files and your backup copy of Windows will still be intact.

To create new partitions on your hard disk for files, perform the following steps, though you should always be extremely careful when managing partitions on your PC. If they are not managed correctly, all manner of things can go wrong, including wiping out your copy of Windows 8.1 and all your files:

1. Press *Win+X* to display the Administration menu.

2. Click *Disk Management.*

3. To create a new partition, you need to make space by shrinking an existing one. In the Disk Management window, right-click the hard disk partition you want to shrink (usually the C:\ drive containing your Windows 8.1 installation).

4. From the options, select *Shrink Volume* (see Figure 12-43). Note that "Volume" is the terminology used here to describe both disks and partitions.

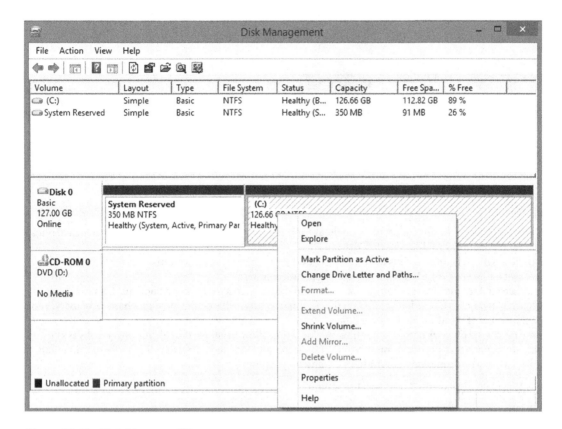

Figure 12-43. *Shrinking a partition*

■ **Note**   How big should you leave your Windows partition? For general light usage, 50 GB is a good size (enter **51200**
in the size box). An enthusiast might want 100 GB to 200 GB (**102400** or **204800**), but a gamer might want up to
300 GB (**307200**).

---

5.   Choose the amount by which you want to shrink the disk. You'll need to leave enough
space for all your files and an image backup. On a larger hard disk (1 TB or more), I suggest
shrinking the drive down to 25 percent of its current size (e.g., 250 GB).

6.   In the *unallocated space* remaining after shrinking the partition, right-click with your
mouse (see Figure 12-44).

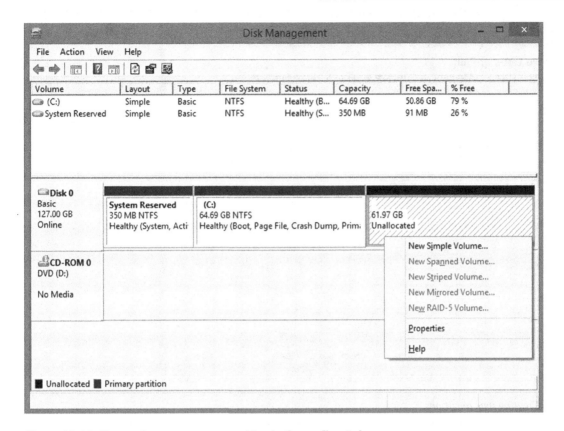

Figure 12-44. *You need to create a new partition in the unallocated space*

7.   From the options, select New Simple Volume.

8.   Create a partition of the appropriate size for files. I recommend 50 percent of the original volume size. Give it a name and drive letter (see Figure 12-45).

Figure 12-45. *Creating new partitions*

9. Repeat steps 6 to 8 for an Image Backup drive. Note that if you are using a professional-grade tablet or an ultrabook that does not have a large hard disk, you might not have enough space for an image drive.

■ **Note**   Many computers come with a backup partition containing a factory system image of Windows 8.1. If your computer didn't come with a Windows 8.1 installation disc, I recommend leaving it and creating your own secondary backup partition as well because you never know when the factory image might come in useful.

Now we need to move the user folders and files to the new files partition.

1. Open File Explorer.

2. Click the small arrow in the File Explorer Address bar at the far left of the current address location.

3. From the drop-down location options, click your username (see Figure 12-46).

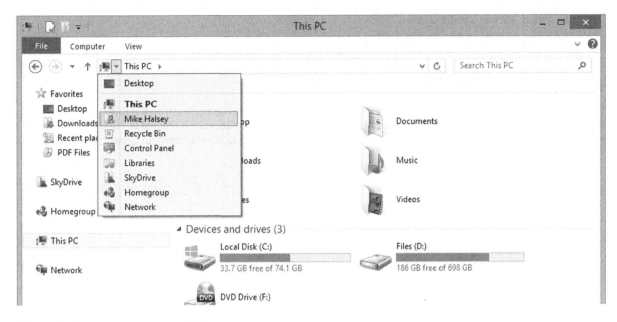

Figure 12-46. *Selecting your user folders*

4.   Select the user folders you want to move, which are usually Downloads, Documents, Music, Pictures, and Videos (see Figure 12-47). Your Internet Favorites are automatically backed up and synced by default in Windows 8.1.

Figure 12-47. *Selecting your user folders to move*

5.   Right-click the selected folders.

6.   From the menu, click Cut. (It is *very* important that you *do not* click Copy!)

7.   In File Explorer, navigate to the new partition in which you want your files to reside.

423

8. Right-click in a blank space.

9. Select Paste from the options that appear.

Taking Ownership of Files and Folders

You can change security options with any selected file(s) or folder(s). Go to the Share tab on the Ribbon to launch Advanced Security Settings (see Figure 12-48). By default, when a new user account is created in Windows 8.1, that user is given full permission to read, write, and modify the files in her user folders (Documents, Music, and so forth).

Figure 12-48. *Setting advanced file security in File Explorer*

At times, you might find that you have permissions set on files and folders from another user or another version of Windows. This is especially true if you have upgraded your system from an earlier version of Windows or if you store your files and folders on a separate partition or hard disk for added security and peace of mind.

When you try to access a folder for which you do not have permission, Windows 8.1 normally asks you if you want to take ownership of the folder; if you say yes, it automatically changes the permissions on its contents.

Sometimes, however, you need to do it manually by following these steps:

1. In the Owner section of the Advanced Security Settings dialog, click Change.

2. In the Enter the Object Name to Select section, type the username of the user you want to make the owner.

3. Click the Check Names button.

4. If the names are correct, they appear. Click the OK button to complete the ownership changes on the files/folders.

Summary

Because Windows has always been a very flexible and adaptable operating system, the options and features available to help you ensure that it keeps running properly and in a healthy way are very refined and advanced. It's ironic that the number of options to safeguard, troubleshoot, and repair increases at the same rate the number of problems and issues associated with the operating system decreases.

That said, by using the tools available to you—and you should never need a third-party tool—you can create a very robust and resilient system.

CHAPTER 13

Advanced Configuration and Customization

Windows has always been renowned for being a very configurable operating system (OS). Despite the new look, Windows 8.1 offers an immense number of ways to customize the OS, tweaked from within the OS itself and with third-party software.

The ability to configure Windows extends to the computer's internal and external hardware as well. In this chapter, I will show you even more Windows 8.1 configuration and customization options. These options enable you to customize your Windows 8.1 installation in myriad ways, from simple changes to more complex customization that can help you build your computer skills.

PC Settings

When Windows 8 was first released, the new Control Panel replacement was somewhere you would visit for a small number of user controls, such as changing your logon settings and adding a new user to the PC. In Windows 8.1, however, PC Settings has been significantly enhanced. Although it doesn't offer the full features of the Control Panel (which I will discuss later in this chapter), it includes every feature a casual or nontechnical PC user will need. So let's take a look at the new PC Settings in detail, where there are a few new gems and treats in store.

Front Screen

The new front screen to PC Settings contains quick links to the settings you are likely to use most often (see Figure 13-1). At the top of the screen are quick icons to get you into controls for your lock screen, account picture, and password. Below them are additional links to settings that you may use most often. It's a neat solution, both for providing a useful front end for PC Settings and for helping people get quick access to the settings they may need the most.

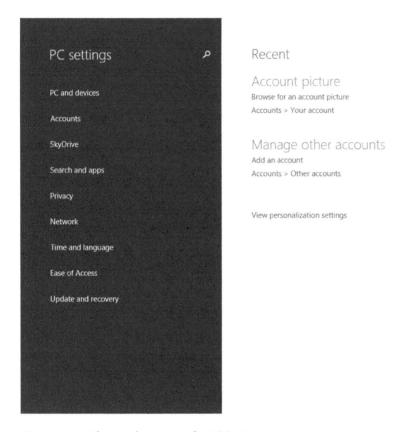

Figure 13-1. *The new front screen for PC Settings*

PC & Devices

The PC & Devices panel contains all the settings you need to control the hardware on your PC and the ways that you interact with Windows 8.1:

- **Lock screen** contains the settings you need to control the main lock screen, including what apps (if any) are allowed to display live information on the lock screen and whether the background image treats your lock screen as a digital photo frame. At the bottom of the controls is a switch to allow the PC's camera to be activated with a *swipe down* movement on the lock screen, as opposed to the swipe upward, which you use to unlock the PC.

- **Display** is where you directly control the monitor(s) attached to your PC (see Figure 13-2). This screen shows you a graphic that shows any displays attached to your PC in proportionate sizes, so you can see the resolutions they are set to and the positions they have. You can drag these graphics around to place them where you want. Below this is a slider that allows you to control the screen resolution. It works independently for each monitor. *More options* provides additional controls for very high-resolution displays (e.g., vertical resolutions of 1440 pixels and above).

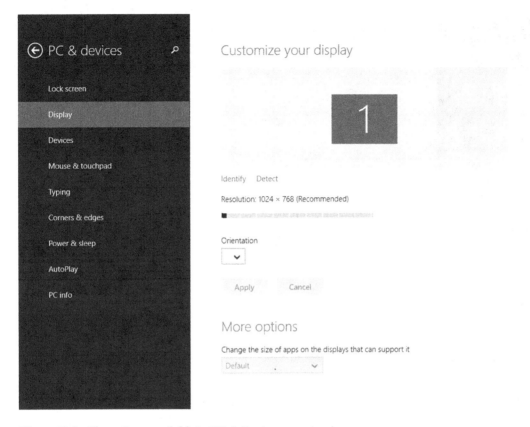

Figure 13-2. *The options available in PCs & Devices are extensive*

- **Bluetooth** provides controls for turning your Bluetooth connection on and off (turning it off can save power if you don't have any Bluetooth devices to connect) and also for making your device discoverable. A quick note here is that if you use your PC in public locations, you should *not* make your PC discoverable because it can pose a potential security risk with people wanting to interface with your PC. Finally, in this panel appears a list of available and currently connected Bluetooth devices. You can tap a device to remove it.

- **Devices** is the PC Settings version of the Control Panel's *Device Manager*, which lists all the main hardware devices attached to your PC, separated by category. As with the Bluetooth devices, you can remove a device from your PC by clicking it (see Figure 13-3). You can also tell Windows 8.1 whether to download drivers over metered (3g/4G/LTE) connections because the data charges on these connections are often expensive.

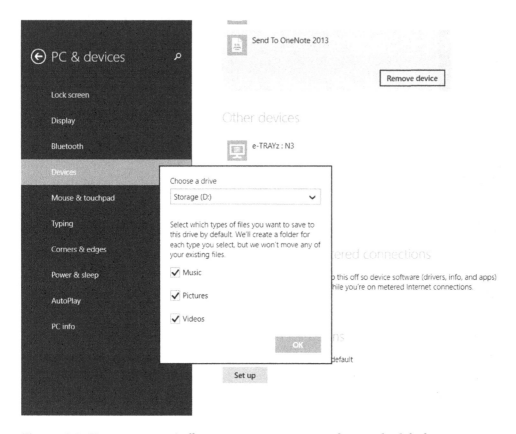

Figure 13-3. *You can automatically save new content to external storage by default*

■ **Tip** If you use a Windows tablet or ultrabook in which you are using a plug-in card (e.g., Micro SD) on which to store some files you can use the *Default Save Locations* setting under the Devices tab to automatically save some new content types to this storage instead of the internal hard disk on your PC (see Figure 13-3).

- **Mouse & touchpad** contains basic controls for the mouse, such as switching the left and right buttons, and scrolling controls.
- **Typing** includes settings for Windows 8.1's built-in spell checker and autocorrect, which can be switched off if you don't want to use them.

■ **Tip** If you use the onscreen keyboard and want the full PC layout—including the function buttons and others such as Home, End, and the Pg Up/Down buttons—you can switch it on with the *Add the standards keyboard layout as a touch keyboard option* control. You can read more about this in Chapter 1.

- **Corners & edges** controls how the hot corners and swipe controls in apps work in Windows 8.1. These include allowing the swipe from left gesture to switch to the last running app and whether moving your mouse to the top left or top right of the screen displays the running apps list or the charms.

- **Power & sleep** are the basic controls you need to help conserve power on your PC (refer to Chapter 9 for more information).

- **AutoPlay** is where you decide what happens when you plug removable storage into your PC, be this a memory card, optical disc (CD/DVD), or USB storage device. You can also turn AutoPlay off completely, which can greatly increase your PC's security by preventing any malware on removable devices form running on your PC automatically.

- **PC info** is where you find information about your PC that you may need if you are on the phone to a support person. You can find the PC name and other details such as its processor, memory, and operating system type. You can also ascertain the activation status of Windows in this panel.

Accounts

The three main sections of the Accounts settings are the following (I discussed this section of PC Settings and how to set up user accounts in Chapter 4):

- **Your account** is where you control settings such as your account picture; you can also connect or disconnect your account from a Microsoft account here.

- **Sign-in option** is where you set a password; PIN; picture password; or, if your hardware supports it, a fingerprint login. You can also specify how long you need to be logged out for before Windows 8.1 asks for your password again.

- **Other accounts** is where you can add and remove other users from the PC. You can also click a user and select *Edit* to change the account type between Child, Standard user, and Administrator.

SkyDrive

You can read all about these settings in Chapter 4, but the main control sections are as follows:

- **Storage space** shows you how much free space you have available on your SkyDrive (if you are logged in to the PC using a Microsoft account). The standard amount of free space you get with a new SkyDrive account is 7 GB, but you can purchase additional storage here to expand it.

- **Files** is where you turn SkyDrive file sync and backup on or off. You can also choose whether (and at what quality) any photos you take with your PC's camera are automatically uploaded to SkyDrive and whether SkyDrive operates over metered (3G/4G/LTE) connections.

■ **Tip**   You can move the default SkyDrive folder in Windows 8.1 by *right-clicking* the SkyDrive link in the left panel of File Explorer and from its properties clicking the *Location* tab. Here you can *Move* the SkyDrive sync and backup folder to a different location.

- **Sync settings** is where you can control what settings on your PC are automatically synced with your other Windows 8.1 PCs, including a master control switch for turning syncing off completely. These controls can be very useful because you might find, for example, that it is difficult to arrange tiles on a Start screen on a small Windows tablet and also have those tiles display as you want them on a larger screen desktop PC. Additionally you might find that your desktop options for a Windows RT device, on which you can use only Microsoft Office, might be very different from your main Windows 8.1 PC.

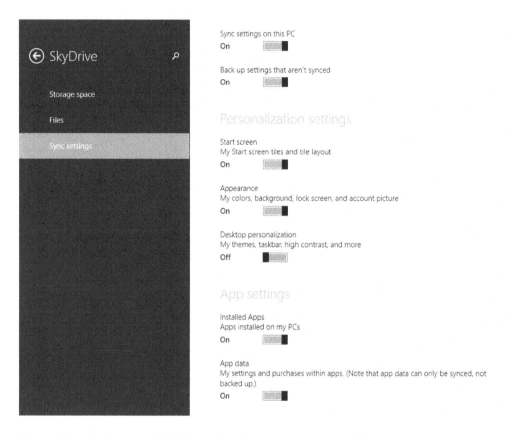

Figure 13-4. *You have control of the settings that are synced on your PC*

■ **Note**   In the Sync settings controls, you can also specify what is synced between the web browsers on your PCs, including your browser tabs, Internet favorites, usernames, and passwords.

Search & Apps

The search system in Windows 8.1 has been greatly improved and now includes searches garnered from the Internet as well as just from your own PC. This does mean however that you will be served advertisements alongside search results. You can control these in the Search and Apps settings (see Figure 13-5).

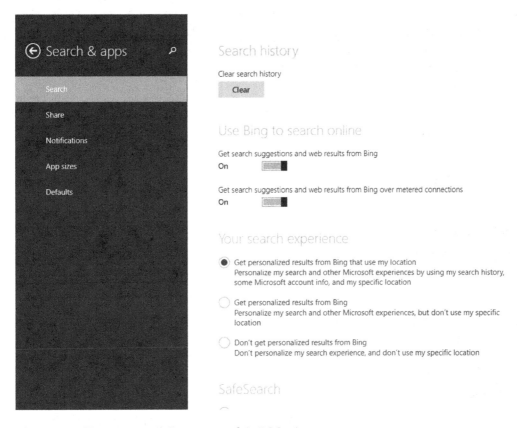

Figure 13-5. *You can manage Internet search in PC Settings*

- **Search** is where you control all aspects of the search system in Windows 8.1, including clearing your search history (useful if you share your PC and have been looking for birthday or holiday presents). You can also turn off Internet searches (from Bing) being included in your PC searches; and optionally changing the *Search experience* settings can disable advertisements from appearing in the results. Finally, the *Safe search* settings can help filter offensive or pornographic content out of search results.

- **Share** is where you control how the Share charm works in Windows 8.1 and which apps are and are not allowed to use it. All the installed apps that support the sharing functions in Windows 8.1 are displayed here, and you can switch individual apps on or off.

- **Notifications** is where you can control how to receive pop-up "toast" notifications in Windows 8.1 and whether they appear on your screen at all; at the bottom of the page, is a full list of all the installed apps you can receive notification from, which can be a lot! You can switch notifications on and off for specific apps here. Perhaps of more interest is the *Quiet hours* feature.

■ **Tip** The Quiet Hours feature in Windows 8.1 is a great way to stop your PC from pestering you with notifications and calls between certain hours; for example, when you're not at work, when you want to relax, or at night (see Figure 13-6). You can set the hours when you are not to be disturbed and you will never receive any notifications (and optionally calls) during these times.

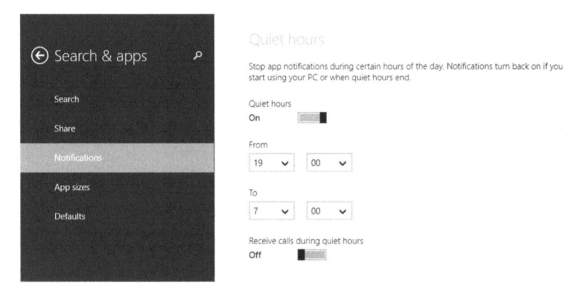

Figure 13-6. *The Quiet Hours feature can be used to stop your PC pestering you when you want to relax*

- **App sizes** is a reporting tool that tells you how large the apps you have installed on your PC are. This can be a useful tool if you are using a tablet or ultrabook with limited storage and you need to clear some free space.

- **Defaults** is where you can choose the default programs and apps that open your files. One of the most annoying aspects of PCs for some people is files opening in the wrong program (for example, a PDF file or photograph opens in an app instead of on the desktop where you want it). Here you can change these programs along with having additional useful controls such as choosing your default *photo viewer* (see Figure 13-7).

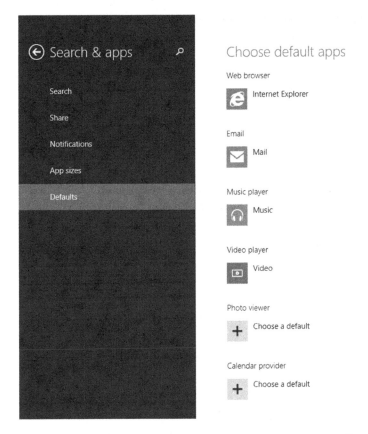

Figure 13-7. *You can change the apps and programs that open different types of files in PC Settings*

Privacy

The privacy options control how apps are allowed to interact with your personal information and what certain hardware in your PC is allowed to do:

- **General** is where you choose whether apps are allowed to access your personal information, though it can sometimes be very useful for the app functionality. The *Turn on SmartScreen filter to check web content (URLs) that Windows Store apps use* is a very helpful security feature that can prevent a seemingly innocent app from trying to install malware on your PC. In this panel you can also change your Microsoft advertising preferences.

- **Location** is where you decide whether apps can use your location; you can set it on an app-by-app basis. You don't need GPS hardware in your PC for this to be possible either as your location can be fairly accurately determined by the IP address assigned by your Internet service provider (ISP).

- **Webcam** is where you can determine which apps are allowed to use your PCs webcam, if you have one installed.

- **Microphone** settings are the same as those for the webcam, but for any microphones you have installed in or attached to your PC.

- **Other devices** is where other hardware in or attached to your PC that can collect data and information about you, such as biometric security devices, appear.

Network

You can connect to Wi-Fi and other networks directly from the Settings charm (as I discussed in Chapter 3), but it is from the Network settings that you can control those networks on your PC:

- **Connections** displays a list of all the available Wi-Fi, mobile broadband, and virtual private networks (VPNs) for your PC. You can tap or click a network here to get more information about it and to turn on or off the estimated data usage display that will appear in the main network connections list from the Settings charm.

- **Radio devices** is used to manage and control any radio receivers built in to or attached to your PC.

- **Proxy** is used if you need to connect your PC to a network via a Proxy server, perhaps because your company has one set up or because you want to maintain your privacy when online.

- **Homegroup** is where you can join, manage, and delete a HomeGroup on your PC (for more on this feature, see Chapter 4).

- **Workplace** is a new feature that allows you to synchronize files with compatible business networks. (For more information on this feature, see Chapter 8.)

Time & Language

Although the full time, language, and region settings are extensive and can be found in the Control Panel (see later in this chapter), you can set many of the common controls here:

- **Date & time** allows you to control whether these settings are set automatically, what your time zone is, and what your chosen date and time formats are.

- **Region & language** allows you to set your current location in the world. You can also install new languages for Windows, although you may need an active Internet connection to do this.

Ease of Access

The Ease of Access features in Windows are discussed in full in Chapter 10.

Update & Recovery

The update and recovery settings contain everything you need to keep Windows 8.1 up to date and restore it from a backup if something goes horribly wrong.

- **Windows update** is where you can check for security, stability and feature updates to your copy of Windows. You can also click the links *View your update history* and *Choose how updates get installed* to get additional information and controls (see Figure 13-8).

① Choose how updates get installed

Important updates

Install updates automatically (recommended) ⌄

When your PC isn't on a metered Internet connection, updates will be downloaded and installed in the background.

Recommended updates

☑ Give me recommended updates the same way I receive important updates

Microsoft Update

☐ Give me updates for other Microsoft products when I update Windows

Apply   Cancel

Note: Windows Update might update itself automatically first when checking for other updates.

Privacy statement

Figure 13-8. *You can control how and when updates are installed in PC Settings*

- **File History** (which is discussed in full in Chapter 12) is a file backup and rescue utility that comes with Windows 8.1. You can control File History from PC Settings, although you can get much finer control from the full Control Panel.

- **Recovery** contains quick links to Refresh (if something go horribly wrong with Windows) and Reset (if you are selling or giving away your PC) if you need them. You can also get quick access to the Windows Recovery Environment (Advanced startup) settings here. I discuss these features in Chapter 12.

Control Panel

The Control Panel is where the full range of Windows controls and configuration options are found. Although throughout this book I've shown you how you can use various Control Panel options to configure specific features within Windows 8.1, there is much more to the Control Panel, including advanced and administrative tools.

The Control Panel is most easily accessed in Windows 8.1 by clicking the *Settings* charm from the desktop, which reveals a Control Panel link in the top right of your screen or by searching for **control** at the Start screen. There have been a few changes since Windows 7, and some Control Panel options aren't where you might expect to find them.

■ **Tip** You can find any Control Panel item by using natural language search in the search box at the top right of the Control Panel window (and from the Search charm). This means you don't need to know the exact name of a control but you can instead search for words such as *password* or *files* to display a list of all the controls that are relevant to that word.

Customizing the Control Panel

By default, the Control Panel appears in the Category view, in which all the Control Panel items are organized into groups, such as network and Internet controls (see Figure 13-9).

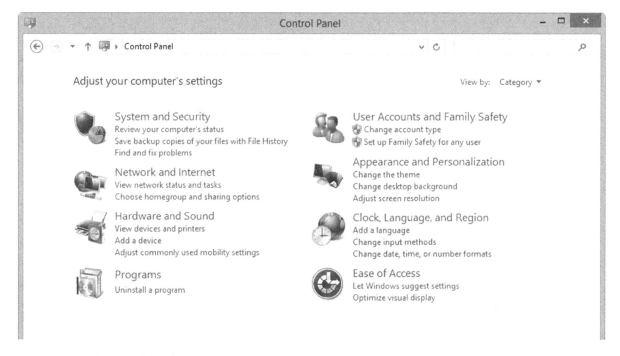

Figure 13-9. The Control Panel Category view

In the top right of the Control Panel window is a View By drop-down list, in which you can choose to display the Control Panel items as either large or small icons. The icon views simply list all the options available to you in the Control Panel (see Figure 13-10).

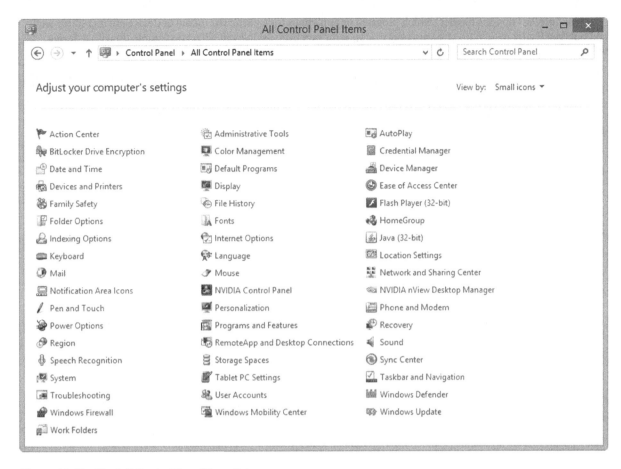

Figure 13-10. *The full Control Panel items list*

Your list of Control Panel items might differ from those seen in Figure 13-2 in that they might show fewer or slightly different controls. If you don't have biometric devices on your computer, for example, you don't see the Biometric controls, and if you don't have a touchscreen, you probably don't see the Tablet PC or the Pen and Touch settings.

The Control Panel shows only the controls that relate to your specific computer, and no more. This ensures that you're not distracted by controls that won't do anything.

I won't discuss every Control Panel item, but I do want to talk about the most important ones and show you how you can use them to configure your copy of Windows 8.1.

■ **Tip**   You can create a folder on your desktop that contains a link to every individual Control Panel item. This folder, which many people call "God Mode," can be created by right-clicking in any blank space on your desktop and creating a *New* ➤ *Folder* that you rename as **GodMode.{ED7BA470-8E54-465E-825C-99712043E01C}**

Choosing AutoPlay Options

Sometimes the AutoPlay options in Windows can be annoying. Do you really want Windows Media Player popping up every time you insert a CD or for File Explorer to appear whenever you insert a USB flash drive?

The AutoPlay options to select which program or app opens for a particular media or device are incredibly well laid out (see Figure 13-11). It's also very easy to stop Windows from asking you what you want to do with a device every time you insert it.

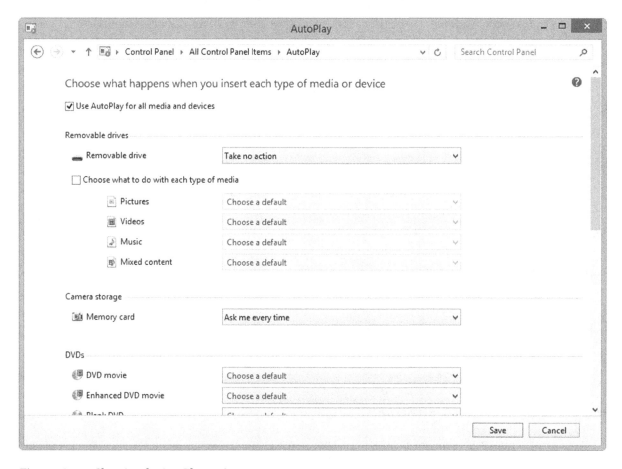

Figure 13-11. *Choosing the AutoPlay options*

It includes all removable drives for all types of media—including pictures, music, and video; storage cards for a camera (you might want to choose between the custom software that came with your camera or Windows importing the images); and DVDs, CDs, Blu-ray disks, and software.

At the bottom of this page is a Reset button to return all the settings to default, in case you make changes that you later decide you want to reverse.

■ **Note** When you insert some USB flash drives, you are asked if you want to use it to speed up your system using a Windows feature called ReadyBoost, a useful feature primarily for older computers with slower hard disks and small amounts of physical memory. It uses the flash drive as cache memory to speed up access to commonly opened Windows files. The speed improvements come with flash memory being much faster than a mechanical hard disk drive.

Setting Default Programs

There are four options in Default Programs:

- Set your default programs

- Associate a file type or protocol with a program

- Change AutoPlay settings (discussed in the "Choosing AutoPlay Options" section)

- Set program access and computer defaults

Set Default Programs lists all the software installed on your computer. Clicking a program in the left pane displays how many of its file defaults are set (see Figure 13-12). This means that the program will open a certain number of file types. The Windows Disc Image Burner, for example, just opens ISO files, but Microsoft Word opens many more files, including RTF, DOC, and DOCX. Windows Media Player opens even more file types.

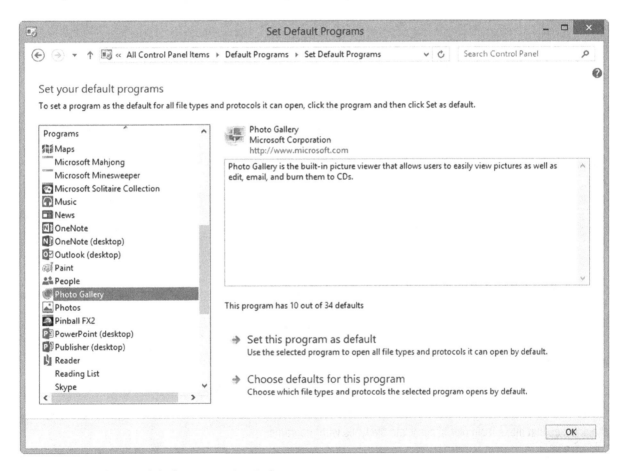

Figure 13-12. *Choosing default programs in Windows 8.1*

Here you have two options. You can **Set this program as default**, which sets the program as the default for *all* the file types it can open. Otherwise, you can **Choose defaults for this program**, which takes you to the **Associate a file type or protocol with a program** options.

Associat[ing] a file type or protocol with a program offers finer control over the program or app that opens with a particular file type by displaying a long list of every file type Windows can open. You have the option to associate a single or multiple file types with a certain program or app (see Figure 13-13).

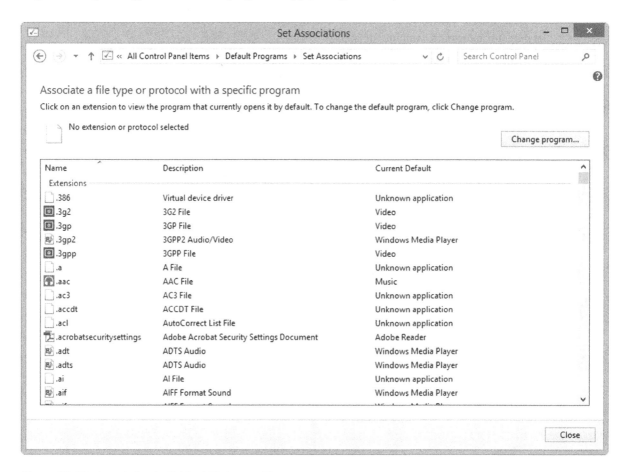

Figure 13-13. *Associating individual file types with programs or apps*

■ **Tip** File types can be set only one at a time. However, if you enter this page from Set Default Programs, you have check boxes that make it simpler to associate file types with programs.

Another way to control the default programs in Windows is through Set Program Access And Computer Defaults, which allows you to easily change the default programs for browsing the Internet, e-mail, media playback, and instant messaging (see Figure 13-14).

Figure 13-14. *Choosing the default web browser, e-mail client, and media player*

Managing Fonts in Windows 8.1

Windows 8.1 doesn't have a dedicated font manager, but the Fonts page is generally an excellent alternative. It shows thumbnail previews of letters and characters in the installed fonts (see Figure 13-15).

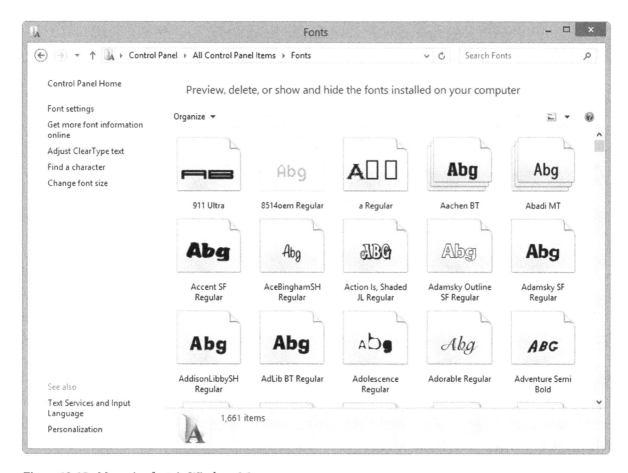

Figure 13-15. Managing fonts in Windows 8.1

■ **Tip**   You do not need to be in the Fonts page to install a font. You can install a font from any location by right-clicking it and selecting Install.

If you want to view more of a font's characters, you can double-click it to open it. Some fonts first open into a font group, but each font shows you more characters, although not the complete character set (see Figure 13-16).

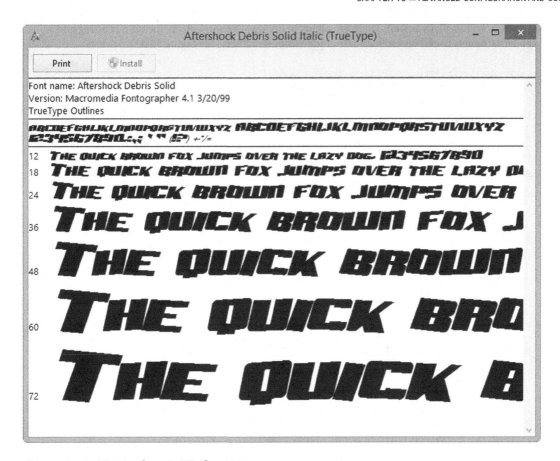

Figure 13-16. *Viewing fonts in Windows 8.1*

Using Location Settings and Other Sensors

In Location Settings, you can turn on (or off) settings that allow apps and other programs to use GPS and other location-aware sensors on your computer. You may not want apps to know your physical location, for example.

Managing Pen, Touch, and Tablet Settings

If your computer supports touch, the Pen and Touch and Tablet PC Settings are visible in the Control Panel. They are separate options, but they are linked in many ways. The Pen and Touch options apply only to using touch on the Windows desktop; you can't change the default controls for the Start screen and apps.

Of particular note, however, are the Flicks controls. They allow you to customize flick gestures on the screen to perform navigational and a variety of other actions, including editing controls such as copy and paste.

The Customize button edits flicks as well. There are plenty of options to choose from, including cutting and pasting, which can be extremely useful on professional-grade Windows tablets (see Figure 13-17).

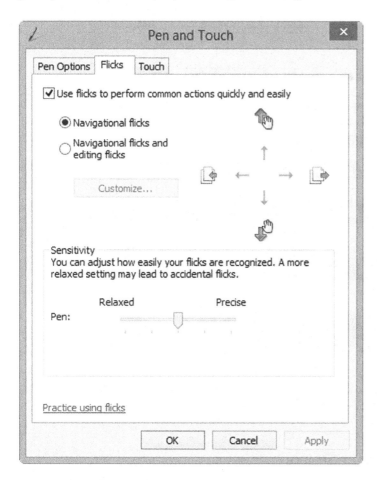

Figure 13-17. *Using flicks*

Tablet PC Settings allows you to tell Windows if you are left- or right-handed. And, if the calibration on your touch panel is out of alignment, you can recalibrate the touch layer on the display (see Figure 13-18).

Figure 13-18. *Changing the Tablet PC settings*

Configuring the Windows 8.1 Advanced System Settings

When you click System in the Control Panel, you are shown information about your computer. The System Properties page is where you find the type of processor and the amount of memory you have, as well as which edition of Windows 8.1 you are using. This information is useful when you need to describe your PC to a support professional.

Clicking Advanced System Settings in the left navigation pane brings up the System Properties dialog, which has settings that you may want to change (see Figure 13-19).

Figure 13-19. *Changing the advanced system settings*

In the Advanced tab of this dialog, there is a page with three sections: Performance, User Profiles, and Startup and Recovery.

To open Performance, click the Settings button. In the Performance Options dialog, the first tab is Visual Effects, which allows you to control some of the ways the Windows 8.1 desktop is displayed (see Figure 13-20). Some of the changes you can make here are purely cosmetic. For example, some people believe that removing **shadows under windows** makes the desktop look cleaner.

Figure 13-20. *Adjusting the visual effects*

If you have an older computer, you can adjust the look of the Windows desktop to get the best possible performance. Stripping the visual look of the desktop back to basics can improve the overall responsiveness of the computer.

Managing Virtual Memory Settings

The Virtual Memory settings are under the Performance Options' Advanced tab. Virtual memory is a file on the hard disk that your computer uses when it runs out of physical computer memory. This is much less of an issue than it used to be because computers ship with increasingly more memory, but you still may want to manage your Virtual Memory settings manually. The reason for this is that the virtual memory (sometimes known as the swap file or paging file) default settings have this file automatically increase and decrease in size. This can lead to disk defragmentation, which ultimately may cause the mechanical hard disk to slow down in accessing your files. If you use a solid-state disk in which hard disk space is at a premium, you may want to reduce the overall size of the paging file. To do this, click the Change button on the Advanced tab. The Virtual Memory dialog appears, as shown in Figure 13-21.

Figure 13-21. *Changing virtual memory*

To manage virtual memory manually, uncheck the box at the top of the Virtual Memory dialog and instead select the Custom Size option. At the bottom of the dialog, Windows 8.1 suggests minimum and recommended sizes for virtual memory. If you have large amounts of physical memory, however, such as 8 GB or more and run Windows from a solid-state drive (SSD), you may want to set virtual memory to the minimum settings. Otherwise, Windows 8.1 suggests a recommended amount for the virtual memory. Setting both values in the Custom Size fields to the same amount prevents the virtual memory file from shrinking, expanding, and ultimately fragmenting your hard disk.

In the drives view on the dialog, you can also move the paging file to a different physical hard disk or partition if you want.

Managing Data Execution Prevention

Data Execution Prevention (DEP), accessed from the Performance Options dialog, is a feature that prevents certain viruses and malware from damaging your Windows installation. On occasion, it can also prevent particular games or other software from running.

If you find that a program isn't running properly, you try allowing it through DEP. To do this, first select **Turn on DEP for all programs and services except those I select** and click the Add button (see Figure 13-22).

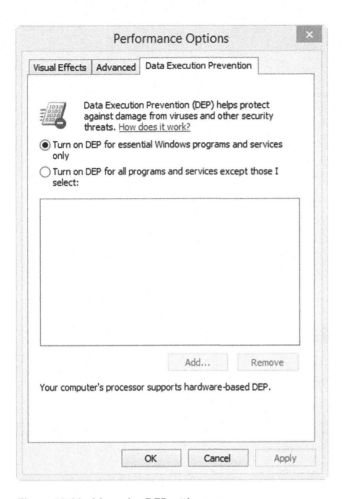

Figure 13-22. *Managing DEP settings*

Now you can navigate to the folder on your hard disk in which the program is located and select it to allow it through DEP. It is possible that this will rectify the problem. You can't turn off DEP completely.

Configuring and Managing System Protection

System Restore allows you to roll back changes to Windows settings if something goes wrong on your computer.

In System Properties, you can turn on System Protection for other drives and add them to the System Restore feature. You can also specify how much space on the disk is allocated to System Restore so that you can increase space if you have plenty available or reduce it if you are using a small SSD (see Figure 13-23).

Figure 13-23. *Managing system protection*

Let's have a look at these two options to see what they do:

- **System Restore** keeps copies of critical operating system files when a major change, such as software installation or an update, takes place. This information is kept in the System Volume Information folders on your hard disk (if you ever wondered what they were for). You can run System Restore to restore system files to an earlier point in time if a recent change has made your computer unstable.

- **System Protection** keeps version-controlled copies of the operating system and other files so that they can be reinstated if an unwanted change is made to a file. This system works closely with System Restore.

Using and Configuring Storage Spaces

Storage Spaces is a feature new to Windows that allows you to aggregate, or pool, several hard disks onto a single large storage drive. This pooled storage then appears on your computer as a single drive that you can expand by adding extra hard disks, as you require.

The advantages that Storage Spaces bring include ensuring that Windows automatically keeps a backup (mirrored) copy of your files in case a hard disk fails. This should not be considered an alternative to a good backup policy, however.

Hard disks that are connected to your computer by SATA, SAS, and USB links can be joined to the Storage Spaces (note that if you remove a USB drive at any time, you lose temporary access to the files stored on it). This means that you can use external hard disks to expand the storage of an all-in-one PC.

■ **Note**   Hard disks that are added to Storage Spaces need to be formatted by Windows. They will be wiped of all data. You will then need to copy files back to them.

When you first set up Storage Spaces on your computer, you are shown a list of compatible hard disks. Windows tells you which hard disks are suitable for use with Storage Spaces, and you can choose which drives to add (see Figure 13-24).

Figure 13-24. *Using Storage Spaces*

There are three different types of storage layout from which you can choose for storage spaces (see Figure 13-25):

- **Basic Space**: The assembled hard disks are aggregated into a single hard disk.

- **Mirror Space**: At least two copies are kept of your files and data on separate physical disks.

- **Parity Spaces**: Saves parity information about the data stored. This information can be used to reconstruct data in the event of a disk failure.

Figure 13-25. *Configuring storage spaces*

Storage spaces are configured via a helpful wizard that allows you to choose the storage layout that best suits you. Windows 8.1 explains what a particular layout does and how it can help protect your data. You can also choose a name for the new pooled drive and assign a drive letter to it.

Consider Storage Spaces to be a software equivalent of a redundant array of independent disks (RAID), which is a collection of physical hard disks in a computer that are configured so the user sees them as a single, large drive. Storage Spaces is very useful in computers that have no RAID system or where storage can be added only via USB-attached hard disks.

■ **Tip** Unlike many RAID systems, you can add hard disks of any size to Storage Spaces.

Working with Hardware Devices

Whatever you do with your copy of Windows 8.1, there is no escaping hardware drivers. These pieces of code interpret the signals between your computer and both internal and external hardware, and enable everything to communicate.

Earlier in this chapter, I spoke about how some hardware can be added through PC Settings. Indeed, Windows 8.1 is excellent at recognizing and installing hardware with network-attached hardware such as Wi-Fi printers.

Drivers can cause problems, however, so I want to talk you through the process of installing, managing, and repairing troublesome drivers.

Device Manager

The Windows 8.1 Device Manager (see Figure 13-26) hasn't changed since earlier versions of the operating system. It contains some extremely useful tools that are commonly hidden.

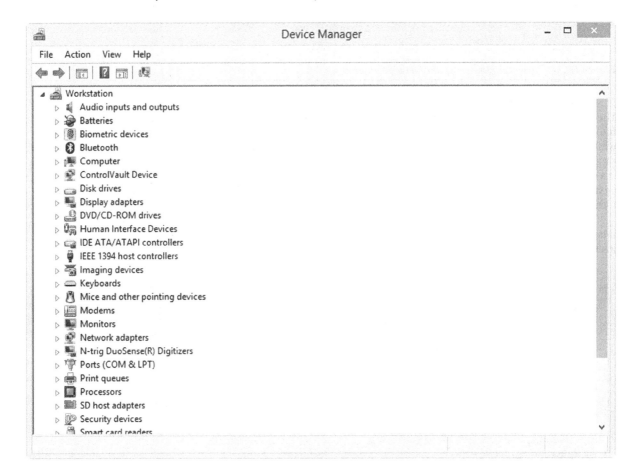

Figure 13-26. *Device Manager*

By default, it shows the hierarchical view of all the computer's attached and installed hardware devices, grouped into collapsible sections. If there are any devices that are not properly installed, have not been correctly configured, or have been disabled, they are highlighted in the list with a small yellow warning triangle. If a device is not working properly, it may have a warning icon superimposed on it.

There are other useful views in the Device Manager that can give you all sorts of additional information about your computer. From the View menu, you have several options. Looking at the resources on your computer provides information such as I/O ports and interrupt requests (IRQs). These are the cycles on which information is exchanged with the processor. If you are experiencing problems, it is useful for determining whether too many devices are set to communicate with the processor at any one time (see Figure 13-27).

Figure 13-27. Viewing resources in the Device Manager

What types of problems might you have with your hardware that you can use the Device Manager to help resolve? The most common are faulty or incompatible drivers, which can come from any source directly downloaded from the Internet or provided through Windows Update. (I will show you how to resolve problems with faulty drivers in a short while.) You can use the custom views to see whether conflicting drivers are trying to use the same Windows Resources simultaneously. This problem is very uncommon and always caused by sloppily written drivers. Another rare problem is a driver inadvertently loaded twice by Windows. By looking at the way drivers are interactive with Windows, such as viewing IRQ requests, you can see whether multiple instances of a driver have been loaded. A restart normally rectifies this problem.

You can also view hidden devices on your computer. These are commonly Windows system drivers that don't relate specifically to a piece of hardware. However, some hardware can also install hidden devices, and you will want to check whether this hardware is causing a problem (see Figure 13-28).

Figure 13-28. Viewing hidden devices

When you want to install a driver for a piece of hardware that isn't visible, select Scan for Hardware Changes from the Action menu in the Device Manager.

You will need to perform actions on hardware drivers when using Windows 8.1, including installing, removing, and updating them. The following sections describe how you to perform these actions.

Installing Device Drivers

Windows 8.1 commonly detects hardware and tries to install a driver for it. If the hardware came out after the release of the operating system, it may be unable to find a driver using Windows Update. If this happens, right-click the driver and click Update Driver Software (see Figure 13-29).

Figure 13-29. *Manually installing or updating a driver*

You will be asked if you want Windows to search for drivers or if you want to install the driver manually. If it is hardware that Windows 8.1 has already failed to correctly install, you should choose the **Browser my computer for driver software** option (see Figure 13-30).

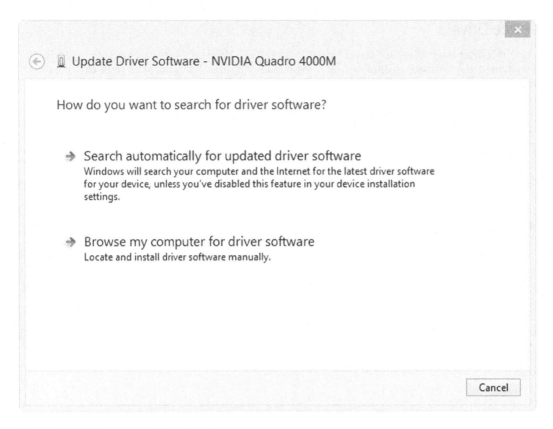

Figure 13-30. *The device driver wizard*

Here you have two options.

- **Search automatically for updated driver software** searches the preconfigured driver folders that come with Windows 8.1. If you have an active Internet connection, it also searches Windows Update. It also looks for drivers on any optical disc or USB-attached drive on your computer.

- **Browse my computer for driver software** gives you additional control. It allows you to manually specify the location(s) on your hard disk(s) or optical drives where the driver might be found. You can browse to a location on your computer, on an attached hard disk or flash drive, or on a network location. You can also choose from a very long list of drivers that Windows 8.1 comes equipped with (see Figure 13-31).

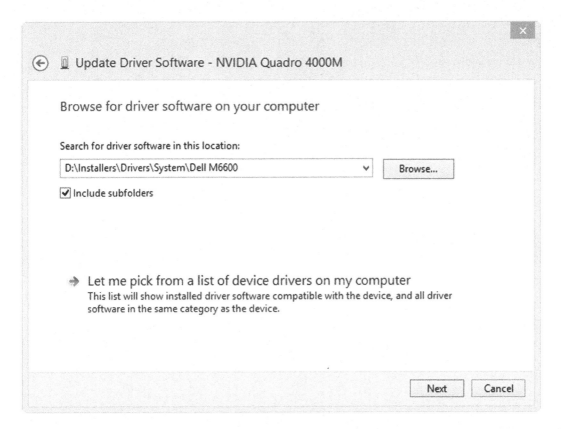

Figure 13-31. *Manually choosing a driver*

When might you want to choose which hardware driver to install? It might be useful if you are using older "legacy" hardware for which you know drivers exist because it's been out for years, but that perhaps Windows 8.1 doesn't recognize.

If you choose the **Browse my computer for driver software** option, Windows will try to identify the hardware for you. It may not get it right, but if it does, select the correct option from the list and then click the Have Disk button to point Windows 8.1 at the correct driver (see Figure 13-32).

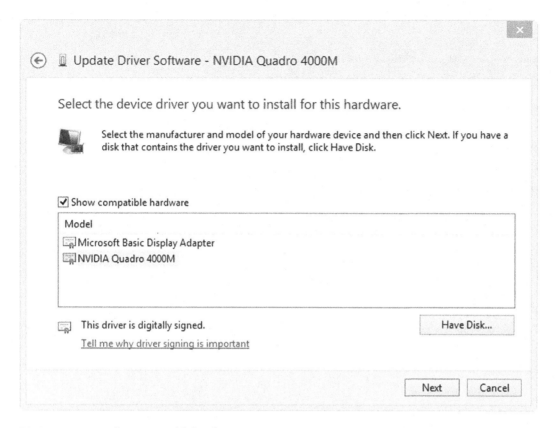

Figure 13-32. *Finding compatible hardware*

If you don't see your hardware in the list, uncheck the **Show compatible hardware** box. You are presented with a long list of hardware by various manufacturers. These are drivers that Windows 8.1 ships with, and if you find your hardware in the list, choose the manufacturer and product name that correctly matches the hardware you are trying to install (see Figure 13-33).

Figure 13-33. *Selecting hardware from Windows 8.1 default drivers*

Uninstalling and Repairing Device Drivers

Sometimes Device Drivers causes problems and needs to be uninstalled or reinstalled. When you uninstall most (but not all) of the hardware on your computer, you are given the option to also completely **Delete the driver software for this device** (see Figure 13-34).

Figure 13-34. *Uninstalling device drivers*

Checking this option will completely remove the driver software from your PC. This can prevent a faulty driver from being automatically reinstalled by Windows. If you need to repair a driver, you can now reinstall it from Windows Update or another source, such as the original driver disc that came with your hardware.

Also, if an updated device driver and is misbehaving, you can roll it back to the previous version of the driver software. You do this in the device driver properties window, as described next.

■ **Tip**   You can disable hardware you don't need to use or that causes problems by right-clicking it and selecting Disable.

Working with Device Drivers

In addition to uninstalling drivers, you can roll a driver back to a previously installed driver (if it has been updated through a service such as Windows Update) by right-clicking the driver and selecting its Properties.

As shown in Figure 13-35, if an earlier version of the driver is available, the Roll Back Driver button is highlighted.

Figure 13-35. Rolling back device drivers

A driver's Properties dialog provides a lot of information about it, but there's nothing here you can change or modify. The General tab is where Windows tells you whether the driver is working correctly.

Manually Connecting to Networks

Clicking *Set up a new connection or network* in the main pane of the Network and Sharing Center allows you to manually connect to a network. You might want to do this if you need to connect to a hidden Wi-Fi network, a virtual private network (VPN), or a dial-up Internet connection (see Figure 13-36).

Figure 13-36. *Connecting to networks manually*

Whichever option you choose, Windows opens a wizard to guide you through the process, including manually entering the SSID of a hidden Wi-Fi network and setting the type of encryption it uses.

Choosing the Connect to the Internet option might be required for some broadband ISPs that require you to log on from your computer to gain access. If you must enter a username and password before getting online, click through **Set up a new connection anyway** and at the next screen select Broadband (PPPoE), as shown in Figure 13-37.

Figure 13-37. *Manually connecting to dial-up or cable Internet*

You are prompted to enter the username and password that your broadband provider has assigned to you. This is required only if you must log on from your computer, not from your router, to get a connection. This probably applies only if you have an ISDN connection.

Windows 8.1 Administrative Tools

So what are the Windows Administrative Tools (see Figure 13-38) and how do you get the best out of them? In this section, I'll focus on the tools that allow you to get the maximum benefit and performance out of your Windows 8.1 PC.

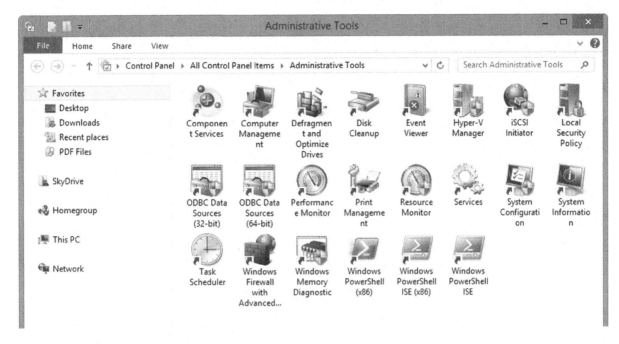

Figure 13-38. *Windows 8.1 Administrative Tools*

Computer Management Console

The Computer Management console provides access to other Administrative Tools, but it is probably most commonly used to access the Disk Management tools. Here you can partition drives; grow and shrink partitions; and change, assign, and remove drive letters.

■ **Tip**   You can also open a dedicated Computer Management window from the Win+X Administration menu.

The main Computer Management window is split into a text details pane at the top and a graphical representation of your hard disks and partitions at the bottom (see Figure 13-39).

Figure 13-39. *The Disk Management console*

You can right-click any hard drive or partition to perform a series of actions on it. These actions include the following:

- **Change Drive Letter and Paths**: If you have two disks that have the same drive letter assignment (perhaps one is an external drive), or if a disk does not appear to have a drive letter, you can change or assign it here. Another task you can perform is to turn the disk or partition into a folder within another disk.

■ **Tip** Some third-party software is available to help fix a USB–attached hard disk to a specific drive letter. They can be especially useful if you use a USB hard disk for backups and your backup software can be set to work only with a specific drive letter. One of the best in my opinion is USB Drive Letter Manager, which can be downloaded from http://www.uwe-sieber.de.

- **Extend Volume** and **Shrink Volume**: These are used to resize the partition. Windows 8.1 has a fairly basic partitioning tool that may not be prepared to shrink a partition as much as you want. If this happens, try using the Defragmenter and then running the partitioning tool again. There is a simple wizard for partitioning and I've never known any reports of Windows corrupting partitions. That said, it is always a good idea to keep an up-to-date backup of all your files.

- Create a **New Volume** and **Delete Volume**: These are tasks that you can perform in blank space on disks or on existing partitions. You can use this to create RAID arrays as well as simple partitions, with Windows 8.1 supporting spanned, striped, mirrored, and RAID-5 arrays (see Figure 13-40). I will show you how to work with partitions in Chapter 14.

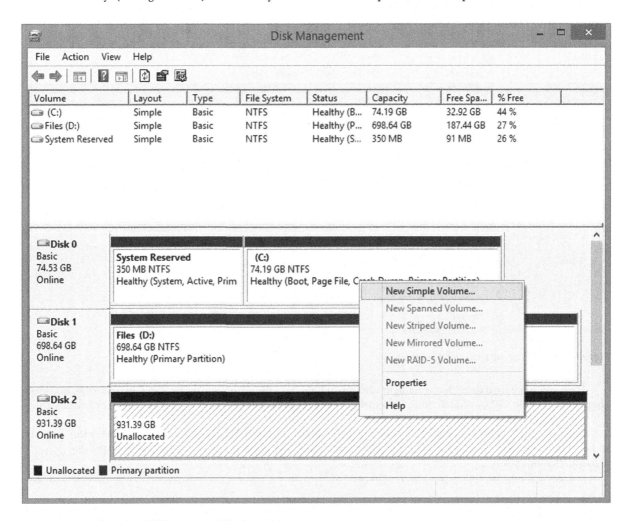

Figure 13-40. *Creating RAID arrays in Windows 8.1*

Defragment and Optimize Drives

The Disk Defragmenter helps keep file access on your computer quick by making sure that all parts of files are stored together on your hard disk. This also helps maintain file integrity and prevents files from becoming corrupt.

By default, it's set to automatically defragment all your hard disks once a week and it automatically adds new hard disks to the defragmentation schedule as well (see Figure 13-41).

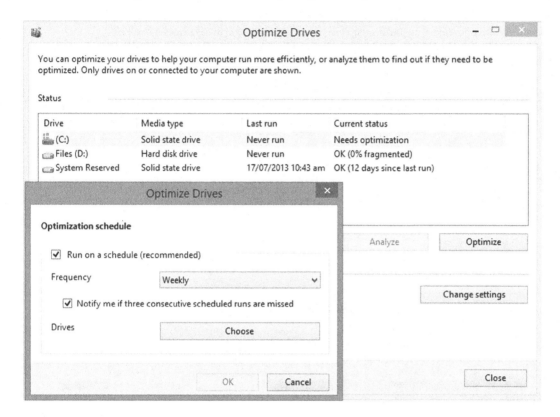

Figure 13-41. *Using the Disk Defragmenter*

There are some hard disks that you might want to exclude from the automatic defragmentation process, however. These disks include SSDs, in which there is no speed advantage to be gained from keeping files together because the drives are random access, anyway.

Defragmentation also puts significant strain on mechanical hard disks, so if you have a disk in which the contents do not tend to change, such as for installers or for an image backup, it is worth excluding it from the defragmentation cycle.

Disk Cleanup

The Disk Cleanup tool removes temporary files from your computer. These files fill up space on a small SSD or generally slow programs down, including Internet Explorer. It's a very simple tool to use and as a basic alternative to more advanced freeware like CCleaner (http://www.piriform.com/ccleaner), it is worth running once in a while.

Event Viewer

No major event happens on your computer without being logged. These events include warnings and critical errors, including Blue Screen of Death errors.

You can view errors by type in the Log Summary to get additional information for clues as to what caused the error—so that you can rectify it. This can include error codes, descriptions, and details of the driver, program, or service that failed (see Figure 13-42).

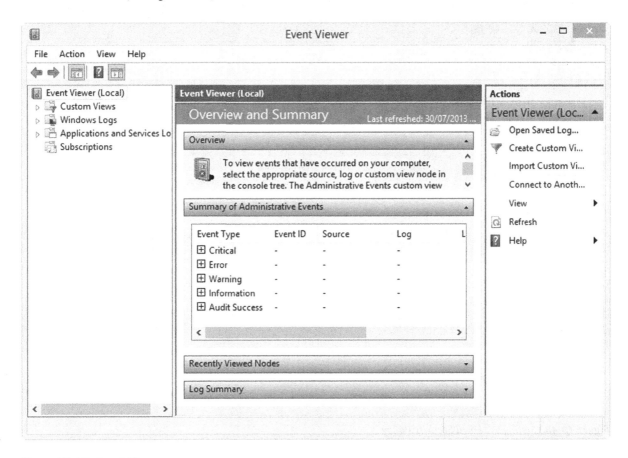

Figure 13-42. *Event Viewer*

Errors are grouped by importance. For example, each event type can be opened with a double-click to display more information such as the error code, description, and any associated system file. You can look up these details online to get more detailed information about what this means, helping you to diagnose and repair the problem. You can find more information about Windows 8.1 troubleshooting on my web site (http://www.theLongClimb.com).

Local Security Policy

You probably won't need to worry about local security policies unless you are a systems administrator, in which case you will be administering group and security policies over a domain. There are a few settings here, however, that small business owners might be interested in.

You can set password expirations and rules governing the strength and length of passwords chosen by users. If needed for additional security, you can also lock out users after a specified number of failed logon attempts.

If you choose to turn on this feature, however, there must be several administrator accounts on the computer; otherwise, Windows 8.1 might be completely locked out to you (see Figure 13-43).

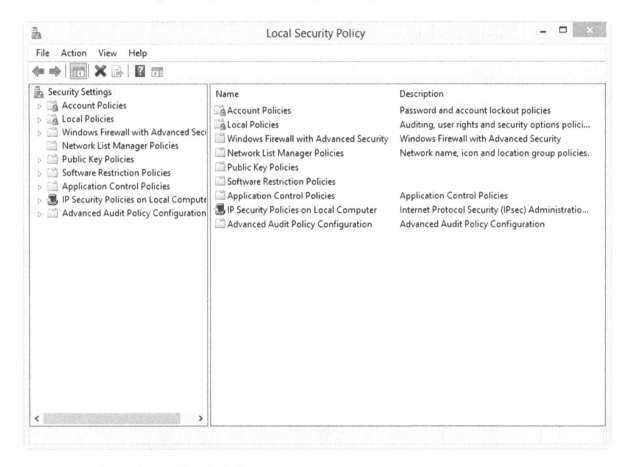

Figure 13-43. *Setting the Local Security Policy*

Performance Monitor

The Performance Monitor provides live graphs that show literally hundreds of metrics about Windows and your hardware. Are you concerned about your Wi-Fi traffic or your hard disk's write capability? To add data to the live graph, click the green + icon on the toolbar and choose the metrics to add from a Category view (see Figure 13-44).

Figure 13-44. *Performance Monitor*

These additional metrics provide valuable real-time information on the processes happening both inside and external to your computer. For example, you can see whether all your processor cores are indeed working or whether there are any bottlenecks with your networking.

Each counter is sensibly labeled, and if you're not sure what counter to add, you can add a whole stack of related counters with a single click of the Add button.

When you are viewing the live data in the Performance Monitor, the graph could become confusing. You can turn a specific graph on and off in real-time by checking or unchecking the box next to its label at the bottom of the page.

Resource Monitor

The Windows 8.1 Resource Monitor provides even more detailed information about processes running on your computer, including the drivers, programs, apps, and Windows' services.

It works with tabs across the top of the page that give quick access to a general overview of your computer and more specific information about your CPU, memory, disk, and network.

Each of these sections contains collapsible panes with huge amounts of real-time information about your computer (see Figure 13-45).

Figure 13-45. *Resource Monitor*

In the top pane of each tab, each item has a check box next to it. Checking one or more of these boxes filters the graph information on the right of the pane to show information only about those particular processes. For example, you might be interested in the amount of data that your SkyDrive app is sending and receiving to diagnose whether it is connecting correctly to the Internet.

Services

Services are programs that perform specific functions in Windows, such as running the print spooler or the firewall. Occasionally, you will want to disable a Windows or third-party service that you either don't need or that misbehaves.

You can do this in the Services page by right-clicking a service. From there, you can start, stop, pause, resume, or restart the service (see Figure 13-46).

Figure 13-46. *Services page*

It was common in the days of Windows XP and especially Windows Vista to completely disable services running in the background that you didn't need. With Windows 7, this was sorted so that only the services that you actually need are running at any one time.

You can disable a service, though, by selecting its Properties and setting its Startup Type to Disabled. Sometimes a service fails, however, especially if it is part of poorly written third-party software or a hardware driver. From this context menu, you can stop and restart services. Sometimes this can be useful if you find that a service is hung up and doesn't respond.

System Configuration

The System Configuration page is most commonly known to Windows users as MSConfig. It has been used in previous versions of Windows to disable unwanted startup programs. This is now managed through the Task Manager, but MSConfig is not without its uses.

The Boot tab allows you to manually set the computer to start in Safe Mode. This can be useful if you have a UEFI firmware system that doesn't allow access to the F8 and Shift+F8 boot menu.

On the General tab are options that allow you to start the computer in a special Diagnostic Startup mode. This offers more functionality than Safe Mode in that it gives you more access to Windows features and controls, and it loads a few more hardware drivers. Diagnostic Startup is a great way to diagnose and repair problems with Windows 8.1 (see Figure 13-47). When you check this option, however, Windows continues to boot into this new mode until you return to MSConfig and change the option back to Normal Startup.

Figure 13-47. *MSConfig System Configuration panel*

I do not recommend that you change the options under the Boot tab, especially not the advanced boot options. On the face of things, controlling the number of processor cores, which is an option here, might look like a tempting way to save electricity when using a high-power computer for lightweight tasks. In reality, though, these features are strictly for IT pros because changing something here can render your copy of Windows 8.1 unbootable.

System Information

The System Information page provides extremely detailed information about your hardware, installed software and devices, running processes, and more. This information can be exported to a file through the File menu if you need to send comprehensive information about your computer to a support person.

Task Scheduler

The Task Scheduler can be used in several ways. First, you can use it to launch programs such as the Disk Cleaner on a set schedule, such as once a month.

You can also set custom tasks that can be triggered in specific events, such as a driver failure. The Task Scheduler can then perform a series of tasks, including popping an alert window onscreen to inform the user that a problem has occurred, to running a Command Line or PowerShell script automatically.

The controls for setting up tasks are found in the right pane, in which you can either create tasks or import them from another computer (see Figure 13-48).

Figure 13-48. *Task Scheduler*

Windows Memory Diagnostic

For many years, Windows has included a very useful and well-hidden Memory Diagnostic Tool (see Figure 13-49) that you can use if you suspect that your computer's physical memory has developed a fault.

Figure 13-49. Windows comes with a memory diagnostic tool

You can access the tool by searching for **memory** at the Start screen. It scans your computer's memory, which can take considerable time so be prepared to walk the dog or have a coffee break. The tool will report any errors it finds.

Further Customizing Windows 8.1

Because of the way that Windows 8.1 is designed, it's possible to customize the operating system in an almost limitless number of ways. My mailbag regularly swells with questions about this. I'll discuss some of the more popular customizations. I should point out, however, that you should always be very careful making these kinds of changes to Windows. You should create a restore point, make sure that you have an up-to-date image backup of the operating system, and follow instructions very carefully because you could be making changes to the core OS. (See Chapter 12 for information on creating backup images and restore points.)

■ **Tip** Metro UI Tweaker is a great little utility for changing various aspects of the Start screen and Windows 8.1 interface. It also provides an easy way to add power buttons to the Start screen. You can download it at www.technobuzz.net/windows-8-metro-ui-tweaker.

Disabling the Windows 8.1 Lock Screen

The new Windows 8.1 lock screen provides valuable information over and above that available in previous versions of Windows, including the number of e-mails and messages received and appointment details.

Opening the lock screen is another step you need to go through to log on to Windows 8.1. You may want to disable it completely and have Windows 8.1 start directly with the logon screen.

The lock screen can be disabled if you are using Windows 8.1 Pro or Enterprise, which includes the Group Policy Editor. To open it, search for **gpedit.msc** at the Start screen.

Once in the Group Policy Editor, you need to navigate to Computer Configuration ➤ Administrative Templates ➤ Control Panel ➤ Personalization (see Figure 13-50).

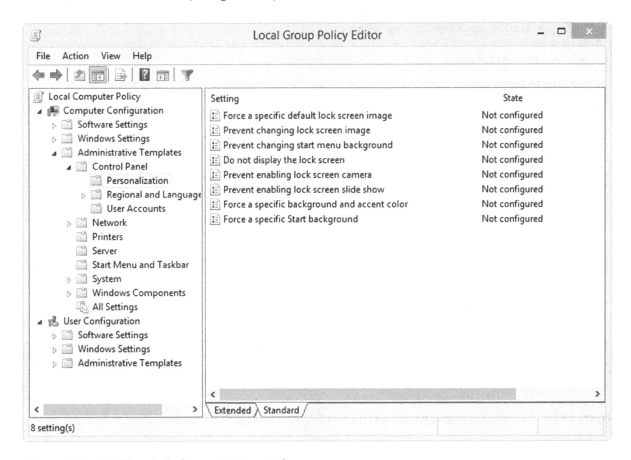

Figure 13-50. *Disabling the lock screen in Group Policy*

Here you will see an option labeled **Do not display the lock screen**. You should right-click it, select Edit from the options, and change the setting to Enabled in the next dialog. The lock screen will no longer appear on the computer.

Automatically Logging on to Windows 8.1

You may want to have Windows 8.1 automatically log on every time you start the computer. After all, if you are the only person using the computer and you log on with your Microsoft account—bringing the benefits of automatically syncing your e-mail and calendar, and allowing you to buy apps, music, and video from the Windows Store—why would you need to type your password every time you start your computer?

It is very simple to do and requires unchecking only a single box. Search for **netplwiz** at the Start screen. In the User Accounts dialog that appears, click your main user account (it is the one labeled Administrator) and then uncheck **Users must enter a user name and password to use this computer** (see Figure 13-51).

Figure 13-51. Automatically logging on users to Windows 8.1

You are asked to confirm your password to provide authorization. Afterward, Windows 8.1 will no longer ask you for your password at logon.

■ **Tip** If you want to restore the Windows 7-style Start menu in Windows 8.1, you need third-party software to do it. Solutions include ViStart (`http://www.lee-soft.com/vistart`), Start8 (`http://www.stardock.com/products/start8`), and Classic Shell (`http://classicshell.sourceforge.net`).

Bring Back the Start Menu with a Toolbar

It is possible to use the desktop taskbar's toolbar feature to reinstate a Start menu of sorts. To do this, right-click anywhere in a blank space on the taskbar; from the menu that appears, click *Toolbars* and then click *New Toolbar*. Navigate to the folder *C:\ProgramData\Microsoft\Windows\Start Menu\Programs* and select it.

You now have a toolbar on the right of the taskbar that simulates a mini-Start menu. You can change the options for this toolbar by right-clicking the taskbar and unlocking it. This displays additional options for the toolbar when you right-click it, including the View change for Large icon if you want and the ability to turn off its Text and Title.

Useful Windows Registry Hacks

One of the best things about the Windows registry is how easy it is to edit, and how much control you can get over Windows by doing so. I'd like to share some of my favorite registry hacks. As with any work in the Windows registry, be very careful adding, deleting, or changing settings; and always make sure that you have both a backup copy of the registry and a backup image of your copy of Windows. Each registry change for a feature within Windows requires you to restart the computer; for registry changes involving programs, restarting the program is normally enough.

Backing Up the Windows Registry

The registry is a database of all the settings and configuration options for Windows, your hardware, and all your installed software. It's the main file (actually a series of files) that tells the operating system what's what and what's where. If you're making changes to the registry, you should make a backup copy of the files.

You can do this from within the Registry Editor. Search for **regedit** at the Start screen to find it. Then, from the File menu click Export and save your backup of the registry file in a safe place (see Figure 13-52).

Figure 13-52. *Backing up the Windows registry*

If you need to restore your backed–up registry keys, open the Registry Editor and from its File menu, click Import. You are asked which file you want to import and then asked to confirm that you *do* want to add this key to the registry. Adding a backed-up key overwrites any changes made to that key.

Add Copy To/Move To Options to the File Explorer Context Menu

Although it's useful for the File Explorer context menu to include Cut and Copy commands when you right-click a file or folder, it's also possible to add Copy To Folder and Move To Folder options to this context list (see Figure 13-53).

Figure 13-53. *Adding Copy To Folder and Move To Folder options to File Explorer*

Here's how to add the Copy To Folder command:

1. Open the Registry Editor by searching for **regedit** at the Start screen.

2. Navigate to the key HKEY_CLASSES_ROOT\AllFilesystemObjects\shellex\ ContextMenuHandlers.

3. Right-click the ContextMenuHandlers key and add a New Key with the name **Copy to folder**.

4. Double-click this new key's Default value and change its value to **{C2FBB630-2971-11D1-A18C-00C04FD75D13}**.

To also add a Move To Folder item to the context menu, repeat these steps but create a new **Move to folder** key with the default value **{C2FBB631-2971-11D1-A18C-00C04FD75D13}**.

Add/Remove Options to the Send-To File Explorer Menu

When you right-click a file or folder in File Explorer, one of the options that appears is Send To, which allows you to send that item to a particular program, piece of hardware or location. You can add and remove items from this menu by navigating to **C:\Users\[Username]\AppData\Roaming\Microsoft\Windows**\SendTo in File Explorer, in which you can paste or delete shortcuts to devices, network locations, and more.

Add Defragment to the File Explorer Context Menu

You can add a Defragment option to the context menu in File Explorer when you right-click a hard disk (see Figure 13-54). This starts a command-line version of the Defragment tool.

Figure 13-54. *Add Defragment to the File Explorer context menu*

Follow these steps to add Defragment:

1. Open the Registry Editor by searching for **regedit** at the Start screen.

2. Navigate to the key HKEY_CLASSES_ROOT\Drive\shell.

3. Create a new key under this called **runas**.

4. Double-click Default Value to open it and set its default value to **Defragment**.

5. Create a subkey under runas called **command**.

6. Double-click the Command subkey and change its default value to **defrag %1 -v**.

Add Command Prompt to the File Explorer Context Menu

You can also easily add the command prompt to the right-click menu in File Explorer.

1. Visit the Registry Key HKEY_LOCAL_MACHINE\Software\Classes\Folder\Shell.

2. Create a new key called **Command Prompt**.

3. Double click the *Default* setting for this key and change its value to *Open Command Prompt* or similar text if you want something different.

4. Create a subkey of Command Prompt called **Command**.

5. Double click the *Default* value for Command and change it to **Cmd.exe /k pushd %L**.

Here the /k switch leaves the Command window open on your screen, rather than executing this one command and closing it. The pushd control contains the name of the current folder, and the %L switch opens the Command window in that folder.

Show Drive Letter Before Volume Name in File Explorer

You might want to turn off the display of driver letters in File Explorer, which you can do by selecting Options and then opening the View tab. Select **Change folder and search options** and then uncheck **Show drive letters**.

You can also have File Explorer display the drive letter before the drive volume name:

1. Open the Registry Editor by searching for **regedit** at the Start screen.

2. Navigate to the following key: HKEY_LOCAL_MACHINE\SOFTWARE\Microsoft\Windows\CurrentVersion\Explorer.

3. Right-click and create a new Dword (32-bit) Value called **ShowDriveLettersFirst**.

4. Double-click the new addition to open it and change its value from 0 to **4**.

Add an FTP Location to File Explorer

If you maintain a web server, you can add a direct link to your FTP service directly to File Explorer. Doing so enables you to manage files on the server as though they were on your own PC, being able to drag and drop files into the FTP site as well as delete them without the need for separate FTP software.

1. In a File Explorer window, click the *Computer* tab on the Ribbon.

2. Click the *Add a Network Location* button.

3. Click *Next* in the window that appears.

4. Click *Choose a custom network location* and then click the *Next* button.

5. Enter the name of your FTP site in the format **ftp://ftp.contoso.com** and click *Next*

6. If you log in to your FTP site with a username and password, uncheck the *Log on anonymously* box and enter your username; then click *Next*.

7. Give your FTP site a name and click *Next*.

8. Leave the *Open this network location* box checked and click *Finish*.

9. In the window that appears, enter your password for the FTP site and optionally check the *Remember my password* box.

You now have direct access to your FTP site from directly within File Explorer every time you log in to your PC.

Change Taskbar Program Previews

With a simple registry tweak, you can change the size of the preview thumbnails for running programs in the Windows 8.1 taskbar:

1. Open the Registry Editor by searching for **regedit** at the Start screen.

2. Navigate to the key HKEY_CURRENT_USER\Software\Microsoft\Windows\CurrentVersion\Explorer\Taskband.

3. Right-click and create a new Dword (32-bit) Value called **MinThumbSizePX**.

4. Double-click this new entry and change its value to the size (in pixels) you want your thumbnails to be. For example, you might want huge thumbnails that are 500 pixels across (change the number to 500) or you might want tiny thumbnails of 50 pixels (change the value to 50).

There are other registry Dword 32-bit Value keys you can create to control thumbnail images:

- NumThumbnails (the number of thumbnail images)

- MinThumbSizePX (minimum thumbnail size)

- MaxThumbSizePX (maximum thumbnail size)

- TextHeightPX (thumbnail title text height in pixels)

- TopMarginPX (top margin in pixels)

- LeftMarginPX (left margin in pixels)

- RightMarginPX (right margin in pixels)

- BottomMarginPX (bottom margin in pixels)

- ThumbSpacingXPx (horizontal spacing between thumbnails in pixels)

- ThumbSpacingYPx (vertical spacing between thumbnails in pixels)

Modifying the Taskbar Using Group Policy

Although there are many controls for modifying the taskbar available from the simple right-click and opening the taskbar's *Properties*, additional controls are available to users of Windows 8.1 Pro, Enterprise, and Windows RT. They exist in Group Policy, which can be opened by searching for **gpedit.msc** at the Start screen.

Once in the Group Policy Editor, navigate to **User Configuration\Administrative Templates\StartMenu and Taskbar**, in which you see a great menu with additional options available, including being able to turn off balloon notifications and hiding the notification area completely.

Disable the ShutDown Command

Sometimes you might not want a PC to be switched off; for example, if it is running as a file or other server type, or performs a critical task. You can disable the Shutdown options in the charms.

1. Find the registry key **HKEY_CURRENT_USER\Software\Microsoft\Windows\ CurrentVersion\Policies\Explorer**.

2. Create a new *DWORD* and call it **NoClose**.

3. Give this DWORD a value of **1**.

This process doesn't prevent people from shutting down the PC by pressing the physical power button, but it does prevent them from shutting down the PC in the normal manner.

Unlock the Hidden Super-Administrator Account

Although main users on a PC are always set up as Administrator, which enables them to make whatever changes they need to the computer, there is also a hidden super-administrator account available if you ever need it. This super account isn't hamstrung by such things as the User Account Control (UAC) and has permissions to do things to files in Windows that you may need, but that are denied to you for reasons of stability and safety in the operating system.

To unlock this account, from an existing Administrator account open *Command Prompt (Admin)* from the Win+X menu and type the following command: **net user administrator /active:yes**. When you log out, the new Administrator account is available to you. You can disable it when you finish with the /**active:no** switch.

Hiding Unused Items from the Control Panel

The Control Panel in Windows 8.1 can get very messy, with all manner of controls listed that you might either never want to use or not want other people who use your computer to see. Fortunately it is possible to remove some of these controls if you want:

1. Search for **regedit** at the Start screen and open the Registry Editor.

2. Navigate in the Registry Editor to **HKEY_LOCAL_MACHINE\SOFTWARE\Microsoft\ Windows\CurrentVersion\Control Panel\don't load**.

3. Here you will see a list of Control Panel items that are already hidden (see Figure 13-55). To hide an additional item, create a new *String* value with the .cpl name for the control that corresponds to Table 13-1.

Figure 13-55. *You can hide Control Panel applets*

Table 13-1. *Control Panel Applet Names*

Control Panel Applet	Name
Accessibility Options	access.cpl
Add New Hardware Wizard	hdwwiz.cpl
Display Properties	desk.cpl
Game Controllers	joy.cpl
Internet Options	inetcpl.cpl
Mouse Properties	main.cpl
Network Connections	ncpa.cpl
ODBC Data Sources	odbccp32.cpl
Phone and Modem Options	telephon.cpl
Power Options	powercfg.cpl
Programs and Features	appwiz.cpl

(*continued*)

Table 13-1. (*continued*)

Control Panel Applet	Name
Region	intl.cpl
Sound	mmsys.cpl
Speech	sapi.cpl
System	sysdm.cpl
Time and Date	timedate.cpl
User Accounts	nusrmgr.cpl

Summary

Windows has traditionally been highly configurable, and Windows 8.1 is no exception with its sheer volume of settings. This chapter could turn into an entire book on its own by just discussing how to configure every setting.

I hope this chapter has given you a good overview of what the settings do, how you can change them, and why you might want to do so. There are some settings, such as changing the virtual memory, that I always recommend you change, but generally speaking, Windows 8.1 is fine out of the box. *Tweaking* Windows 8.1, on the other hand, is something entirely different.

CHAPTER 14

Getting Started with Virtualization

Each new release of Windows, whether major or minor, brings not just new features and new ways of working, but also fresh challenges. One of those challenges is maintaining compatibility with the older software that we've used for years and that are as comfortable as an old shoe.

I am not excluded from this scenario. I have used the same graphics package, Microsoft PhotoDraw, for more than a decade. I love it—it does everything I want and it's extremely easy to use. Why should I change?

Sadly, with upgrades to Windows come software incompatibilities. The biggest change came with the move from Windows XP to Windows Vista. The whole core of the operating system was rewritten from scratch. It included some major restructuring, such as removing, replacing, or rewriting features. With PhotoDraw, I found that although most of the package still worked, some features treated me to only an annoying *"donk!"* noise when I tried to use them.

There are also times when you want to be able to use or try a different operating system on your computer, such as Linux or even the prerelease of the next version of Windows. Setting up a dual-boot system can be extremely complex, especially because Windows 8.1 usually needs to be installed last (see Chapter 15 for notes on this). A good option is to install the second operating system in a virtual machine (VM).

When Windows 7 was launched with the accompanying Windows XP Mode virtualization client, I was delighted. At long last I could use PhotoDraw again on the desktop without worry or problems.

The bad news is that Windows XP Mode is no longer supported and it isn't a feature of Windows 8.1 because all support for Windows XP ends (or ended, depending on when you're reading this) in April 2014, before the release of Windows 9.

It's not all bad news, though. Windows 8.1 Pro and Enterprise editions contain a feature called Hyper-V. This is Microsoft's latest virtualization client ported from Windows Server. It's more than powerful enough to get your legacy software working again.

Virtualization isn't just about maintaining compatibility with older software, however, because it also has important roles to play in testing stability in software and updates for deployment, and also for providing customizable working environments for users. In this chapter, I'll show you how to set up and maintain Hyper-V for all these roles.

Note that using virtualization is an advanced feature and something that less-technical Windows users will likely avoid. You can't do anything to harm or damage your current Windows installation, but if you want to use Hyper-V and you're not completely comfortable with computers, you should follow the instructions in this chapter very carefully to ensure the best results.

Note   Hyper-V is available only in the 64-bit versions of Windows 8.1 Pro and Enterprise if running on compatible hardware.

What Is Virtualization?

Virtualization allows any operating system to run inside another in a specially configured environment that simulates the hardware of a full PC. Think of it a bit like the "virtual world" as it appeared to people trapped in the Matrix in the popular film trilogy. Virtualization effectively tricks the virtualized operating system into thinking that it's running on its own hardware. Older VMs that simulated the hardware were very slow because every hardware action had to be re-created in software.

Newer VMs, including Hyper-V, enable the virtualized operating system to access your computer's own hardware. They manage the sharing of that hardware between the host OS and the virtualized OS on the machine to make sure that conflicts don't occur. This means that Hyper-V acts on your computer and your network as if it's just another computer attached to that network.

The main benefit of virtualization is that the hardware management allows VMs to harness the full power of modern computers with multiple processor cores and large volumes of memory. For example, if you have a quad-core processor and 8 GB of memory in your computer, a good VM can assign each of three operating systems a single processor core and 2 GB of memory, each with the host OS using the remaining core and memory—thus maximizing the computer's potential and reducing overall costs.

When Should You Use a Virtual Machine?

There are several scenarios in which the use of a VM is helpful, including keeping your older legacy software working. If you really must use software that worked fine in Windows XP but doesn't work in Windows 8.1, installing a copy of Windows XP into a VM is a way to continue using that software.

VMs are also commonly used for testing scenarios. Let's say you want to roll out a patch or software upgrade across your computers, but you're unsure of how it will interact with the existing software that you use. You can test it first in a VM so that you are certain that all works fine beforehand and avoid the risk of any downtime.

You might also use virtualization to provide custom working environments. On one machine, you could set up VMs for design, accounting, or other purposes that provide workers with the tools and environment they need to be productive, while also making the environment easy to transport between computers in different locations.

I used Hyper-V while writing this book so that I could install a clean copy of Windows 8.1. There are all manner of scenarios in which it is useful to have a VM running.

■ **Note**   You need a valid license (product key) for each operating system you install in a VM using Hyper-V.

Why You Should "Sandbox" Windows XP

For those who want to run Windows XP on a VM, I want you to examine whether you should really continue using Windows XP to run your legacy software. Although there is one scenario in which it's perfectly safe to run Windows XP (I'll come to it shortly), there are a couple of very good reasons why you should not.

Windows XP, although very well-liked by many people, is an extremely insecure operating system. After shipping with Internet Explorer 6, it was responsible for many major security scares in the decade after it was released.

Those problems have never gone away. In countries such as China, Windows XP usage was still very high when Windows 8.1 was released. Malware writers and criminals still want to target the OS and its vulnerabilities to steal personal data from users.

At the end of extended support for Windows XP, all patches and updates for the operating system stop forever; any vulnerabilities that still exist, or any new vulnerabilities created through third-party software or malware, will be left unpatched. You can be certain that when Windows XP support ends, malware for any remaining vulnerabilities—the ones that the criminals have identified but not yet exploited—will be released.

Tip Always make sure that Windows Updates is turned on and that antivirus software is installed on any operating system in a VM with Internet access.

I do not recommend that anyone continue using Windows XP, either on its own or within a VM, in Windows 7 or Windows 8.1. There is one scenario however, in which it might be considered okay to use Windows XP in a VM: when you use software in Windows XP that never requires Internet access. You can set up the VM with no networking or Internet support.

This "sandboxed" VM is completely isolated from your network and the Internet, with no traffic able to get in or out. You can still give it local file storage access so that you can work with files on your computer; but without direct ability to contact the Internet, the only way it can succumb to virus infection is if the host PC or the files on it are already infected.

Note Although Windows XP Mode in Windows 7 enabled you to pin Windows XP–installed software to the Windows 7 taskbar and use it on the Windows 7 desktop, Hyper-V does not support this. To use this functionality, you need to use Microsoft Enterprise Desktop Virtualization (MED-V), which is part of the Microsoft Desktop Optimization Pack (MDOP). It is available to businesses only through Software Assurance volume licensing. There is a way to "sort of" get Windows XP-mode running on the Windows 8.1 desktop using Oracle VirtualBox. HowToGeek.com has published a guide at `http://www.howtogeek.com/howto/12183/how-to-run-xp-mode-in-virtualbox-on-windows-7/`.

Can't Find Hyper-V on Your PC?

Hyper-V exists in the Pro and Enterprise versions of Windows 8.1, but it is commonly hidden in Windows 8.1 Pro. You can activate it, however, by searching for **programs and features** at the Start screen, which is the Control Panel applet you use for uninstalling desktop programs. This panel contains a link on the left of its window called *Turn Windows feature on or off* and you should click it.

The new window that then appears (see Figure 14-1) contains a full list of all the Windows 8.1 features that can be either enabled or disabled. Hyper-V appears in this list. To activate it, check the box to its left, click OK, and then restart your PC. Hyper-V now appears in your All Apps view.

Figure 14-1. *Enabling Hyper-V in Windows 8.1 Pro*

Installing an Operating System in Hyper-V

How do you install an operating system into Hyper-V and what types of operating system does it support? You can install any version of Windows or other Intel (x86 and x64)–based operating systems into Hyper-V, including GNU/Linux, by following these steps:

1. Find Hyper-V in Windows by searching for **Hyper** at the Start screen.

2. Click Hyper-V Manager. The Hyper-V Manager (see Figure 14-2) looks and operates much like the other administration windows in Windows 8.1. Your main controls are in the right pane.

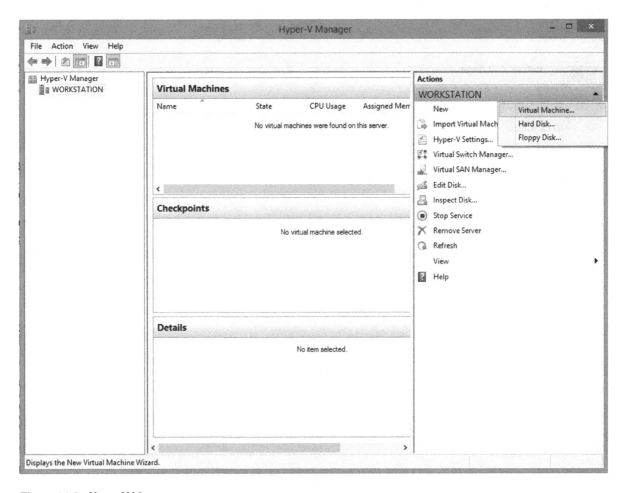

Figure 14-2. Hyper-V Manager

3. Click New ⇧ Virtual Machine to create a new VM.

■ **Tip** When you set up your first VM in Hyper-V, it has no networking available to it, either local or Internet. You might want to jump ahead in this chapter to the "Setting Up Networking in Hyper-V" section to configure it before creating the VM.

---

4. Click the Next button at the bottom of the New Virtual Machine Wizard (see Figure 14-3) to set up your own VM.

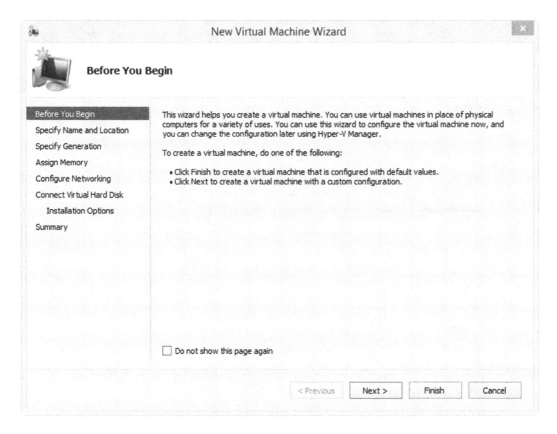

Figure 14-3. *New Virtual Machine Wizard*

5. Give your VM a name and a store location (see Figure 14-4). By default, Windows 8.1 suggests storing it on the same hard disk on which Windows is installed. You may want to specify a different hard disk, however. Click Next.

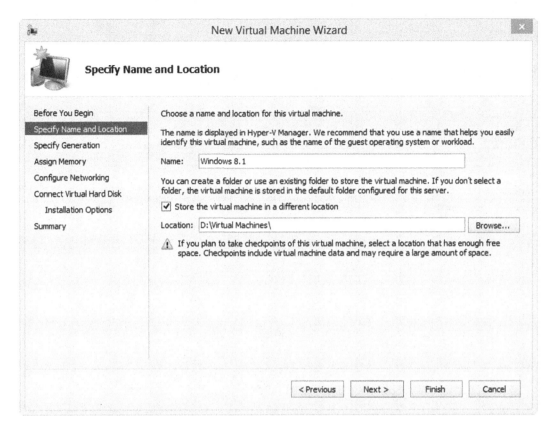

Figure 14-4. *Specifying a name and store location for the VM*

■ **Tip** Storing your VM on a different disk or partition to Windows 8.1 excludes it from any custom Refresh image you make, thus bringing down the overall size of that backup. If you always want to use the VM *with* your installed copy of Windows, however, keeping it on the same hard disk as Windows (and therefore included in backup Refresh image) might be the best choice.

---

6. One of the improvements made to Hyper-V in Windows 8.1 includes a new type of VM container file that supports features such as different boot types (see Figure 14-5). This *Generation 2* VM type is fully compatible with Windows 8 and Windows 8.1 as well as Windows Server 2012, but it doesn't work on Hyper-V installations on earlier operating systems such as these. If you think you will want to use your VM on computers running Windows Server 2008, for example, you should choose the Generation 1 option to maintain full compatibility.

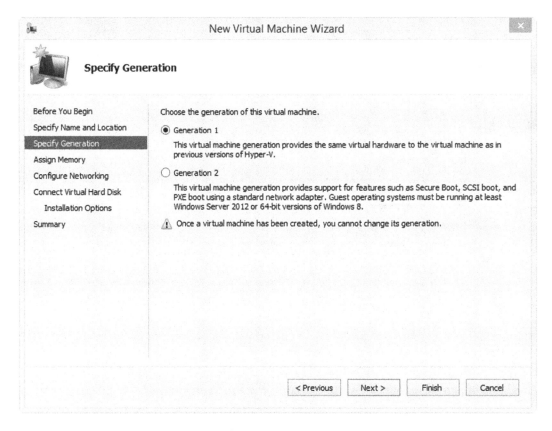

Figure 14-5. There are now several types of VM you can create

7. Assign the amount of memory you want to dedicate to the VM (see Figure 14-6). The amount depends on the type of operating system is running in the VM and how much physical memory your PC has.

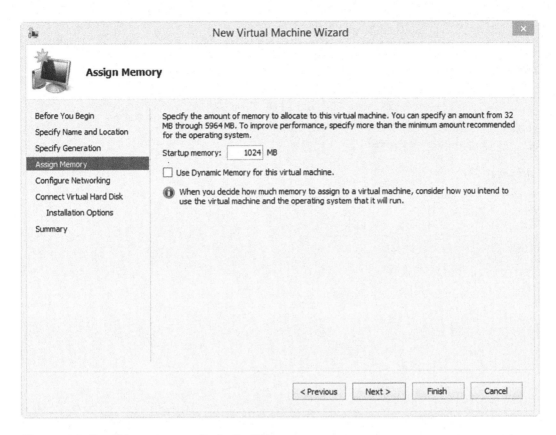

Figure 14-6. *Specifying a memory size for the VM*

For example, you might be installing Windows XP into the VM, which means you would need only 512 MB of RAM. If you plan to do graphics work in the VM, however, more memory would be required. If your PC has only 4 GB of memory, you should probably not specify more than 1 GB for the VM; if you have 8 GB, you could dedicate a healthier 2 GB of memory to the VM.

There is also the option to use Dynamic Memory. This feature allows the VM to automatically assign additional memory through Hyper-V if it is required and if there is available memory on your PC. You may find this option useful because it is used only when required. Click Next.

8. Configure the networking options for the VM by choosing from a drop down-list of the preconfigured networks you have set up for Hyper-V (see Figure 14-7) and click Next.

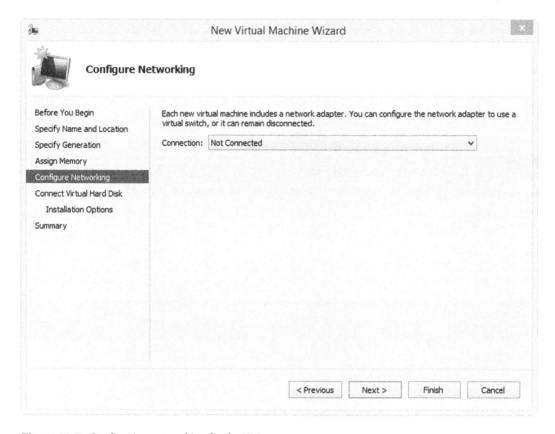

Figure 14-7. *Configuring networking for the VM*

If you want a completely sandboxed operating system with no local computer, network, or Internet access, there is no need to configure a network adaptor to work with the VM. This isolates the VM completely from the outside world, but it also means that you can't access the files and documents on the host computer and that you don't have access to the VM using Remote Desktop.

■ **Note**   You may not be able to add networking options at this time because networking in Hyper-V must be configured independently of any individual VM. VMs can share individually configured networks to give them Internet access, access to the local computer, or access only to other VMs. If this is the case, you need to install Integration Services into the VM when it is installed, and set up a virtual switch. I show you how later in this chapter.

---

9.   Connect the VHD. This wizard page lets you specify the size of the VM's hard disk (see Figure 14-8). It suggests a size, though you can change this if you require the VM to be larger or smaller. An alternate option is to reattach an existing VHD. Click Next.

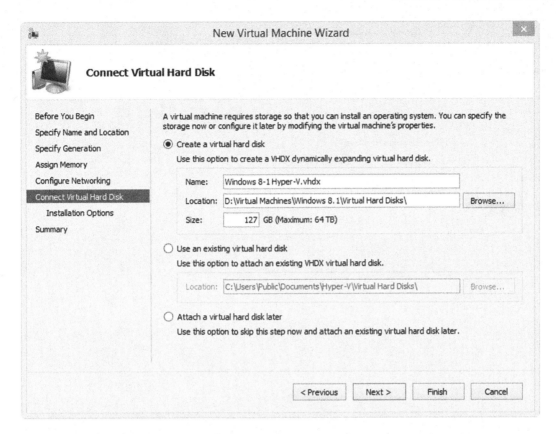

Figure 14-8. *Specifying virtual disk properties*

10. Install an operating system (see Figure 14-9). You can do this from a virtual floppy disk, CD, DVD, USB flash drive, or ISO file.

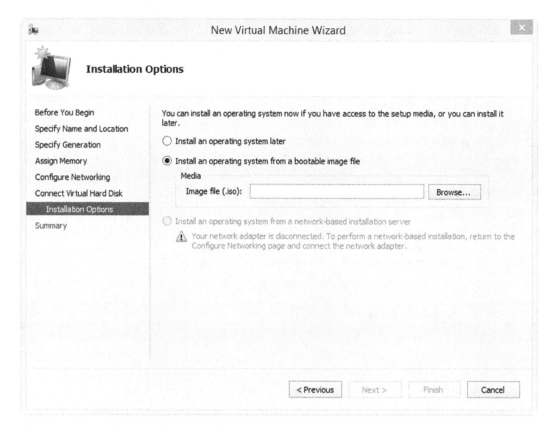

Figure 14-9. *Installing the OS into the VM*

11. Confirm all the details you have entered (see Figure 14-10). Click Finish when you are done.

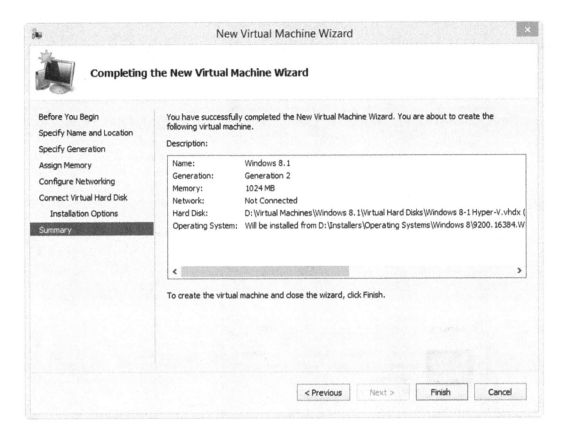

Figure 14-10. *Confirming the VM details*

12. Start the VM. In the Hyper-V Manager, you now see your VM listed in the top-center pane (see Figure 14-11). Click it. In the bottom half of the right pane, click Connect to connect to the VM.

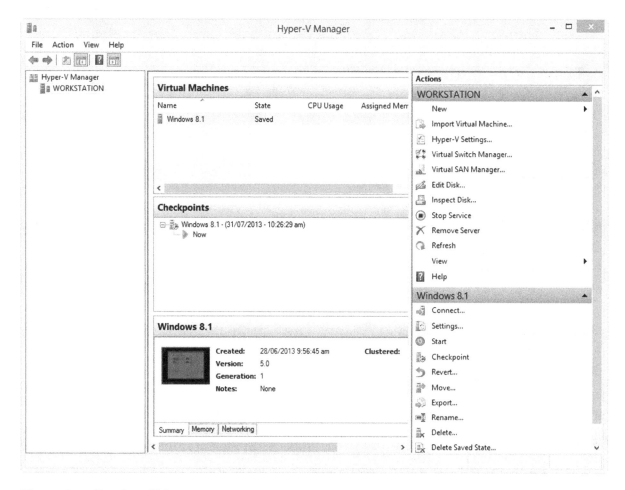

Figure 14-11. *Running a VM*

13. Open the Action menu and select Start to launch the VM (see Figure 14-12).

Figure 14-12. *Launching a VM*

After you start the VM, you see a window with the virtualized OS running inside it.

When you start a VM, you see a connection options dialog (see Figure 14-13) that asks at what screen resolution you want to run the VM, and the slider goes all the way up to your full-screen resolution. This makes it simple to run the VM as different resolutions depending on what you're doing with it without having to change the resolution within the display properties of the VM every time. At the bottom of this dialog is a *Show options* button that includes more settings, including audio for the VM.

Figure 14-13. *You are presented with additional options when launching a VM*

Setting Up Networking with Hyper-V

By default, all Hyper-V VMs are sandboxed and completely isolated from the computers and networks around them. When you want a VM to interact with other VMs, your physical computers, the network, and the Internet, you need to create a virtual switch. You can do this from the main Hyper-V Manager, in which you click Virtual Switch Manager in the right pane.

You need to decide what type of virtual switch you want to create. The Virtual Switch Manager gives you a text description of each type of switch (see Figure 14-14).

Figure 14-14. *Creating a virtual switch*

If you want your VM to see and access files on the host PC and on your network, you need to select External, which is also the option that gives the VM access to the Internet (so be careful with it if using Windows XP). The Internal and Private options allow Hyper-V VMs to communicate only with each other.

After you highlight the option you want, click the Create Virtual Switch button.

You now need to configure the options for your virtual switch (see Figure 14-15). It is important to determine which network adapter in your computer you attach it to. You may have both wired and wireless network adapters in your computer; you need to choose the right one.

Figure 14-15. *Setting virtual switch options*

■ **Tip** Let's say that you want a VM to access files on the host PC, but you do *not* want it to have access to the network or the Internet. If your PC has wired and wireless connections, connect the switch to the one that you *don't* use to get online. If you don't have a physical network cable plugged into the PC, choose the non–Wi-Fi connection. This gives the VM access to the host PC *only* and helps isolate it from malware and attack.

After you create your virtual switch, you need to attach it to your VM. Click the appropriate VM in the top-center pane in the Hyper-V Manager. Then in the bottom-right pane, click Settings, which brings up the settings for the VM (see Figure 14-16).

Figure 14-16. *Connecting a VM to a virtual switch*

Click Network Adapter option in the left pane. If you do not see this option, click Add Hardware to add a network adapter. A useful feature is Bandwidth Management, which ensures that whatever the VM does, it can't use more than a specified amount of your network bandwidth. This throttling control is a useful way to ensure that the VM has the network connection it requires without becoming a bandwidth hog.

Where you choose the virtual switch at the top of the Network Adapter settings, select the switch you created and press OK. No further configuration should be necessary. Your VM now has network access.

Although other options can be changed in the VM Settings, some settings that are set when you first create the VM can't be changed. To change these settings, the VM needs to be switched off.

Saving VM Checkpoints

When a major change is made to Windows 8.1, such as the installation of a desktop program or a Windows Update, a System Restore point is kept. It keeps copies of critical operating system files such as the Windows registry from just before the change was made. Thus if something then goes wrong, this change can be rolled back to revert your copy of Windows to its earlier state. In Hyper-V, this procedure can be a pain, however, because you first have to start the VM and then run System Restore from within it. This process can be annoying and time-consuming.

Hyper-V gets around this annoyance by having a feature called *Checkpoints*, each of which is a snapshot of the VM taken at a specific time. You can create a checkpoint at any time by selecting the VM you want to create one for in the top center of the *Virtual Machines* panel of the Hyper-V Manager and then clicking the *Checkpoint* link in the bottom right of the management window.

Created checkpoints are then listed in the center of the Hyper-V Manager (see Figure 14-17), and you can click one to either apply it (to roll the VM back to that point), export it (more on exporting VMs in the next section), or delete it.

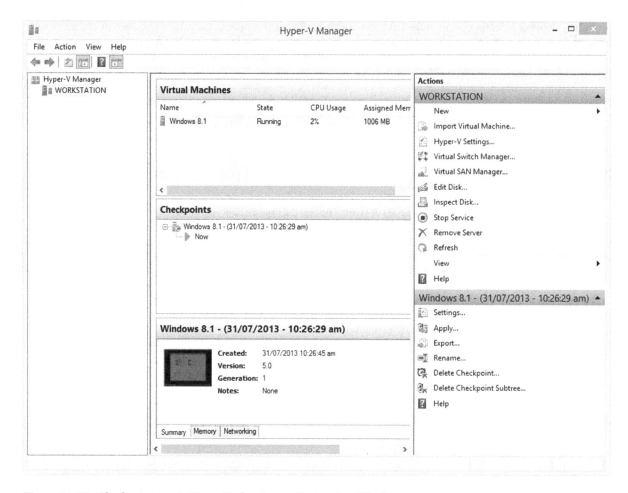

Figure 14-17. *Checkpoints are to Hyper-V what System Restore is to Windows*

Importing and Exporting Virtual Machines in Hyper-V

You may want to create VMs that are to be used on other PCs or that you want to keep copies of. Just creating a VM and then opening that VM file after copying it to another computer doesn't work for importing VMs in Hyper-V, which is why a special import and export option is available. To export a VM, select it in the Hyper-V Manager. In the bottom right of the Hyper-V Manager window, the *Export* option displays (see Figure 14-18). Click it and you are asked which folder you want to store your exported VM in. The export process is both invisible and fairly quick.

Figure 14-18. *You can export VMs from the Hyper-V Management console*

1. You can import previously exported VMs into Hyper-V by clicking the *Import virtual machine* link in the top right of the Hyper-V Manager window (see Figure 14-19) when no VM is currently selected.

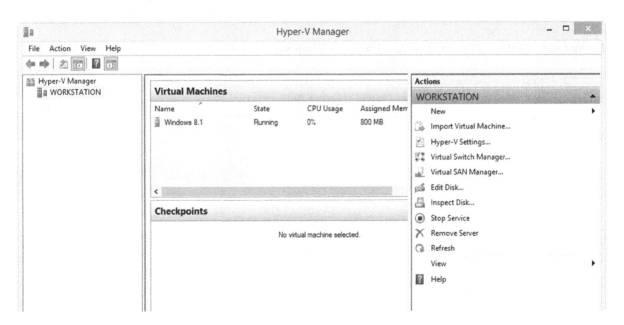

Figure 14-19. *VMs are also imported using the Hyper-V Management console*

2. The Import Virtual Machine Wizard opens, which first asks you to specify which folder (not which file) has the stored VM (see Figure 14-20).

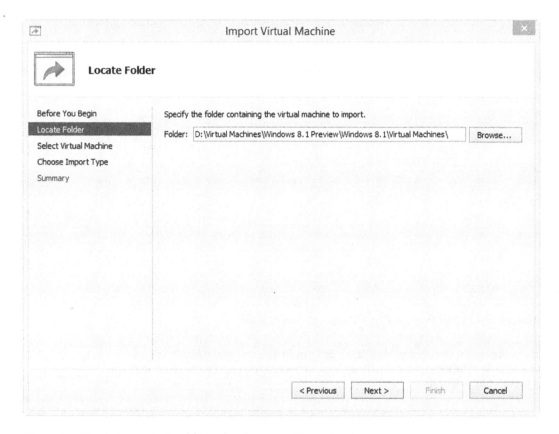

Figure 14-20. *The import wizard first asks where your VM is stored*

3. Next you are shown the name of the VM along with details of when it was created (see Figure 14-21). If this is the correct VM, click *Next*.

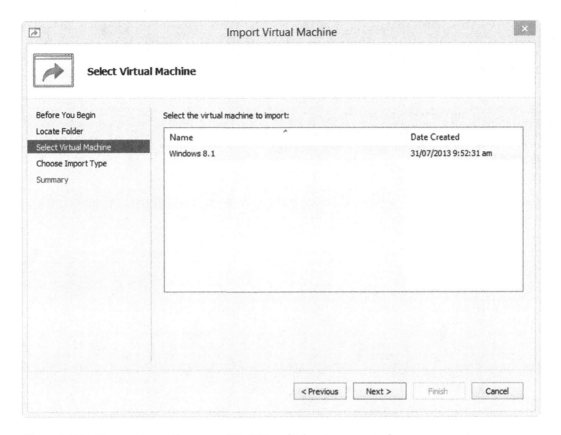

Figure 14-21. You are shown the name of the VM and when it was created

4. You are now asked how you want to import the VM (see Figure 14-22). The three options are as follows:

- **Register the virtual machine** is used when you are performing a straight import, the VM is still in the same folder location it was exported to, and you want to leave it there.

- **Restore the virtual machine** is used if the VM is not in the same folder location it was exported to; for example, if it is a copy taken from a master image on a server.

- **Copy the virtual machine** is used if you want to create a local copy of an existing VM, leaving the "master" VM intact for importing later on this or another PC if required. This option is also used if you want to create a copy of an already imported VM.

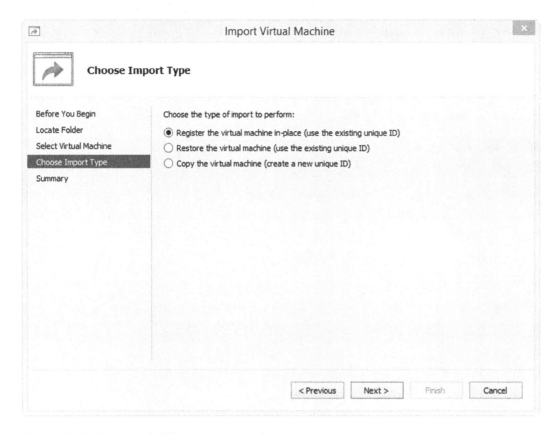

Figure 14-22. *You are asked if you want a straight import or a copy*

■ **Note**   If you import a VM without making a copy of it, any changes you make to the VM and any problems that occur with it become part of it, and you effectively lose your clean *master* copy.

---

5.   If you choose to create a copy of the VM, you are asked where you want to store it in your PC (see Figure 14-23).

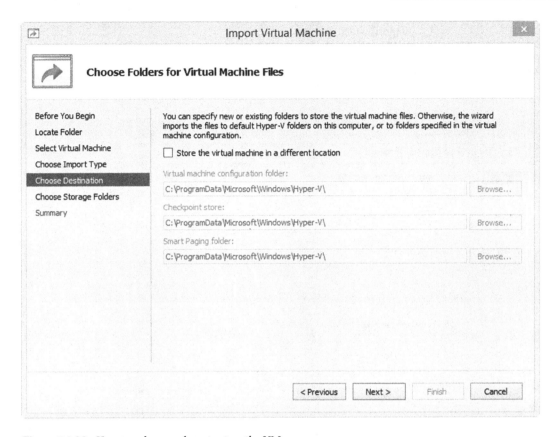

Figure 14-23. *You can choose where to store the VM copy*

6.   The last step is for Hyper-V to confirm all your chosen settings with you (see Figure 14-24) before it completes the VM import process.

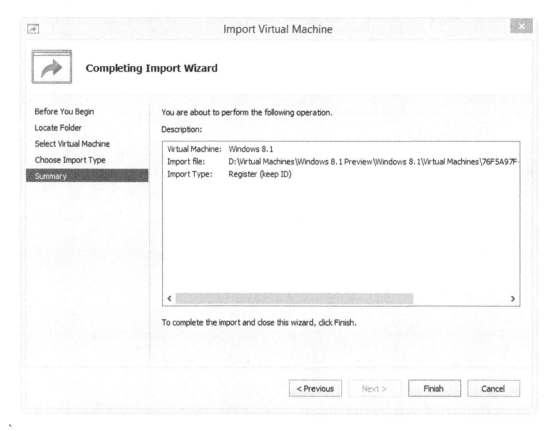

Figure 14-24. *Hyper-V confirms all your choices before importing the VM*

Integrating Additional Services into a VM

Some operating systems, especially earlier versions of Windows, won't give you network access or other features at this point. This is where you need to plug extra features into the VM. You must do this with the VM running.

These additional features, which are required for some operating systems, include the ability to move your mouse cursor freely between your main desktop and open VMs without having to first unlock it from the VM window. They also include networking and USB support for some operating systems.

From the Action menu, click *Insert Integration Service Setup Disk.* This loads an ISO file containing software that enhances the functionality of the VM.

Using Virtual Hard Disks

You can also use virtual hard disks (VHDs) within Windows both as file containers and as boot drives for the operating system. You can create a VHD within Hyper-V, but also from the Windows 8.1 Disk Management console (available by using the Win+X keyboard shortcut).

On their own, VHDs are of limited use because you need to manually reattach them to Windows 8.1 when the computer is restarted. It is in booting from a VHD that they become useful. Let's say you have a laptop that you repurpose for different roles within a company, such as sales, accounting, or management, for example. Rather than having a complicated multiboot system that is difficult to maintain, you can create a series of VHDs and copy the correct one to the laptop when you need to assign the laptop a different departmental role.

Creating a VHD in Windows 8.1

Create a VHD from the Disk Management console (press Win+X to open options). From the Action menu, click Create VHD (see Figure 14-25).

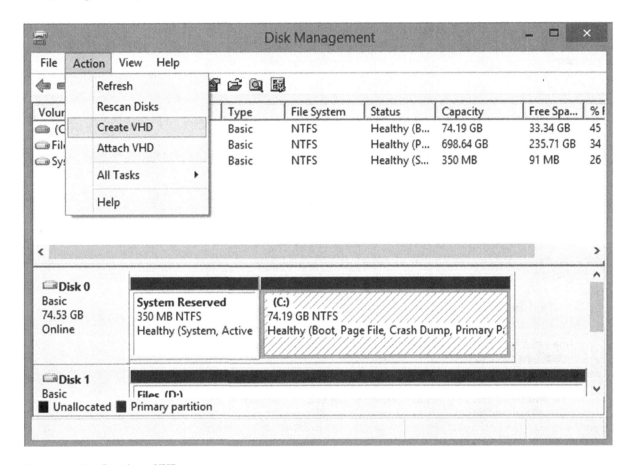

Figure 14-25. *Creating a VHD*

A dialog allows you to specify the VHD size and the hard disk location for VHD storage (see Figure 14-26).

Figure 14-26. *Choosing VHD options*

When you choose the location for the VHD, you also specify its name. The size options are interesting, however, because you can specify a fixed size or you can have the VHD expand in size dynamically as and when you need more space within it. Note than when specifying a size for the VHD the size drop-down list offers megabytes (MB), gigabytes (GB) and terabytes (TB). Don't accidentally choose the wrong one; they're all very different.

When the VHD is created, you can attach it to Windows 8.1 in the Disk Management console by selecting Attach VHD from the Actions menu.

Booting Windows from a VHD

Creating a VHD doesn't let you install an operating system in it or boot from it. To do this, you need to start your computer from your original Windows 8.1 installation media. After you select your installation language, perform the following steps:

1. Press Shift+F10 at the installation screen to open a Command window.

2. Type **diskpart** and press Enter.

3. To use an existing VHD, type **Select vdisk file=C:\Path1\Path2\disk.vhd**, substituting the path and disk names for the location on the disk of the VHD and its name.

4. To create a new VHD, type **Create vdisk file=C:\Path1\Path2\disk.vhd maximum=20000 type=dynamic**, again substituting the path and disk names with where you want the VHD to be created and what you want it to be called (the path folders must already exist). Also, substitute the number of megabytes and create either a fixed or dynamic disk.

5. Type **Select vdisk file=C:zPath1\Path2\disk.vhd** and press Enter to attach the VHD if you have just created one.

6. Type **attach vdisk** and press Enter.

7. Type **exit** and press Enter.

8. Type **exit** again and press Enter.

9. Click Install ➤ Custom: Install Windows Only (Advanced).

10. Locate the newly attached VHD in the hard disk pane in which you want to install Windows. This is Disk 1 if you have only one hard disk in your computer. You can identify it by its size. Click Next when you are ready to install Windows onto the VHD.

You can install Windows 7 Enterprise and Ultimate, Windows 8.1 Pro and Enterprise, and Windows Server 2008 and 2012 into a VHD.

■ **Note**   Each operating system and software package you install into a VM needs to have its own license and, if necessary for that product, its own product key. Some versions of Windows are not licensed for use inside a VM. You can find out more about licensing for your particular copies of Windows and other Microsoft software at http://www.microsoft.com/About/Legal/EN/US/IntellectualProperty/UseTerms.

You now need to add the VHD to the Windows boot menu:

1. Press Win+X to open the Administration menu.

2. Click Command Prompt (Admin).

3. Type **bcdedit /v** in the Command window. Press Enter.

4. Locate the VHD you installed and make a note of its globally unique identifier (GUID) code. It is a long string of numbers and letters in the Identifier section for the OS (see Figure 14-27).

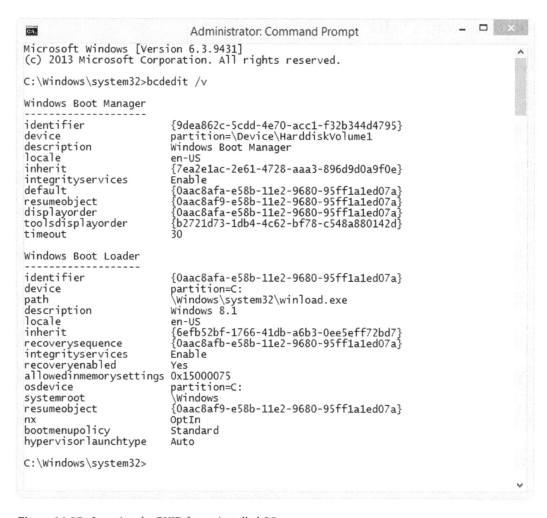

Figure 14-27. *Locating the GUID for an installed OS*

5. Type **bcdedit /set {GUID} description "OS Name,"** substituting the actual GUID for the OS for the letters *GUID* and assigning the OS its proper name. Press Enter.

6. Optionally, you might want this VHD to be the OS that loads by default. Set this by typing **bcdedit / default {GUID}**. Press Enter.

You can now boot your computer from the VM in the same way that you boot into your normally installed copy of Windows. In fact, you won't even be able to notice the difference. Most people booting into a VM have no idea that they're not using an operating system that's installed onto the computer's hard disk.

■ **Note**   The Secure Boot feature in Windows 8.1 on UEFI-equipped motherboards might prevent some VHDs from booting. You should check in the UEFI firmware settings to see if this feature can be turned off on your computer.

Summary

The virtualization options in Windows 8.1 are powerful, but remember that they are available in only the Pro and Enterprise editions.

I have shown you how it is also possible—as long as you have two network adapters in your PC—to isolate a VM from the Internet while still giving it access to your own PC. It can really be done only if you connect to the Internet via Wi-Fi and *do not* have a physical network cable plugged into your computer. Doing so helps to protect an older Windows XP installation from viruses and other malware infections.

CHAPTER 15

Installing Windows 8.1 on Your Computer

Whether you get your copy of Windows 8.1 with a shiny new PC, off the shelf from your local store, or on a software subscription package from Microsoft, you have to install it at some point—either to replace an earlier version of Windows on your computer or when something goes wrong.

Installing Windows 8.1 is something that can be done fairly simply and without fuss. In fact, it's the least fussy version of Windows ever. It allows you to upgrade from an earlier version of the operating system or wipe out an existing one while keeping all your files intact.

Back Up Your Files and Documents First!

When you install Windows 8.1 onto an existing computer, make sure that you keep all your files and documents intact. To guarantee this, you should *always* make an up-to-date backup of all your files and documents beforehand.

Although the Windows installation process is generally very robust, there's no knowing when and how something might go wrong. Problems could be due to a power outage, a driver failure, or simply forgetting that you had some important files in a different folder that Windows 8.1 doesn't save because it doesn't know it needs to do so.

The best place to keep a files backup is on an external USB hard disk, but if you have a second physical hard disk or a hard disk that's split into several different partitions on your computer, you can keep your files there. Bear in mind, though, that a *proper* backup should be one that's external to the computer, which covers you in case of fire, theft, or hard-disk failure. (See Chapter 12 for information on performing backups.)

Windows 8.1 Edition Differences

There the several editions, (sometimes known as flavors or stock-keeping units (SKUs) of Windows 8.1. Be aware that some are available only to certain customers and in certain ways:

- **Windows 8.1** is the general consumer version and comes preinstalled on most new PCs. It is also available through retail purchase.

- **Windows 8.1 Pro** is the version aimed at IT professionals and enthusiasts. It comes preinstalled on some PCs and is available for purchase.

- **Windows 8.1 Enterprise** is available only to business volume-licensing customers.

- **Windows RT** (Runtime) is the ARM version of Windows 8.1. It is available only to Microsoft's hardware partners. It is not available through retail purchase and cannot be installed on a blank tablet by the end user.

- **Windows 8.1 Pro with Media Center** isn't actually an official version of Windows 8.1, but it is sold by some hardware partners or preinstalled on some media and entertainment-focused PCs. It is available for purchase only by upgrading Windows 8.1 or Windows Pro through the Add Features to Windows option in the Control Panel.

Deciding How to Install Windows 8.1 on an Existing Computer

One of the perennial questions asked in computing circles when migrating from one version of Windows to another is whether to perform an upgrade over an existing copy or completely wipe the old installation and start from scratch. So what are the pros and cons of both?

Upgrade pros:

- Upgrading is much faster and easier overall, especially if you have a lot of software on your computer, because it saves reinstalling everything afterward.

- Performing an upgrade leaves your files intact if your files and documents are on the same hard-disk partition as your old copy of Windows and you don't have an external backup (more on this shortly because it's very important).

Upgrade cons:

- Any problems associated with your software or Windows installation might be carried forward into Windows 8.1.

- Upgrading does not guarantee that your software will work properly afterward, and some software programs might need to be uninstalled and reinstalled.

Clean install pros:

- Your new installation is fresh and clean with no problems associated with it.

- There are no bugs and incompatible software.

Clean install cons:

- Installation and configuration can be time-consuming, especially if you have a lot of software.

- You need to have an up-to-date external backup of your files and documents.

In truth, you might not have a choice but to perform a clean installation, at least as far as the Windows 8.1 upgrade options go, because Windows 8.1 might not be able to migrate your software.

Now let's look at the process of actually upgrading to Windows 8.1. Once you have physical media for installing Windows 8.1, be it a DVD or a USB flash drive, you can set about the process of installing the operating system (OS) on your computer. If you want to upgrade from a version of Windows other than Windows 7, you have to reinstall your software, as I will explain shortly.

When Is an Upgrade *Also* a Clean Install?

Each and every upgrade path to Windows 8.1 allows you to move *Just* [the] *personal files* for each user on the computer. Is this a clean install and is it a clean installation alternative? The answer to this question depends on the version that you're upgrading from and the setup that you have in place.

When Windows performs an upgrade, it copies your old Windows installation, complete with programs, into a `Windows.old` folder. You can then recover any files from the installation that you need to—such as Internet Favorites from Windows XP, which weren't stored in a separate User folder and weren't considered part of the user's files.

All new folders are thus created for the new operating system containing all new files. You essentially have a clean installation because there's nothing left over from your old Windows installation that can cause problems, malware infection, or incompatibilities.

When You Should Perform a Clean Install

So when shouldn't you choose Upgrade to perform a clean installation? There are a few scenarios in which you should just choose to perform a completely clean installation, formatting your hard disk and starting from scratch:

- **You already store your files and documents on a different physical hard disk or partition to your copy of Windows**: I always recommend storing your files on a separate partition of Windows for data security, and there is simply nothing to be gained from creating the `Windows.old` folder. In this circumstance, it's best to reformat the Windows drive, which removes any trace of doubt that the former installation might cause problems.

- **Your Windows disk isn't large enough to store both Windows 8.1 and your old Windows installation in a Windows.old folder**: If there isn't enough space on your hard disk to upgrade Windows, the installer informs you before the upgrade process begins.

- **You are upgrading from Windows XP**: You should always reformat your hard disk because Windows 8.1 (as with Windows 7) wants to create a System Reserved partition at the beginning of your primary hard disk (Disc 0) in which it places its startup and system repair files. This partition contains the boot information for Windows and, crucially, all the rescue tools and utilities for when the operating system doesn't start. If the Windows installer can't create this partition, you lose valuable Windows 8.1 features.

- **You have UEFI firmware on your computer**: Windows 8.1 might create support and rescue partitions in addition to the System Reserved partition. If you have a Windows 7 computer that you are upgrading to Windows 8.1, performing a format and clean installation is the only way to create these additional troubleshooting and rescue partitions.

Acquiring Windows 8.1

Windows 8.1 is the first version of the operating system that you can purchase online direct from Microsoft. You have the choice of downloading the operating system or ordering it on a DVD. You can purchase the operating system as a download on an existing computer that is running another version of Windows. There is no requirement, however, to install the downloaded copy of Windows 8.1 on the computer you download it to; you can install it on another computer if you want.

If you choose to purchase a packaged DVD product, you can skip ahead to the "Preparing to Install Windows 8.1" section in this chapter.

Downloading Windows 8.1

The Windows 8.1 Upgrade Assistant is at http://www.microsoftstore.com. It helps you through the process of downloading and paying for your new copy of Windows 8.1. At the end of the process, it presents you with several options (see Figure 15-1).

Figure 15-1. *Using the Windows 8.1 Upgrade Assistant to purchase Windows 8.1*

When you download Windows 8.1, you should keep a copy of the installer because you never know when you might need to reinstall it. When you are prompted to **Install by creating media**, this is exactly the option you should choose because it gives you physical media that you can safely store in case you need it.

You can create this media on a USB flash drive or an ISO file that can be burned to DVD (see Figure 15-2). *I strongly recommend* that you choose the ISO file option to create an installer file that can be used later because the ISO file can later be burned to a DVD or copied to a USB flash drive (I will show you how to do this shortly). If you create a USB flash drive, you can't ever use that flash drive for anything else unless you want to delete the copy of the Windows 8.1 installer that is on it. The ISO image file is saved to your computer for later use.

Figure 15-2. *Choosing where to create your bootable installation media*

The other important part of this purchasing process is to keep a safe record of your Windows 8.1 product key, which is displayed in the Windows 8.1 Upgrade Assistant. You should always keep a record of it in a safe place with your installation media.

Once the installation media is created, you can install Windows in place or from a restart. I will show you how to do this later in this chapter.

Creating Bootable Media from a Windows 8.1 ISO File

Once you have created your Windows 8.1 ISO file, you will want to create bootable media from it by using either a DVD or a USB flash drive. The easiest way to do this—the way that's supported in every edition of Windows—is by downloading the Windows 7 USB/DVD Download Tool. You can search for it online or get it directly from `http://www.microsoftstore.com/store/msstore/html/pbPage.Help_Win7_usbdvd_dwnTool`.

This tool allows you to burn a DVD of an ISO image file or copy it to a USB flash drive (see Figure 15-3). It first asks you to select the ISO image file you have downloaded and then it prompts you to create an installer on a USB device or a DVD.

Figure 15-3. *The Windows 7 USB/DVD Download Tool*

If you are using Windows 7 and want to burn a DVD of your Windows 8.1 installer, you can double-click the ISO file in Windows Explorer to open a dedicated DVD burning tool. This option might be quicker and easier for some people.

Preparing to Install Windows 8.1

After you download or buy a retail copy of Windows 8.1, or if you need to reinstall it, the process varies, depending on whether you are upgrading an existing Windows installation or performing a clean installation. If you are upgrading, the process depends on the version of Windows from which you are upgrading.

The options that present themselves to you therefore can vary quite considerably, so in this section, I'll show you what those options are and how the installation will vary depending on how you choose to perform it. I'll also help you make sure that the installation you perform is stable and reliable.

Upgrading from Windows XP

Unlike Windows 7, Windows 8.1 *does* support a direct upgrade path for users of Windows XP, although you can't transfer your programs, user accounts, and settings. The upgrade process only enables you to migrate your personal files and documents to the new operating system (see Figure 15-4).

Figure 15-4. *Upgrading from Windows XP*

The reason you can't upgrade your full Windows XP installation to Windows 8.1 is because Windows XP and Windows 8.1 are based on completely different core code (the OS kernel) and are largely incompatible. When Microsoft migrated Windows to a new kernel with Vista, many Windows XP features became obsolete as they were replaced by newer, faster, and more efficient features. This is the primary reason for software incompatibilities with XP software. If you want to upgrade from Windows XP to Windows 8.1, you have to reinstall all your software afterward.

■ **Note** Some software packages never run happily in Windows 8.1, not even in compatibility mode. To use older software in Windows 8.1, you may need to install it in a (VM). I show you how to do this in Chapter 14.

Upgrading from Windows Vista

If you are upgrading to Windows 8.1 from Windows Vista, you may be surprised to see that you still can't migrate your software to the new OS. Why not? After all, I did state in the last section that Microsoft moved to a new core kernel with Windows Vista and that this is what makes XP software incompatible.

This limitation may seem all the more unusual because you could migrate software when upgrading from Vista to Windows 7. However, parts of the core kernel changed during Windows 7's tenure, and those changes have carried over into Windows 8.1. To avoid any risk of problems due to software trying to call Windows Vista functions, Microsoft has disallowed software migration from Vista to Windows 8.1.

In Figure 15-5, the upgrade path from Windows Vista allows you to migrate your personal files and Windows Settings. This makes the process of configuring Windows 8.1 simpler and quicker.

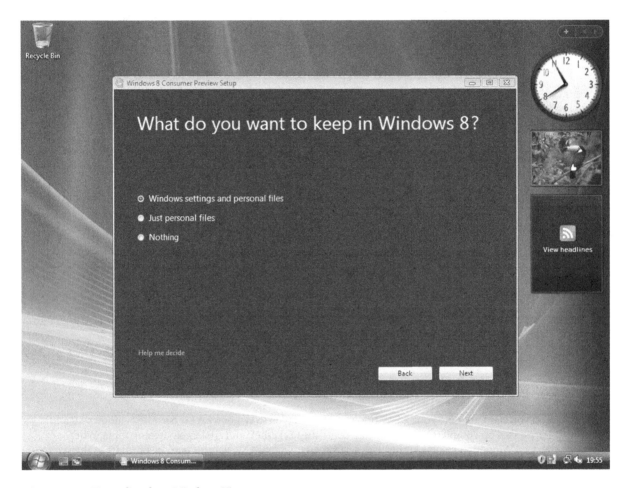

Figure 15-5. *Upgrading from Windows Vista*

Upgrading from Windows 7

It is only when upgrading from Windows 7 that you can actually migrate all your software to the new OS. Windows 7 and Windows 8.1 are similar in many ways, but this doesn't mean that software incompatibilities don't appear. I have encountered a couple of software packages that worked fine in Windows 7, but that were buggy or produced errors when ported to Windows 8.1.

As you can see in Figure 15-6, the Windows 8.1 installer gives you the options when upgrading from Windows 7 to migrate all your *Windows settings, personal files, and apps* (for this, read desktop software) or just your *personal files*.

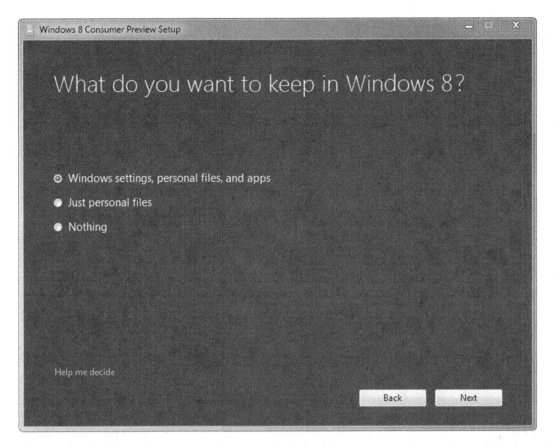

Figure 15-6. *Upgrading from Windows 7*

Moving from 32-bit (x86) to 64-bit (x64)

If you are currently running a 32-bit (x86) version of Windows, either because you're using Windows XP (in which the 64-bit version was withdrawn some years ago), or you're using the 32-bit version of Vista or Windows 7 and you want to upgrade to the 64-bit version of Windows 8.1, there are some things you should know.

First and most important, you simply can't upgrade any 32-bit version of Windows to the 64-bit version, not with XP, Vista, or even Windows 7; the installer simply doesn't support it (see Figure 15-7).

Figure 15-7. *You can't upgrade from a 32-bit version of Windows to a 64-bit version*

You can't upgrade because the differences between the 32-bit and 64-bit versions of Windows are very pronounced, not the least of which is with the hardware driver support, for which the x86 and x64 drivers are very different from one another.

This means that if you want to move to a 64-bit version of Windows 8.1, perhaps because you have already upgraded the memory in your computer to more than 4 GB (including your graphics memory), you have to reformat your hard disk and perform a clean installation of Windows 8.1.

This 4 GB memory limit is important because it *does* include your graphics memory. Let's look at an example. Your computer has three 1 GB memory cards installed, and your graphics card has a memory standing at just 512 MB (0.5 GB). In this situation, the 32-bit version of Windows happily sees *all* 3.5 GB of your memory.

If you upgrade the graphics card, though, to one with 2 GB of installed memory, you have a total of 5 GB. Windows discards your memory in chunks of entire memory cards, so the total amount of memory your PC sees is only two of the three 1 GB memory cards on your motherboard (in some configurations, it might see only one of them!).

In this circumstance, the only way to see above the 4 GB memory ceiling is to install the 64-bit version of Windows 8.1, which can see *all* your installed memory.

Windows 8.1 Minimum Hardware Requirements

If you have an older computer, you might wonder whether Windows 8.1 will run on your computer. The good news is that the minimum hardware requirements for Windows 8.1 are very low, meaning that it runs on most computers:

- **Processor**: 1 GHz or faster

- **Memory**: Minimum 1 GB (32-bit) or 2 GB (64-bit)

- **Hard Disk**: 16 GB free (32-bit) or 20 GB free (64-bit)

- **Graphics**: DirectX 9 with WDDM 1.0 or higher driver

- **Resolution**: 1024×768 pixels for Start screen and apps

Bear in mind that these are the *minimum* requirements. You should not expect the full Windows 8.1 experience to run on older hardware as well as it does on a newer computer.

Installing Windows 8.1 on Netbooks

It is very important to carefully consider whether to install Windows 8.1 on your netbook. Windows 8.1 Start screen and apps don't work on screens with a vertical resolution of fewer than 768 pixels. Many netbooks, especially older ones that originally shipped with Windows XP, have a vertical resolution of only 600 pixels.

■ **Tip** You can check the vertical screen resolution on your netbook in Windows XP by right-clicking in an empty space on the desktop and then clicking Properties in the options. Then click the Settings tab and check whether the second number in the Screen Resolution section is 768 or higher. In Windows Vista, right-click in an empty space on the desktop, select Personalize from the options, and click Display Settings. Check whether the second number in the current resolution is 768 or higher. With Windows 7, right-click in an empty space on the desktop and select Screen Resolution to show the current resolution of your monitor.

Upgrading to Windows 8.1

There are several ways to upgrade Windows 8.1, but you might find that you upgrade Windows 8 from the Windows store. This will happen if you are already using Windows 8 on your PC. You will be alerted when an update such as Windows 8.1 is available for your PC when you visit the store (see Figure 15-8. Installing Windows 8.1 in this way doesn't remove any of your apps, user accounts, settings, or desktop programs. Everything remains exactly as it was before the upgrade.

Figure 15-8. *Windows 8.1 is installed from the Windows Store on existing Windows 8 systems*

Clicking the Store tile for the Windows 8.1 update displays information about the OS update and what it means for you and your PC (see Figure 15-9).

Figure 15-9. *The Windows Store tells you what the upgrade will involve*

The installation of Windows 8.1 occurs as it would with any app (see Figure 15-10), though if you are installing Windows 8.1 on an ultrabook, laptop, or tablet PC, make sure that it is plugged into the main electricity before committing to the installation because it can take some considerable time.

Figure 15-10. *Windows 8.1 installs from the store like any app*

You can also upgrade to Windows 8.1 from a DVD or USB flash drive, or through a digital download. All operate in the same way once started, except that if you choose to download your copy of Windows 8, this download (between 3.5 GB and 4.5 GB) has to complete before the upgrade process can begin. When the download completes, you are asked if you want to make a bootable DVD or USB flash drive from it, and you need to supply this item yourself. You can install Windows 8.1 directly, but I always recommend making a backup copy of the installer onto a DVD or a flash drive because you never know when you will have to reinstall Windows 8.1 or need to perform a clean installation. You can later capture it as an ISO file for backup using software such as WinISO (http://www.winiso.com).

1. When you first start the upgrade process from a DVD or USB flash drive, you are asked if you want to get updates to the installer online. This is important and very worthwhile because it includes stability updates and new hardware drivers that can make the installation process more stable and robust (see Figure 15-11).

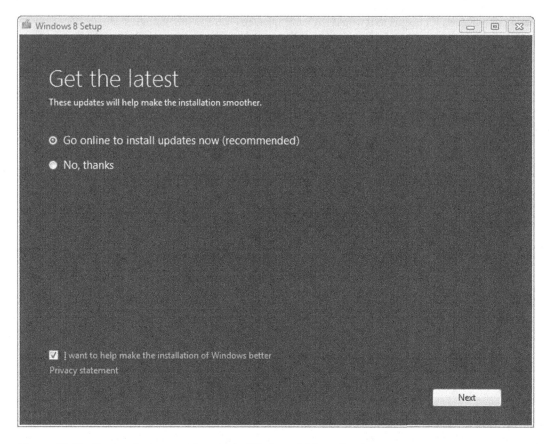

Figure 15-11. *Getting the latest updates to the Windows 8.1 installer*

2. After this process completes, you are asked to enter your product key for Windows 8.1 and accept the license agreement.

3. Next, you are asked what you want to keep from your previous installation. As I showed you earlier, you can choose files, settings, and apps (programs); only files and settings; only files; or if you want a clean installation, nothing at all (see Figure 15-12). This screen varies, depending on the version of Windows you are upgrading from.

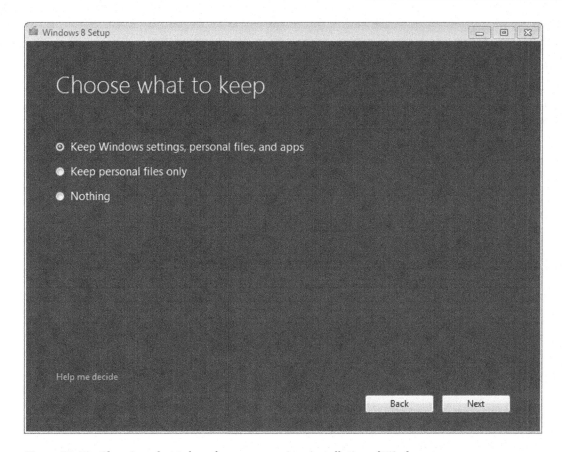

Figure 15-12. *Choosing what to keep from your previous installation of Windows*

4. The Windows 8.1 upgrade advisor runs automatically as part of the installer and informs you of any incompatible software and hardware (see Figure 15-13). As part of the upgrade process, it might recommend that you uninstall some hardware or software, that some hardware of software might need manual updating after the upgrade, or that some software or hardware might not function correctly or work at all.

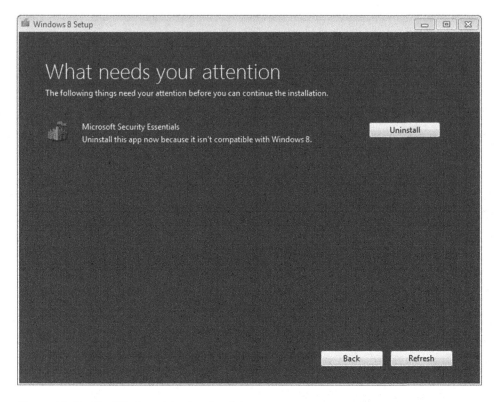

Figure 15-13. *The Windows 8.1 upgrade advisor*

■ **Note**   Don't be concerned if the upgrade advisor says you should uninstall your antivirus software. Windows 8.1 includes antivirus software by default.

Note that the Windows 8.1 installer might not let you proceed with the upgrade unless certain tasks that it deems important have been completed, such as uninstalling software identified as incompatible with Windows 8.1. The installer helps you uninstall this software.

Once these steps are complete, Windows 8.1 installs. You can't use your computer during this time, and the computer might restart several times during installation.

Performing a Clean Install

To perform a clean installation of Windows 8.1, you need to start your computer from the boot media that you created (either a DVD or USB flash drive) or from your retail copy of Windows 8.1 (note that you don't receive an installation disc with a new computer that has Windows 8.1 preloaded onto it). You may need to enter the boot menu of your computer (normally F12 when you start the PC, though this may differ on your computer) to tell the PC to start from the media that you have inserted.

1. When the Windows installer starts, you are asked to enter the country and language you want to install (see Figure 15-14). Click Next when you have selected the appropriate options.

Figure 15-14. *Installing Windows 8.1 from bootable media*

■ **Note**   The Windows 8.1 installer fully supports touch interfaces to make it easy to install on tablet computers.

---

2. The next screen is important. Because you are installing Windows 8.1, click the Install Now button in the center of the screen (see Figure 15-15). In the bottom right of the screen, notice Repair Your Computer, which can be useful if you later need to rescue and repair a faulty Windows 8.1 installation.

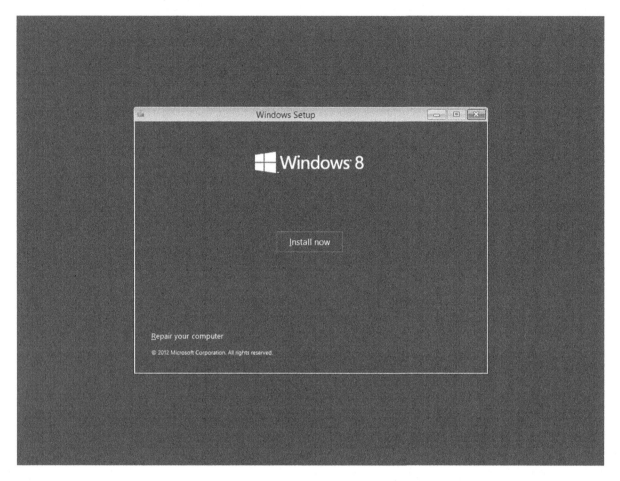

Figure 15-15. *Click Install Now to install Windows 8.1*

3. At the next screen you can upgrade your current copy of Windows to Windows 8.1 through the bootable installer. This feature is most useful when rescuing a faulty installed copy of Windows 8.1 because it creates a completely new and fresh (i.e., without your software and apps installed) installation of Windows 8.1. It also places your old installation, complete with all your files, in a Windows.old folder so that you can save them.

To perform a clean installation of Windows 8.1, click Custom: Install Windows Only (Advanced), as shown in Figure 15-16.

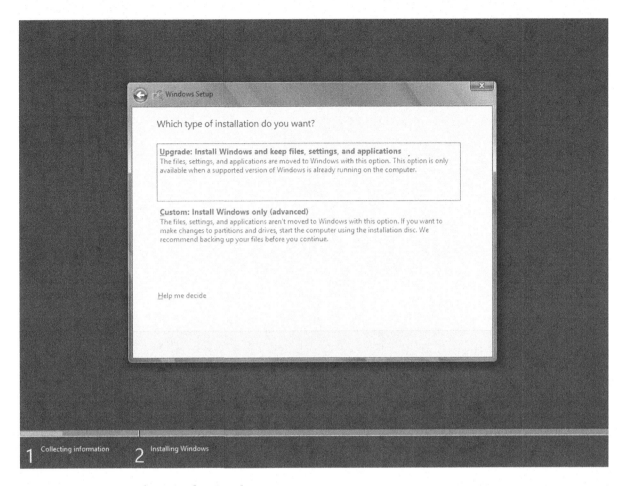

Figure 15-16. *You can also upgrade to Windows 8.1*

4. You are presented with a list of hard disks and partitions in your computer on which you can install Windows 8.1 (see Figure 15-17). On most computers, you likely see only a single disk listed, which is where you will install Windows 8.1. You should choose to install Windows 8.1 on Disc 0 (zero) because this is where the System Reserved partition with the OS boot files will be placed. If you have UEFI firmware in your computer, the Windows 8.1 installer will possibly create other startup and rescue partitions as well). The installer *always* places them on Drive 0 (zero).

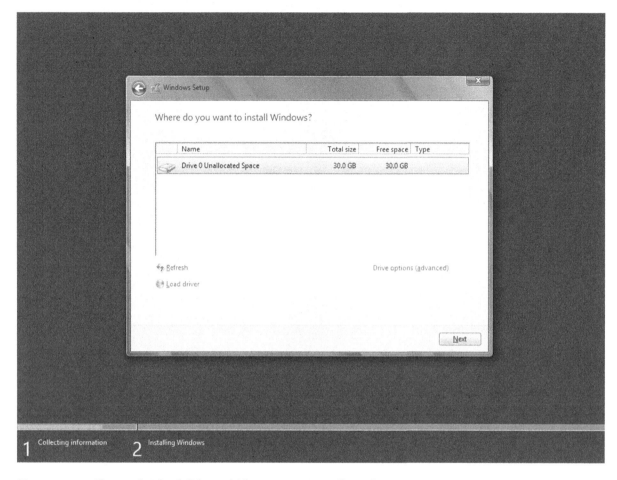

Figure 15-17. *Choose what hard disk on which you want to install Windows 8.1*

5. The installation process is completely automated from here. You aren't required to do anything with your computer until Windows 8.1 is completely installed. When this happens, you are asked to choose the color scheme for Windows and to either log in to the computer with a Microsoft account or to create an account.

Best Practices for Installing Windows 8.1

Installing your copy of Windows on Drive 0 is important because in computers with more than one physical hard disk, you might find that your *second* hard disk, which contains your files, might read as Drive 0 in the drives list (because of the motherboard socket you plugged it in to), and your Windows drive might read as Drive 1.

■ **Tip**   In a tower PC with more than one physical hard disk, unplugging all but the Windows disk drive before installing Windows 8.1 mitigates any problems associated with the Windows and System Reserved partitions ending up on different disks. It ensures that the System Reserved partition is on the correct disk.

The problem arises when you come to create a system backup of your computer. With the System Reserved partition *always* residing as the first partition on Drive 0, if that hard disk already has files on it, Windows will insist that you back up the entire files disk as part of your Windows image backup.

■ **Note** Windows Vista and Windows 7 created a System Reserved partition of 100 MB in size. Windows 8.1 contains more tools and creates a System Reserved partition of 350 MB in size. If you have a System Reserved partition that is too small, Windows might not allow you to create an image backup.

The upshot is that your image backup file can be huge, and when you restore it, it is an older copy of your files, wiping out all your new and updated files.

You should also make sure that you install your copy of Windows 8.1 onto Drive 0. With the System Reserved partition always on Drive 0, if your Windows installation is on another hard disk—let's say Drive 1—removal or failure of Drive 0 (where the boot menu resides) will result in a Windows installation that won't start and that will be very difficult to repair.

In the bottom half of the Where Do You Want to Install Windows? page is Drive Options (Advanced), which provides the basic partitioning and formatting tools you need to create a clean installation of Windows 8.1 successfully (see Figure 15-18).

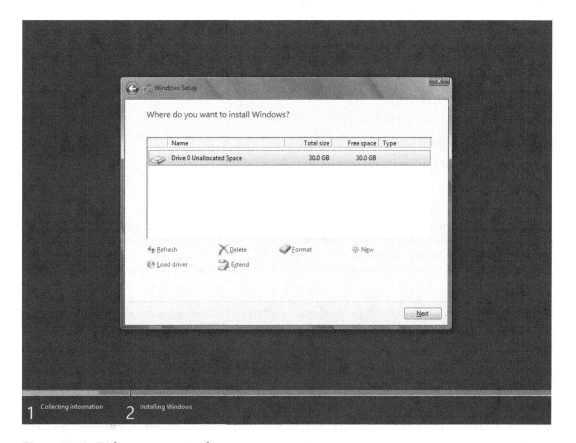

Figure 15-18. *Disk management tools*

Using these tools, you can perform the following actions:

- **Delete** an existing partition on a hard disk

- **Format** a partition or disk

- Create a **New** partition on a physical hard disk

- Join partitions to create an **Extend**ed partition

Sometimes, however, your hard disks don't appear in the drives list in the Windows installer. This happens if your computer contains RAID drives, but you can specifically load the driver required for the Windows 8.1 installer to be able to work with those disks if they don't appear in the drives list by clicking Load Driver. You need a copy of the driver on CD, DVD, or a USB flash drive.

My best recommendation is to *always* delete your existing Windows partition and create a new one where one already exists (i.e., if you used another version of Windows on the computer). You should do this because the boot and system partitions that Windows 8.1 creates are different from the ones used by Windows 7 and Windows Vista, and if you are upgrading from Windows XP, you don't have these partitions—but you do need them.

On some computers, the Windows 8.1 installer might create four of these partitions, and you need to make sure that there is space for them. The reason you want these partitions is because they contain all the tools you need to troubleshoot and repair Windows 8.1 when it doesn't start. If you don't allow the installer to create them, the troubleshooting and repair tools might not work when you need them.

If you have enough hard disk space, I also recommend that you create two (preferably three) partitions so that you can keep your Windows installation and your files (and optionally a backup copy of Windows) separate. Moving your files away from Windows 8.1 in this way helps make sure that if something goes wrong with Windows 8.1 and you need to reinstall it, there is no question about the integrity of your files.

I recommend that you create partitions. The size of your main Windows partition varies, depending on how you use your PC. The following are some recommended Windows 8.1 partition sizes for different types of users:

- **General business user**: 50 GB (enter **51200** in the partition size box)

- **General home user**: 50 GB to 100 GB (51200 to 102400)

- **Power user**: 100 GB to 200 GB (102400 to 204800)

- **Developer:** 100 GB to 200 GB (102400 to 204800)

- **Gamer**: 100 GB to 300 GB (102400 to 307200)

If you create a separate backup partition for a Windows image backup, it should be the same size as your Windows 8.1 partition, or double the size if you want to keep both a System Image Backup and a custom Refresh image. You should also add any additional space you need for a backup copy of the hardware drivers and software installers for your computer, perhaps an extra 5 GB.

Finally, the files drive should occupy all the remaining space. Obviously, this setup is suitable only for computers with very large hard disks of at least 1 TB, and preferably 1.5 TB or more. You might be installing Windows 8.1 on a tablet or ultrabook with precious little storage space, perhaps just a 64 GB or 128 GB solid-state drive (SSD). If this is the case, you can install Windows 8.1 into a 30 GB partition and save the rest for files, or you can simply create one big partition that occupies the entire hard disk. If you do this, however, you should make sure that you keep regular up-to-date backups of all your files and documents.

■ **Note**   Many enthusiasts and power users keep a copy of their hardware drivers handy on a hard disk, either internal or USB-attached. You can install all the hardware drivers in this folder at one time, as long as all the files are in the same folder and not located in subfolders through a Command Prompt (Admin) control. Type **pnputil –a <DriversFolder>/*.inf** in the command window.

Transferring Files and Documents from an Old Computer

The Windows 8.1 install disc contains a tool called Windows Easy Transfer (see Figure 15-19) that is used to transfer files and settings from one physical computer to another. This tool is extremely useful if you bought a new computer with Windows 8.1 preinstalled.

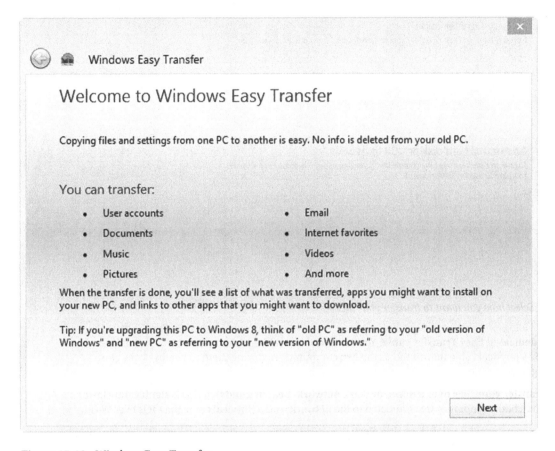

Figure 15-19. Windows Easy Transfer

Put your Windows 8.1 install DVD or USB flash drive into your *old* computer running Windows XP, Vista, or Windows 7. From its Support/MigWiz folders, run the **migsetup** program.

This tool allows you to easily transfer files and settings from your old computer in a variety of ways (see Figure 15-20):

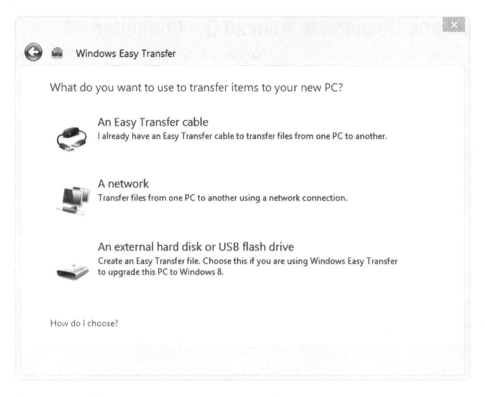

Figure 15-20. *Select how you want to transfer your files*

- **A dedicated Easy Transfer cable**: You can buy these cables at computer stores and online. It is a physical cable that connects the two computers, requiring them to be physically close together.

- **Transfer your files over a home or work network**: Bear in mind that this is significantly faster when both computers are connected to the network with a physical cable than it is over Wi-Fi.

- **Via an external hard disk or USB flash drive**: This option has the added benefit of giving you a backup copy of your files.

After you select your preferred transfer option, you need to specify whether it is the old PC or the new (destination) PC (see Figure 15-21).

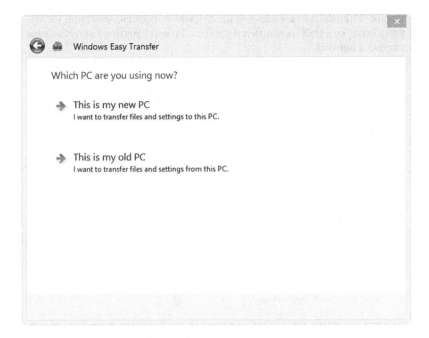

Figure 15-21. *You need to specify which PC you are using*

If you are transferring files and settings across your home or work network, you are given a code and asked to run Windows Easy Transfer on your new Windows 8.1 computer (see Figure 15-22). You can find it by searching for **transfer** at the Start screen. You need to specify on the Windows 8.1 computer that you are receiving files over your network and input the code provided on the old computer.

Figure 15-22. *You can transfer your files over a network connection*

Click Next. You are then asked what you want to transfer and are told how much space is required (see Figure 15-23). This space requirement could run to many gigabytes, so a USB hard disk is a good idea if you have one handy because it is a much faster way to transfer files than across a network.

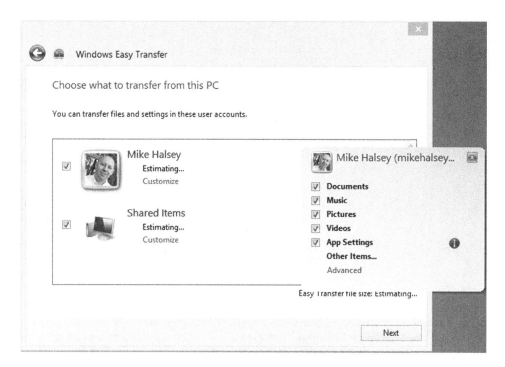

Figure 15-23. *You can choose what to transfer*

Windows Easy Transfer now begins the process of copying your files. To accept imported files on your new Windows 8.1 computer, you have to be running Windows Easy Transfer on that computer. Search for **transfer** at the Start screen to find it.

When you are running Windows Easy Transfer on the destination PC, you are asked whether you have already created a files backup (see Figure 15-24). If you click *No*, Windows Easy Transfer terminates; if you click *Yes*, a dialog opens and asks you to specify the location for the files. This works differently than if you are transferring your files across a network

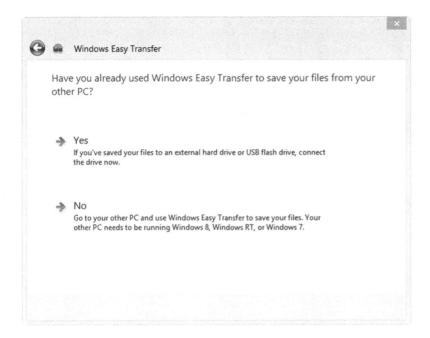

Figure 15-24. You are asked if you have already created a files backup

The files transfer process is then automated, but might take some time if you have a great many files to transfer. For this reason, if you are transferring from or to an ultrabook, laptop or tablet, you should make sure it is plugged into mains electricity during the process.

Summary

Migrating from an earlier version of Windows, even Windows XP, is simpler with Windows 8.1 than with any other version of the operating system, and moving your files and documents is relatively straightforward, even from a completely different computer.

Microsoft worked hard with Windows 8.1 to make the installation experience as straightforward as possible and it has succeeded with Windows 8.1 in ways that make moving to this OS a joy.

When it comes to the choice between performing an upgrade or a clean install, it's relevant only when migrating from Windows 7 or reinstalling Windows 8.1. This is because you can't bring your software and hardware drivers from Windows XP or Windows Vista, and you also can't bring any problems associated with them.

Some tools are relatively hidden—such as Windows Easy Transfer, which is an excellent tool that supports new features, including the transfer of files across a network.

Then there are the advanced administrator tools, such as Unattended Setup and SysPrep. These tools, especially when coupled with the Windows Automated Installation Kit, make very powerful ways to deploy Windows 8.1. If you are interested in learning about Windows deployment, this is a great next read for you. And you can find out about creating unattended Windows 8.1 installations at technet.microsoft.com/en-us/library/ff699026.aspx.

As for this book, I have covered all you need to be able to really come to grips with the power that lies under the surface of Windows 8.1, from ways to customize the look and feel of the OS to hidden tools and utilities that can make you more productive.

I hope you have found this book useful and informative.

—Mike Halsey

APPENDIX A

■ ■ ■

Windows 8 Touch Gestures

For many people, touch will be new to their Windows experience. In many ways, such as with tapping and double-tapping, touch operates in the same way you would expect a mouse click to work. Table A-1 contains a complete list of the touch gestures you can use with Windows 8. Those who already have been using touch will be pleased to hear that the gestures haven't changed. Some new gestures have been added, though, and those are included in the table.

Table A-1. *Windows 8 Touch Gestures*

Touch Gesture	Command	Action
Tap	Click	Tap the screen with your finger.
Double tap	Double-click	Tap the screen twice in the same place with your finger.
Drag vertically	Scroll	Touch the screen and vertically drag your finger upward or downward.
Drag horizontally	Drag selection	Touch the screen and horizontally drag your finger left or right.
Press and hold	Right-click	Touch and hold the screen with one finger while tapping it briefly with another finger.
Zoom	Zoom	Move two fingers apart (zoom in) or toward each other (zoom out).
Rotate	Rotate	Move two fingers in a circular motion.
Two-finger tap	Programmable in some apps	Tap the screen with two fingers.
Flick	Pan up, down, back, forward	Flick your finger up, down, left, or right on the screen.

Narrator Touch Gestures

The Accessibility features in Windows have long been a strength of the operating system, but with Windows 8, they have been extended to add support for touch gestures that work with the Narrator. To use Table A-2, the touch gesture listed in the left column will execute the corresponding command in the right column.

Table A-2. *Narrator Touch Gestures*

Touch Gesture	Command
Tap or drag	Read aloud the item under your finger.
Double tap **or** **Hold with one finger and tap with a second finger**	Activate an item (equivalent to a single mouse click).
Triple tap **or** **Hold with one finger and double-tap with a second finger**	Select an item.
Flick left or right	Move to the next or previous item.
Hold with one finger and two-finger-tap with additional fingers	Drag an item.
Two-finger tap	Stop the Narrator speaking.
Two-finger swipe	Scroll.
Three-finger tap	Show or hide the Narrator settings window.
Three-finger swipe up	Read the current window.
Three-finger swipe down	Read from the current text location.
Three-finger swipe left or right	Tab forward and backward.
Four-finger tap	Show all commands for current item.
Four-finger triple tap	Show the Narrator commands list.
Four-finger swipe up or down	Enable/disable semantic zoom(semantic zoom provides a view of large blocks of content; on a web site, for example).

APPENDIX B

■ ■ ■

Windows 8 Shortcut Keys

Table B-1. *Keys with No Modifier*

Key	Function
Space	Select or clear active check box.
Tab	Move forward through options.
Esc	Cancel.
NumLock	Hold for 5 seconds: ToggleKeys.
Del	Delete file (File Explorer).
Left arrow	Open previous menu or close submenu.
Right arrow	Open next menu of open submenu.
F1	Display help (if available).
F2	Rename item.
F3	Search for next instance in a search.
F4	Display items in active list.
F5	Refresh.

Table B-2. *Windows Logo Key Combinations*

Windows Logo Key+	Function
No other key	Toggle Start screen/last app.
PrtScr	Capture screenshot (saved in Pictures as screenshot.png, screenshot(1).png, screenshot(2).png, etc.).
C	Open the charms.
D	Show desktop.
E	Open File Explorer.
F	Open files in Search charm (+Ctrl to find computers on a network).

(*continued*)

Table B-2. (*continued*)

Windows Logo Key+	Function
H	Open Share charm.
I	Open Settings charm.
J	Switch focus between snapped and larger apps.
K	Open Devices charm.
L	Switch users (lock computer if on a domain).
M	Minimize all windows (desktop).
O	Change lock-screen orientation.
P	Open the second screen and projection options.
Q	Open Search charm.
R	Open Run dialog box.
T	Set focus on taskbar and cycle through running desktop programs.
U	Open the Ease of Access Center.
V	Cycle through notifications (+Shift to go backward).
W	Go to Settings in the Search charm.
X	Quick-link power-users' commands (opens Windows Mobility Center, if present).
Z	Open the App bar.
1-9	Go to the app at the position on the taskbar.
+	Zoom in (Magnifier).
−	Zoom out (Magnifier).
, (comma)	Peek at the desktop.
. (period)	Snap an app to the right (+Shift snap to the left).
Enter	Narrator (+Alt to open Windows Media Center, if installed).
Spacebar	Switch input language and keyboard layout.
Tab	Cycle through app history (use Ctrl to use arrow keys).
Esc	Exit the Magnifier.
Home	Minimize nonactive desktop windows.
PgUp	Move Start screen to left monitor.
PgDn	Move Start screen to right monitor.
Left arrow	Snap desktop window to the left (+Shift to move to left monitor).

(*continued*)

Table B-2. (*continued*)

Windows Logo Key+	Function
Right arrow	Snap desktop windows to the right (+Shift to move to right monitor).
Up arrow	Maximize desktop window (+Shift to keep width).
Down arrow	Restore/Minimize desktop window (+Shift to keep width).
F1	Open Windows Help and Support.

Table B-3. *Ctrl Key Combinations*

Ctrl+	Function
Mouse wheel	Desktop: Change icon size, Start screen: Zoom in/out
A	Select All
C	Copy
E	Select search box (Explorer)
N	New window (Explorer)
R	Refresh
V	Paste
W	Close current window (Explorer)
X	Cut
Y	Redo
Z	Undo
Esc	Start screen
NumLock	Copy
Left arrow	Previous word
Right arrow	Next word
Up arrow	Previous paragraph
Down arrow	Next paragraph
F4	Close active document

Table B-4. *Alt Key Combinations*

Alt+	Function
D	Select Address bar (Explorer)
Enter	Open Properties dialog box
Spacebar	Open Shortcut menu
Tab	Switch between apps
Left arrow	Move to previous folder (Explorer)
Up arrow	Go up one level (Explorer)
F4	Close active item or app

Table B-5. *Shift Key Combinations*

Shift+	Function
No other key	Five times: Sticky keys
Tab	Move backward through options
Esc	Open Task Manager
NumLock	Paste
Left arrow	Select a block of text
Right arrow	Select a block of text
Up arrow	Select a block of text
Down arrow	Select a block of text

Table B-6. *Ctrl + Alt Key Combinations*

Ctrl + Alt+	Function
D	Toggle Docked mode (Magnifier)
I	Invert colors (Magnifier)
L	Toggle Lens mode (Magnifier)
Tab	Switch between apps using arrow keys

Table B-7. *Alt + Shift Key Combinations*

Alt + Shift+	Function
PrtScr	Left Alt + Left Shift + PrtScr: High contrast
NumLock	Left Alt + Left Shift + NumLock: Mouse keys

■ ■ ■

Advanced Query Syntax for Search

In addition to the search methods that I detailed in Chapter 5, there is a large volume of Advanced Query Syntax options that you can use when searching (especially for files) in Windows 8. These options are available both at the Start screen and in File Explorer.

Data Store Location

Table C-1. *Data Store Location*

Restrict Search by Data Store	Use	Example
Desktop	desktop	Gilbert store:desktop
Files	files	Mike store:files
Outlook	outlook	Jed store:outlook
A Specific Folder	foldername or in	foldername:MyDocuments or in:MyVideos

Common File Kinds

Table C-2. *Common File Kinds*

Restrict Search by File Kind	Use	Example
Calendar	calendar	kind:=calendar
Communication	communication	kind:=communication
Contact	contact	kind:=contact
Document	document	kind:=document
E-mail	email	kind:=email
RSS Feed	feed	kind:=feed
Folder	folder	kind:=folder
Game	game	kind:=game

(continued)

Table C-2. (*continued*)

Restrict Search by File Kind	Use	Example
Instant Messenger conversations	instant message	kind:=instant message
Journal	journal	kind:=journal
Link	link	kind:=link
Movie	movie	kind:=movie
Music	music	kind:=music
Notes	note	kind:=note
Picture	picture	kind:=picture
Playlist	playlist	kind:=playlist
Program	program	kind:=program
Recorded TV	tv	kind:=tv
Saved Search	saved search	kind:=saved search
Task	task	kind:=task
Video	video	kind:=video
Web History	web history	kind:=web history

Properties by File Kind

Table C-3. *Properties by File Kind*

Property	Use	Example
Title	title, subject or about	title:"Windows 8"
Status	status	status:pending
Date	date	date:last week
Date modified	datemodified or modified	modified:last week
Importance	importance or priority	importance:high
Deleted	deleted or isdeleted	isdeleted:yes (no)
Is attachment	isattachment	isattachment:yes (no)
To	to or toname	to:mike
Cc	cc or ccname	cc:chris
Company	company	company:Microsoft
Location	location	location:"office"
Category	category	category:pilot

(*continued*)

Table C-3. (*continued*)

Property	Use	Example
Keywords	keywords	keywords:"pending"
Album	album	album:"equinoxe"
File name	filename or file	filename:Report
Genre	genre	genre:metal
Author	author or by	author:"Mike Halsey"
People	people or with	with:(jed or gilbert)
Folder	folder, under or path	folder:downloads
File extension	ext or fileext	ext:.txt

Filter by Size

Table C-4. *Filter by Size (Note that the NOT and OR operators here must be in uppercase.)*

Size	Use	Example
0KB	empty	size:empty
0 > 10KB	tiny	size:tiny
10KB > 100KB	small	size:small
100KB > 1MB	medium	size:medium
1MB > 16MB	large	size:large
16MB > 128MB	huge	size:huge
> 128MB	gigantic	size:gigantic

Boolean Operators

Table C-5. *Boolean Operators (Note that the NOT and OR operators here must be in uppercase.)*

Keyword/Symbol	Use	Function
NOT	draft NOT edition	Finds items that contain *draft*, but not *edition*.
–	draft –edition	Finds items that contain *draft*, but not *edition*.
OR	draft OR edition	Finds items that contain *draft* or *edition*.
Quotation marks	"draft edition"	Finds items that contain the exact phrase *draft edition*.
Parentheses	(draft edition)	Finds items that contain *draft* and *edition* in any order.

(*continued*)

Table C-5. (*continued*)

Keyword/Symbol	Use	Function
>	date:>10/23/12	Finds items with a date after October 23, 2012.
	size:>500	Finds items with a size greater than 500 bytes.
<	date:<10/23/12	Finds items with a date before October 23, 2012.
	size:<500	Finds items with a size less than 500 bytes.
..	date:10/23/12..10/11/12	Finds items with a date beginning on 10/23/12 and ending on 10/11/12.

Boolean Properties

Table C-6. *Boolean Properties*

Property	Use	Function
is:attachment	draft is:attachment	Finds items that have attachments that contain *draft*. Same as isattachment:no (yes).
isonline:	draft isonline:yes (no)	Finds items that are online and that contain *draft*.
isrecurring:	draft isrecurring:yes (no)	Finds items that are recurring and that contain *draft*.
isflagged:	draft isflagged:yes (no)	Finds items that are flagged (Review or Follow up, for example) and that contain *draft*.
isdeleted:	draft isdeleted:yes (no)	Finds items that are flagged as deleted (Recycle Bin or Deleted Items, for example) and that contain *draft*.
iscompleted:	draft iscompleted:yes (no)	Finds items that are not flagged as complete and that contain *draft*.
hasattachment:	draft hasattachment:yes (no)	Finds items containing *draft* and having attachments.
hasflag:	draft hasflag:yes (no)	Finds items containing *draft* and having flags.

Dates

Table C-7. *Dates*

Relative to	Use	Function
Day	date:today	Finds items with today's date.
	date:tomorrow	Finds items with tomorrow's date.
	date:yesterday	Finds items with yesterday's date.

(*continued*)

Table C-7. (*continued*)

Relative to	Use	Function
Week/Month/Year	date:this week	Finds items with a date falling within the current week.
	date:last week	Finds items with a date falling within the previous week.
	date:next month	Finds items with a date falling within the upcoming week.
	date:last month	Finds items with a date falling within the previous month.
	date:this year	Finds items with a date falling within the current year.
	date:last year	Finds items with a date falling within the next year.

Attachments

Table C-8. *Attachments*

Property	Use	Example
People	people	people:gilbert

Contacts

Table C-9. *Contacts*

Property	Use	Example
Job title	jobtitle	jobtitle:author
Instant messaging address	imaddress	imaddress:mike@MVPs.org
Assistant's phone	assistantsphone	assistantsphone:555-1234
Assistant's name	assistantname	assistantname:Darren
Profession	profession	profession:designer
Nickname	nickname	nickname:Gilby
Spouse	spouse	spouse:Victoria
Business city	businesscity	businesscity:Seattle
Business postal code	businesspostalcode	businesspostalcode:96487
Business home page	businesshomepage	businesshomepage:www.thelongclimb.com
Callback phone number	callbackphonenumber	callbackphonenumber:555-555-2345
Mobile phone	mobilephone	mobilephone:555-555-2345
Children	children	children:Gilbert

(*continued*)

Table C-9. (*continued*)

Property	Use	Example
First name	firstname	firstname:Jed
Last name	lastname	lastname:Halsey
Home fax	homefax	homefax:555-555-1234
Manager's name	managersname	managersname:Tom
Business phone	businessphone	businessphone:555-555-1234
Home phone	homephone	homephone:555-555-1234
Mobile phone	mobilephone	mobilephone:555-555-1234
Office	office	office:sample
Anniversary	anniversary	anniversary:1/8/11
Birthday	birthday	birthday:1/8/11
Web page	webpage	webpage:`www.thelongclimb.com`

Communications

Table C-10. *Communications*

Property	Use	Example
From	from or organizer	from:Jed
Received	received or sent	sent:yesterday
Subject	subject or title	subject:"Editing Report"
Has attachment	hasattachments, hasattachment	hasattachment:true
Attachments	attachments or attachment	attachment:presentation.ppt
Bcc	bcc, bccname or bccaddress	bcc:Gilbert
Cc address	ccaddress or cc	ccaddress:mike@MVPs.org
Follow-up flag	followupflag	followupflag:2
Due date	duedate or due	due:last week
Read	read or isread	is:read
Is completed	iscompleted	is:completed
Incomplete	incomplete or isincomplete	is:incomplete
Has flag	hasflag or isflagged	has:flag
Duration	duration	duration:> 50

Calendar

Table C-11. *Calendar*

Property	Use	Example
Recurring	recurring	recurring:yes (no)
Organizer	organizer, by or from	organizer:Rory

Documents

Table C-12. *Documents*

Property	Use	Example
Comments	comments	comments:"needs final review"
Last saved by	lastsavedby	lastsavedby:mike
Document manager	documentmanager	documentmanager:mike
Revision number	revisionnumber	revisionnumber:1.0.3
Document format	documentformat	documentformat:MIMETYPE
Date last printed	datelastprinted	datelastprinted:last week

Presentations

Table C-13. *Presentations*

Property	Use	Example
Slide count	slidecount	slidecount:>20

Music

Table C-14. *Music*

Property	Use	Example
Bit rate	bitrate, rate	bitrate:192
Artist	artist, by or from	artist:Lacuna Coil
Duration	duration	duration:3
Album	album	album:"shallow life"
Genre	genre	genre:metal
Track	track	track:12
Year	year	year:> 2006 < 2013

Pictures

Table C-15. *Pictures*

Property	Use	Example
Camera make	cameramake	cameramake:sample
Camera model	cameramodel	cameramodel:sample
Dimensions	dimensions	dimensions:8×10
Orientation	orientation	orientation:landscape
Date taken	datetaken	datetaken:yesterday
Width	width	width:1600
Height	height	height:1200

Video

Table C-16. *Video*

Property	Use	Example
Name	name, subject	name:"Family holiday in Germany"
Ext	ext, fileext	ext:.avi

APPENDIX D

■ ■ ■

Upgrading Your Computer

A PC isn't just for Christmas, it's for life. You'll want to make sure that your computer lasts for as long as possible because, let's be honest, these things are expensive and you can't afford to be buying a new one before the current machine is out of its warranty period.

In this appendix, I'll talk you through not only the options for upgrading your copy of Windows 8 and its features, but also upgrading your entire PC—and even buying a new one. It's most likely you'll get Windows 8 with a new computer because it is the cheapest way to buy a copy of the operating system.

Choosing a New Windows 8 Computer

I went through the specific hardware requirements for Windows 8 in Chapter 15, but most computers you buy today can run Windows 8 with no problems whatsoever. This makes it more important to know what you need to buy, so that you don't get ripped off by unscrupulous salespeople when choosing and paying for a new computer.

I've split this section into three categories: desktop PCs (including all-in-ones), laptops, and ultrabooks and tablets.

Do You Need a New Computer?

So do you need a new computer anyway? Well, if you are using a computer that's running a copy of Windows Vista or Windows 7, then you probably do not need a new one because the hardware requirements for Windows 8 are the same and it'll run fine.

The only considerations you need to think about here are

1.   Do you want to take advantage of the new multitouch technology in Windows 8?

2.   Is your current computer more than four years old?

If the answer to either one of these is yes, then it could be the right time to buy a new computer. Any computer more than four years old is more prone to failure than you might like, and the new touch technology in Windows 8 enhances usability considerably. Also, if you have a laptop more than three years old, I recommend replacing it.

Remember that if you buy a new PC, your copy of Windows 8 is effectively free. That $500 budget-computer the salesman tried to steer you away from will probably be perfectly good for years to come.

Choosing the Right Desktop PC

When it comes to buying either a desktop PC, by which I mean a separate tower and monitor, purchasers have traditionally had the hardest time avoiding over-zealous salespeople. "You want to edit photographs? Then you'll benefit from having the fastest processor. . ." commonly goes the line.

The first decision to whether you want a desktop PC or an all-in-one. Both have their advantages and disadvantages.

Desktop PC pros

- More easily upgradable by the user

- If one part fails, the entire PC doesn't need to go for repair

- As you upgrade the PC, old parts can be sold secondhand

- More powerful than all-in-ones, making them more suitable for some tasks

Desktop PC cons

- Can look big and unsightly in the home

- Can be noisy

All-in-One pros

- Stylish and won't look unsightly in the home

- Commonly very quiet computers

- Only one power lead is required, reducing overall power consumption

All-in-One cons

- If one part fails, the entire PC needs to go out for repair

With computer parts changing so rapidly these days, you'll commonly find that all you can ever do with a tower is add more memory, add a second hard disk, and change the graphics card. You might be surprised how big a difference these changes can make, so if you want a tower case, even a small one, ask to see how easy it is to work with the components inside.

Does it have any spare memory sockets? Does it have a spare hard disk bay? If/when the internal power supply fails, how easy is it to replace? Is it a custom-made unit (common in small towers) or a standard, big-box PC PSU (power supply unit)? Does the PC have any expansion ports, and can these take a graphics card?

Never let the salesperson dictate to you what type of processor you *must* have to get the maximum benefit. These things change often, but Intel's Core series (which should be around for a few years yet) provide us with a good guide.

If you only want a PC for light e-mail, web browsing, and basic photo editing, then an inexpensive Core i3 is a great option. If you want to watch HD video but don't need a separate graphics card, you'll want a Core i5 with integrated graphics. That leaves the faster Core i7 processors for enthusiasts and those doing design, animation, HD video editing, and gaming.

You'd be hard-pressed to find a modern PC with less than 4GB of RAM, but do you need any more than this? For very light duties, such as e-mail and Internet browsing, this amount of memory is fine. Hard-core gamers and people using their computers for the other intensive tasks I mentioned need more RAM. You might need more if you want to edit your digital photos and videos. Go for the fastest speed memory you can get, such as 2 GHz instead of 1,333 MHz, because this is where the benefits are.

Next, do you need a solid-state (SSD) hard disk? These are expensive and do not yet come in big capacities at an affordable price. If you are a gamer, then you'll certainly benefit from the extra speed; but with modern games occupying 24GB or more or space, and Windows itself requiring up to 40GB with software and temporary files taking up room, you won't get more than two games on an average SSD before filling it up. This doesn't give you space for any of your files and documents.

If you use a mechanical hard disk, try to get a 7,200 rpm (revolutions per minute) drive, which operates faster than the 5,400 rpm hard disks.

You should only buy a dedicated graphics card if you have to do thoroughly intensive work such as HD video editing, gaming, or graphic design. For general use, including watching Blu-Ray discs, the onboard graphics of a modern PC are perfectly adequate.

When it comes to choosing between a tower and an all-in-one it's worth considering where the computer will live. If it's in a home office or a work office, then a tower is fine; but in your living room you may want something less intrusive and with a smaller overall profile.

Finally, does the monitor have a touchscreen or a built-in Kinect sensor? With Windows 8, these are two options well worth having.

Choosing the Right Laptop or Ultrabook

Many of the considerations for choosing a desktop or an all-in-one PC are the same for laptops and ultrabooks. One of the main differences is that whereas you can upgrade the memory and the hard disk in a laptop, you can never upgrade an ultrabook. What you get is what you're stuck with!

There is the consideration of how you will use a mobile computer. If you want to do serious work, storage is probably important and thus you should choose a laptop. Ultrabooks are perfect for light use if you enjoy working at the local coffee shop or if you want something that you can put in a bag and easily carry.

Get a touchscreen if you can, though it can make some smaller and lighter laptops topple over backward. A big factor is in the build quality. Poke the back of the screen to see if you can distort the picture).

Test the keyboard too. Is it genuinely comfortable to type on? Are all the keys a sensible size and in a sensible place? Is the touchpad usable? Does the touchpad have additional functions, such as multitouch? A keyboard with a backlight is a welcome addition.

More importantly with laptops and ultrabooks is the length of the battery life like and whether the battery be changed by the user.

Choosing the Right Tablet

With Windows 8 tablets there is a simple choice: Intel/AMD or ARM? On Intel and AMD chipsets, you'll have the advantages of the full version of Windows, with the full desktop, probably the same power as a modern laptop but with poor battery life and a high price.

With an ARM-based tablet, you'll get fantastic battery life but the machine won't have anywhere near the power, storage, or memory of an Intel/AMD machine, and you won't be able to install desktop software—ever!

There's also an argument on what size screen to get with a tablet. With a professional-grade tablet, a screen around 12 inches should be the maximum, otherwise it's far too big to hold and your arm will tire quickly. With an ARM tablet, I personally find 10-inch tablets (original iPad size) to be too bulky to carry around and even use casually on the sofa. Personally, I prefer smaller 7-inch screens.

Microsoft's Surface tablets provide a great deal of flexibility. They come with both lower power ARM processors that offer long battery life, and Intel processors that provide the full Windows 8 desktop experience. The integration of a keyboard in the cover is a bonus that may make a Surface tablet a suitable alternative to an ultrabook.

Windows 8 and OEM Installation Discs

I want to tackle one of the biggest problems facing people buying new computers. This is the omission of a Windows 8 installation DVD.

Original equipment manufacturers (OEMs) have worked with Microsoft for years now to reduce the number of pirated copies of Windows. Most OEMs no longer ship new computers with a copy of the Windows installation DVD; instead they provide recovery partitions with a copy of the installed factory image that can be restored if need be.

The downside is that if you need to restore the operating system and you haven't backed up your files and documents (which you have, right!?), then you will almost certainly lose them all because restoring the rescue image that came with your computer always destroys any files you have stored on the same partition as your Windows 8 installation. You will also take the machine back to its default state, reinstall all your software, and reconfigure the computer from scratch.

Sure, you can create your own custom disc image, even wiping out the factory one to save disc space, but haven't you paid for a copy of Windows, which includes the installation disc?

My best advice here is to always check the manufacturer's policy regarding installation discs before you buy. High-end and business computers commonly come with an option to get the disc, or they provide it automatically, but budget computers don't.

Many OEMs allow you to get a copy of the disc separately for a small shipping fee (usually $10) and many people think this is reasonable. If an OEM flatly refuses to provide a disc under any circumstances, however, I recommend that you spend your money elsewhere.

■ **Note** If you buy a Windows 8 ARM tablet, you can never get an installation disc. This version of the operating system is *only* available to OEMs and is not user-installable.

It is important to note that OEM discs are commonly tied to the computer's BIOS or UEFI firmware purchased with a new PC. This means that if you try to install them on another computer, they will not work.

SHOULD YOU BUY EXTRA SOFTWARE?

The subject of discs brings me to the age-old question of should you buy all the extra software that salespeople want you to buy because they make more money on that than on the PC itself. Most often, they try to sell you an antivirus suite and a full copy of Microsoft Office saying you need both because what comes with Windows 8 is just not good enough.

What comes with Windows 8, both in terms of antivirus and Office, is good enough for most people. The advice I've included throughout this book helps you get the most out of them. Perhaps you'd find a copy of Adobe Photoshop Elements very useful. Windows 8 doesn't come with DVD or Blu-Ray players, so you might like one of these. But antivirus and general Office—forget it!

Adding More Memory to a PC or Laptop

It is widely known and accepted that the quickest, cheapest, and fastest way to get a performance increase out of an older computer is to add more memory to it. You always need to make sure that you add the correct type of memory, however.

When you open the computer's case or the panel where the memory is located (see Figures D-1 and D-2), you see that the memory sticks have labels on them. The information you need from the labels are memory type (DDR, DDR2, DDR3, etc.) and speed in MHz.

Figure D-1. *Adding memory to a desktop PC*

Figure D-2. *Adding memory to a laptop or all-in-one PC*

These are the two things you need to match when buying additional memory. You also need to check if there are any free memory slots. The documentation that came with your motherboard can tell you what types of memory are compatible.

There is a clip at each end of the memory slots on a desktop PC. When you insert the memory, you need to make certain that these are clipped into place firmly.

When adding memory to a laptop, you also find small clips that need to be firmly fixed in place on either side.

■ **Note** If you are using the 32-bit (x86) version of Windows, adding more than 3GB of memory won't result in greater speed because Windows won't see it. A 32-bit operating system can only see a maximum of 4GB of memory, including what's on the graphics card. You can determine which version of Windows you are using in the System section of the Control Panel.

Changing or Adding a Hard Disk

In Figure D-3, you see two SATA hard disks and an SSD. The power and data plugs that attach to the back of these drives only go in one way. You shouldn't force them because the plastic on the connectors could snap.

Figure D-3. *Adding hard drives to a desktop PC. The drive on the far left is the SSD*

You should always make sure that hard disks are properly screwed into the computer's case.

When it comes to laptops and all-in-one PCs, hard disks commonly come in a slide-out caddy (see Figure D-4). They are less accessible than the memory in some laptops. You should check your computer's manual to determine whether the hard disk is a user-serviceable component.

Figure D-4. *Changing the hard disk in a laptop or all-in-one*

Changing or Adding a Graphics Card

At times, people want to change the graphics card on their computers. Doing it is usually a simple matter of pulling out the old card and slotting in the new one. Each type of card only fits in the correct slot (see Figure D-5). You should check the documentation that came with your motherboard to determine the type of slot it has before buying a graphics card.

Figure D-5. *Changing the graphics card in a PC*

You should always check if your graphics card requires additional power, usually provided by a six- or eight-pin plug, because not all power supplies come equipped with these.

If your power supply does not have the relevant plugs (apart from the question of whether you need a new power supply to supply the additional current the graphics card requires), you can buy a power lead adapter cable to give you the plug you need.

Changing the Power Supply in Your PC

The power supply is commonly the first thing in a PC to fail. The power supply is the big box in the back of the computer into which you connect the mains electricity cable. In the desktop PC, a power supply is simple to change. The leads coming from it need to be unplugged (make a note of what it's plugged into so you can easily reconnect everything again). There is a power lead for each drive, perhaps one for the graphics card and two for the motherboard.

There are four screws on the back of the case, at the top and bottom corners of the power supply (not the ones on the fan) that, when undone, allow the old power supply to pop out (see Figure D-6). Screw the new one in place and reconnect the wires, and all is done.

Figure D-6. *A power supply*

If you have an all-in-one or a small form-factor PC with an internal power supply, you will probably need to take the computer to an authorized service center to have it replaced.

Safely Working with Your PC, Laptop, or Tablet

To work safely with your computer when you are adding or changing hardware, you should always follow these instructions:

- Place the computer on a firm, flat surface.
- Make sure the computer is switched off and unplugged from the main electricity.
- Touch unpainted metal inside the computer's case to ground yourself and release any static electricity discharge from your body.
- Avoid working on nylon carpet or other locations where static electricity build-up is common.

Upgrading Windows 8

Throughout this book, I have made reference to features that are only available in the Pro edition of the operating system, such as Group Policy, or that need to be bought separately, such as Windows Media Center and DVD/Blu-Ray playback functionality.

You can add these features to Windows 8 by upgrading it. In the Control Panel, there is an Add Features to Windows 8 option (see Figure D-7). You can purchase upgrades and add-ons for the operating system that gives you new features.

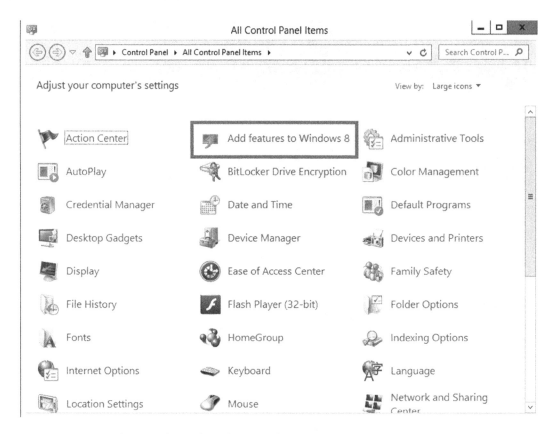

Figure D-7. *Upgrading Windows 8 from the Control Panel*

Summary

The instructions on how to upgrade and change the parts inside your computer are fairly short. This is because it is actually much simpler and easier to perform these actions than you might think.

On a computer, every cable only plugs into the right thing, so you never need to worry about incorrectly plugging in something somewhere it will cause harm or damage. Laptop and all-in-one PC sockets and plugs are all hard-wired and fixed in place, so you can only slot in components.

The short instructions prove just how easy it is to upgrade a PC and breathe new life into it.

Index

X, Y, Z